Reflections on Biography

Reflections on Biography

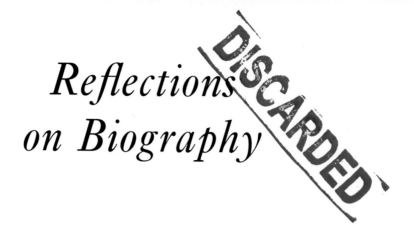

PAULA R. BACKSCHEIDER

OXFORD
UNIVERSITY PRESS

OXFORD

UNIVERSITY PRESS

Great Clarendon Street, Oxford OX2 6DP

Oxford University Press is a department of the University of Oxford.
It furthers the University's objective of excellence in research, scholarship,
and education by publishing worldwide in

Oxford New York

Athens Auckland Bangkok Bogotá Buenos Aires Cape Town
Chennai Dar es Salaam Delhi Florence Hong Kong Istanbul Karachi
Kolkata Kuala Lumpur Madrid Melbourne Mexico City Mumbai
Nairobi Paris São Paulo Shanghai Singapore Taipei Tokyo Toronto Warsaw
and associated companies in Berlin Ibadan

Oxford is a registered trade mark of Oxford University Press
in the UK and certain other countries

Published in the United States
by Oxford University Press Inc., New York

British Library Cataloguing in Publication Data

Data available

Library of Congress Cataloging in Publication Data

Backscheider, Paula R.
Reflections on biography / Paula R. Backscheider.
Includes bibliographical references (p.   ) and index.
1. Biography as a literary form.   I. Title.
CT21.B28   1999   808'.06692—dc21   99-34521
ISBN 0-19-818641-X (Hbk)
ISBN 0-19-829995-8 (Pbk.)

1 3 5 7 9 10 8 6 4 2

Typeset by Best-set Typesetter Ltd., Hong Kong
Printed in Great Britain
on acid-free paper by
Biddles Ltd. Guildford and Kings Lynn

To
JAKE, JORDAN, ZACHARY, JOCELYN,
and their GREAT-GRANDPARENTS

Acknowledgements

THIS BOOK WAS born and nurtured in two National Endowment seminars, and I offer warm thanks to the seminar members, especially Anna Battigelli, James Cook, Catherine Ingrassia, Mary Jo Kietzman, Kathryn King, Paula MacDowell, and Carol Shiner Wilson. At different times and in different ways, these people have contributed to my thinking about biography and offered steady encouragement: the late James Breslin, Martine Watson Brownley, Ruth Crocker, William Epstein, David Haney, Peter Holland, Linda Merians, Margaret Osler, Diane Wood Middlebrook, Natasha Trethewey, James Winn, Elly Welt, and Jan Wojcik; Diane, Tina, Natasha, and Jan have kindly read and commented on chapters, and Catherine, Ruth, Diane, and James brought important books and articles to my attention. This book has taken so long that there are dozens of other scholars, critics, biographers, and lecture audiences who have discussed and reflected upon biography and biographies with me, and I remember them with gratitude. For practical help and unflagging generosity in sharing his amazing fund of knowledge, I thank James P. Hammersmith, and, with special delight, I acknowledge the steady help and advice with Chapter 4 from my daughter, Andrea Backscheider, and her professional friends. Many student assistants have shared the research and the endless checking of facts and references; without their energy, ingenuity, and encouragement this would be a very different book: Hope Cotton, Patsy Fowler, Jessica Smith, Adlai Trone, and especially Elizabeth Anne Cater. For special photographic help, I thank Robert Dean and Willie Robinson. Sophie Goldsworthy, my editor, believed in the book from the beginning and her interest and suggestions improved it in many ways. My greatest debts are to the late Lewis White Beck, whose conversations about the duties and possibilities of biographers and his ways of posing intellectual challenges animated my work; and to my husband, whose enthusiasm for biography and this book, and his ability to ask stimulating and challenging questions as he read successive drafts, never flagged. Without the support of the National Endowment for the Humanities and the Pepperell–Philpot Research Fund, Auburn University, this book would not exist.

P.B.

Contents

List of Illustrations x

Abbreviations xi

Introduction xiii

I. THE BASICS I

   1. The Voice of the Biographer 3

   2. Living with the Subject 30

   3. Evidence: 'Bare Patches and Profusions' 61

   4. Perspective, Personality, and Life Shapes 90

II. EXPANSIONS 125

   5. Feminist Pressures 127

   6. Pushing the Envelope 163

   7. Eyeing the Future: British Professionals and African-American Academics 182

   Conclusion 226

Notes 236

Bibliographies 253
   Biographies 253
   Theory and Practice of Biography 262
   General 268

Index 281

List of Illustrations

1. Life mask of John Keats by Benjamin Robert Haydon. Courtesy of
Walter Jackson Bate.   47
2. Postcard of David Hilbert, one of a set honouring the great
mathematicians of the University of Göttingen. Courtesy of Springer-
Verlag Publishers.   56
3. Mary Curzon as one of the original Gibson Girls. Courtesy of
Nigel Nicolson.   131
4. Mary Curzon in her 'peacock gown', designed for the State Ball on the
last day of Durbar, the celebration acclaiming King Edward Emperor of
India. Courtesy of Nigel Nicolson.   131
5. Eleanor Roosevelt with her hand on the knee of her bodyguard Earl Miller.
Courtesy of the Franklin D. Roosevelt Library, Hyde Park, New York.   158
6. Eleanor Roosevelt holding hands with Hilda Smith, a dean at Bryn
Mawr College. Courtesy of the Franklin D. Roosevelt Library, Hyde Park,
New York.   158
7. Vita Sackville-West in her favourite clothes. Photograph by Jane Bown.
Courtesy of Nigel Nicolson.   195
8. Detail from Benjamin Robert Haydon's *Christ's Entry into Jerusalem*, with
likenesses of Wordsworth, Keats, Voltaire, and Newton. Reprinted by
courtesy of the Athenaeum of Ohio, Mount St Mary's Seminary,
Cincinnati, Ohio. Photograph by Virginia L. Backscheider.   196
9. Horace Pippin, 'Mr. Prejudice'. Courtesy of the Philadelphia Art
Museum.   217

Abbreviations

NYRB   *New York Review of Books*
NYT   *New York Times*
NYTBR   *New York Times Book Review*
TLS   *Times Literary Supplement*

Introduction

Tell me whose life you read.
'Tell me who haunts you; I will tell you who you are.'
André Breton, *Nadja*

The last literary genre to be read by a very wide cross-section of people is biography. Publishers can count on steady sales of biographies of film stars, military heroes, bank robbers (historical and S&L [Savings and Loan]), rock stars, adventurers, writers, sports figures, and murderers, and the readers of these books defy the usual marketing categories based on age, sex, occupation, education, race, and class. In England a 1994 survey found that of the people who read one book a month, 19 per cent preferred biography. The biographer Stephen Oates quotes a survey by the Library of Congress that discovered that more people had read a biography in the previous six months than any other kind of book (*Biography as High Adventure*, ix). Biographies, even of nearly unknown people (Gilbert White, the Earl of Sandwich, Dorothy Jordan), are widely reviewed and on the shelves in bookstore chains. Young men who appear to be cutting school can be seen on subways reading *The Hammer of the Gods*, a biography of Led Zeppelin that came close to best-seller status. The A&E television show 'Biography' has one of the four highest ratings of any cable programme in the USA and the result is what some are calling 'a mini-industry in biographical programming'. For instance, Lifetime's 'Intimate Portraits' is on every weekday night, the Nashville Network's 'The Life and Times' is now a weekly, and both 'Celebrity Bio' on E! and 'Legends' on the Learning Channel appear increasingly frequently. MTV began a biography show, BIOrhythms, with the life of Steve Tyler of Aerosmith in June of 1998. A&E has expanded to five nights and added 'Biography: This Week' (on a person in the news), 'Biography for Kids' on Saturday mornings, and 'Biography International' on Sunday mornings.

A&E began a glossy magazine, *Biography*, and a series of audiocasettes and biography books in the autumn of 1997. Launched with glossy advertisements featuring books on Jacqueline Onassis, Muhammed Ali, and Pope John Paul II, the series is yet to reflect that the top-rated television lives were Sam Walton, founder of Wal-Mart, and the Gambinos (*NYT*, 5 April 1998, Arts and Leisure, 37). The rush to books is academic as well and includes Blackwell's Critical Biography Series, Greenwood Publishing Group's Bio-Bibliography Series, and the St Martin's Press Literary Lives Series. Scattered among the predictable Coleridge, Conrad, and Hardy are John Barrymore and Tony

Richardson, and Greenwood in particular is trying to reach something of a general audience.

And yet almost everyone who writes about (or around) biography remarks that it is the least studied and understood of the major literary genres. Since the mid-1960s publication of literary criticism, fired by the 'publish-or-perish' mentality of universities, has grown exponentially. And yet, in 1994, Ira Nadel commented on the fact that 'with few exceptions, what has been so far absent from this recrudescence is a sustained theoretical discussion of biography incorporating some of the more probing and original speculations about language, structure, and discourse that have dominated post-structuralist thought.'[1] Joan Hedrick, winner of the Pulitzer Prize for her biography of Harriet Beecher Stowe, gave a paper at the 1996 Modern Language Association in which she asked, 'Where are the articles in *PMLA* [the association's official journal] devoted to analyzing patterns of selection and modes of organization that inform a particular biography? Why do we not have essays with titles such as "Voice and Argument in Nancy Milford's *Zelda*"?'

Bypassed, then, by traditional genre critics and by the trendy theorists, biographers might expect that reviews of their books would be uneven, whimsical, and largely unhelpful—and, generally, they are. Writing quite recently, Elisabeth Young-Bruehl, biographer of Hannah Arendt and Anna Freud, said, 'One of the things that I think makes the biography-writing business so complicated today is that people who review biographies and even write about them don't have any . . . critical perspective. . . . people who review biographies generally content themselves with retelling the story of the life . . . and you have no idea what the strategy for the biography is. There's no cultivated readership for biography, because people are only reading for life story. If you asked most people, "Well, what kinds of things make a good biography?" you would draw a blank.'[2] Like most biographers, I have turned away from review after review of my *Daniel Defoe: His Life* that narrate pieces of Defoe's exciting life and never engage questions of selection, organization, or presentation. Those that have addressed these issues often record wishes and personal preferences rather than exhibit the kinds of reflections coloured (some would say 'tainted') by 'lit. crit.' judgements. The very few, like John Carey and Rosemary Dinnage, who consistently evaluate the biographies they review from the perspective of the expert connoisseur of biography as a literary form have yet to write helpful books on the subject.

It is quite routine for reviewers of fiction to write thus: 'Much of *Wonder Boys* possesses this fever-dream quality of narration' (*TLS*, 21 April 1995, 20) or, 'In a series of chapters at once stark and resonant, it follows the lives of half a dozen characters' (*NYTBR*, 14 November 1993, 66). Biographers, however, discover their best new material recited as though the reviewer just happened to know it. In an analysis of over 500 reviews, I discovered that the average space devoted to criticism, the discussion and evaluation of the biographer's style and technique, was 10 per cent; lucky biographers find 15 per cent. Leon Edel, the biographer of Henry James, observed years ago what is still true: 'Biographers are left with only one course: to teach critics how to read a biography with proper judicial awareness' ('Biography and the Science of Man', 11).

Although my book may contribute to developing more cultivated readers of biography and, I hope, lays the groundwork for future detailed studies of many of the aspects of biography that I touch upon, rather than 'teaching' I see myself sharing some of the wonders, frustrations, and realities of a genre we find endlessly fascinating. Neither a visit-the-workshop, theoretical study, nor scholarly survey, my book is an invitation to turn 'biography' over in the mind as we turn a beautiful vase or well-crafted dodecahedron in our hands. *Reflections on Biography* is just that, reflections and cogitations on biography from many angles; devoted to stimulating thought about biography, it offers a tour of the decisions biographers make and some of the implications of those choices. Its governing premiss is that by being more analytical about biography, readers (and biographers and their reviewers) will discover another enjoyable dimension to the reading experience and gain important insights into the art of writing biography.

Catherine Drinker Bowen began her *Biography: The Craft and the Calling* with the statement that it was in the question periods after lectures that she felt that she and her audiences 'came closest to the issues' related to biography writing. That has been true for me, too. Questions such as 'Would Defoe like for you to be his biographer?' made me rethink the relationship between subject and author, between human needs and the biographical act. Startling questions such as 'Who would burn your biography?' have increased my understanding of how important biography is to a nation and what its relationships are to society. Like Bowen, I have found that these question periods have clarified and organized my opinions, sharpened my awareness, made me truly analytical about the biographical act, and, not insignificantly, persuaded me that this book is worth writing.

This book, like writing biographies, is both cerebral and passionate. There is nothing like writing biography. The biographer becomes the subject's closest ally and bitterest enemy. All biographers must be their subjects' advocates, taking up the burden of explaining lives and why they were led as they were. And so they become closer than mother, wife, school friend; they see through the subject's eyes, try to feel exactly what hurt about each painful event. But only an enemy touches the very soul, probes until the deepest, most shameful secrets and the most raw aches lie exposed, trembling in the light under the surgeon's dissecting tool. We do that no matter how passionately we love and respect our 'subject'.

A flood of quotations comes back to me. Oscar Wilde once said that every person has disciples, but 'it is usually Judas who writes the biography'.

Alexander Pope greeted a series of extended obituary–biographies of distinguished contemporaries with the remark: 'It gives a new fear to death'. W. H. Auden spent his last months attempting to destroy every letter he had ever written, every deeply personal piece of evidence about his life. Charles Dickens and Henry James also burned their letters, and the struggle over letters and other personal documents between Ted Hughes and the would-be biographers of his wife Sylvia Plath often made headlines.

Getting to the person beneath, the core of the human being, is the biographer's job, and few willingly submit themselves to that. I had taken great care to find out and present the human weaknesses and fears that had led to Defoe's most reprehensible actions. I had described so many things that he was surely ashamed of; I had counted the times he was imprisoned and documented his desperation, despair, and bravado, as well as his acts of courage, honour, and endurance. He was a proud man, and I had sought out and found long-hidden griefs and petty acts of revenge.[3] As another biographer, Paul Mariani once said, 'There are certain things that are so close to the bone that you don't talk about them. You don't want to name them, because to name them is to give power to somebody else.' An example of just how intimate the biographer–subject relationship can be is John Berryman's remark when he heard that Ernest Hemingway was dead: 'The bastard shot himself, didn't he?'

At every step, biography is wonderful and terrible. Finding a single fact can take an hour, a month, years, or elude the seeker forever. When I began the life of Defoe, I was sure that I would find at least one letter written by Defoe's wife to him. They were apart for months at a time, and evidence suggests that they wrote to each other several times a week. I never did. I did find other undiscovered letters to him and numerous letters about him that pulled aside a curtain on his private life. But no letter from his wife.

Conversely, there are moments of triumph so intense that time seems to stop and the pen shakes in the biographer's hand. Earlier biographies of Defoe had mentioned his imprisonments and bankruptcies, but significant details that would allow the full reconstruction of events remained maddeningly elusive. For example, no one had yet explained exactly how Defoe got out of jail after standing in the pillory in 1703. For answers I turned to the 'KBs' in the London Public Record Office. These records of the King's Bench Court were stored in 'croker sacks,' some as high as 4 or 5 feet and filled with filthy, nearly illegible, 280-year-old documents—they are one of the horrors of the PRO. By the time I carried the first sack to my seat, I looked as if I had been mining coal. Inside were parchment rolls: each case from indictment through trial and sentencing was written on a separate page, then *all* the cases for a court session were bound together by a leather thong through one corner, rolled tightly, and tied. The most awful thing was that they prefer to remain rolled up. The real fun, then, would begin when I unrolled the documents to search for Defoe's cases. I would move along the document putting lead weights along the edges, or, when I ran out of the office's weights, sneakily using books or the edges of readers' book stands (strictly forbidden). The slightest shift of the document, and suddenly there would be a hideous clap, a series of crackling snaps, and the document would roll itself back up. The other readers and I would be sprayed with dirt, the weights would fall in laps or on toes, and all the readers would glare.

After weeks of poring over entire letter books, boxes of correspondence, and those filthy parchment rolls of legal records—everywhere official notation or gossipy accounts might have been—I took the advice of a friend and began to read the Treasury Books at the Public Records Office at Kew. I was no longer looking for the explanation of the means of his release. But one day, I apathetically turned over a scrap of paper that was stuck down on only one edge and found the note a government official wrote detailing the clandestine way he would make the payment that would free Defoe. In that moment, nearly three centuries of speculation gave way to fact, and to a good story about the consummate skill of a politician who wanted to cover his tracks and who would employ Defoe for most of the next twelve years.

Writing a biography is obsessive. Not only does it require meticulous record-keeping, painstaking filing, and prodigious feats of memory, but the writing is difficult. In lives like Defoe's, such things as the Act of Uniformity, the Bangorian Controversy, and the South Sea Bubble must be explained clearly but also briefly enough that the story is not interrupted. Paul Mariani describes vividly what happens during the writing process: 'Berryman said, "You belong to me. You Belong to me." As it got darker and darker, there was nothing else I could do except Berryman. Nothing else. Nothing. He just took all my energy'.[4]

When I was about halfway through the biography, James Winn, the biographer of John Dryden, told me that at the end, 'it' got worse—biographers become, he said, 'like the horse that smells the barn door'. I recoiled. I had had horses as a girl, and knew they looked undignified and ungainly as they rushed towards the barn. They stuck their necks out, and, if opposed, flattened their ears back. Even the best trained broke stride and had no recognizable gait. It was true. And yet a new horror revealed itself. When completed, my biography weighed 11 pounds. You don't polish and proofread an 11-pound manuscript easily. You don't even carry it around or mail it comfortably.

But then there are readers—long-imagined, magic beings. Their interest, not just in the life but in the writing, is also different from readers' relationships with other kinds of books. A man on a plane flight between Boston and London shows me a biography he has brought on board to read and asks questions about what sources biographers trust. A man from New York asks if I can tell him how to write a biography of Averell Harriman. A woman from Tennessee writes thanking me for telling her something she always wondered about—'why Defoe sold wool socks'. A man from Japan writes to find out if I think Defoe was a better writer of *modern* English prose than was Addison. A former student sends me a picture of herself with a statue of Defoe in Scotland. Physicians, personal friends, and colleagues have confessed that they are writing biographies or 'have always planned to'. Many people like these have contributed to this book, and they are my magic, imagined readers.

★

The International Bibliography of Biography, 1970–1987 listed 10,481 published biographies in 1982 alone, and the project leaders acknowledge freely that it is not comprehensive. Recent US publication figures are equally remarkable: 1992: 2,007; 1993: 2,071; 1994: 1,758. In 1993, the latest year for which reliable figures are available, only 1,247 books were published in education and 2,169 in all other kinds of literature.[5] Obviously I have had to be selective in my reading and even more so in my writing. In making up a 'fair sample', I began by choosing biographies that have won major prizes (the Pulitzer, National Book, Bancroft, Whitbread, or Critics' Circle) and added to that biographies that seemed to offer useful comparisons to them. This large group was augmented with personal favourites, special interests, and biographies that opened new lines of inquiry or special insights. Some selections were driven by my desire to explore where biography is going and by my interest in experiments and in biography's relationship to such current cultural preoccupations as gender; all of these themes run through the book.

There are kinds of biographies and uses of biography that I confess are not my central interests here and will not receive their due. I see the primary purpose of the genre of biography to be to give a vivid picture of an interesting person whose life matters. Somewhat regrettably, I see as outside my book's subject the partial life such as Richard Wendorf's *Sir Joshua Reynolds: The Painter in Society*, now much in fashion, and 'critical' biographies written primarily to demonstrate how a writer's life illumines the works. For some people, the work *is* the life, but others of us believe that the work is part of a larger canvas, that rich, nuanced portraits reveal quite varied degrees to which the work was the life. There are many of this kind of literary biographies included in my book; not only are they a major form of contemporary biography but this type has won surprisingly many prizes.

Although some will disagree with my choices, and even perhaps with this distinction, I have included biographies that seem deeply concerned with integration and balance rather than with literary criticism, the *use* of the life to enrich our understanding of texts. The genre biography assumes that what a person does expresses an inner life—personality, motives, aspirations, character. To some extent a military campaign, a symphony, and serial murders can be used to interpret a human being just as reliably as many novels. This is not to deny the life in the works; rather it is an emphasis on the common purposes and strategies that biographers share when their primary purpose is to tell the life of a fascinating person rather than, for instance, to commit an act of literary criticism.

By using prize-winning books as my core 'fair sample', I unintentionally set a direction that resulted in some neglect of academic biographies. In truth, I never intended to write about quite specialized biographies, such as Jerome Christensen's *Practicing Enlightenment: Hume and the Formation of a Literary Career*, which are intended for other specialists. Some of the very best prize-winning biographies were written by academics, but analysis shows they are not really representative of what we call academic biography. In many ways, the academic is especially poorly prepared to write biography. A psychologist might say that they were conditioned to avoid its most essential skills and consistently negatively reinforced for practising them. Almost unnoticed is the contrast in attitudes; to write on a living or recently dead subject, one academic observed, 'I had to be aggressive, devoid of shame, and rude . . . and I had never to take no for an answer. Nothing in graduate school had ever prepared me . . .' (Weinberg, 2). At least since Sputnik and the glorification of science in our culture, academic writing that displays rigorous argument, carefully detailed 'proofs', and the appearance of clear-headed, open-minded neutrality has been exalted in the USA and to a somewhat lesser but still high degree in Great Britain. Biography requires passion and the selective presentation of evidence; academics are taught to 'survey the literature', to locate and know everything written on the subject. Obvious dangers of the academic approach are tendencies towards encyclopaedic recitations of facts—what Tony Tanner once described as an archive that feels like a mausoleum (*TLS*, 23 August 1996, 3)—and an unwillingness to assign and exploit the drama suggested by configurations of facts. Therefore, many academics' biographies become essential reference works but seldom-read books.

The recent sensational, very public discussion of when it is legitimate for a biographer to borrow from the techniques of the fiction writer is likely to caution and inform the professional biographer but to terrify the academic one. For an academic to be accused of 'making up things' or 'conflating' quotations and evidence is the most serious charge that can be levelled against him or her and may discredit that person forever. Those who turn life into art are always vulnerable to some degree to such charges, and biography is art. 'Biography seeks to do what only the greatest art has ever done: to convey the feel of an individual's experience, to see the world as a single person saw it' (Homberger and Charmley, xi); such an act of, first, projection and then interpretation and communication is always a risky kind of truth-telling.

The best biographers probably feel a strong kinship with readers, a sense of shared interest in a subject and a kind of person, life pattern, and story; most academics feel at least some degree of distrust for average readers. Crazed from explaining at least ten times each year that 'a lot' is two words and wary from encounters with students who confuse the dates of the Revolutionary and Civil Wars or who are completely unmoved by the greatest poetry in the language, academics often struggle to establish a tone and level of diction appropriate for a general audience.

Just as the writers of the literary biographies included in *Reflections on Biography* seem to believe that there is far more to life than the work, the academics who won prizes are unusual in that they usually think of themselves as biographers first and academics second. They are aware of the climate in which most of them work. As Robert Skidelsky, biographer of John Maynard Keynes, writes, 'True enough, distinguished writers and scholars dabbled in biography. But they were not distinguished *because* they did so; and indeed their distinction was a little tarnished by their excursions into the genre' (*Troubled Face*, 1). Arnold Rampersad explains the development of his biographical art in part as being 'less concerned with impressing fellow scholars' (*Life into Art*, 49). But academics in Great Britain and against more odds in the USA have become distinguished by writing biographies; the path that Leon Edel, Nick Furbank, Richard Ellmann, and Walter Jackson Bate broke is now recognized. And yet even academics who have succeeded often make self-conscious statements about their departure and identities. Joan Hedrick describes how she 'learned the hard way' how ambivalent universities are about biography: 'It took me three attempts and eighteen years to achieve tenure.' The academics who managed to escape the crippling ambivalencies and define themselves as biographers are included but not treated as academic biographers.

Reflections on Biography, Part I: The Basics, begins with four chapters on four decisions that are most influential in shaping the biography and the reader's experience. The first chapter is on the voice of the biographer, because it is the invisible bridge between biographer and reader and between reader and subject, and it is a good means to make obvious that things are hidden from the ordinary reader of biography. In choosing a voice, a point of view, biographers decide their relationship to the reader, to the subject, and to the genre; above all, they decide how much of themselves to make audible. The second chapter, on the selection of the subject for the biography, like the first, takes into account conceptions of the genre and market forces, but highlights the biographer as creative, individual intellect. Specifically, it focuses on the complex dynamic between a biographer choosing a person to write about and the possibilities, which are driven in complicated ways by personality and the culture. Kenneth Silverman, biographer of Cotton Mather, has adeptly likened the choice and its dynamics—both immediate and long term—to Hemingway's bullfighters sizing up a bull: 'Some will show off your talents, others will probably kill you.'

The third chapter takes up another aspect of biographers' relationship to their material: evidence, its sources, uses, and problematic aspects. A fourth controversial part of biography is the subject of the next chapter, 'Perspective, Personality, and Life Shapes'. Whether or not a biographer should have a strong theory of personality (and, if so, which one) is much debated, and recent work in the life sciences and by feminists in many fields has raised questions about traditional theories of personality, life course, and even maturity. Together these four chapters encompass the major means of presentation and influence, the forces biographers marshal to give narrative power, credibility, and utter persuasiveness to their accounts of lives.

The next three chapters, Part II: Expansions, extend the discussions of the multiple forms of biography and are organized around additional kinds of choices. The first suggests some of the ways that feminist biographers of the last twenty years problematized earlier decisions and permanently influenced the expectations and demands of readers. The second discusses briefly some illuminating recent experiments, and the third argues that two groups of biographers are making equally revisionary choices and are impacting the form as profoundly: those I am calling the 'British professionals' (for example, Holroyd, Ackroyd, Holmes, Glendinning) and the 'Black biographers', African-Americans writing the lives of African-Americans. The book concludes with a brief postscript on the form and its directions.

Richard Holmes, biographer of Shelley, Coleridge, and author of *Dr. Johnson and Mr. Savage*, says that since Samuel Johnson's life of Richard Savage, 'biography became a rival to the novel. . . . It began to pose the largest, imaginative questions: how well can we know our fellow human beings; how far can we learn from someone else's struggles about the conditions of our own; what do the intimate circumstances of one particular life tell us about human nature in general?'[6] As Hannah Arendt wrote, 'In dark times we have a right to expect some illumination, and some lives cast a light upon the world' (Josselson and Lieblich, 190). And so readers come back and back to biography, ceaselessly seeking to understand the way human beings have lived, the shapes of life, how individuals fit into history, and the ways humankind has grappled with the advantages and obstacles that life inevitably entails.

The biographer is explorer, inquirer, hypothesizer, compiler, researcher, Researcher Extraordinaire, selector, and writer. Today the biographer is seen benignly as guide, companion, interpreter, analyser (not necessarily analyst), literary critic, classifier, and artist. Or else as manipulator, propagandist, exploiter, critic, and competitor with the subject for being the site of truth and genuine understanding. Readers can see biographers as omniscient judges, skilled drivers of well-tuned machines, harmless drudges, or in the words of one very hostile critic, 'a humanist machine of aggression'.

Above all, biographers are decision-makers whose decisions matter. From a variety of perspectives, they judge and evaluate, and the act of interpretation is ever present, inseparable from every other action. Making sense of the material, identifying the interesting and significant, making the material and the life memorable, and revising endlessly are but the last—and sometimes the easiest—of the responsibilities.

Reading this book can change the ideas and reading practices of those who regularly read biographies. I hope that it will increase enjoyment, but some parts of it may have unpleasant effects such as one of my students described after close study of the evidence in lives of Richard Savage, the eighteenth-century poet and friend of Samuel Johnson: 'Now I trust nothing.' By analysing and thereby laying bare the implications of choices in presentation even biographers may be unaware they are making, I have done more than offer a tour of the biographer's decisions; I have offered fruit from the tree of the knowledge of good and evil.

I

THE BASICS

1. The Voice of the Biographer

> In Miss Nightingale's own eyes the adventure of the Crimea was a mere incident—scarcely more than a useful stepping-stone in her career.
>
> Lytton Strachey, *Eminent Victorians*

The most invisible person in a biography is the most powerful—the author. At every moment his or her voice can be heard—but isn't. Indeed it has been said that when we notice the biographer we have found an artistic and technical flaw. When we don't notice, however, we risk forgetting how much of biography is interpretation rather than 'fact' and why that matters so much.

It is the job of the biographer to interpret, but the more invisible interpretation and even judgement are the better the book reads—and the more subversive it is. Consider Henry Pringle's narrative of Roosevelt and the Rough Riders. The chapter begins, 'This was the adventure glorious. "San Juan was the great day of life", said Theodore Roosevelt . . .'. Pringle immediately observes, 'War, in 1898, was still romantic' (p. 181). As a post-World War I person, he describes Roosevelt's 'anxiety to get into action' as 'a little ludicrous' and his enthusiastic behaviour as 'rather weird' (pp. 184, 192). He also entertains the idea (one other biographers do not mention) that Roosevelt and his men were ambushed and probably took Kettle, not San Juan, Hill. In other words, the voice has embedded a splash of anti-war sentiment in the narrative. The bridge between reader and Roosevelt, between biographer and reader is not a neutral grey.

Some biographers want to trigger analysis or focus attention on a process, and they do so in ways that increase the reader's admiration for the subject. In *Peter the Great: His Life and World*, Robert Massie carefully highlights and subordinates, as he does in the description of Tsar Peter moving the capital of Russia and turning the nation's eyes West. He writes,

Many things about St. Petersburg are unique. Other nations, in the flush of youth or a frenzy of reform, have created new national capitals on previously empty ground: Washington, Ankara and Brasilia are examples. But no other people has created a new capital city in time of war, on land still technically belonging to a powerful, undefeated enemy [p. 355]. . . . low and marshy and sometimes covered by flood, the first stage of work was to bring in earth. . . . Lacking wheelbarrows, they scraped dirt into their shirts . . . [p. 356]. Noble families were required to build houses with beams . . . 'in the English style' . . . [p. 362]. With its merging of wind and water and cloud, its 150 arching bridges . . . its golden spires and domes . . . [it] would be called the Babylon of the Snows . . . [p. 366].

On and on Massie catalogues the wonders of the city and the achievements wrought out of Tsar Peter's imagination and iron will. Peter's spirit seems to live on for 'through the centuries, none of the conquerors . . . Charles XII, Napoleon, Hitler—was able to capture Peter's Baltic port, although Nazi armies besieged the city for 900 days . . .' (p. 354). And in a few lines there is a glimmer of another, attenuated story: 'The actual number who died building the city will never be known . . . it was estimated at 100,000. . . . St. Petersburg was "a city built on bones" ' (p. 361).

Some biographers remind the reader of their special positions. When Laura Howe Richards and Maud Howe Elliott write in their life of Julia Ward Howe, 'Our mother . . .', 'Our liveliest association with . . .', and 'We cannot resist quoting our . . .', we are being invited to share memories and information about Julia Ward Howe, not to give ourselves over to a smoothly unfolding life story. In a quite different way, Walter Jackson Bate never lets us forget that it is through his eyes we see. Park Honan calls Bate a 'narrator–commentator' and concludes that his 'humane, intruding, generalizing "I" ' is a 'major instrument of present-ness', by which he means the avoidance of trapping the biography in a retrospective or distant past (*Authors' Lives* 38–9). This 'present-ness' does contribute to absorption, but Anglo-American readers are already conditioned to allow the verb tense called 'historical present' to sweep them into another time and place. The 'I' in Bate's biographies is a familiar biographical voice, and this venerable 'instrument' has had its detractors. Virginia Woolf once wrote of her pleasure in reading a book with a direct, straightforward, confident tone.

But after reading a chapter or two a shadow seemed to lie across the page. It was a straight dark bar, a shadow shaped something like the letter 'I.' One began dodging this way and that to catch a glimpse of the landscape behind it. Whether that was indeed a tree or a woman walking I was not quite sure. Back one was always hailed to the letter 'I.' One began to be tired of 'I'. (*A Room of One's Own*, 103)

Bate's commentary goes beyond 'readings' of Johnson's development such as, 'In most of what we have touched on, there is usually—up to a point—a genuine, if precarious, innocence' (p. 305). 'Despite the circumstances and speed in writing, the result is one of the short classics of world literature', he writes of Johnson's *Rasselas* (p. 337). Because this is judgement, not the more typical guidance, Bate, for me at least, approaches Virginia Woolf's great capital 'I', and I wonder if I am seeing Johnson or Bate and how much I need to 'dodge this way and that' to see past the 'dark bar'. I know, however, that I am seeing a great interpretative, literary critic at work. In contrast, Victoria Glendinning, who is a masterful user of the unobtrusive guiding sentence, constantly moves us along and supplies leads that seldom arouse our evaluative faculties. 'Even this experiment was not enough for [Trollope]', she writes of his investments in the *Fortnightly* and another periodical (p. 345).

As these examples show, the perspective supplies continuous commentary and the voice is a nearly inseparably integrated blend of narration and interpretation. How this coexistence functions can perhaps be seen most easily by comparing accounts of the same events. Henry Pringle, David McCullough, and Edmund Morris wrote prize-winning biographies of Theodore Roosevelt, and they all describe the sudden death of Theodore Roosevelt's first wife, Alice, shortly after the birth of their daughter. In a horrible and remarkable coincidence, his wife and his mother died in the same house within a few hours.

Pringle, whose book won the 1932 Pulitzer Prize, begins the section by noting that 'Here, the story of Alice Lee becomes increasingly unsubstantial.' He gives a few domestic anecdotes before the birth of the baby and gives a sentence to Roosevelt heading home 'having been told only that a daughter had been born and having left the New York State Assembly Chamber in the midst of effusive, good-natured congratulations'. He narrates how Roosevelt then spent the night holding Alice in his arms as she died of Bright's disease except for a brief time when summoned to be with his mother as she died. Then he quotes in full Roosevelt's memorial written the year after her death: 'She was beautiful in face and form, and lovelier still in spirit . . .' (p. 51). There is a section break in the chapter, then Pringle gives an account of public reaction, and interprets: 'Somehow, Roosevelt went on with his work; if proof were needed that he had courage and an iron will this fact would serve' (p. 52).

Morris, who won the 1980 Pulitzer and National Book Award for his biography, begins the account with the scene of congratulations on the birth of the baby daughter and for the remarkable successes Roosevelt was having in the Assembly, the Lower House of the New York State Legislature. He speculates that a second telegram was very close to the words spoken by a family member: 'There is a curse on this house . . .'. He emphasizes the long train ride, and then he reports the deaths in three tightly-wrought paragraphs. Next he quotes Roosevelt's terse diary entry: a Christian cross and 'The light has gone out of my life.' After reporting that his family thought him 'unable to understand the condolences of friends' and 'The family were afraid he would lose his reason', the rest of the chapter turns on this interpretation: 'Actually he was in a state of cataleptic concentration on a task which now preoccupied him above all else. Like a lion obsessively trying to drag a spear from its flank, Roosevelt set about dislodging Alice Lee from his soul' (p. 243). He tells us that after her death, all their love letters were destroyed, pages of his Harvard scrapbook torn out, photographs of Alice removed, and captions under pictures in scrapbooks 'erased so fiercely the page is worn into holes' (p. 244). From this picture of fierce grief, however, Morris concludes 'that Alice, had she lived, would have driven Roosevelt to suicide from sheer boredom' (p. 245). He pronounces her death 'more kind than terrible'.

McCullough, whose biography, *Mornings on Horseback*, received the 1982 National Book Award, builds up to the deaths with information about the large New York city house Roosevelt had recently bought, the decision to build a house on their Oyster Bay land, and his trips home from Albany for three-day weekends. We see the happy couple playing backgammon in a pleasant room and Theodore proudly bringing friends he met on the street home to meet Alice. McCullough tells us, 'he knew no greater happiness than to be with her in his own sitting room' (p. 278). The Oyster Bay house was to be called 'Leeholm' after his wife's maiden name and 'was to be enormous, suggesting a future for Alice, at least, of unending pregnancies'; McCullough also calls it Roosevelt's 'first commitment to the future' (p. 181). He cleverly tells us that someone remembered Roosevelt 'full of life and happiness' after receiving the first telegram but 'worn' after receiving the second. After an account of the funeral, again with telling details such as the officiating clergyman's tears, he weaves Roosevelt's working life back into the story quickly and more smoothly than the others: 'Yet three days later Theodore was back in Albany, and the day following, at ten in the morning, he was in his seat as usual. Now week after week, on into March and April, he did little but work' (p. 285). He, too, quotes the tribute written a year later and tells us it was a memorial for private publication.

Reading these accounts beside each other reveals differences in material selected and even in fact. The mild sentiment in Pringle's account, which is of a piece with the time in which the biography was written, still seems appropriate within the story of young love and sudden, unexpected death. McCullough's relation largely substantiates it and can be read as carrying the tone of the prosperous, materialistic time in which it was written with a modern sensitivity to the wife as a person and a 'political asset' (p. 279). That both of them choose the same memorial to quote while Morris, with his harsher opinion, omits it is also worth noting as interpretative strategy. Pringle may not have known facts the others do, such as about the second telegram—his is, after all, much the earliest biography of the three. McCullough quotes a letter Roosevelt wrote to Alice (p. 282) but not one of those from her that Morris has characterized as 'totally uninteresting' (p. 245). This letter and the other information he gives suggest that rather than being bored by Alice, Roosevelt shared what was important to him, his intimate feelings at least about those with whom he socialized, and found what men of the time sought in a wife— a woman creating a gracious, pleasant home that was both haven and site of career-related entertaining. Some differences could undoubtedly be explained by the fact that Pringle covered Roosevelt's entire life; Morris concludes at the moment he becomes president; and McCullough ends even earlier with Roosevelt's second marriage and election as Mayor of New York. The existence of earlier biographies certainly could have had some influence, especially perhaps on McCullough because his follows Morris's so closely; there is, however, a high probability that McCullough's book was already in press when he saw Morris's.

To a considerable extent, of course, the selection and presentation of details shape interpretation, but it is worth pausing to reflect on direct statements, the explicit interpretative assertions that each biographer makes, since they flow easily and credibly past the reader in all of these books. Each biographer decides to impose a strong interpretation on Roosevelt's rapid return to the Assembly, and, in the flow of the narrative, how strong and how subjective each is can easily be missed. Pringle's man of 'courage and iron will', Morris's man of 'vitality', susceptible to sentiment but determined to 'suppress' any painful thoughts in order to move ahead, and McCullough's fuller, more leisurely account of a Roosevelt incrementally schooled in a *carpe diem* philosophy of life are the men we see throughout their biographies and, either because each has captured an aspect of Roosevelt's personality or because their narratives are powerful enough to make us believe so, we leave the episode, no matter who told it, feeling we understand Roosevelt better. Interpretation is a major responsibility of all biographers, and all three of these men exercise it in exemplary ways, but how it is made credible or even at what points it enters narrative to what effect deserves sustained critical attention—and almost never receives it.

For both narrative and interpretative strategies, biographers draw heavily on literary devices. The passages on Alice's death, for instance, ring with the conventions, indeed clichés of novels. One builds as much suspense in as possible, another moves the scene from one deathbed to the other, another describes the details of houses to give material forms to expectations for the future, and each turns documents into approximations of charged conversations.

All biographers borrow what they can from fiction, and, because it is such an effective condensing tactic, metonymy is a favourite, perhaps necessary strategy. Its use, too, is far from neutral. Metonymy comes from the Greek word for 'substitute naming', and it is the term for using the name of an attribute or object closely associated with something for the thing itself. The Holman *Handbook to Literature* offers 'the Crown' for king and 'In the *sweat of the face* shalt thou eat bread' for 'hard labour'. Robert Massie uses it in the opening chapter of *Peter the Great* to give us context and atmosphere economically. Descriptions of the Assumption Cathedral and the Palace of Facets stand for the temporal and spiritual life and history of Moscow and introduce major themes of power and of change.

Metonymy can also assure that an incident or even an allusion will carry tremendous power, greater emotional weight than the actual noun (Nadel, *Biography*, 166–9). Edmund Morris uses metonymy adeptly, first to make the

Rough Riders distinctive and memorable, and, second, to reinforce themes about Roosevelt's personal history, philosophy, and character:

Roosevelt had enlisted fifty of these 'gentlemen rankers', as he called them, in order to give the [cavalry] regiment its necessary tone. He made it clear, however, that no man would earn a commission save through bravery and merit, and that once in Texas, 'the cowboys and Knickerbockers ride side by side'. . . . There was his old classmate Woodbury Kane, a yachty dandy who 'fought with the same natural ease as he dressed'. There was Joseph Sampson Stevens, the world's greatest polo-player. There were Dudley Dean, the legendary Harvard quarterback; Bob Wrenn, tennis champion of the United States; and Hamilton Fish, ex-captain of the Columbia crew (pp. 619–20).

Roosevelt reached San Antonio on the morning of May 15, 1898. . . . These weather-beaten faces and sinewy, bowlegged bodies were as familiar to him as the aristocratic lineaments of Woodbury Kane (who, he noticed with approval, was cooking and washing dishes for a troop of New Mexicans). He had ridden many a roundup with such men in his youth, and proved himself as tough as they. . . . Here was young Douglass Campbell, grandson of the man who led the cavalry up King's Mountain in 1780. Here was an Indian named Adair. . . . Here was another Indian, named Colbert—perhaps one might trace his origins back to the half-Scottish, half-Chickasaw Colberts who dominated the eastern Mississippi in the eighteenth century. . . . a Clark and a St. Clair, no Boone but two Crocketts (pp. 620–1).

The weave of striking individuals, references to Roosevelt's unusual past, and traditional American 'values' is obvious and artful. Morris brings out the contrasts within Roosevelt, and he brings to mind ways Americans believe they prove their toughness and merit. That the Eastern élite must win over the Westerners and fit in is an example of a nearly invisible value system—the Westerners are assumed tough and brave, the Easterners must prove it. Morris is also defining and reinforcing 'Americanness' with its faith in rising through merit, its insistence on the ability of diverse people to get along and unite in a cause they define as patriotic, and even its glorification of cowboys and quarterbacks. Morris, as he so often does, subtly reinforces an interpretation he has worked to create through detail, narrative form, and direct comment: 'the Rough Riders buried . . . in a common grave . . . "Indian and cowboy, miner, packer, and college athlete, the man of unknown ancestry from the lonely Western plains, and the man who carried on his watch the crest of the Stuyvesants and the Fishes"' (pp. 646–7). That he uses some of Roosevelt's own words makes his picture doubly credible, and Roosevelt becomes the epitome of the romantic leader mourning fallen patriots whose symbolic value he understands better than anyone else.

The biographer carries in his voice the power to define people and their places in history, to characterize a nation and transmit its value, and to support or undermine accepted cultural values. Given the sophistication even teenagers show in understanding how advertising works to persuade and manipulate and the amount of attention professional scholars have given to political or ideological content, it is astonishing that the degree of power biographers have to influence the selection and perception of a nation's heroes, reformers, villains, and 'players' has been largely neglected. Clayborne Carson, director of the Martin Luther King Papers Project, in a review of David Garrow's *Bearing the Cross* emphasizes this point. He impressively evaluates Garrow's sources and interpretations of Martin Luther King as a 'sexual athlete'. He rightly sees that Garrow's biography greatly increased the now-commonplace opinion that King was promiscuous and obsessed with sex; he points out that this idea has gone beyond 'racist propaganda' and 'a scholar's interpretation' to being 'a widely accepted notion of historical reality'. With a carefully constructed chronology that interleaves such things as Hoover's racist statements and failed attempts to verify that King was a 'tom cat' with what was actually on the FBI tapes, Carson argues that Garrow has been at least careless if not irresponsible. Carson reminds the reader of the stakes and the politics at work, the power biography has to fix opinion, and the importance of 'sufficient precision and sensitivity to make possible an understanding of . . . historical or biographical significance'.[1]

Extremely rarely, and perhaps only with personalities central to a culture's history and identity, does a reviewer make biography's ethical function central to the review as Carson does. Recent biographies of Churchill drew an especially fine group of reviewers who were well aware of the power biography has to reinforce, attack, and help create national character and values. A fine example is Gaddis Smith's review of John Charmley's *Churchill: The End of Glory*, a book that, in the outraged words of another reviewer, Gertrude Himmelfarb, argues that Churchill 'should have negotiated a peace settlement with Hitler in 1940' and 'succeeded in destroying the British Empire, establishing Socialism in Britain and aggrandizing the two enemies of Britain, the Soviet Union and the United States' (*NYTBR*, 16 July 1995, 6). Smith asserts that the biography is immoral, and he emphasizes that fact carefully: 'it is the argument's immorality—immorality, not amorality—that makes it truly offensive' and 'To imply that Britain should have trusted Hitler and not the United States is morally sickening' (*NYT*, 29 August 1993, 3). In a review very much concerned with defining moral courage and even heroism, Henry Kissinger condemns Norman Rose for lack of insight into Britain's place in Europe and the world, specifically into Churchill's insights and assessments 'that define a society's freedom of action' and his actions, taken 'before they are generally understood'. Kissinger finds *Churchill: The Unruly Giant* immoral because it fails to comprehend the pursuit of 'success as the outgrowth of inner values' (*NYTBR*, 16 July 1995, 7). He, Himmelfarb, and most reviewers of Churchill biographies are outraged that little or no recognition is given to 'Churchill's most singular achievement, holding Britain together to fight alone against Nazi Germany' (Kissinger, 7). Treating these actions as aberrant rather than expressions of his core personality, the reviewers point out, intersects with morality in numerous ways. Not the least is that practising the biographer's profession 'irresponsibly' is immoral, as is denying a nation of the representative, the symbol, of its 'finest hour'. Anyone who has heard tapes of Churchill speaking to his people, quoting the African-American poet Claude McKay's 'If We Must Die', can understand the outrage and the terms of objection.

★

Readers carry away from a biography with an established and consistently maintained voice an understanding of the subject's life that they are now persuaded is accurate and reliable. The biographer's X is now their X; Walter Jackson Bate's Johnson is now their Johnson, Lewis's Wharton is now their Edith Wharton, and Garrow's King is now their Martin Luther King.[2]

A good way to think of the voice is as the contract the biographer has established with the reader. More than a bridge, it is the primary signal of the writer's relationship to readers and to content. As readers accept and come to trust the contract, they feel that they are in expert hands, as if they are being conducted on a tour by a superb driver who knows the landscape, its historical markers and contemporary significance. To develop the idea of the contract with the reader and to 'unpack' the phrase 'in expert hands' is a fruitful way of approaching the successful and persuasive voice.

The most obvious and important part of the contract biographers have with readers is simply that the biographer must know what he or she is talking about and tell it accurately, fairly, and with comprehension of related contexts. Rightly, a few mistakes in such things as dates, names, and locations of squadrons on a battlefield will throw the accuracy and, therefore, value of the entire work into question. And, rightly, a well-crafted paragraph will allow readers to relax and give themselves over to the experience:

Hilbert was now involved in investigations of his own which he had long wished to pursue. . . . The Law of Quadratic Reciprocity, known to Euler, had been rediscovered by Gauss at the age of 18 and given its first complete proof. Gauss always regarded it as the 'gem' of number theory and returned to it five more times during his life to prove it in a different way each time. It describes a beautiful relationship which exists between pairs of primes and the remainders of squares when divided by these. (Constance Reid, *Hilbert*, 55–6)

Beyond accuracy, the voice of the biographer must demonstrate grasp and penetration, range and depth, and this passage illustrates a lot of these things. The mathematics and its personal, historical, and mathematical significance is stated correctly, clearly, and economically. The Law of Quadratic Reciprocity is characterized for the reader—it fascinates mathematicians, they fall in love with it and return to it with pleasure, and it is 'beautiful', a 'gem'. Here Reid's voice is reassuring not only because of its easy mastery but also because she allows her appreciation to creep in; 'beautiful', she says. Her companionable voice assumes the reader's and her enjoyment of mathematics and pleasure in its special history.

Done well, such grasp earns spontaneous admiration, even awe. In *Here I Stand*, Roland Bainton's mastery of history, documents, doctrine, Martin Luther's life—perhaps especially the massive number of documents that formed church history and then the controversies associated with Luther's writings—and Bainton's sustained, pleasing tone and prose style quickly create the sense of going on a ride with that driver who handles the scenery and the machine with seldom equalled skill. Over and over, the great biographer will cut to the heart of what something means and why it matters and engage readers with the story, the person, and the issues. Doing all of this is a complex task. In a daring move, David Garrow begins his biography of Martin Luther King with the story of Rosa Parks and the Montgomery bus boycott. It is page 17 before King is introduced, and page 32 before we are given substantial information about him. In retrospect, we see that Garrow has begun with the event that set King on the course that led to his greatness and his assassination, but in the short run we receive an efficient, memorable, 'applied' lesson in the politics of the African-American church, the city of Montgomery, and groups associated with both. We know what is at stake and what is being asked of the 26-year-old Dr King.

Part of the contract the best biographers have with readers is dedication to careful, lucid, lively writing. For instance, Carol Brightman calls Mary McCarthy 'a whistle-blower in the House of Culture' and adds the characterization of a fellow writer: 'You've got to remember . . . her as she was. . . . When Mary stroked your arm, that was real blood that came out' (*Writing Dangerously*, xii–xiv). Awkward, ungrammatical, pedantic, chatty, convoluted prose jars the reader and destroys the absorption in the book that makes for the best reading experience. Uninteresting sentences with difficult syntax or repetitive lengths and structures work against absorption and entrancement, which are technical terms for deep reading. In a state of absorption, the reader is transported into the content of the book and is hard to distract; in entrancement, she or he is harder to distract and, when interrupted, feels a momentary confusion as though awakening from sleep. Research has proved that during the latter, the consciousness of readers is altered, and their respiration, skin tension, and heart rates fall.[3]

Strong narrative in particular aids in absorption and it is an especially powerful and dangerous part of the biographer's art. It is, after all, a mode of understanding, a structure within which questions are raised and answers tested, a fiction of possibilities and hypotheses.[4]

The lives of literary people provide a good test of narrative skill. As all biographers do, the work—writing a novel, composing a symphony, choosing a political office to run for—must be related to the events and responses to experiences, but the biographer is also expected to point out when and how the life is infused in the work. Unfortunately too many biographical narratives come to a complete halt and a section of literary criticism is inserted, but others keep the focus on the life and the works smoothly become a part of that life.

Most people would probably agree with Park Honan's judgement that Richard Ellmann is the best literary biographer to have written in English in the twentieth century. Honan bases that opinion in part on the fact that 'in Ellmann's practice, everything *in effect* becomes narrative' (*Authors' Lives*, 61, 65). In *Golden Codgers*, Ellmann himself reflects on the correspondences between biography and fiction and reveals the way his mind works, 'since the mode of translating characters from the one universe to the other must be close to basic movements of the mind, and so of critical as well as biographical consequence' (p. 17). The opening of his *James Joyce*, for example, quotes one of Joyce's characters on family and then spins out, with a few gracefully interspersed quotations from the novels, what his family was like and some of the ways Joyce drew upon his background and them later. Ellmann seems to be able to make art and life touch at nearly every point: 'The name of Joyce is derived by genealogists from the French *joyeux* . . . and James Joyce, who held that literature should express the "holy spirit of joy", accepted his name as an omen' (p. 10).

Ellmann explains, 'This book enters Joyce's life to reflect his complex, incessant joining of event and composition. The life of an artist, but particularly that of Joyce, differs from the lives of other persons in that its events are becoming artistic sources even as they command his present attention. Instead of allowing each day, pushed back by the next, to lapse into imprecise memory, he shapes again the experiences which have shaped him.' The awareness that events *first* 'command present attention', shape the man, and form the fabric of the life even as they are transformed into artistic sources, into single lines or extended episodes or striking characters, gives his biographies a narrative unity unusual in literary lives.

Also engaging the reader immediately in the life, the works, and the relationship between them, Victoria Glendinning manages in her first chapter of *Trollope* to trace his family history, his childhood, and without the appearance of forcing to suggest some of the ways the personal history and experience influenced them. Because she works with broad themes and recurrent concerns, notably disappointed grievance and marriage, rather than with individual anecdotes, she persuades but also arouses readers' interest in these themes in both domains. Interweaving 'the life'—the feelings, motives, thoughts (or whatever the biographer can guess they were) and the private life with the subject's work, no matter what that work was, is always difficult, but the stationary, repetitive, even invisible work of a writer may be a unique challenge.

As many critics have noted, Ellmann tends to work from the literary works towards the life, but he also works from the life towards the works and, perhaps more crucially, proceeds from a series of questions that are as much about the man as the life and works. For example, in his chapter on *Salome* in *Golden Codgers*, he explains what grips him and, in so doing, reveals the underlying motif that gives the sections in the biography of Oscar Wilde its tension and air of heightened significance: 'To read . . . other writers about Salome is to come to a greater admiration for Wilde's ingenuity. The general problem . . . is what the play probably meant to Wilde and how he came to write it. Villainous women were not his usual subject, and even if they had been, there were others besides Salome . . .' (p. 41). In both places, Ellmann conveys honesty, because he believes that many aspects of the life are revealed in the works, but he also pleases most readers since the fame of James Joyce and Oscar Wilde is based on their works and readers seek to understand the relationship between life and significant literary achievement; many even believe that it was Ellmann's job, the point of the biography, to deliver this illumination.

Another part of the contract with readers involves content and the ability to deal with massive amounts of information. Park Honan, biographer of Jane Austen, Matthew Arnold, and Robert Browning, says, for instance, that 'ten or twelve revisions of a chapter may not be enough: I once wrote one biographical paragraph more than seventy times', and Paul Mariani casually admits that 'each biography is rewritten four-five-six-seven-eight times'.[5] The occasion for Honan's rewriting was 'to do exact justice to an excessive amount of material' (p. xi). Catherine Drinker Bowen affirms Mary Roberts Rinehart's hard-earned insight: 'the more easily anything reads, the harder it has been to write'. Bowen goes on to observe, 'Misrepresentation . . . occurs not only through factual error . . . but by faulty organization, the clumsy construction of page, paragraph or sentence.'[6]

Mountains of material, sorting and mastering them, and full, fair, and accurate presentation pose, of course, the most intractable, frustrating problem biographers encounter in writing (there are numerous other horrors that compete for number 1 problem in other categories such as researching). As early as 1929 Virginia Woolf was describing 'biographical style' as tacking 'together torn bits of stuff, stuff with raw [ragged] edges'.[7] It is easy to be overwhelmed by material, to forget important pieces of information and notes, and to be unable to marshal potentially telling, 'perfect' information. But, sometimes, out of drudgery perfection. Henry Pringle begins the section on Roosevelt's career with the Rough Riders with an account of what seems like everyone's amazement and resistance to Roosevelt's desire to leave his government post. Pringle remembers (or has the filing system to yield) exactly what he needs. In the fourth paragraph of the first of these chapters, he quotes Secretary of the Navy J. D. Long's diary: '[Roosevelt will merely] ride a horse and . . . brush mosquitoes.' Then he gives us Long's later annotation of this diary page, 'Roosevelt was right. . . . His going into the army led straight to the Presidency' (pp. 181–2). Thus, the reader enjoys Roosevelt's unpromising and even odd desire to leave his exceptionally successful career as Assistant Secretary and is also well prepared to watch the train of events that led to his election as William McKinley's Vice President. Above all, what Ellmann, Glendinning, Lewis, and the biographers of Roosevelt do is maintain the voice they have established. Readers leave these biographies with a sense of having been in expert hands; nothing distracts them, nothing awakens them from their absorption in the story.

Virginia Woolf wrestled with an aspect of voice that all biographers stumble upon and then struggle with: 'the difficulty is to choose whether to speak oneself or let him speak—and how to combine the different voices. But of course it is immensely interesting' (*Letters*, 6: 271). After the biography was out, she wrote, 'I did my best to let Roger tell his own life, but of course one can't simply do that. And it was a question, how far to intrude, and how far to suppress, oneself' (6: 423). 'How far to intrude', 'how far to suppress', how present to be in the biography—this question becomes another part of the contract. No reader wants a perspective that shimmies wildly from ever-present companion to a neutral, 'scientific' observer and back again. Some readers will be charmed by sentences such as this, 'The documents . . . suggested the possibility of rethinking the meaning of Lafayette's career and challenging the modern, ironic accounts of his life, but . . . other subjects seemed more important, and I assumed that writing about a "mediocre idol" would be the academic equivalent of supporting the losing side in a revolutionary war . . .' (Kramer, *Lafayette in Two Worlds*, 6). Others will find such bits of personal history distracting and inappropriate.

Woolf complains about biography in particular, 'Of course the great difficulty was not to intervene oneself, and yet not to be colourless. I've never done anything so devilishly difficult . . .' (6 August 1940, *Letters* 6: 411). In fact, Woolf and every other biographer intervenes at almost every moment. Years earlier Leonard Woolf had told her that a life 'must be seen from the writers [*sic*] angle' (*Diary*, 5: 271). He believed that the writer should be the primary speaker, and certainly their friends Lytton Strachey and Harold Nicolson provided influential examples, as Strachey's devastatingly revisionary judgement of Florence Nightingale does: 'the Crimea was a mere incident . . . a useful stepping-stone in her career'. The degrees and ways of intervention are what vary.

★

What should a biography sound like? It has long been agreed that all the best literary genres have a 'poetics', a body of principles and rules governing composition and, in turn, readers' expectations. From the poetics are derived the essential qualities of each form, the 'laws' governing it, and a hierarchy of values—the range of its voices and the perimeters of its contracts.

Biography resists a poetics. The problem with a 'poetics' is inseparable from its venerable origin and heritage. When Aristotle wrote a poetics, as we can tell from his surviving work, he looked at many, many examples of a literary kind and wrote a definition of 'tragedy' based upon the characteristics that were frequently found and appeared to make the examples successful. He could, therefore, provide a theory of literary structures and principles or, in other words, a means to understand the evolved and recognized nature, form, and laws of a 'genre'. It is notable that 'literary kind', a term signifying works that show a family resemblance and are 'obviously related', becomes 'tragedy'. The limitations of Aristotle's definition of 'tragedy' did not become fully apparent until the twentieth century, when debate tended to focus on Arthur Miller's *Death of a Salesman* and whether or not it was 'really' a tragedy.[8]

The type of controlling, prescriptive definition that Aristotle wrote with its carefully-argued discussion of each element of the definition and its 'scientific' method has been widely imitated in literary study. Students can reel off neat definitions of almost all of the most frequently studied literary forms, and those forms with the definitions that work best have been awarded the greatest admiration ('epic', 'sonnet'). 'Genre' became inseparable from form, content, and mode, and students and literary critics chafed at its restrictions and puzzled over texts that resisted any category even as they retained and used genre categories to maintain hierarchies of literary achievement and value. Brooks Atkinson's review of *Death of a Salesman*, for instance, described Miller's play as 'epic', 'poetry', and 'wraithlike tragedy', while John Gassner talked of the 'prosaic masonry' of modern creators of 'low tragedy' and found *Hamlet* 'more expressive'.[9]

Another kind of normative definition comes from mathematics and is characterized by its 'rigour' as mathematicians use the word. It is even more effective in ruthlessly including and excluding and in identifying beauty and also success in 'actualizing' the full potential of the form as we speak of that in literature as ἀρχέτυπον/ἀρχέτεκτονική [*archetupon/archetectonike*]. An example of this kind of definition is that for a circle: 'a set of points lying in a plane and equidistant from a given point'. Kenneth Burke's description of the Aristotelian definition has the force of uniting it to the mathematical: 'a definition so sums things up that all the properties attributed to the thing defined can be as though "derived" from the definition' (*Language as Symbolic Action*, 3).

There is a third kind of definition, and it is probably not a definition at all. In recent years, definitions of the novel, the literary kind most similar to biography, have increasingly been argued from conceptions of when the novel becomes a dominant form in a culture, from what 'work' the novel does in society, and from its effect on other genres. For instance, in the most important recent book on the early English novel, Michael McKeon says that the novel 'can be understood *comprehensively* as an early modern cultural instrument designed to confront, on the level of narrative form and content, both intellectual and social crisis simultaneously' (my emphasis).[10] Nancy Armstrong and Leonard Tennenhouse have recently called the English novel 'the perfect creole' and argued that it constituted itself as an exception to the European tradition of letters, much as American culture did.[11] Mikhail Bakhtin's *The Dialogic Imagination*, which is not a unified book but a series of essays, succeeds better than these American examples because it develops and refines what the novel does in great detail and locates functions and configurations that no other genre shares.[12] Therefore, his work most closely approximates a definition because it can be used to distinguish. Much could be understood about biography from this kind of theorizing. Bakhtin begins 'Epic and Novel': 'The novel is the sole genre that continues to develop, that is as yet uncompleted. . . . the birth and development of the novel as a genre takes place in the full light of the historical day' (p. 3). These things—with the same kinds of literary, cultural, and social ramifications—are equally true of biography; in fact, modern biography came into being in the same century as the English novel. Thinking, for instance, about the times the form biography waxes, wanes, or is transformed; about the ways other genres mimic it and biography sometimes parodies them; about how the subject of the biography both illuminates the world and is illuminated, and especially about biography as in the zone of direct contact with developing reality are but a few of the challenging, tantalizing lines of enquiry.

And there is the fourth kind of definition, one characterized by the stubborn insistence, 'I know it when I see (meaning "experience") it.' This descriptive or functional definition has precedents at least as ancient and venerable as the first two kinds. Cicero, for instance, wrote in *De optimo genere oratorum*, 'in the kinds [genres], each to his own tone and voice, *which the educated recognize*' (my emphasis).[13] Today we are more likely to substitute 'experienced' for 'educated', and to recognize Jonathan Culler's useful 'literary competence' (*Structuralist Poetics*, 113–30). There is no question but that this kind of functional definition dominates in our thinking about biography and even in reviews of biographies.

From our experiences, enjoyments, and functional definitions we can identify some of the assumptions about the art of biography and some strategies and concerns that seem essential to the 'biographical'. Although there has probably never really been a time when 'biography' could be 'comprehensively' and satisfactorily defined as, for instance, 'an account of a person's life, and a branch of history,'[14] numerous books published since the mid-seventies have spotlighted the inadequacies of such comfortable totalizing definitions as surely as did *Death of a Salesman*. A sign of the result is that a 1987 book, one of the few genuinely theoretical books on biography, is

entitled *Recognizing Biography*. Composite and group biographies, imaginatively 'mingled' biography–autobiographies, and studies of what sociologists
call 'the underclass' or even 'the underworld', as well as experimental
strategies within more conventional 'biographies' have extended the limits of
the genre, and what no one in 1950 would have called a biography is now
recognized and reviewed as such.

The problem—or rather the glory—of biography is that a poetics is based
on conceptions of a genre against which individual texts can be measured and
assessed, in Rosalie Colie's wonderful phrase, to 'live up or down to generic
regulation'.[15] As she points out, genres and genre characteristics are really
modes of thought and literary kinds are really metaphors for views or 'fixes'
on the world. Biography, unlike any other category of literature, bears the
responsibility of encompassing and transmitting all modes and fixes. It is read
so avidly and seriously because readers recognize that ways of understanding
and relating to the world and human experience in the world are the subject
of biography. Just as the novel's infinite variety captures the breakdown of the
political and religious certainties during the Renaissance, biography—and
we cannot forget that modern biography was born in the same century as
the modern English novel—captures humankind's *various* experiences and
interpretations of those experiences. Because the great subject of biography is
modes of thought in and about the world, the form speaks to readers' searches
for an understanding of life that will give them coping skills and a satisfying
'philosophy' of life. Biography offers us an array of ways of looking at the
real world.

Georg Lukács noted that the novel 'appears in the process of becoming'
(*The Theory of the Novel*, 72–3). Because biography is representing, even
actualizing, a subject that is in the process of becoming, it, too, is in the process
of becoming, and so the reader experiences a doubly unstable genre. In
recognition of the way the self experiences itself, Lillian Hellman called one
of her autobiographical books, *An Unfinished Woman: A Memoir*. And Walt
Whitman wrote in *Leaves of Grass*,

> When I read the book, the biography famous,
> And is this then (said I) what the author calls a man's life?
> And so will some one when I am dead and gone write my life?
> (As if any man really knew aught of my life,
> Why even I myself I often think know little or nothing of my real life,
> Only a few hints, a few diffused faint clews and
> indirections
> I seek for my own use to trace out here).

> (ll. 1–7)

No wonder that Virginia Woolf wrote, 'My God, how does one write a
Biography. . . . And what is a life? And what was Roger [Fry]?' (*Letters* 6: 226).

The best biographers know that they are inventing through their selection and arrangement of materials; they are establishing cause–effect and other relationships, and they are determining what was most formative and important for someone else, someone they do not know. They must choose what to include, leave out, emphasize, and subordinate, and when they do, they have constructed a narrative that, whether they are aware of it or not, partakes of cultural stories with expectations for resolutions and interpretations built in. As Martin Stannard says, biography is an art 'precisely because it gains its effects by the imagination of its form' (*The Literary Biography*, 40). Narrative becomes the life and the basis for the judgements that will be rendered about the subject.

★

So what does a biography sound like? Most commonly, like history or like one of the great realist novels of the nineteenth century. Those seem to be the voices that biography 'lives up or down to'. Both history and these novels usually employ an omniscient narrator—a neutral, all-knowing, all-seeing observer. No one calls a biographer omniscient; instead the bar is set at magisterial, and it sounds like this: 'The span of Edith Wharton's lifetime— 1862 to 1937—can be measured in other ways, and the enormous changes that were wrought in it go far to account for one of her major literary themes: significant historical change and its impact upon the individual' (Lewis, 6). The perspective, the method, and a number of themes are stated in this economical sentence that promises mastery of history, the life, and the works.

Woolf called her biography of Fry 'an experiment in self suppression' (*Letters*, 16 August [1940], 6: 417). Aware of the difference between her approach and that recommended by Leonard Woolf and practised by her friends, Woolf described Harold Nicolson as following 'the path which had been already trodden by Mr. Strachey and others' by 'writing about people and about himself'. She concludes, 'Indeed, by the end of [*Some People*] we realize that the figure which has been most completely and most subtly displayed is that of the author' (*Collected Essays*, 4: 231–3). She was also self-conscious about how different she was from Fry: 'My own education and my own point of view were entirely different from his. I never went to school or college. My father spent perhaps £100 on my education' (*Letters*, [24 August 1940], 6: 419).

Turning over and over in her mind how much to intrude, the contrasts between herself and the men in her life, and the conflicts between her instincts and the magisterial 'I', Woolf created *Orlando*, the playful biography of the young aristocrat who is by turns male and female, the book that Bill Epstein described as a feminist deconstruction of the patriarchal mainstream of English biography,[16] and *Flush: A Biography*, the life of Elizabeth Barrett Browning's spaniel that ends in a delightful imitation of Strachey's biographical voice. Such are the games that can be played with 'magisterial', and, as Woolf makes clear, if we begin to think about gender new facets of 'biography' rotate into focus.

'Magisterial' often sets off a biography and gender quest. One day, friends asked what I intended to do now that I had finished a book, and I told them I was going to write a biography of Defoe. The immediate response—and subject of a lively, intellectually sweeping conversation—was that I couldn't because women did not have the 'magisterial voice' that great biography required.

Without saying a word, I saw Virginia Woolf's great capital 'I'—'a shadow [lying] across the page. . . . a straight dark bar, a shadow shaped something like the letter "I"' (*A Room of One's Own*, 103). More interested in content, especially evidence and what survived of my subject's voice, I had not yet reckoned with 'magisterial'. The imposition of such a magisterial 'I' might produce something akin to the work of the great Victorians, Macauley perhaps. The Voice would take over, appropriate, and silence the subject. Where, after all, is Queen Victoria in Lytton Strachey's biography of her? Woolf's reflections on this 'dark bar' portray her as 'dodging this way and that to catch a glimpse of the landscape behind it. Whether that was indeed a tree or a woman walking I was not quite sure' (p. 103). Just as Strachey and the men through whose eyes Queen Victoria is portrayed obscure the woman who was queen, so the magisterial voice might by definition compete with the subject.[17]

For biographers in the late twentieth century, a vision of a massive stack of books and articles drawn from the huge bibliography of feminist works on language and especially from theories that argue that women have no language appears. Some of this work has been on biography. So formidable and confident a woman as Carolyn Heilbrun seemed to agree with the perception that a handicap does indeed exist; in *Writing a Woman's Life*, she says bluntly, 'there is no model for the female who is recounting a political narrative. . . . Nor do women have a tone of voice in which to speak with authority.' 'There is no "objective" or universal tone in literature, for however long we have been told there is. There is only the white, middle-class, male tone.'[18] When women use the academy's voice of authority, even if they have earned the right, they are likely to be criticized. Descriptions of Simone de Beauvoir's style when she wrote French philosophical discourse include the adjectives, 'peremptory, condescending, even arrogant', and negative responses outnumber positive ones.[19] And de Beauvoir had indeed earned the right to this language; in the very competitive *agrégation* examinations, she came second to Jean-Paul Sartre, there was debate over whether or not she deserved the first, and 'everybody [all the examiners] agreed that she *was* Philosophy'.[20]

What should a biography sound like? Is the voice gendered—consciously? unconsciously? necessarily? The biographies that had won the Pulitzer,

National Book, Bancroft, Whitbread, or Critics' Circle awards for biography can be seen as a laboratory. These books will be used more because they provide an intriguing source for a statistical sample and are prominent and widely read and reviewed than because I believe they are 'the best'. A fascinating book on the part editors, presses, and even friends play in the nomination and selection process could be written.

Counting the women: the first Pulitzer in biography was awarded in 1917, and a collaborative group of women won with *Julia Ward Howe*.[21] The other women were Ola Elizabeth Winslow for *Jonathan Edwards* (1941), Linny Marsh Wolfe for *Son of the Wilderness* (of John Muir, 1946), Margaret Clapp for *Forgotten First Citizen: John Bigelow* (1948), Margaret Coit for *John C. Calhoun: American Portrait* (1951), Elizabeth Frank for *Louise Bogan* (1986), and Joan D. Hedrick for *Harriet Beecher Stowe* (1995). Also in 1995 Doris Kearns Goodwin's *No Ordinary Time: Franklin and Eleanor Roosevelt* received the history prize. The cluster of biographies in the forties is perhaps not surprising considering the massive mobilization of men during World War II; their subjects, too, could be classified as distinctly nationalistic.

The National Book Award, not established until 1950 and one with numerous category revisions during its history, has been won by three women for biographies, four if Aileen Ward who won the 'arts and letters' prize for *John Keats: The Making of a Poet* (1964) is counted.[22] The winners were Catherine Drinker Bowen for *The Lion and the Throne* (of Edward Coke, 1958), Deirdre Bair for *Samuel Beckett* (1981), and Judith Thurman for *Isak Dinesen* (1983). The Bancroft, first awarded in 1960, has been given to two women, if we include Laurel Thatcher Ulrich's *A Midwife's Tale: The Life of Martha Ballard* (1991). Jean Strouse received the prize for *Alice James* in 1981. The Whitbread, dating from 1971, went to four women, one a two-time winner. Victoria Glendinning's *Vita* and Kenneth Rose's *King George V* in 1983 received the only shared Whitbread for biography, and her *Trollope* won in 1992. Winifred Gérin had received the Whitbread in 1976 for *Elizabeth Gaskell*, and the judges chose Ann Thwaite's *A. A. Milne: His Life* in 1990. Brenda Maddox's *D. H. Lawrence: The Story of a Marriage* won in 1994. The National Book Critics Circle Award was first given in 1975, and one woman's book (Carol Brightman's *Writing Dangerously: A Critical Biography of Mary McCarthy*, 1992) has been honoured.

Counting generously, 8 per cent of the books chosen for these major awards were by women. Most were clustered in or immediately after the World War II years or in the years of the flowering of the women's movement, the period between 1976 and 1986. There are, however, heartening signs in the number of women winners in the early 1990s. I knew these figures raised major statistical issues and would have to be the concern of others: how many biographies were published in each year? considered for prizes? how many by men? by women? can 'major' or 'serious' biographies be separated from 'popular' ones? how many of the female authors had been educated in predominantly male graduate programmes? Do women educated in such programmes learn a different voice, or different voices, from other women?

I read the opening hundred or so pages of numerous biographies, winners as well as non-winners, and listened to the voices of men and women. The cynic in me noted that an improbable number begin with a reference to weather, and that fact raised the suspicion that most biographers were generalizing about what the weather was most often like in, for instance, mid-November. The most useful weather openings were grounded in some verifiable record and could subsequently be recognized as consistent with the character the subject was given. R. W. B. Lewis, for instance, began *Edith Wharton*, the biography that won the Pulitzer, the Bancroft, and the Critics Circle Award, 'On Tuesday, January 24, 1922, Edith Wharton wrote in her diary. . . . The weather was rainy and windy, she noted with precision' (p. 3). Most, however, seemed to be generalizations along the lines of these: 'There had been week upon week of the cold grey fury of the North Atlantic . . .' (Esther Forbes, *Paul Revere and the World he Lived in*, 3), or 'About halfway from Albany to New York the Hudson River flows into a narrow channel. . . . January 30 of that year dawned cold and windy, with a hint of snow in the air' (James Burns, *Roosevelt: The Lion and the Fox*, 3). (What else would we expect of the Hudson in January?) I knew just how lucky I had been to find out what the weather had really been on the days Defoe stood in the pillory, and I didn't believe all of them had been so fortunate. I also noticed what I considered an unlikely number of rainy birth days. Had thousands of psychologists studied birth order when they should have studied birthday weather as a predictor of achievement?

Were references to the weather 'magisterial'? Were they part of the poetic fallacy that, read as a group, became as ridiculous as all that rain introduced as backdrop for Catherine's death in Hemingway's *A Farewell to Arms*? Were they intended to suggest that the rain falls on the just and unjust alike? to predict a stormy future? to set up the rise of a shining light from cheerless beginnings?

I went back to the winners and narrowed the social science sample: all of the books by women that seemed to me to be indisputably biographies (eighteen by seventeen women) and a sample of books by men numbering twenty-four. I excluded Thatcher's *A Midwife's Tale* because it is predominantly a literary and social history interpretation and contextualizing of a diary; it prints entries and then extrapolates on them. Although most of this sample could be called by any definition a random sample, I was careful to include R. W. B. Lewis's *Edith Wharton* because of the unequalled number of prizes it had won as well as most of the biographies written by men who won for two books. In the latter group are Samuel Eliot Morison's Pulitzers for *Admiral of the Ocean Sea* in 1943 and *John Paul Jones* in 1960, Walter Jackson Bate who did the same with *Keats* in 1964 and *Samuel Johnson* in 1978 (also National Book and Critics

Circle awards), and David McCullough *Mornings on Horseback* (National Book Award, 1982) and *Truman* (Pulitzer, 1993). I also chose biographies by Leon Edel and Richard Ellmann because they were multiple-prize recipients and both men have written extensively about writing biographies. Edel, for instance, won the Pulitzer, National Book Award, and Critics Circle awards for the second and third volumes of his life of James in 1963 and wrote several books on biography including *Writing Lives*. Ellmann received the National Book Award for *James Joyce* and a Pulitzer and Critics Circle for *Oscar Wilde*; in addition, he published a number of excellent theoretical essays and *Golden Codgers: Biographical Speculations*. I also included all of the winners about Theodore Roosevelt in order to consider whether Roosevelt had attracted exceptional biographers or was just a great subject. The result of this selection was that eighteen male biographers made up the sample of twenty-four books.

It was indeed possible to hear the 'magisterial voice'. Leon Edel had written in *Henry James: The Untried Years*: 'James stands astride two centuries and reaches backward to a third; with him the American novel, in a single leap, attained a precocious maturity it has never surpassed. And it is now recognized that with Henry James the novel in English achieved its greatest perfection' (1:10). Many of these books evoked a sweep of time and showed a similar grasp of the individual in an era made to seem significant and interesting. Kenneth Rose, whose book had shared the Whitbread with Glendinning's *Vita*, wrote, 'King George V spanned the centuries. At his christening in 1865 the minister in attendance on his grandmother, Queen Victoria, was Lord Palmerston. Shortly before his death in 1936 he handed the seals of office to a new Foreign Secretary, Anthony Eden' (p. xiii). Rose goes on in his introduction to establish briefly that those years were ones of great social restlessness and change. Women could do this, too. Catherine Drinker Bowen begins the preface of *The Lion and the Throne*: 'Sir Edward Coke—Lord Coke, his contemporaries called him—was Queen Elizabeth's Attorney General and Chief Justice under James, first Stuart King of England' (ix).

My analysis led to a useful refinement of 'magisterial' voice. Although language is an issue, and it is true that our culture does not yet have an acceptable, accessible language to describe many of women's experiences (or the experiences of persons of colour or of the lower classes or the culturally stigmatized),[23] 'voice' is not primarily 'language'. 'Voice' is part of the contract with the reader, the primary signal of the writer's relationship to readers and to content, and it is not always magisterial. In the prize-winning biographies, it is with very rare exceptions audibly authoritative and can slide almost imperceptibly into authoritarian.

At the beginning of these books—the prefaces, introductions, and opening chapters—where the establishment of the contract begins and readers expect set pieces of information, the voice that transmits the 'magisterial' or 'in expert hands' is conveniently available for comparison. Not only is this the place where an authoritative presence must be established and quickly reinforced but here controlling themes are introduced and the reader is swept away—or not. As Bowen says, a good result 'is worth any amount of trouble and revision' (p. 21). Some common denominators in the sample emerged, and I will begin with them.

The most common opening lines of the prefaces or introductions of winning biographies are personal remarks or anecdotes (18 or 43 per cent); second is impressive identification of the subject (12 or 29 per cent). In fact, a little less than half of the personal statements point out the great challenge their biographical subjects are. The difficulties are varied: Gaskell was hostile to biography; Bogan 'seldom talked about her life'; an 'overwhelming' amount of documentation survives about de Staël; many lives of Keats have been written. Most of the personal remarks describe how the subject was selected, and ranged from David McCullough's humorous account of seeing his brother play Theodore Roosevelt in a school play to Charles Capper's somewhat self-indulgent tracing of his intellectual path from a course he taught as a teaching assistant to his fascination with Margaret Fuller. Samuel Eliot Morison, in a move I confess to finding both bizarre and fascinating, identifies himself as a sailor-biographer and proclaims cheerily: ' "You have heard o' [John] Paul Jones." . . . Of course you have! But have you read what a sailor has to say about him? That is the reason for this biography' (p. xxxi). Having established the same point of view in the Columbus biography, *Admiral of the Ocean Sea*, perhaps he had prepared his readers and reviewers for this persona. Ann Thwaite skilfully weaves her experiences as a reader of Milne's stories into her introductory tracing of his career. Like music with a flowing melody punctuated with strong, harmonious chords, her opening gives us a double account of his achievement and can evoke experiences readers may have shared with her: 'Pooh and the other animals, if not Milne himself, seem to pervade our daily lives. People call their pets, their friends, their shops after them' (p. xv).

These two categories, personal remarks and impressive identifications, account for 72 per cent of the openings of the winning biographies in the sample. Five others, four by men, begin with a philosophical or highly abstract statement. Richard Sewall, for instance, writes, 'Great poets, like great dramatists, need great audiences' (*Emily Dickinson*, xi). Other openings used by at least two biographers were pre-emptive strikes on received opinion and arguments for the value of the subject's life to the reader. It would be possible to absorb these categories into one, for they seem partly aimed at explaining why the biography is worth while. Sometimes the reason for the pre-emptive strike is clear and cleverly done. Alice James seems to have spent most of her life in bed, and it would be easy to joke that the only interesting things about her life are her famous brothers. Jean Strouse begins, ' "When I am gone," Alice

James wrote to her brother William as she was dying, "pray don't think of me simply as a creature who might have been something else, had neurotic science been born"' (p. ix). Not only does this introduce the puzzle that was her life but also associates her dying plea to her brother with the biographer's task of representing and preserving a life. Walter Jackson Bate probably widens his audience by promising that Keats's life 'provides a unique opportunity for the study of literary greatness and of what permits or encourages its development' (p. vii).

Close analysis demonstrates that effective introductions often combine two categories of winning openings. Victoria Glendinning uses the pre-emptive strike in both of her biographies but combines them with witty personal remarks. For instance, she tells us that *Gypsy Lips* was her working title for *Trollope*. In *Samuel Johnson*, Walter Jackson Bate combines an unusual slant with a strong statement implying the value to the reader: 'Johnson loved biography before every other kind of writing. It gives us, he said, "what comes near to us, what we can turn to use"' (p. xix). In two tight sentences, Bate demonstrates his grasp of his subject's voluminous writings and of one of the major appeals of biography. In a masterful stroke, R. W. B. Lewis makes a statement about his personal experience with his subject, that what he found 'shook to pieces most of the preconceptions' he had about Edith Wharton. This, joined with the opening sentence that uses the impressive identification mode to tell us that Wharton was 'the most renowned writer of fiction in America', prepares us for a serious rethinking of her fiction and her significance. Lewis exploits the technique of the impressive identification with the beginning of his first chapter. In it, Wharton is celebrating her sixtieth birthday, and she is at the height of her success. With the house of her dreams, a dazzling set of friends, a recent Pulitzer, and a typist picking up (off the floor) the pages of her work-in-progress, Lewis has impressed even the most cynical reader. Brightman's beginning is somewhat similar: 'Mary McCarthy belongs with a handful of American writers whose lives embody legends. . . .' When she joins this assertion to personal reflection, however, she directs the reader to what she wants her biography to do. She moves into an account of a personal meeting with her—the movement is, thus, not towards an intense intellectual experience, as Lewis's was, but towards an intense engagement with what McCarthy's life means to her and, by extension, others.[24]

Analysis of opening chapters gives what might be predictable results. The most common beginning was as exciting a description of the family as possible (eleven examples); any unusual or novel anecdote is sure to appear. Eight more began with the birth of the subject and quickly moved to the family, and an additional nine began with a strong description of the place with which the family and the subject were strongly associated. Some people enjoy genealogy, even in chart form, but biographers seem to recognize that this obligatory information is a challenge to present. At what stage in the subject's life the biographers begin and how long they sustain that moment varies greatly. James Miller begins *The Passion of Michel Foucault* with his death, and the theme is Foucault's preoccupation with death.

Only a few openings seem daring or especially creative. Among the daring ones are Garrow's *Bearing the Cross* and McCullough's *Truman*. Just as Garrow delays Martin Luther King's entrance, McCullough gives many initial pages to an account of the Kentucky farmer and the others who 'decided to stake their future on new land in the unseen, unfamiliar reaches of westernmost Missouri, which was then the "extreme frontier". . .' (p. 15). As part of the great story of very ordinary people settling this vast land with 'their Bibles, farm tools, and rifles', Truman becomes part of a beloved American myth.

Bowen's *The Lion and the Throne*, Burns's *Roosevelt: The Soldier of Freedom*, and Ellmann's *Oscar Wilde* have unusually creative opening chapters. Evoking the myths of London as powerfully as McCullough did of the settling of the West, Bowen moves leisurely up the Thames, gradually elucidating the time and the contemporary conflicts in a visually detailed story. Time after time, she points out things that were changing and the vested interests in the change. By the time Edward Coke appears, we are not surprised that he is 'walking gingerly on the edges' of the system. Just how skilful a politician he was is strikingly done in an economical five pages, and Bowen wraps the chapter up with one of the sentences she admits to labouring over: 'Such were the factions, such the scene and such the royal philosophy when Coke took upon himself the Speakership in 1593' (12). Burns begins on 5 November 1940 with Franklin Roosevelt, his family and friends celebrating his re-election to a third term as president, and then the neighbours with a drum and bugle corps congratulate him like strange carollers. One carries a sign, 'safe on third'. As visually rich and narratively pleasing as this is, it is Burns's next move that is brilliant: he portrays reactions to the election in London, Berlin, Tokyo, and then concludes with Roosevelt's challenge to the nation to make Lend–Lease work, a programme not yet passed by Congress. The drama of the war and of Roosevelt's relationships with Congress and the people who would fight the war and fulfil his vision, the country as 'the great arsenal of democracy', is set up. Ellmann begins with an apparently awkward sentence: 'Oscar Wilde first emerges for us into articulate being in 1868. . . .' Then he uses the childhood letter to his mother to tease out aspects of Wilde's personality, sense of humour, and formative influences.

As might be expected, the biographies can be divided into those of subjects who require identification and those who do not. Some biographers want to emphasize a lesser known aspect of the life, or to change opinion, or spur reassessment. Burns can begin with the wonderful description of Roosevelt's family and neighbours gathering to celebrate his election, and Morris can open with the scene of lines of people waiting to shake hands with Theodore Roosevelt upon his re-election (8,150 hands shaken by the end of the chapter). Kennedy, however, uses Margaret Sanger's eulogy both to remind us who she was, how famous she was, and why significant; Clapp begins by telling us that 'the policeman . . . straightened his shoulders and saluted. . . . Citizens bowed . . .', and then gives us the necessary highlights of John Bigelow's career. Hedrick cleverly begins, 'Few in the *nineteenth* century could have doubted that Harriet Beecher Stowe's life was worth writing' (my emphasis). Next she produces the famous Abraham Lincoln anecdote: 'So you're the little woman who wrote the book that started this great war!' She quickly documents Stowe's success as a writer and takes head-on the 'challenge twentieth-century notions of art and excellence' will be.

These openings accounted for 67 per cent of the sample. Characterizing incidents and quotations was the only other significant category (19 per cent). Brenda Maddox takes D. H. Lawrence's life-threatening bout with double pneumonia at age 26 as the subject for her prologue to *D. H. Lawrence: The Story of a Marriage*. Through the illness and the setting, she brings together Lawrence's lifelong susceptibility to chest ailments, his fraught relationship with women (his sister, his fiancée, the wife and daughters of his landlord are all characters in this mini-drama), and some of his aspirations and anxieties. The first chapter extrapolates on the ideas introduced in the prologue and leads smoothly into the second chapter, 'In Want of a Wife', which calls to mind the subtitle of the book: 'Lawrence was fascinated by marriage and marriages' (p. 46). Brightman, in what may be indicative of a trend towards prologues, describes the 16-year-old Mary McCarthy's visit to a Seattle lesbian bohemian.[25]

I had begun this survey sometimes expecting to find gender differences but more often thinking education, socialization, date of publication, editorial practices, or that invisible poetics of the genre would determine that I would not. There are some significant gender contrasts. The time Forrest Wilson spends on Harriet Beecher Stowe's father and his creation of the jolly-man's-story that asserts, 'The "great gun of Calvinism" had begotten a major prophetess' (p. 21) contrasts starkly with Joan Hedrick's steady attention in chapter 1 to the bleak, depressing life of Stowe's intelligent mother. Hedrick gives us a thesis that assures a more balanced consideration of her parents: 'In contrasting ways, Harriet Beecher's parents embodied important spirits of the age' (p. 4). Perhaps no post-women's-movement biography regardless of the sex of the author would include Wilson's narrative of an 'impatient' Lyman Beecher waiting for another son through, first, a 'hiatus of three years in the rhythm of [his wife's] productivity', and then two more years after a daughter who lived but a single month was born. Nor would, perhaps, friends be depicted offering 'humorous consolation' and appreciating 'Beecher's chagrin' at the birth of another daughter (pp. 20–1).

The treatments of the death of the baby, however, reveal different sensibilities. Wilson passes over it with a single sentence, but Hedrick comes close to blaming Beecher. The baby has whooping cough, and infants 'were more likely to wake up choking than coughing. After Roxana had been up night after night with the baby, Lyman told his exhausted wife to get some sleep; she obeyed, and while she slept the child died' (pp. 5–6). Hedrick quotes Beecher's *Autobiography* in which he remembers Roxana's 'resignation to God', but she does not give us his reaction, if any. The effect is a darkening of his character and a reinforcement of the impression that Roxana was trapped in a marriage requiring courageous endurance. David McCullough notes in passing that today a serious inquiry might have been made into the disastrously late diagnosis of Alice Roosevelt's Bright's disease. Here, perhaps, we see these biographers' generational similarities; we now believe medicine can be a science—identify illness almost at its onset and treat it successfully, and, when this illusion is shattered, blame and legal action are contemplated. In both Beecher's and Roosevelt's time such demands were not made on medicine; infants in our own country die of whooping cough, and a one-month baby would still be at serious risk. Nevertheless, both Wilson and Hedrick portray a Beecher whose mind was seldom on his family and whose attention to detail minimal. It is in what the biographers leave out as well as include that determines our interpretation. Wilson gives us that 'cop-out' impression that death was so common then that it was expected, but he also asks, 'What price a woman-child in 1811?' (p. 21). Hedrick tells us nothing about Beecher's reaction to the death—if there was none recorded, that, too, is evidence.

Women have rightly pointed out that we would never find a great man's biography entitled 'Philanthropist in Boxers'. Wilson's *Crusader in Crinoline* calls attention to Stowe's underwear and her sex—that she is not the usual type of crusader—and offers a figurative, titillating peak beneath the crinoline. Nigel Nicolson's unsympathetic description of Mary Theresa Carver Leiter, his portrayal of the appeal of Marshal Field (the family store) to women, and the lament that he could not 'name for certain Mary's many suitors' or find out if Balfour and Kitchen were 'in love with her' smell of gendered images of women. Strangely, this perspective can be a strength. Mary Curzon, who became Vicereine of India, 'the highest position which any American, man or woman, has ever held in the British Empire', led a fascinating life, and Nicolson's prose evokes a glittering late-Victorian world which we have been conditioned to believe in. We learn that she arrived for her wedding in an open carriage between 'banks of spectators' and that she 'wore no gloves, which excited comment' (p. 78). At a dance in her honour, she arrived with what the press called 'a mailbag over her shoulder', presumably to contain the ' "favours", an odd assortment of ribbons . . . , sachets, match-boxes, and thermometers' (p. 29). The summing up in these terms, however, is problematic:

'The purpose and triumph of her life was to be loved by such a man as George Curzon' (p. 211). That she once wanted to organize and finance a group of women to educate and help the poor would in the hands of a feminist biographer of either sex receive serious attention.

Another gender difference is that women were much more likely to put personal information in their prefaces and introductions than were men. Even when men did it, they tended to share intellectual rather than private connections and thoughts, as R. W. B. Lewis does. Personal remark becomes the leading category in the popularity poll because of the number of women biographers in the sample I extracted from the total number of winning books. In fact—and I'm not sure what to make of this—all of the personal comments about the difficulty of writing their subject's life by men were by men writing about women, and two-thirds of the personal openings by men were in books about women. This does not mean that women confined themselves to recollections of occasional conversations with the *grand dame* or Master. For instance, the personal statements by Elizabeth Frank's 'Foreword' to *Louise Bogan* seem to handle delicately her subject's reticence, depression, and painful life; she comments sensitively, 'privacy that is violated for the sake of literary and cultural history remains violated' (p. xvi). The differences are, however, significant, and many could be identified with already gendered categories. Both David Kennedy's and Deirdre Bair's biographies began as Ph.D. dissertations; Kennedy begins with an 'impressive identification' of Margaret Sanger and tells us late in the preface how his study began. Deirdre Bair confesses her naïve, even gauche, graduate student behaviour, but then effectively weaves comments by Beckett and her reactions to them into her narrative and sometimes teases out Beckett's bluff stoicism.

Sometimes women were disarmingly themselves, as when Victoria Glendinning writes, 'I have never been so happy researching and writing any book. . . .' Some take up deeply feminist issues, as Thurman does when she recites the many names Isak Dinesen had. Sometimes they admit deeply private connections; for instance, women biographers' fascination with intellectual women appears often. Carol Brightman describes the moment in which Mary McCarthy told an entire audience that she had given Brightman so much access because she was 'writing about herself'. Brightman's master's thesis, we are told, was on Simone de Beauvoir and Anaïs Nin, and her fascination with these women becomes an invitation to share it.

As I read, I began to recognize new kinds of balances that needed to be struck, the artful ways biographers engage readers, new dangers in perspective, gender, and ideology, and subtle differences in the contract being established and maintained between the writer and the reader, between the writer and the biographical subject.[26] What fosters the experience that my friends were calling 'magisterial' is the quality of the contract and begins in the establishment and inobtrusive maintenance of an authoritative tone, one that is far more complicated than has been thought. The biographer, Edmund Wilson admonished, 'has not only to choose and place every detail of his picture, but to calculate the tone of every sentence' (quoted in Nadel, 154). Certainly selecting, establishing, and maintaining the voice of the biography is the most personal decision biographers make and the aspect of the book requiring the most sustained effort.

2. *Living with the Subject*

Some will show off your talents, others will probably kill you
Kenneth Silverman, comparing choosing a subject
to the way Hemingway's bullfighters sized up bulls

Virginia Woolf wrote: 'A career in biography is a costly investment.'[1] That is certainly true—even a single foray into biography is an expensive undertaking. Writing a biography ordinarily takes between five and fifteen years and a significant amount of travel, often to distant places. Commitment to any topic and sustaining interest and freshness for that length of time is a daunting challenge. It would seem, then, that the selection of the subject of a biography would be a serious undertaking—a decision reached reflectively by heart and head. This is rare. Every biography, however, bears the traces of what lured the writer into the investment, and each is even more strongly marked by what the relationship between subject and biographer became. The subject's life, representation, and reputation is at the mercy of these motives and shifting feelings. Therefore, in addition to the biographer's qualifications—the talents to be shown off—motives matter and infuse the biography as surely as the voice does.

★

Sometimes the talents to be shown off and a sensible motive for selecting a particular person are obvious. Once a historical period or the rituals of something like a political campaign have been mastered, that knowledge can be mined and deployed in a series of lives. We can understand, then, the biographer who writes several lives of prime ministers or presidents. Richard Holmes specializes in the Romantic period (*Shelley*, *Coleridge*), and Michael Holroyd exploited and developed what he had learned writing *Augustus John* and *Lytton Strachey* in his life of Bernard Shaw. At home in a time period or with an occupation, fascinated by it, and sensible enough to see the reasons for taking advantage of the investment in time, money, travel, and research already made, biographers often move easily from subject to subject, and readers experience the biographer's deep familiarity—familiarity that can be taken to such amusing lengths as Richard Holmes dating a cheque '1772' while working on his life of Percy Bysshe Shelley (Atlas, 64).

Lifelong students of time periods, events, or writers sometimes see biography as the natural apogee of their work and the showpiece of their mastery. N. John Hall wrote *Trollope: A Biography* after editing the letters; R. H. Super had written about Trollope's career in the post office before writing *The*

Chronicler of Barsetshire: A Life of Anthony Trollope, and most of the biographers of Daniel Defoe had written at least one book about him before writing a biography. Sometimes the connections are not so obvious, but the relationship of themes and dominant contextual and social issues is fascinating. Catherine Drinker Bowen speaks of her biography of Edward Coke, which followed lives of Oliver Wendell Holmes and of John Adams and won the National Book Award, as 'quite naturally rounding out, carrying the story of our form of free government back to England, where it had its inception' (Bowen, *The Lion and the Throne*, ix). One of the explanations for the number of second and third biographies that win major prizes may be this almost invisible honing of technique and immersion in periods of political or intellectual history.

Years of teaching, research, and publishing provide a nearly unmatchable foundation upon which to base an interpretation of the life and art, and mature scholars sometimes turn back to subjects and approach them from new perspectives or with completely different questions. As a student, Isobel Grundy worked with Robert Halsband, the distinguished expert on Lady Mary Wortley Montagu. Now, years after Halsband's death, she is writing a new biography of Lady Mary and has published a collection of manuscripts that twenty years ago might have been dismissed as 'fragments' or 'dabblings in romance' (*Romance Writings*, 1996).

Most decisions to write a biography of a specific person have an element of intellectual or personal passion. Deirdre Bair describes ruminating with her agent about possible subjects for her second biography; when Simone de Beauvoir's name came up, 'it was something like those comic-strip characters who suddenly have light bulbs flashing as the word "Eureka!" explodes above their heads'. The questions that fired her imagination came from the realms of literary, intellectual, and feminist biography: 'How could that well-brought-up little Catholic girl have found the courage to become the fearless, free-spirited adult, who gave as good as she got in the often vicious arena of Paris intellectualism? And as for *The Second Sex*, from what place within her creative consciousness had that book come?' (*Simone de Beauvoir*, 12–13). These questions animate and shape the biography and become the organizing themes. Bair discovers the fact that 'almost every time she put her pen to paper' for twenty years, de Beauvoir wrote about a different subject in a different genre (p. 545) and celebrates what she believes to be true about de Beauvoir's life: that the last sixteen years, when she was giving support to feminist causes, effaced the 'High Priestess' of existentialism, Sartre's 'disciple'. As Bair worked, the feminist, the intellectual, and the personal relationship grew, and she became intensely engaged with de Beauvoir's mind and her self-conscious womanhood. The relationship changed repeatedly and veered in ways that deeply affected the content and presentation of the biography, for Bair moved from studying de Beauvoir's development to feeling intimate friendship and admiration. At one point, she even suggested that she and de Beauvoir collaborate on the final version.

The kind of blend of intellectual and personal engagement has many points of origin. Sometimes the researcher in quest of something else stumbles upon a cache of letters or a set of diaries. Sometimes a scholar is offered or shown a document or object that haunts the imagination until a biography is inevitable. Richard Ellmann describes such an event, which led to his biography of Joyce: 'Twelve years ago in Dublin Mrs. W. B. Yeats showed me an unpublished preface in which Yeats described his first meeting with James Joyce . . . (*James Joyce*, vii). Sometimes a question haunts the mind. Charles Capper found, as he expected, that Margaret Fuller was 'the most written-about woman in early American history' but found nothing to satisfy his desire to know how she established herself as the first woman in America to be a 'dominant figure in highbrow culture at large'.[2] After all, Julia Ward Howe had written her biography, and Emerson sent Thoreau to the Fire Island beach to search for 'any fragment of manuscripts or other property' that might have washed up from the shipwreck that killed her. Capper wrote her biography setting her among, beside, and in competition with her most educated and cultured contemporaries. Samuel Eliot Morison had a much less predictable but equally haunting question. He wanted to know how good a sailor Columbus was, and so he chartered a boat, followed Columbus's four routes, and wrote his prize-winning *Admiral of the Ocean Sea*. Perhaps navigation is one of the less-frequently showcased talents biographers possess, but Morison brings readers to share this means of evaluating Columbus and making comparisons between the states of navigational methods. The ways Morison's questions affect the narrative emphases are often unexpected and original.

Some biographers' intellectual passions draw them to new methods they have read about, and if they are fortunate many circumstances often converge. About the time T. Harry Williams became intrigued by the Columbia Oral History Project of the 1950s, he chanced upon a letter from Russell Long. His interest in Russell's father, Huey, knowledge of a configuration of research methods, and his Louisiana background and deep knowledge of the state allowed him to write virtuoso sections of *Huey Long*, such as the chapter on Long and Louisiana State University in which Williams moves quickly through the almost incredibly sudden changes Long made, including building a medical school from scratch on the campus. Williams tends to structure discussion of each change in the same way. He begins with what appears to be speculation but because of the material before and after it, he is actually supplying interpretation. He writes, 'As though obsessed with a determination to lift up the educational condition of the state overnight, Huey turned his attention to . . . the appalling illiteracy rate among adults' (p. 523). The sentence is filled with judgements. In a few sentences, Williams tells us what Long did and gives the data to support it: 'Over a hundred thousand adults, most of them Negroes, attended the classes. . . . The effect . . . was reflected in the census table of 1930. The illiteracy rate for whites, ten per cent in 1920, was reduced to seven per cent, and the rate for Negroes from thirty-eight per cent to twenty-three per cent' (p. 523). Quickly Williams uses a quotation from Long to demonstrate that, in Williams's words, 'the social implications of illiteracy [were] more important than the political ones' to Long (p. 524). Williams uses census data and Long's programme to give the past and present and this quotation and other information to show the implications and significance for the future. The result is a nuanced account of Long and an unusual diversity of sources that, among other things, show us Long through the eyes of different classes and races and measure Louisiana State University against other American universities and academic revolutions.

It is familiar folklore that biographers have an 'affinity' for their subjects, may have long 'identified' to some extent with them, and 'like' them. In some cases, these statements are true. According to a number of people, Scott Berg, who began his biography as a senior thesis at Princeton, had 'a perfect feel for Max Perkins—who he was, what he represented'.[3] Ann Thwaite, who felt resistant to writing a third biography, describes how she saw 'immediately that [A. A.] Milne was exactly the right subject' for her when he was suggested by an editor at Faber.[4] Here the 'liking' went back to childhood, and the affinity was deeply intellectual and perhaps psychological. Her father had written a Milne-style children's book, in imitation of Christopher Robin she had been called by a double name, and she treasured pictures of her brother holding Kanga and Roo.

Thwaite's 'Introduction' teases out what this subject and her earlier subjects had in common and some of the powerful interests they fed. She notes that she is particularly interested in writers and the literary and theatrical worlds, and she is clearly fascinated by class—both social and literary. She tells us that she and Christopher Robin had 'down-market' London childhoods and that Milne once said that a writer who 'stooped to write advertisements' ' "would deem it necessary to slink past Sir Edmund Gosse [one of Thwaite's earlier biographical subjects] with his hat over his eyes" ' (p. xiv). Thinking about questions people asked her leads her to talk about gender:

People have often asked me whether I would not rather be writing a biography of a woman. I find that surprising. I am interested in people—men *and* women—and the way they live their lives. . . . But it occurs to me that the lives of Gosse and Milne shared many of the characteristics of the lives of women. They were both for men of their time unusually concerned with childhood. . . . Their lives as writers were home-based . . . They were . . . interested in words rather than actions and in people rather than power. The worst time of Milne's life was the only time when he lived as a man among men. (p. xix)

Although Thwaite describes her ideal relationship to her subject as 'a discriminating love', she sees herself as detective and tireless researcher and turns a sympathetic but thorough microscope lens on him from every angle. Milne's son wrote, 'My father's heart remained buttoned up all through his life.' Thwaite finds the same phrase in musings by others of Milne's generation and concludes, 'This "buttoning up", I think, was not a "natural" aspect of Alan Milne's character but, at least in some sense, a consequence of being born a Victorian' (p. 79). Over and over, she uses her personal voice not to excuse but to explain, to convey compassionate understanding without exoneration.

Sometimes a biographer believes that the subject is misunderstood or unjustly neglected. James Winn mentions several times that he hopes that his biography of Dryden will 'send readers back to [Dryden's] works' and help them hear 'his mighty music' (pp. 513, xiv); Paul Mariani freely admits that he hoped to 'canonize' Williams with his biography of the poet and cites a lead-up article entitled, 'Toward the Canonization of William Carlos Williams' (Mandell, 22–3). Some of the most gripping parts of Maynard Mack's biography of Alexander Pope are the sections in which he shows Pope to be part of a circle of affectionate, lifelong friends rather than to be the lonely, peevish wasp of legend and those in which he argues the costs of Pope's Roman Catholicism and the poet's stubborn dedication to his faith.

The affinity of biographer with subject colours the tone and enriches the book. Thomas Congdon, a partner in Congdon and Weed and publisher of many biographies, writes, 'In choosing biographies to publish, there is a consideration beyond the subject, beyond the material, beyond the analysis of the competition. It is the author himself [sic]. The material may be fine from every point of view—but is this author the right person to write this particular book?' (p. 5). Sometimes someone else first notices that the biographer is especially capable of understanding the subject, the contexts of that life, and that there will be dynamic engagement with the person's life. A group of Hannah Arendt's friends gathered at her memorial service discussed a biography and turned to Elisabeth Young-Bruehl with the suggestion that she write it. A reviewer, who knew both Arendt and Young-Bruehl, later wrote that she saw 'them as very much alike—breathtakingly brilliant and informed by a rare moral passion. Both as young women struggled with the impact, the force, of their personalities on the world around them.'[5]

Sometimes what outsiders know of a writer's work or personality leads them to identify a good potential biographer and in that identification may be an investment both in learning more about the subject and in being themselves better understood. Diane Wood Middlebrook tells the story of the phone call from one of Billie Tipton's wives, who exclaimed at one point: 'I expected you to understand.' Later Tipton told her, '*I* want to understand.' Arthur Ashe had read and admired Arnold Rampersad's biography of Langston Hughes and asked Rampersad to collaborate on his autobiography, *Days of Grace*, and, before that, the executor of Langston Hughes's estate had asked Rampersad to write the authorized biography of Hughes.

In these cases, an outsider has observed the biographer and identified him or her as the right person—one whose affinities, insights, personality, and even prose style are likely to yield an illuminating, sympathetic biography. Linnie Marsh Wolfe recounts how John Muir's older daughter asked her to do the biography that would win the 1946 Pulitzer Prize: 'Many people know of my father as a naturalist, but the world has never understood him as a man. I wish you would write of him from that point of view and tell of his human relationships' (*Son of the Wilderness*, vii). Nigel Nicolson invited Victoria Glendinning to write *Vita: The Life of V. Sackville-West*, his mother's life. A senior editor and his agent suggested the tantalizing mathematical genius, Srinivasa Ramanujan, to Robert Kanigel, author of *Chaos*, and Kanigel, as he says, 'came under Ramanujan's spell'. Many biographers record similar events.

It is not uncommon for people to remark on the similarities between a biographer and the subject and to believe that the biographer at some level recognized the affinity and was influenced by it. Whether these similarities—and in my experience they are almost invariably superficial—existed before the biography was written, were written into the biography and, therefore, imposed on the subject, or were adopted by the biographer from long and intense exposure to the subject's habits, mannerisms, and speech patterns will always be a tangled question. Toril Moi, who was deeply involved with Simone de Beauvoir throughout her book, comments, 'Like other intellectual women I recognize myself in some, but by no means in all, of Beauvoir's experiences . . .' (*Simone de Beauvoir*, 10). Claire Tomalin is certainly correct and commonsensical: 'I don't know whether biographers can claim intimacy with their subjects; in one sense, obviously not—the woman [Dorothy Jordan] died nearly two hundred years ago—but in another, yes, since four years living with somebody does tend to put you on first-name terms' (letter to *TLS*, 4 November 1994). One could note that Isobel Grundy and Lady Mary are dignified, even stately, are gracious, socially adept women, and write with precision and elegance. It is possible to imagine Isobel conducting herself with the ease, charm, and alertness that Lady Mary did with the European and Turkish court ladies. Did Grundy see herself in Lady Mary? Did she come to see herself in Lady Mary? Over the many years that she worked with Lady Mary and her writings did Lady Mary's story become for her one of the many 'plots' for a woman's life that fiction, history, and biographies provide? After all, as Bettina Aptheker wrote in *Tapestries of Life*, 'Stories transform our experiences into ways of knowing', and surely stories provide us with models of conduct and relating to people and situations. Carolyn Heilbrun has gone so far as to say that 'lives do not serve as models; only stories do that' (*Writing a Woman's Life*, 37).

These questions have some intrinsic interest, and all biographers are asked questions such as those posed above. Some would argue that the kinds of similarities between Grundy and Lady Mary are important and parallel a theory about fiction writers, that, for instance, a low-born, grammar-school-educated person could not write a convincing novel about aristocratic life conducted in New York city penthouses, four-star European hotels, and the garden parties of aristocratic acquaintances in England. Carolyn Heilbrun notes graciously that James Brabazon had two advantages in writing the life of Dorothy Sayers that she would not have had: 'he is English, with that inherent understanding of a culture that cannot be learned; and he is conversant with and sympathetic to Sayers's religious beliefs' (p. 50). The crippling handicap of not having a good grasp of this kind of contextual resonance can result in a biography such as one J. P. Kenyon judged 'riddled with clownish errors'. The 'lack of "feel" for the period makes [the biographer] incompetent to assess the effect of Puritanism on Pepys's thinking', Kenyon writes of Vincent Brome's *The Other Pepys* (*TLS*, 30 July 1993, 23). When the voice wavers or the contract between reader and biographer is stretched, speculations about the relationship between writer and life bubble to the surface. For instance, it has been said that the alert reader can tell what Walter Jackson Bate's therapist said to him at the time he was writing Part 3 of his biography of Samuel Johnson.[6]

It seems to me that 'affinity' and 'identification' usually play little part in the actual decision to write a biography. The statement that John Wain makes claiming that he has special insight into Samuel Johnson because he was 'born in the same district as Johnson', went to the same university, and 'since then [has] lived the same life of Grub Street . . . and the unremitting struggle to write enduring books against the background of an unstable existence' (14) is striking not just because of its bizarre forthrightness and arrogance but because, even in ameliorated form, it is nearly unique. Certainly the biographer has to believe that the subject is worthy of a biography and is interesting and important enough to engage him or her for many, many years of dreary research and careful writing. Here Wain's claims that he wants to reach intelligent, general readers in order to correct 'certain stereotyped misconceptions' and to make Johnson better known outside the English-speaking world by writing an accessible book are solidly mainstream biographical motives.

Were biographers entirely practical people and their decisions about whom to write about completely rational, they would ask themselves a series of questions, some dictated by their own abilities and interests, some by their culture, and some by the literary market-place. Most biographers, if not before they begin but at least at the stage they propose the book to a publisher or granting agency (and only a fool writes a biography without a contract or the solid hope of one), ask themselves these questions:

Value of the Undertaking

◆ What is the significance of the person? how worthy a subject?

◆ What is the significance of the person's work?

◆ What is the significance of the person's life?

◆ What is interesting about the person's life? work? is it interesting enough to hold my attention for years?

◆ In what ways is this life of interest to my own contemporaries? the work? has it to any degree shaped the world in which we live?

As they begin to develop the voice and identify the themes and emphases in the book, a new set of questions comes into play.

Contribution of the Undertaking

◆ In what way will my biography be original? what's new? what can be related in a new way? what new aspect of the life can I explore?

◆ How will it fit into the existing scholarship on the person and the subjects?

◆ How can people use it? (to extend knowledge, to develop other aspects of the life and work, to teach better, etc.)

And there are questions that come to biographers in the dead of night. Many of these questions are completely unanticipated until some unpleasant discovery or event forces them into consciousness. Biographers do meet people in libraries who are working on lives of the same person—and are three years ahead. They discover important manuscripts that they can't read or can't have access to or can't quote. In year five, they discover they have done it all wrong, as Bowen did after writing 50,000 words on Tchaikovsky only to start over (*Biography*, 27–8). Or find they loathe or are bored by their subject. As Justin Kaplan, winner of the Pulitzer and the National Book Award for *Mr. Clemens and Mark Twain*, says, biographers are the authors of many unwritten books. Among the many examples, all resonant with fellow biographers, he gives is his flirtation with Ulysses S. Grant, 'the sort of archetypal figure I had been looking for: a shabby firewood peddler divinely endowed with strength and a charisma so powerful that [Sherman] said he fought under Grant with "the faith a Christian has in his Savior." ' 'But after about a year of living with Grant I began to develop such a long list of reluctances . . . that I was left with an idea for what could only be a tiny book about Ulysses Grant and his rapport with horses.'[7] Trust me; it happens. Just like that.

So, although being able to pose these questions before a biography is begun would require the combined talents of Merlin and Tiresias, here are the questions that trigger nightmares during the writing:

Bedrock practical

◆ Can I do this? do I have the skills and knowledge?

◆ How long will it take? (triple that) can I afford that?

◆ What are some of the known costs? (double that) can I afford that? (sadly, some people simply cannot manage to do research in France or England or the USA year after year)

◆ Is there too much or too little material about the subject?

◆ Is there new material available?

◆ How accessible is the material?

◆ Who are the competing experts? can I compete?

◆ How can I be sure it is original?

◆ Who is the audience? do I know how to write for them?

◆ How will it fit into my career plan?

◆ How much do I want to do it? (often the answer to this question, cancels out all negative answers)

From the culture and the publishing world comes another group of unpleasant questions:

Questions a publisher will ask

◆ Will it sell? is there a market?

◆ Will it contribute to the prestige or special niche of the press?

◆ What will be its length and cost to produce?

◆ What kind of reviews and reviewers will it attract?

◆ Will it endure?

These questions suggest the interweaving of the personal, the cultural, and the commercial. Even if it can be done—the writer has the knowledge, skill, time, and means—no one may publish it—or read it. 'St Defoe won't do, this is a secular time, his religion, even if it is the key to his actions and emotions, just isn't interesting', friends cautioned in the materialistic 1980s. Richard Sewall's biography seems hopelessly of a piece with its time and, therefore, dated: 'She set herself the task—a task that developed gradually into a vocation—to mediate to "every man" the infinitely varied facets and phrases of the central "dazzling" truth as it was vouchsafed her in her moments . . . of inspiration' and 'But the "Dream" was always there. Immortality was the . . . pursuit . . . that gave form and coherence to her life and work. . . . her "pilgrim" life, her "Puritan Spirit"' (2: 724).

That it won tells much about the prize's era and the connections between the time, society's sensibility, and the plots and stories it enjoys and believes in.

★

Cultural interests, economics, and ambition merge with the personal and may even be the primary motives for choosing a particular subject.[8] Biographers do, after all, write the lives of people they consider monsters or repellant human beings. Biographies, though seldom capable of competing with a novel by Irving Stone or Danielle Steele, can attract a steady readership and, over years, reward the biographer with higher royalties and more recognition than a book of literary criticism. The possibility of the equivalent of a gold strike, however remote, exists; R. W. B. Lewis's *Edith Wharton* and Diane Middlebook's *Anne Sexton*, for instance, moved traditional academics into enough prominence that their books made best-seller lists and their names became widely recognized.

It is not uncommon to hear 'We need a biography of . . .', and a cultural history of any nation, its anxieties, needs, and aspirations decade by decade, could be built out of its biographies. Agreeing with 'need', recognizing opportunity, being engaged with the issues of the time, and wanting to work through or present interpretations of events encourage biographies. For example, as race relations in the USA have become more confrontational, a stream of biographies of nearly forgotten Civil Rights workers have appeared, and the meaning, issues, and resolutions of that period are being reconsidered and contested. As Bill Clinton's small-state political world gains world wide attention, biographies of Orville Faubus, another former governor of Arkansas, and even Harry Truman emphasize what a *TLS* reviewer called 'local American politics' (17 May 1996, 8). England, in many ways the world's biographer, is reaffirming its international sensibility and financial and diplomatic position with biographies of people from continental Europe and the Middle East and especially of people who lived or served in foreign countries during the Empire.

Leon Edel has written that there was almost no literary figure for whom a new biography could not be profitably written because of newly discovered information. Moreover, as Kenneth Silverman says, each new age wants to know different things about historic figures.[9] Each generation asks new things from its writers and new questions about the people who shaped the world we live in. For instance, each new biography of D. H. Lawrence treats his marriage, his anger, and the effects of his strange vagabond lifestyle on his temper and his art. Biographies of women have become a boom industry, and until we have more of early women writers, we will not be able to construct a picture of what the literary experience was like for them, what pressures influenced their decisions and shaped their books, and how and when the truisms we repeat about, for instance, the 'modesty' of early women writers began.

Sometimes the critic discovers that the most interesting, even essential, remaining questions about a famous person are biographical; this situation is often true for writers. A reviewer of Hazel Rowley's biography of the Australian writer Christina Stead wrote

Most literary biographies follow on from their subjects' fame. But in Christina Stead's case, one suspects, her acceptance as one of the century's great writers will depend on getting a full picture of her as a person. The story of her life gives her stories a context and a continuity they otherwise lack, and helps you believe that they are indeed this savage, this intense, this demanding.[10]

Daniel Defoe's fiction has often been treated as similarly puzzling. Peter Earle, author of a very good book about Defoe wrote, 'The Defoe who wrote the novels seems to be a very different man from the Defoe one gets to know in the rest of his works' (*World of Defoe*, 230). Until recently critics often treated Defoe as outside the canon or as a precursor rather than a part of the mainline history of the English novel. Why indeed would a successful journalist and writer of non-fiction prose suddenly at age 59 write a novel?

As in Stead's case, knowledge of Defoe's life and of the historical and literary context in which he worked gives his novels roots and continuity. For example, Defoe had been experimenting with fictionalized lives as a form of political propaganda and with extended *exempla* complete with characters and lively dialogue as central parts of books of 'practical divinity' for nearly ten years. In *Robinson Crusoe* he brought these techniques and forms together, and this 'novel' can be read partly as a highly original and effective contribution to debates associated with colonization and especially with the Salters' Hall controversy, the dispute among Defoe's religious group over whether the Bible was an adequate test of doctrine or if the confessions of faith needed to be applied as well.

Biographies move readers a tiny bit closer to understanding genius—how an individual transforms experience and even personality into art.[11] It is perhaps only biographical evidence that can give us access to the personal intensity that, like the point of greatest pressure that creates the diamond, stands behind the most powerful passages and episodes in literature. Douglas Bush identified the blind poet John Milton's line 'O dark, dark, dark, at brightest noontide dark' as 'impersonal art charged with personal meaning',[12] but a legal decision or a land acquisition can be equally charged and resonant. As John T. Noonan, a judge of the United States Court of Appeals, argued in a review of Andrew Kaufman's *Cardozo*[13] 'Americans are blessed with a much fuller literature on their judges' lives, reflecting, I believe, an American appreciation of the truth that the law a judge makes is a projection of values that are inescapably personal' (*NYTBR*, 21 June 1998, 7).

★

The reasons for choosing a particular person as the subject for a biography can be deep, even unreachably deep in the psyche, utterly pragmatic, idealistic, romantic, blatantly ambitious, carried over from childhood, born in a chance encounter—the range is nearly infinite. In fact, the choice is far less personal than it seems, but regardless of how ambitious, crass, or financial the decision is, it becomes *very* personal and the movement from choice to ongoing commitment is a major factor in how the life story and its meaning begin to be perceived.

James Breslin explained in an interview about writing his *Mark Rothko* that he was trying to distance himself from 'the tendency of biographers to project themselves onto their subjects, to write their autobiographies in the form of biographies'.[14] And yet in the afterword to the biography, he explains as explicitly as any biographer ever did some of the personal, autobiographical things that drew him to Rothko. He describes his personal life and his mood and then his response to an exhibit of Rothko's paintings, especially to one period of them: 'Empty and luminous, they seemed ebullient, ecstatic, a visionary alternative to the entanglements of my daily life. Yet their emptiness sometimes seemed a void, an annihilating vacancy that came from some profound sense of loss. Both Rothko's elation and his despair were moods I was particularly ready to experience. . . . how was Rothko at forty-seven—just three years older than I was then . . . able to re-form his work, his life, his *self*' (*Rothko*, 554).

In a fascinating recognition and analysis of his personal and his intellectual experiences during the writing of the biography, he observes, 'I was also moved to find out how Rothko, at mid-life, managed to liberate himself and his work and then, a little more than fifteen years later, how Rothko, now eminent, wealthy, and productive, felt trapped within his format, his marriage, his success. . . . exploring how Rothko did it and then how he undid it was not, for me, a mere intellectual exercise. . . . [these] are the issues that originally activated me' (pp. 554–5). At every point, the biography explores these questions of remaking and redirection, and provides a unified narrative that integrates events, his work, and his psyche. The rightness of Breslin's narrative of Rothko's suicide is certainly the result of this dynamic intellectual and personal engagement, and he captures both its likelihood, indeed near inevitability, but also the complex, entangled motives for it.

Paul Mariani recalls how he began to hear John Berryman saying, 'You belong to me. You belong to me.' Soon, he relates, 'there was nothing else I could do except Berryman. Nothing else. Nothing.'[15] Every biographer knows this feeling: obsession, absorption, an intensity of concentration that few can even imagine and that becomes a memory we long to experience again. James Atlas describes 'The old sensation of being drawn into another life began to assail me almost with a sense of fatality.'[16] Assailed, sucked into, consumed by, a kind of writing unlike any other.

Sometimes the accounts given by biographers are frightening. Phyllis Rose sank into a depression when she came to the point of writing about Virginia Woolf's suicide: 'I narrate her death from the point of view of the cook. For me, it was a way of getting out of a psychological box: I identified with her and she was terribly depressed, in fact suicidal, and I just couldn't write at all, until I figured out this way of breaking out of that identification' (Mandell, 105). Joan Weimer imagined that she had begun to read with Constance Fenimore Woolson's eyes and think her thoughts and that her husband was 'wildly jealous . . . of the way Connie soaks up my time and attention'.[17] Bonny Vaught experienced a 'total entanglement' of her life with Charlotte Forten Grimké's that she described as 'deadly'. She describes periods during which she feels that she and her subject are 'sad, childless women of middle age' and not only blends but compounds their difficult situations: 'My depression became entangled with hers in a way I still do not fully understand. It may have been a classic identification of biographer with subject. . . . Adding the weight of another woman's life and another century's problems brought me nearly to a halt.'[18] 'As in [Stephen] Crane's story ['The Monster'], my father had no face. Crane had written my nightmare', Linda Davis writes in a moving account of what drew her to writing his biography.[19] While some of these experiences seem extreme to me, Carol Ascher's dreams about de Beauvoir are probably fairly common. Shortly after Jean-Paul Sartre's death, for instance, she dreamed that she went to Paris to interview de Beauvoir (p. 112).

As they write, some biographers find encouragement and validation for what they feel they are and want to be or fear they might be. Every modern biographer of Simone de Beauvoir has to come to grips with her life with Sartre and many actions and statements that distress mainline feminists. Yet female biographers of Simone de Beauvoir often say in one way or another with Carol Ascher that de Beauvoir's life reinforced their 'own sense of being an intellectual'. Deirdre Bair entitles chapters 'The Girl with a Man's Brain' and 'The Young Girl Who Worked Too Much'—jibes often made at smart girls who enjoy learning. As Moi argues in detail, being an intellectual is usually considered an asset for a man but a 'liability' for a woman.[20]

In her prize-winning book, Bair tells the story of a journey that concludes with de Beauvoir earning her place as a feminist icon by her writing and the life she led after Sartre's death. In writing, Bair's relationship to de Beauvoir became complicated in a variety of ways. Her working through her reactions contributed to the unfolding story of de Beauvoir's multi-faceted complexity and her changing actions and ideas. Her book becomes a circuitous, fascinating journey that is a metaphor for de Beauvoir's life and concludes with a description of a funeral procession joined by thousands of people, including groups of African women and elderly people, that provides a symbolic canonization as, in Bair's words, 'the mother of us all' (p. 618). In her biography, Carol Ascher addresses a personal letter to de Beauvoir and puts the letter in the biography: 'I have been badly troubled by you . . . Often in the morning as I go to my desk, I feel resentful. . . .' 'Unfortunately you aren't that "good mother" I long for in my weakest moments.' 'With you the relationship has always been ambivalent.'[21]

Toril Moi insists she is not writing a biography of de Beauvoir, but her book fits comfortably within a group of neo-biographies that are ideological, consider a portion of a person's life or work, or are a blend of intellectual biography and cultural studies. On nearly every page, Moi engages with what de Beauvoir's life and work mean to the twentieth century and especially to intellectual women. By defining 'intellectual woman' as 'any woman who has ever taken herself seriously as a thinker, particularly in an educational context', she casts her circle wide enough to include a large audience (p. 3). In the chapter analysing the ongoing responses to and representation of de Beauvoir, she observes, 'I realized just how difficult it is for a woman to be taken seriously as an intellectual, even in the late twentieth century' (p. 74). She makes us aware of the stakes and the politics in reviewing and writing, and, because France continues to have such complex responses to de Beauvoir, how the representation of a person in a biography is always the 'site of ideological and aesthetic conflict'. Chapter by chapter, she studies de Beauvoir and her life with the most sophisticated of contemporary theoretical tools, and the result is that we understand de Beauvoir's life at least as well from her book as from Bair's, and we understand a great deal about the literary, intellectual, and social milieu and how it impacts intellectual women. Like Bair's study, Moi's shows signs of discomfort and struggle with portions of de Beauvoir's life and, like the others, especially with the way de Beauvoir sometimes sacrificed autonomy and even self-respect for Sartre and consistently privileged masculinity in her writings, but her conclusion is original and strikingly tough-minded. 'There is something heroic about her cast-iron determination to make that central relationship work in spite of everything', Moi insists. Her book comes full circle when Moi speaks in her own voice to explain why de Beauvoir's life is so important: she teaches us 'courage, patience, and fortitude' through her 'persistent and patient efforts to become an independent woman, to build a literary career for herself, and to devote herself to the solitary task of writing' (p. 256). Moreover, 'More than any other woman in this century, her life invites us to consider the questions of love and the intellectual woman' and leaves us with a vision of possibilities both 'comforting and . . . utterly daunting' (p. 257). Bair and Moi got out of writing de Beauvoir's life what readers seek, and the openness of their responses to de Beauvoir admits troubling questions with great cultural resonance.

All of these biographies have their experimental elements, and lives such as de Beauvoir's seem to encourage or even demand departures from traditional approaches and shapes. Jean Gattégno gives his biography of Lewis Carroll the subtitle *Fragments of a Looking-Glass* and arranges his numerous, short sections in alphabetical order ('Assets and Expenditure' is chapter 2, 'Early Years' chapter 7, and 'Papa and Mama' chapter 19). 'What, then, can we say? . . . we have a few highlights, but no picture—even a distorted one—of the total reality', he muses (p. 70). The problem that Gattégno saw was bringing together the 'three men' he believed Lewis Carroll to be (and to have been perceived to be). In addition to the immortal creator of *Alice in Wonderland*, Carroll was Charles Lutwidge Dodgson, a rather distinguished Oxford University mathematician, and also an uncommonly quirky human being. By arranging his biography by alphabetical topics, Gattégno attempts, he says, to suggest the many worlds in which Carroll lived.

Gattégno is exceptionally self-conscious about the fact that the biographical subject is both at the centre of the work and not the centre, because he is to be discovered by being looked at, described, and discussed. In a daring move, Gattégno uses Dodgson's term as Curator of the Christ Church College Common Room to begin to bring the three 'men' together. Gattégno notes, 'As to the Wine Committee, Carroll's biographers have often been dismayed to see how much time he devoted to anything so frivolous. They fail to understand both its seriousness and the English taste for good wine' (p. 46). In Dodgson's actions and especially his memos, minutes, letters, and forms, the writer of both *Alice* and *Symbolic Logic, Part I* stands forth, and a 'coherent, efficient, and sound' person emerges.[22] Dodgson's quirkiness and the readers' preconceptions of the kind of person who would write *Alice in Wonderland* make for resistance to traditional biographical presentation, and Gattégno, who had already written a book on Lewis Carroll, saw this probability as well as his subject's odd personality and unusual combination of writings.

Edith Gelles calls her biography of Abigail Adams a 'collage' and foregrounds in each chapter a defining identity: female patriot, mother, wife to a founder of the country, news-hungry, flirtatious correspondent, and loyal member of a family machine as pervasive as the Kennedys.[23] Andrew Field in *Nabokov: His Life in Part*, which is presented as conversation, may also have been motivated by both a sense of his subject's unusual personality and a dawning realization that different methods of representing his identity would be necessary. Like Gattégno, he had written an earlier, more conventional book on his subject. In *Nabokov: His Life in Art* (1967), his first biography of him, Field remarked that Nabokov had 'managed to make his private self all but invisible . . . moving . . . never leaving more than a puzzled shrug . . .' (p. 33). He described his biography as a 'sea chest containing excerpts from and allusions to hundreds of valuable and precious documents, forgotten or completely unknown' (p. 6). Using these neglected works by Nabokov is, he says, one of the innovative features of his book, and the other is his construction of 'parabolic' chapters that treated Nabokov's works as 'characters in a novel'.

Field's second biography is written as a continuous dialogue with Nabokov. Sometimes the words in bold are Nabokov's, sometimes they are what Field imagines Nabokov would say, and, rarely, they are the words of people who know Nabokov intimately. As the book unfolds, what Field already knows, what Nabokov tells him and reacts to, what Field observes and finds out through, for instance, interviews, and what he comes to understand from recognizing themes in Nabokov's discourse give the biography the flavour of both collaboration and sparring. Like so many of the experimental biographies, this is a place where the biographical enterprise and stance and the biographer's complex relationship to the subject are revealed starkly. Good biography must be collaboration—even with a dead subject, there must be empathy and a real or developed understanding of the social, emotional, and historical world. But good biography is always at its heart somewhat adversarial. The biographer must ferret out the hidden, the buried, the most shameful secrets. At one point Field describes a conflict, 'He was defending his life. I was defending my task and my independence' (p. 13). About that time, Nabokov 'grew progressively more alarmed at what he chose to regard as the wildly unreliable memories of my informants, who also of course happened to be relatives and friends' (p. 13). And Field re-evaluates interviewing—whom to talk to and how much to believe.

This biography, like those by Gelles and Gattégno, is arranged primarily by topic, includes gaping holes in the 'story' of the person's life, and depends more heavily on themes and images for unity than traditional biography. Just as we come incrementally to understand the central importance of Abigail Adams's relationship with her daughter, we begin to realize the part Aleksander Pushkin played in the formation of Nabokov's identity. Pushkin becomes a central image that allows the reader to move out to understanding Nabokov as man, writer, and Russian. Nabokov is represented as understanding himself by defining how he is like and unlike Pushkin and how Pushkin might react to him. Moreover, through Pushkin, Field creates a way of seeing what the city of St Petersburg and the special legacy of the city's Russian writers mean (pp. 90–1, 102). He concludes that Russia is as Nabokov describes it in a poem, 'the murmur of his blood and the riot of his dreams' (p. 105).

Like many of the other experimenters, Field strives for intimacy and the depiction of the intimate. He often represents himself in the home of the Nabokovs, at a meal with them, or in a position to overhear a private question or remark. We learn, for instance, that Nabokov writes standing at a lectern, that he takes a daily, morning bath ('a long steeping affair'), and that he has a 'homely butterfly-shaped mail catch' hanging in his foyer. Obviously fascinated by the Nabokovs' marriage, Field has a gift for striking details and anecdotes. He overhears Nabokov ask Véra Evseevna in Russian, 'Darling, can I really not write about him?'[24]

Just as some high-order fiction writers are tireless experimenters, so are some biographers. They are drawn to a different kind of subject, a different way of presenting a life. Sometimes the experiment is as mild as writing the life of an almost unknown person (Margaret Clapp's 1948 Pulitzer Prize winning biography of John Bigelow; William Willcox's Bancroft Prize winning life of Sir Henry Clinton) or writing the part of the life that has interested people least (David McCullough's *Mornings on Horseback*). In his biography of Sir Joshua Reynolds, Richard Wendorf concentrates on how the painter conducted himself with friends and got along in society. By so doing, he brings Reynolds's time alive, both the details of how people lived and its social values, but, most originally, he gives us unforgettable vignettes. We see one of Reynolds's rather chaotic dinner parties where, typically, too many people crowded around a table set with an inadequate number of knives, forks, glasses, and even plates, and guests quickly learned to grab the inadequately supplied wine and bread. Yet the company and the conversation were always animated and without equal—Johnson described the servants as 'gaping upon' the famous guests (pp. 50–1). Wendorf also emphasizes what portrait painting meant and how it was conducted, and especially in the description of Reynolds's rather collaborative work with the actors Sarah Siddons and David Garrick he explains with insight the performative elements of portraiture.

More commonly, however, biographers, like their readers, are drawn to the culture's favourite stories and kinds of achievement. Many times the choice of a subject is born in a complex desire to answer lingering questions about a particular kind of life story and in the hope of better understanding it—or even sharing in it by recording or celebrating it. Some of these stories are familiar. From fiction we recognize certain life patterns that can be depended upon to make satisfying stories. We see, for instance, in Colin Powell's life the contrast between his childhood and his adult achievement and are perennially fascinated by such success stories. How men such as Powell or Eisenhower or Nelson or Marlborough came to be the kind of military leaders they were is an unfolding, progressive story that we find familiar and pleasing. We also enjoy watching how early promise plays out. General P. G. T. Beauregard, for instance, graduated first in his class at West Point, and that adds an intriguing element to the story of his life as a Civil War general. In other cases, there is a quest. A man, it is usually a man, decides at a young age that he wants to be an MP, and he achieves his goal. The overcoming of extreme hardship or physical handicap to reach great achievement is another. Samuel Johnson with his severely damaged sight is a good example, as is Franklin D. Roosevelt and his triumph over polio.

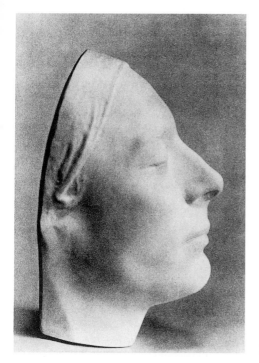

1. Life mask of Keats by Benjamin
Robert Haydon

Some biographers find a satisfying archetype of our culture and enjoy dramatizing it. Walter Jackson Bate opens his preface to the life of John Keats by invoking a powerful one: 'The life of Keats provides a unique opportunity for the study of literary greatness and of what permits or encourages its development. The interest is thus deeply human and moral, and in the most capacious sense of both of these words.' Bate concludes the paragraph by asserting that 'many readers' find Keats 'Shakespearian' (*Keats*, vi). The portrait opposite the title page is Benjamin Haydon's life mask of Keats, a mask that presents a smooth, sensuous, marble visage. The face seems to be of one who has closed his eyes to experience music or some other sensation more deeply. As David Bromwich points out, Bate makes Keats into the epitome of his own 'Ode on a Grecian Urn' ('Uses of Biography', 163–4). This Keats seems far from the man who wrote,

> There's a blush for want, and a blush for shan't
> And a blush for having done it:
> There's a blush for thought and a blush for naught
> And a blush for just begun it.[25]

Thus, in Bate's hands, the myth of the writer and especially of the poet-genius burning brightly and dying prematurely gained strength, and the political radical that Keats also was faded. Similarly the political commitments and intensity of Coleridge and Shelley did not appeal to the biographers of Bate's generation, but recent biographies written by people shaped by the activism of the 1960s and 1970s attend to these aspects of the poets' lives.

Toril Moi, like Bate, begins her book with a deliberate invoking of an archetype: 'Simone de Beauvoir is the emblematic intellectual woman of the twentieth century' (p. 1). Each nation, each century seems to allow—even glamourize—a few intellectual women. As strange and fascinating as the great seductresses (Dalilah, Cleopatra, Greta Garbo), they, too, must create themselves. Sometimes, like a commemorative coin an 'emblematic' archetype is struck: Queen Elizabeth I and the Renaissance women who followed her, Madame de Staël and the French salon, the upright Elizabeth Montagu and her *Essay on the Writings and Genius of Shakespeare*, George Sand and her late-night, passionate creativity, Madame Curie with her two Nobel prizes bent over the radon experiments that killed her, Virginia Woolf, Simone Weil—and, for our time, Simone de Beauvoir and Hannah Arendt.

Biographical subjects may be chosen because they shed light on perennially absorbing questions. Consider 'the great man theory of history' and its attendant concept of the 'man of destiny',[26] which conceives change as the result of the actions or even genius of a compelling personality. Historical eras are ushered in by, for instance, Confucius, William the Conqueror, Napoleon, and Hitler. The purest kind of person of destiny is one whose nature and actions were such that he or she singly and strongly influenced the unfolding of events. Others are children of destiny caught in the crucible of the times; what happened to this person would have happened to someone—must indeed have happened to several others. Destiny seizes them rather than their actions making them Authors of Destiny who create what from a retrospective point of view seems destiny. Time seems to snatch the Children of Destiny away from the life they expect and that might be expected of them.

We like to think that meticulous scholarship and long study will make clear to us whether we are writing about Authors or Children of Destiny. In fact, careful work emphasizes to what extent the biographer chooses and then represents the choice, thereby imposing one of these powerful cultural narratives. Oliver Cromwell seems to be an Author of Destiny. It is hard to imagine there being another man with all the personal, administrative, and military qualities he had. Although others might have the strong Protestant Reformist family and his rich experience in parliamentary committee work, his particular leadership qualities, radical principles governing leadership appointments, and imperial, diplomatic perspective seem individual.[27] John Bunyan, in contrast, seems to be a Child of Destiny. England was awash in itinerant, evangelical, 'Nonconformist' preachers and, only one hundred years later, Bunyan might have been a Charles Wesley, the father of a new denomination, rather than a prisoner for nearly twelve years.

Most often there are illuminating intersections of patterns that the biographer must take seriously and that underscore the fact that the biographer chooses rather than finds an indisputable type. Martin Luther might seem to be the true man of destiny, and, yet when he tacked up his ninety-five theses, he intended to start discussion and debate, not become the father of Protestantism. He quickly found out that no one was interested in debating, and he was swept up. And yet, a person other than Luther in a similar position might have had the ability to heal the breach. Roland Bainton's *Here I Stand* captures the many realities, including the well-known corruption and decadence in the Vatican and the abuses in the parishes, that could have made Erasmus or Frederick the Wise or Luther heroes or martyrs. Bainton's even-handed consideration of the circumstances peculiar to Luther, of his temperament and opinions, and of the immediate, historical, and doctrinal contexts is relatively rare. It hints at the fact that the biographer must not feel hurried, must be willing to engage with subtle questions, and must attempt what Clifford Geertz has called 'thick description'.[28] If the book is widely read, the power of biography to shape opinion, national image, and even a culture's metaphysics reveals itself.

Another attractive subject is a rather ordinary person in whose life many significant social forces and events converge. The biographer can implicitly argue that we can understand the times through this person. Rather than being a special type, such as the 'emblematic intellectual', the person becomes representative of the times. Such people have experienced more but not in extreme degrees. Thomas Benjamin Chaplin owned a South Carolina plantation, fought in the Civil War ('obscurely'), and after the war returned and 'tried with bitter results to reassert control over his family and free black workers' (*Tombee*, 10). Theodore Rosengarten recognized the representative nature of Chaplin and the way his life was ordinary and illustrated the effects of history on individuals; in an unusual move, he appended Chaplin's journal to his biography, which won the Critics Circle Award. The biographies of such subjects make more events and forces visible, and, perhaps, articulate more clearly the experiences and their implications than biographies of more influential people. Written at the same time as Garrow's *Bearing the Cross*, *Tombee*, like Sewall's book is very much a product of its time, for it shows the sensitivities and engages the issues of the US Civil Rights movement even as it draws out Chaplin's problems making his crops, including some seldom discussed such as language and vocabulary barriers, first with slaves and then with free Blacks (cf. pp. 152–67, 271–6). Many readers enjoy biographies that show the sweep and impact of history through the eyes of one person, and the biographies of Fanny Lou Hamer and Martha Ballard, subjects of, respectively, Kay Mills's *This Little Light of Mine* and Laurel Thatcher Ulrich's *A Midwife's Tale: The Life of Martha Ballard*, are examples, and many biographers choose to handle their subjects this way, as Christopher Hill does his of Cromwell (*God's Englishman*).

Then there is the fascination some biographers and readers have with forms of 'genius'.[29] Some of the lives of those so-labelled, of course, follow the patterns of the success story or the quest, but other subjects seem to possess a special fire burning inside their minds. In such cases, the interest is divided not just between interior and exterior but among the exterior, interior feelings and thoughts, and this special mental dimension that sometimes flashes out and awes us. Asked in elementary school to write down all the whole numbers from 1 to 100 and add up their sum, within seconds Carl Friedrich Gauss brought his slate to the teacher and 'said in his Braunschweig dialect: "Ligget se" (there it lies). On Gauss's slate . . . there was only one number: 5050.' And it was correct (Tord Hall, 4). Johann Bernoulli, a mathematics professor at Basle, wanted to know if Isaac Newton could compete with Gottfried Wilhelm Leibniz in the new field of calculus. He mailed Newton two challenge problems. Newton arrived home, 'very much tired', read the problems, worked until four that morning, and published their solution anonymously. Bernoulli saw them there and knew Newton had done them: 'I can tell the lion by the mark of his claw', he wrote.[30]

We ask: How did he think of that solution to that problem? How did she imagine that design? What inspired that painting? In a time when it is far more popular, and indisputably easier—as it always has been—to write of the 'constructed' rather than the creative person, the biographer has much to offer and special obligations and challenges when describing genius and geniuses. Leon Edel writes of one of the most familiar kinds of genius:

> for surely the writing of a literary life would be nothing but a kind of indecent curiosity, and an invasion of privacy, were it not that it seeks always to illuminate the mysterious and magical process of creation. That process belongs to the inner consciousness, those deeper springs of our being where the gathered memories of our lives merge and in some cases are distilled into transcendent art   (*Literary Biography*, 3).

'Distilled into transcendent art'—the phrase captures the biographer's most difficult and intriguing problem. That distillation must be reconstructed, the elements restored and identified, and the succession of chemical reactions described.

And beyond even that is the mystery of genius. From classical times well into the Renaissance, each person's 'genius' influenced his or her character, conduct, and fortune, and was personified into an attendant spirit. In the late Renaissance, it often meant simply a special aptitude or natural ability, as 'he had a genius for mending tools'. In the early eighteenth century, it came to be associated with a willingness and capacity to undertake infinite pains, to persevere in perfecting an endeavour. Soon, however, it also came to mean 'native intellectual power of an exalted type'; for a long time, an inclination towards a kind of study was coupled with it. Thus, the older association with long study and infinite pains did not disappear at once, for a musical genius would, for instance, not only have extraordinary talent but a desire to learn more, to practise, and develop this ability. As late as Thomas Carlyle, we find, 'Genius . . . means the transcendent capacity of taking trouble.'[31]

In the eighteenth century philosophers made attempts to categorize the manifestations of genius and spoke of 'extraordinary capacity for imaginative creation, original thought, invention, or discovery' (*OED*). In the early nineteenth century 'genius' was most often applied to poets and artists and came to be contrasted to ability that could be gained through study. The example the *OED* gives from Froude's *Short Studies on Great Subjects* (4. 2. 3) captures the idea of genius as an irresistible, mysterious force well: 'a spring in which there is always more behind than flows from it'. 'Genius does what it must, talent does what it can', his contemporary Edward Lytton wrote, and statements about its awesome power abound: 'Talent is that which is in man's power; and genius is that in whose power a man is.'[32]

In fact, it is worth while to pause over some biographies of scientific geniuses, for analysing them can increase our enjoyment of reading all kinds of biographies and contribute to our understanding of fundamental problems in the writing of biography. These lives highlight the art required to make accessible what the subject accomplished and how—what actions or thought patterns or even coincidences made possible those achievements. Many believe the work of high-order mathematics is as little within the ability of the average person as composing a sonata. Thus, the mystery of the classical and medieval 'attendant spirit' which was the individual's genius, takes a modern form. The wit might also note that artists inspired earlier generations and lifted their spirits and pride, but scientists, not poets, have shown us 'heavenly harmony' and 'A broad and ample road, whose dust is gold, | And pavement stars.' The biographer must 'biographize' the mathematics, weave it into the fabric of the life and into the person's patterns of thought; although the latter is difficult enough, the next step is to show the mathematics as an expression of the personality.

In contrast to biographers' growing confidence in their understanding of their subject, biographers of geniuses often become more uncertain during the process of writing the life. Even Richard Westfall who had spent a lifetime studying Isaac Newton and his intellectual contexts concluded:

The more I have studied him, the more Newton has receded from me. It has been my privilege at various times to know a number of brilliant men, men whom I acknowledge without hesitation to be my intellectual superiors. I have never, however, met one against whom I was unwilling to measure myself, so that it seemed reasonable to say that I was half as able as the person in question, or a third or a fourth, but in every case a finite fraction. The end result of my study of Newton has served to convince me that with him there is no measure. He has become for me wholly other, one of the tiny handful of supreme geniuses who have shaped the categories of human intellect. (p. x)

Westfall's experience is something of a functional definition of genius. Ramanujan, surrounded by the élite Cambridge faculty and G. H. Hardy, and Richard Feynman, at Los Alamos with the greatest scientists of the time including J. Robert Oppenheimer, who privately recorded that Feynman was 'the most brilliant young physicist at the atomic bomb project' (Gleick, 6), finally led those around them as well as their biographers to the same results in comparative measuring. These people strike all others as exceptionally bright, then as extraordinarily intelligent, and finally as figures of wonder and even awe. That all are very hard working momentarily clouds but then spotlights the contrast, for people come to admit that no matter how hard they worked, they could not do what these subjects have. As one of Feynman's colleagues said of him, 'Even after we understand what they have done, the process by which they have done it is completely dark' (quoted in Gleick, 11).

Making mathematics and its significance comprehensible to the ordinary reader is a balancing act over a vipers' pit. Kanigel's cheery denial of difficulties (and trivializing) in *The Man Who Knew Infinity* becomes as tiresome as Tord Hall's succumbing to pages of proofs in his life of Gauss that never lead to an understanding of the intrinsic triumph or the contribution to the advancement of the field. The greatest difficulties are in the language, not merely in translating from the language of mathematics to the language of the reader, but in making sure that the reader recognizes that many mathematical terms have distinct, precise meanings either slightly or vastly different from the word's standard use ('OR', 'field'). Moreover, difficulties come from the fact that most readers have little training in mathematics and little experience in dealing with abstract, rigorous argument, which is the standard language of mathematics. Thus, they will have difficulty in reading a theorem and recognizing its logical form, let alone understanding the content.

Without question, the greatest challenges for the biographer of a mathematical genius are in 'biographizing' the mathematics itself. Specifically, biographers need to answer *organically* such questions as what the subject did and why it mattered. In other words, they must deal with the mathematics and its significances:

Historical (Hilbert spaces, Nonstandard Analysis and the previous use of infinitesimals, Fermat's last theorem, in what contexts they arise)

Applied (what questions did this answer?)

Mathematical (how did this affect mathematics? did it consolidate separate theories; provide a more intuitive way of looking at a complex problem; provide groundwork for new advances? how was it seen by the mathematical community of the day?)

Cultural (perhaps Gödel's incompleteness theorem had cultural impact)

Philosophical (occasionally)

Here what led to the selection of the subject, the questions with which the biographer began, the varying degrees of recognition and interest in the contexts, and the evolving relationship with the subject and the changing amount of engagement with the contexts are part of the ongoing commitment to the life and determining factors in how the life story and its meaning come to be perceived. The desired outcome is that the biographer is able to explain how the mathematics is a reflection of the life, an entrée into the person's mind and heart.

Joseph Dauben's biographies of mathematicians offer an example of how readers might test biographical presentation with an eye to why the subject was selected and how the relationship between his life and the biographer affected the narrative. Dauben mentions that a Cal Tech (California Institute of Technology) acquaintance who had heard him lecturing on his biography of Georg Cantor asked if Dauben might not be interested in writing Abraham Robinson's life. After assuring himself of the necessary people's co-operation and the survival of adequate materials, he began. He tells us that he and Abraham Robinson's widow hoped the biography 'might be finished in a matter of years', but it took fifteen (p. xviii). Dauben mentions that he came to recognize the intersections of 'history' and Robinson's life, and the part World War II played and Robinson's complex feelings about Germany, England, and especially Israel become major interests for Dauben that sometimes overshadow the mathematics completely. He makes geography, topology, and regional differences bear thematic weight with increasing interpretative power.

Dauben came to feel at home working in Robinson's study, and he concludes the acknowledgement, 'His study, downstairs, in the home . . . on Blue Trail in Sleeping Giant State Park . . . is cool and quiet. The window to his study looks out onto a world full of serenity, contentment, peace' (p. xix). These are exactly the adjectives that characterize the Yale years, the concluding chapters of the biography. What had begun as the biography of 'another' mathematician becomes increasingly rich as Dauben sinks into Robinson's life-mind and imaginatively shares a part of it he didn't know about when he began the book. *Abraham Robinson* stands in stark contrast to Dauben's first biography. *Georg Cantor: His Mathematics and Philosophy of the Infinite* gives 270 pages to Cantor's mathematical thought and its contexts and concludes with a single chapter, 'Epilogue: The Significance of Cantor's Personality'. This imbalance is particularly regrettable because Dauben asserts that 'Cantor's cycles of manic depression contributed in a unique and heretofore unsuspected way to his own interpretation of the nature of transfinite set theory.'[33] One reviewer has complained that the result can be that it seems to make no difference whether the mathematics (or philosophy or scientific discovery) was done 'by a human being, rather than by a computer or a visiting Martian'.[34]

Another test of changing commitments: at the very heart of Dauben's biography of Robinson is the discovery of Nonstandard Analysis, which happened to be the topic of Dauben's college honours thesis in 1966. It could be expected, then, that Dauben would not only be able to explain his subject but would recall the excitement Nonstandard Analysis generated in the beginning. Dauben was, then, 'showcasing a talent' and doing something he knew how to do, since he was writing his second biography of a mathematician. In fact, Dauben's grasp of the mathematics and especially of the problems Robinson selected, their contexts and challenges, and their applications never flags. In a typical section, he describes Robinson working at IBM on programming languages, and the state of the field, the needs addressed by Robinson's research, and his accomplishment are presented economically and clearly.

Throughout the book, Dauben elected to assume that his audience has a strong understanding of the language and methods of mathematics, especially of mathematical logic. Specifically, he uses logical notation, easily misunderstood technical terms such as 'elementary', and technical terminology such as 'maximal ideal'. By making this choice, Dauben avoids having to make many translations and explanations. An analysis of the key section of the book on the discovery of Nonstandard Analysis (NSA) (pp. 281–9) shows that his statements are correct; that the arguments presented are not rigorous but give a good sense of Robinson's construction of NSA and application of it to the calculus; the understanding of its historical significance depends on the reader's mathematical sophistication (reference to the use of infinitesimals in the 'classic work in differential geometry' suggests that NSA will provide rigour here as Cauchy did for analysis); the description of the reactions of the mathematical community is weak.

For a mathematically literate reader, this section is workmanlike. The ideal, however, is that the presentation be correct *and* presented so that the general reader will understand and a mathematician reader not be troubled by the presentation, perhaps even be charmed or intrigued by the analogies. It is often illuminating to compare how the subject himself has written on a subject discussed by the biographer, and a comparison of 'On the Construction of Models', Robinson's paper for Abraham Fraenkel's *festschrift*, suggests what might have been done. The complexity, simplicity, and breadth of Nonstandard Analysis are understood in light of its being a particular, although quite clever, outcome and instance of model theory, and some of the excitement of the first readers and learners of NSA comes through.

In the best biographies, the mathematics is woven into the fabric of the lives and shown to be an expression of the personality. Robinson's carefully narrated life here, however, seems to offer no explanation of the discovery of NSA. The life is told as a variant on the overcoming obstacles story. Little Abraham Robinson, nearly lost at train stations not once but twice in Nazi Germany, then nearly swallowed up in the Holocaust again when his immersion in studies at the Sorbonne deafened him to the advance of the German army, a homeless refugee in London after his flat was bombed, and marooned forlornly there while his companion, who already had his master's degree, left for Cambridge, becomes the successful, much-sought professor whose tranquil life and death at Yale is measured in Dauben's book by a series of major papers presented at international gatherings.

Dauben writes, 'one day, as he walked into Fine Hall, the idea of non-standard analysis suddenly flashed into his mind' (p. 281). Here we have a technical if not evidentiary flaw. No evidence is presented for this very dubious statement. In general, readers object, as this expression of outrage by Ramanujan's biographer shows: 'Abruptly, on page 71 of "B. F. Skinner: A Life", we learn that the young aspiring writer "made a decision to enter graduate school in psychology." How, pray tell, did the thought even pop into his head? We come away with scarcely a clue.' (Robert Kanigel on Daniel Bjork's *B. F. Skinner. A Life*, *NYT*, 3 October 1993, 26).

Following the statement of sudden revelation are eight pages summarizing his paper at the Association for Symbolic Logic in January 1961. G. H. Hardy once generalized from his experience with Ramanujan: 'a mathematician usually discovers a theorem by an effort of intuition; the conclusion strikes him as plausible, and he sets to work to manufacture a proof' (Kanigel, 225). Close reading of Dauben's life of Robinson suggests that that is what probably happened and allows the reader to piece together some of the foundations of his sudden conception of Nonstandard Analysis, but the reader must do most of the work. For instance, Dauben has made it clear that Robinson began very early to apply symbolic logic within pure mathematics, especially abstract algebra, in productive, creative ways, and he has presented a wealth of evidence that Robinson was broadly educated and deeply engaged with the history of mathematics. In a 1950 paper, Robinson said,

The concrete examples produced in the present paper will have shown that contemporary symbolic logic can produce useful tools . . . for the development of actual mathematics, more particularly for the development of algebra and, it would appear, of algebraic geometry. *This is the realisation of an ambition which was expressed by Leibnitz (sic) in a letter to Huygens as long ago as 1679.* (quoted in Dauben, *Robinson*, 174)

Robinson's education, like Newton's, is best described as rooted in the liberal arts, and his work is highly distinctive in its drive to relate the branches of mathematics to each other. What is most disappointing in Dauben's biography is the lack of any sense of the excitement that Robinson and the mathematical community felt, as well as the failure to make Nonstandard Analysis anything like the product of an individual personality and mind, the equivalent of a novel or a sculpture. Dauben seems to lose his personal engagement with Nonstandard Analysis.

2. Postcard of David Hilbert,
one of a set honouring the
great mathematicians of the
University of Göttingen

In contrast, Constance Reid employs a variety of strategies for biographizing the mathematics in her much-praised life of David Hilbert. Most of the
time, she conveys an ease with mathematics and, at times, a true affection
for it:

Hilbert was now involved in investigations of his own which he had long wished to
pursue. . . . The Law of Quadratic Reciprocity, known to Euler, had been rediscovered
by Gauss at the age of 18 and given its first complete proof. Gauss always regarded it
as the 'gem' of number theory and returned to it five more times during his life to
prove it in a different way each time. It describes a beautiful relationship which exists
between pairs of primes and the remainders of squares when divided by these.
(*Hilbert*, pp. 55–6)

Here she fits Hilbert's work into the history of mathematics with emphasis on
lineage and appeal and with the easy insertion of evocative words such as 'gem'
and 'beautiful'.

Her biography develops themes incrementally that characterize his work and
provides succinct summaries at key moments. We are persuaded because we
are shown that his career was marked by the variety of his investigations, the

importance of the problems attacked, the elegance and simplicity of the methods, the clarity of the exposition, and the care for absolute rigour (p. 125). That the summaries are often quotations from, for instance, his great contemporaries, for instance Henri Poincaré, are especially telling; in the citation for the Bolyai Prize, which Hilbert won in 1910, Poincaré recited example after example of Hilbert's work, usually ending, 'we should not be surprised at the number of investigators who are now engaged on the path opened up by M. Hilbert' (p. 126).

Reid weaves the mathematics completely into Hilbert's life. She captures the importance of the daily walks with other mathematicians, his preference for working at a blackboard hung on his garden wall, and his co-opting of everyone around him in the service of his work. She transmits Hilbert's love of nature, his deep need to be outdoors and physically active, and in a series of telling metaphorical passages, some written by Hilbert himself, she shows how, indeed, the mathematics was an expression of his personality, how it united the fibres of his life and mind: once Hilbert said '[Mathematics] appeared . . . as a flowering garden. In this garden there were well-worn paths where one might look around at leisure and enjoy oneself without effort, especially at the side of a congenial companion. But we also liked to seek out hidden trails and discovered many an unexpected view . . .' (Reid, 121). In this biography, the work and life are integrated; in Dauben's, we have a 'life *and* works'.

Loneliness and eccentricity seem inseparable from the life of genius. Bertrand Russell observed that he frequently felt in social situations like a ghost who was trapped in soundless invisibility or imprisoned in a shell. Subjects are quoted as saying that they felt they possessed knowledge that isolated them, and the degree and duration of their concentration when working is extraordinary. We find biographers' voices reveal their relationship to the subject as they deal with this topic. For instance, the obsessions and the intensity can be off-putting. Isak Dinesen 'exploited' her need for 'absolute silence and privacy', Judith Thurman tells us. She 'begrudged her mother the visits of friends and grandchildren'. Like so many 'geniuses', she was described as 'bad-tempered, selfish, hypersensitive to intrusion' (Thurman, 259). And the books record envy and problematic working relationships. Gleick writes of Feynman: 'He was a master calculator . . . slashing his way through a difficult problem. Thus scientists—believing themselves to be unforgiving meritocrats—found quick opportunities to compare themselves unfavorably to Feynman' (p. 9).

Westfall tells us that Isaac Newton struggled to make friends at Grantham school, often by making things such as lanterns and mechanical marvels for his schoolmates, but when he moved on to Cambridge, he left behind a record of fighting, erratic bursts of academic excellence, and pathetic attempts to ingratiate, befriend, or best his schoolmates. They knew and commented on his long, strange retreats to the attic in his boarding house to build models of windmills, then new to England, and to sketch designs for a perpetual motion machine. One of the girls for whom he made doll furniture called him 'a sober, silent, thinking lad', but the general opinion seems to have been one recorded by William Stukeley, a contemporary: they 'rejoic'd at parting with him, declaring, he was fit for nothing but the 'Versity' (Westfall, 65). Westfall marshals a wealth of evidence and leads us to the kind of generalization about human nature that the biographical form can manage. Specifically in Newton's, as in many of these lives, the desires of any child manifest themselves in ways that reinforce their differences, even their particular talents and obsessions, and Westfall has demonstrated that.

Westfall writes what is true for many brilliant people: 'Never fully at ease with others, [Newton] held his distance and lived largely in the setting of his own study. His books furnished the context of his life more than Cambridge or London did' (p. xi). Drawing several strands in descriptions of genius together, Catherine Drinker Bowen explains, 'They know they are not as other men. . . . Work and work only—painting, writing, composing music—gives them a blessed conviction of function in the world which they feel is alien. Work tells them they can be themselves—unique, defiant—yet share with and contribute to the life around them' (*Biography*, 151–2). Most have experiences in which they are misunderstood, both personally and professionally, and the biographers' feelings about the subject as well as interpretations of evidence determine sympathy or disapproval.

Like the work of a poet, mathematics can indeed 'tell them they can be themselves—unique', and the biographer must be careful to give examples that are not so elementary as to miss the point or so full of incomplete pieces that they mislead the reader into thinking that the presentation is more substantial than it is. The resources of fiction writers and of the biographers of writers are available and, when used, can have the effect of Reid's quotation about Hilbert's real and mathematical gardens. Gleick, for instance, uses the published *Feynman Lectures on Physics* as a touchstone. He quotes illustrations that Feynman intended to capture students' imaginations to help convey the remarkable way he thought and the quality of his mind. Through such strategies, genius becomes what we believe it to be—a mysterious characteristic of the personality, not just of the mind.

If we stand on the shore and look at the sea . . . we see the water, the waves breaking, the foam, the sloshing motion of the water, the sound, the air, the winds and the clouds, the sun and the blue sky, and light; there is sand and there are rocks of various hardness and permanence. . . . Is the sand other than the rocks? That is, is the sand perhaps nothing but a great number of very tiny stones? Is the moon a great rock? If we understood rocks, would we also understand the sand and the moon? Is the wind a sloshing of the air analogous to the sloshing motion of the water in the sea? (p. 22)

Whoever chooses to write about genius struggles to explain the bright, hard intelligence that glows like a mysterious, alien coal. With scientists they must communicate what Hall impressively and accurately identifies as 'the creative intuition, the numerical virtuosity, the logical rigor, the experimental proficiency' (p. 169)—but so must all biographers.

Just as readers are drawn to the mystery of genius, so some biographers are drawn to the challenge of finding words, anecdotes, and narrative strategies to unravel them. Can it be done? To some degree, biographers of poets, musicians, and painters have succeeded. Some, like James Breslin, are as aware of the difficulties of describing a non-verbal achievement as of capturing the subject's genius in words, and cultural strategies for expressing artistic genius are better developed and more familiar than those for scientists. The intriguing analogies, shared responsibilities, and possible tests among types of biographies are greater than the contrasts.

★

In choosing a subject, the relationship need not be those most commonly assigned—identification or affinity or sympathy. It can be a deep understanding of the pressures the time brought to bear on the subject. It can be deep engagement with the 'puzzles' that remain unsolved about the life. It can be intellectual engagement with the challenges of the act of writing a particular life or kind of life. The great questions of biography are the essential questions about human experience in the world. What did Defoe want? Did he get it? How did he express and live out these desires? What stood in his way? How did he cope with obstacles, opponents, and adversity? They are the stuff of humankind's puzzling out its relationship to the world, how individual desire and ambition are confounded or aided by social, historical forces and other human beings, and the implications of various conceptions of religious, ethical, or moral imperatives. The answers to these questions reveal a Defoe who often suffered intensely because he felt that God's plans for him retarded and even worked against the successes he imagined for himself—not the stereotype of the Puritan servant of God.

The personal aspirations, struggles, and emotions of the subject offer vicarious experience, hope, and even inspiration to readers. In the most successful biographies, the writer also has a clear conception of what that life represents and in what ways it was significant and has significance for us. Lloyd Kramer makes questions of reciprocity between understanding the life and understanding cultures a thematic emphasis of his *Lafayette in Two Worlds*. As he says, the 'meaning of a particular life is always changing in conjunction with the evolving experiences and perspectives of other people' (p. 8), and he demonstrates that truth not only with Lafayette's reception in America and France but with his reputation in both countries at various time since his death. How, Kramer asks, does biography participate in the processes that create identities and meanings, historical as well as national? Deirdre Bair poses the issue in a lovely passage in which she explains that biography is 'one of my preferred forms of critical inquiry': 'how did X's life and work illuminate our cultural and intellectual history; how did X influence the way we think about ourselves and interpret our society; . . . what can we learn from X's life and work that will be of use to us once we have read his/her biography?' (p. 19). Biography explicates the symbolism of lives, can turn lives into symbols, and is itself always a socially symbolic act.

Samuel Johnson once wrote 'The stage but echoes back the public voice | The drama's laws the drama's patrons give.' In large measure, so biography. The complex dynamic between a biographer choosing a person to write about and a culture, its peoples, its various influences on the biographer, and its audiences for biography, always carries the potential for a magic combination—the right biographer with the perfect subject at an important moment of need, quest, and desire.

3. Evidence: 'Bare Patches and Profusions'[1]

Kenneth Murdock is said to have flown to South America for a footnote.
When to stop? When you drop.

Kenneth Silverman

Biographers' relationships to evidence and to the culture's attitudes towards it are almost as psychologically revealing as their attitudes towards their subjects. Just as poets court, bless, fear, and rail at the Muses, so biographers relate to evidence. The intensity of their mixed experiences is recorded in numerous places. Virginia Woolf finds the biographer's evidence to be the 'very cruel distinction' between the 'restriction' of a life-writer and the freedom of the artist.[2] In her diary, she writes of her biography of Roger Fry, 'I can't broach another chapter—too tired of facts'; 'I'm stuck in a bristle of dates.'[3] But Elizabeth Young-Bruehl's feelings are equally familiar to biographers: 'I had such incredible material! That's one of the things that's addictive about the biography business—you start on a small scale and unearth things, and the story grows and grows and grows. There's more and more to tell, and each time you find something, it leads you to something else. You get caught up in the detective work, which becomes very fascinating.'[4] This chapter is a meditation on how biographers work with evidence, on some controversies associated with evidence, and on some issues specific to biography.

In a review of Frank McLynn's *Robert Louis Stevenson: A Biography*, 'The True Stevenson?', Ernest Mehew neatly states a basic truth: 'A good biographer first assembles and examines the facts before developing his theories and interpretations' (*TLS*, 2 July 1993, 15). Just as matter-of-factly, Geoffrey Strickland asserts, 'If Zola is to receive proper justice, it can only be through the closest possible examination of his career and of the far from transparent relationship between the novelist and the man' (*NYTBR* 4 June 1995, 10). Any biographer reading these sentences experiences in rapid succession recognition, agreement, irritation, despair, challenge, and perhaps finally hysterical laughter.

Mehew says 'facts' quite casually; biographers know there are few real 'facts'. The birth date of a person born in Great Britain in the twentieth century ought to be 'a fact', but Deirdre Bair tells us that Samuel Beckett 'insists' that he was born on a day different from the one somewhat belatedly entered on his birth certificate. 'Facts' are very often disputed or even simply unavailable. I spent uncountable hours trying to determine when or even where Defoe was born. Not only did I survey all the London parishes and every county where he was known to have family or even business connections (Essex, Surrey, and more), but I worked systematically in widening circles around London. The most promising find was the record of 'Daniel, son of a stranger' in the records in Essex, but unfortunately 'the vellum book' to which the records referred me for 'full information' had been taken home by a staff member or patron when such things were allowed at too many record offices and never returned. Even the most persevering, lucky biographer with two filing cabinets of material could extract only two or three file folders of 'facts'. Mehew's 'facts' must be crossed out, and 'evidence' inserted.

Most readers probably believed the record that Bair found of Beckett's birth. But we all know errors are made in records, and that 'data-input' mistakes keep us on the telephone bickering with credit card companies and benefits offices. Bair even says, 'there is a certain validity to the question of the actual date' (p. 3). What is the evidence for each date? Besides, which is more important for the biographer and the reader? the 'real' date of birth or the one Beckett claims and what that date means to him? Once some 'fact' is in hand anyway, intelligent things have to be done with it, and the inordinate compression of the process that Strickland's sentence casually accomplishes is horribly evident. James Knowlson, authorized biographer of Beckett, treats the competing dates matter-of-factly in *Damned to Fame* (1996). He begins chapter 1, 'Samuel Barclay Beckett, who was to become one of the major writers of the twentieth century, was born at Cooldrinagh in Foxrock, Country Dublin, on Good Friday, 13 April, 1906' (p. 23). He immediately asserts that the date on the birth certificate is wrong and offers as evidence that an adult friend wrote in his notes of conversations with Beckett that Beckett's mother had told him the certificate was in error and that 'everyone who knew Beckett as a child thought of his birthday as being on April 13' (p. 23). This evidence is hardly better than Bair's; how many people can remember the birth dates of *any* of their childhood friends? Knowlson's presentation, however, is notably different from Bair's, especially in the way it dismisses the 'myth' of April 13. The following has been often quoted: 'Knowledge is good, method is good, but one thing beyond all others is necessary: and that is to have a head, not a pumpkin, on your shoulders, and brains, not pudding, in your head.'[5] This is true for finding, recognizing, evaluating, and using evidence.

Both Mehew and Strickland are right; the biographer must begin with 'the closest possible examination' of what can be known about the life and career. One of the peculiarities about writing biography is that only about 20 per cent of the time taken to 'write' it is spent writing. The rest is spent collecting evidence, organizing and filing it. Most of us begin by constructing a detailed chronology from what has already been published and documented. This apparently straightforward activity invariably turns up discrepancies—often major ones—as well as gaps. Moreover, we have to care about the sources of each item we put in our chronologies. Here again we find shocking gaps, or trace things back to a blatant speculation now recorded repeatedly as 'fact'. Unfortunately some of the best stories may be purely fictitious. Sometimes it takes bravery to explode such myths; long survival generally signals cultural usefulness. For example, biographer after biographer used and even ornamented the tale that William Blake died singing praises to God, making the room resound 'with the beatific Symphony'.[6] This picture of the mystical artist contributed to keeping Blake's place in the humanist myth of the artist existing outside of time and social forces who can produce an 'unfolding' body of work with its own internal coherence and development.[7] Where the narrative is so attractive and works so well, we often find dubious sources and material that seems highly questionable. We have no choice but to subject them to scrutiny and face the consequences of making the life a site for the struggle of meaning.

Biographers usually have a good knowledge of what the subject has written, if anything, and they may begin by reviewing it and completing their reading. Cynthia Griffin Woolf prepared for her biography of Emily Dickinson by very nearly committing all of the poems to memory. No matter which is the first or second step, reading everything written by and about the person is indispensable preparation. For some subjects, this is a nearly overwhelming task; the number of biographies and literary critical studies alone of Charles Dickens or George Eliot seems to supply reading for years to come. Unfortunately, even articles in *Notes and Queries* and popular periodicals need to be included because they may be the only source of useful, even important, information and may help the biographer begin to develop a sense of the subject's reputation and reception in different decades. Pertinent material of all kinds must be read or reread; Catherine Drinker Bowen, for instance, reread the Federalist papers in preparation for writing her life of Oliver Wendell Holmes. This reading also hones biographers' awarenesses of what their books will contribute, correct, or compete against. 'The price of biographical truth appears, indeed, to be eternal vigilance, and eternal skepticism.'[8] It has been said in many ways that biographers should doubt everything; equally important, I would say, is not to be afraid to agree. The foolish striving for originality or revision can be as destructive as a lack of scepticism and the omission of running routine checks.

The most dreaded drudgery is filing, and, unfortunately, biographers may be only as good as their filing systems.[9] In the few books on life-writing and in collections of essays, authors describe their systems and those of others with a detail and gusto that must strike most readers as a kind of group fetish. The essential file is chronological, and I kept a schematic version of it posted on my wall for all the years I worked. By the writing stage, I had an entire four-drawer filing cabinet of chronological files. What had begun as '1660–5' (birth and childhood) became a dozen files including three on genealogy, one on the plague, one on the Great Fire of London, two on Nonconformist-government relations, one on Defoe's minister (later a vice-president at Harvard), and one on his teacher (one of the rocks of early religious Dissent). As you can see, chronology began to acquire topics. Defoe would later write two long prose fictions, including his still-moving *Journal of the Plague Year*, about the epidemic, and this file included important historical and personal information. Therefore, it would become relevant for several chapters.

Some files strike me now as strange but ingenious; I had 'Ink'—what it cost, how to mix it, what the ingredients were—in the 1704 group, because Defoe was exceptionally poor and complained about the cost of it. (An advertisement explained that a pennyworth of ink powder would make $1\frac{1}{2}$ pints and as much as a quart for 'ordinary writing'. Also, Defoe wore glasses by 1710; he had Button fix them. These leftovers have preyed on my mind.) Some topics, however, were life-long concerns ('Apparitions', 'Happy Marriage'), and I began to develop a topic-filing system that eventually filled three more drawers of a filing cabinet. In the 'Memoirs' group were files on each of the many fictional memoirs Defoe wrote, several files of literary studies of memoirs, and several files on important memoirs by other writers that were published at the time his were. 'Crime' became a huge group of files, as Defoe was concerned with its causes, the legal system, and the possibilities of rehabilitating criminals; since I knew little about eighteenth-century crime and punishment, the historical files multiplied. The final set of files I had, and they mercifully occupied only a single drawer, were quite miscellaneous. They included five folders of attacks on Defoe—he was much hated by his contemporaries—and many other thin folders with labels like 'Pantomimes of *Robinson Crusoe*' that I hoped would become useful.

All three sets of these files began in the initial reading stage. Most biographers move next to diaries, journals, letters, and other personal records. In other words, we begin to deepen, or thicken, our chronologies and to invest them with the subject's personal feelings and experiences. If we are lucky, these are printed. If not printed, we are fortunate if they are collected in a few, easily accessible places with good lighting, comfortable furniture, and a decent ventilation system. Few biographers are lucky, however. It would be easy to become indignant here, as other biographers have. Why, one wonders, if the average *man* was 5 feet 7 inches not very long ago, are tables far too high for the chairs in every record office and library in Great Britain? A six- to seven-hour work stretch (which we all put in) presses our shoulders up near our ears and delivers hours of backaches. What modern lunacies (division of labour, unions, and supervisory indifference?) put opening the windows to allow air into the North Library of the British Museum in the hands of the 'museum staff' while the library staff and readers experienced an atmosphere in summer that duplicated in temperature and smell the London Underground (the unairconditioned, overcrowded subway system)? And I still remember the outrage I felt after taking a train and booking a hotel room to work for a day and a half at a record office in Kingston-on-Thames only to discover that the office would be closed all afternoon—without prior announcement—for a staff birthday party. In fact, I found out when I returned from lunch to locked doors and an index card notice taped to the door.

At this point, the reasonably orderly process becomes an exercise in simultaneous, strenuous activity. Intimately tied to the locating and reading of journals, letters, and other documents is the search for new material. Not only must all of the personal material and manuscripts for the subject be found, but almost as much effort needs to be put into locating personal diaries, journals, and other materials kept by family members and close friends. The notes of earlier biographers may be extremely useful, as they may include important material that never found its way into print or information about the locations of sources. The letters of all the correspondents also need to be located and interleaved with the subject's letters. Giant matrixes of how important events are described to different correspondents need to be constructed.

One of the most useful things that I did was begin to develop circles of friends, contacts, rivals, and acquaintances at different periods of Defoe's life. Jeffrey Meyers did something similar for Ernest Hemingway, beginning with the acknowledgements, notes, and index to an earlier, good biography of Hemingway. I would sit around and deliberately try to imagine everyone who might be related to Defoe's life and to expand into different domains— surviving relatives and schoolfellows, civil servants, booksellers, and so on. After all, the friends of our college years are largely replaced by the friends of our young adulthood and with professional relationships, and these, in turn, are augmented and sometimes replaced with the relationships of our mature years. People move, and those whom we once saw frequently become correspondents. Some people may briefly be important parts of our lives, only to be swept away by distance and the press of other life concerns. I began to carry alphabetized packs of 3″ × 5″ index cards with every member of Defoe's family and every other person who might have written to or about Defoe or received a letter from him. These had to be arranged in packs broken into years, and in some cases, countries, because of the size of the archives in Great Britain. The American researcher, even those privileged to use the great resources of places such as the Houghton at Harvard or the Folger in Washington, cannot imagine the difficulties of working in, for instance, the Public Record Office in London with its 40 million documents. On my first visit, I had a chronology filled with entries of years alone. I quickly realized that, to make the job possible, not only did I need months but, whenever possible, exact days. To have a year meant going through seven to ten mammoth boxes and books; to have the full date cut that to one or two.

Some researchers work rather chronologically. In other words, they attack genealogy and the early years, or only genealogy, then move on to early years, schooling, and so on. By breaking the life into its natural segments, they have coherent research units. I did not have this luxury and am not persuaded that this method is a good one, anyway. Because of the number of places I needed to read and search for Defoe material and their distances from Rochester, New York, where I then taught, I worked by record office, and it turned out to be efficient in more ways than anticipated. For instance, each library, record office, and archive has its own organizational system, rules and procedures for seeing materials, and idiosyncrasies. My method allowed me to master each one, get to know a few helpful staff members, and establish a routine. I would, then, work through Defoe's entire life in each research place, take sheaves of notes and note cards back to the USA and then gnash my teeth through hours and hours of sorting, copying for double filing, and filing. Following a distinguished tradition was no comfort; Boswell once recorded in his journal, 'Sorted till I was stupefied'.[10] A few generous students would combine discussions of their honours theses and papers with friendly conversation while I filed, and that always raised my morale.

Every archival or library visit needs to begin with taking the time to master the system. It is natural to be impatient to order something and begin reading, but because of the complexity and individuality of record offices that simply does not work. After all, each group of records in the archive was created for the original administrative office or parent organization, and no thought was given to future Record Office users' convenience. Because they are not grouped by subject, material on any subject or person may require consulting many different groups of records. I always ask the reading room staff to show me the major 'finding aids' and give me a brief introduction to them and the procedure for getting materials. They are always glad to do it, because it saves them time and frustration, too. Many hand out useful printed guides to, for instance, doing research on family history or criminals (Defoe was arrested more than thirteen times). I also try to take two references from a good printed source that I need to check, and my first requests are for these items. They serve as nice test cases and allow me to work through the process with something that I know is there. It is necessary to check almost all references to manuscript documents anyway, because the quotations may be greatly abbreviated, taken out of context, attributed to the wrong writer, year, or situation, or miscopied.

Most places maddeningly allow the request of only three to five items, and no more can be requested until those are delivered. During the time I wait for their delivery (and this can be up to two hours), I read the finding aids, calendars, and inventories, and make lists of the reference items with call numbers that I want to see. As soon as one set of documents is delivered, I turn in the next set of requests. With luck, then, I can go from document to document with no more loss of wait time. As I order a document, I put a circle beside it on my list, and when it is delivered cross through the circle. Request slips are sometimes lost (or something) and, with long lists of items to be seen, it is easy to forget what has been requested and delivered.

In every place manuscripts are held, I look up each name that might possibly appear in catalogues and lists. Some amazing material turns up that way; unpublished letters to Defoe were listed in the Advocates Library, Edinburgh, for instance. Some researchers always order up indices to records first. My own experience is that this is a mistake with pre-1900 material and largely a waste of time. Most indices are incomplete, and they are always only as good as the indexer, who may have had trouble with the handwriting, been careless or rushed, or, and, this is certainly common, uninterested in women and various kinds of people. I once asked an archivist for help; she was surprised I hadn't found what I was looking for already, and, as we talked, she said dismissively, 'Oh, he was a *Dissenter.*' And so that Church-of-England biased county office had either not saved or not indexed material about the Nonconformists, even those of the stature of Defoe. I have found useful, even important, manuscript entries on the backs of indexed items and folded inside other documents. No index will pick up every mention of the people about whom you care. Even if the index is good, I find examining the material around the item useful as I build up a sense of the time, its issues, and how people worked and thought.

As this chapter implies, serious research of any kind requires diligence, but biographical work requires dogged, unflagging perseverance. Jeffrey Meyers read 8,000 Wyndham Lewis documents at Cornell University alone, and he abandoned the idea of writing a life of Ezra Pound 'with considerable relief' and retired to the Kinsey sex museum at Indiana University after 'contemplating the 12,000 pages of letters and manuscripts written by Pound in his madcap backwoods dialect and realizing there were even more papers at Yale'.[11] Leon Edel describes reading 15,000 Henry James letters—and that was what was left after the Lamb House fire.[12] He writes that he does not 'disparage archives. I simply groan when I see one.'[13] Richard Altick exhorts, 'He [*sic*] must comb every library, large and small, every archive, every institution where manuscripts may conceivably be kept; he must go through innumerable catalogues of book dealers and auctioneers [to find manuscripts] . . . and then try to trace them as they passed from collector to collector; he must try to communicate with every single person . . .'.[14] Day after day can pass with nothing found, with nothing concrete accomplished. Just as scientists know that no evidence is evidence, biographers learn that by bitter experience. They must, for instance, go through volumes of tax records to ascertain that their subject did not live in a district.

In recent years many useful sources of information have become available. The National Registry of Archives in Quality Court, Chancery Lane, London, continues to grow, and the subject, the family, and all of the circles of relationships can be checked there. Where many, many letters once had to be written to county record offices and a kind of scatter-gun approach taken to possible private-family holdings, now the National Registry, although not complete, largely accomplishes the same thing. The *Directory of Archives and Manuscripts Repositories in the United States* is useful but more limited. Many archives and record offices, especially the large national ones, have produced books such as the *Guide to Genealogical Research in the National Archives* and *The Library of Congress: A Guide to Genealogical and Historical Research.* Genealogical societies not only offer on-site research help but offer books such as the American Society of Genealogists' *Genealogical Research: Methods and Sources.*

Biographers constantly learn from each other, and it is usually true that each one has such specialized needs that only other specialists can offer advanced help and that much will be learned that can then be shared with others. For instance, without the friendly advice of J. M. Beattie, author of *Crime and the Courts of England*, I would not have found many of the legal documents I needed. I also remember insisting that merchants were given passes to travel to other parts of England during the troubled years of the Exclusion Crisis, when the Catholic James II was driven out of England in favour of King William III. Persisting doggedly in spite of vehement discouragement from staff, I found these records and now both the Public Record Office and the Corporation of the City of London Record Office list them in finding aids.

Many beginning researchers do not realize that records are in layers; they find one item, rush out of the archive thrilled, and leave behind many related documents. For example, as interesting and important as the indictments, decrees, orders, fee books, and transcriptions of trials are, the examinations, depositions, exhibits, and affidavits usually yield more valuable information. The latter group tends to be narrative and filled with all kinds of detail from the names of people involved with the subject to daily habits and even what the subject wore. Note how many kinds of documents there are; not all will survive for every year for every court, but with a clear idea of the possible number and kinds of documents the chances of finding new information and also putting together a complete narrative of the proceedings increases greatly. With this kind of systematic effort, I was able to find out where Defoe was imprisoned in Newgate, that he did appear at the required times after he was released 'on good behaviour', and when he was finally dismissed. In another case, I found depositions that filled in many details about his work habits—what hours he worked, how he employed his sons, and that he always corrected his own proofs even though he or the printer had to travel 23 miles. Behind the printed calendars of the actions of the House of Lords are the full records, including minutes, which are always much fuller than the calendars, and the minutes of committee meetings and the 'main papers', which are petitions, statements, evidence, and other documents. The calendars, like indices, reflect the interests, opinions about significance, and time limitations of the compilers. By working through the layers, I found the realistic acrimony of the first divorcing couples, and the moving words of an abused wife under great pressure to reconcile: 'I have bourn, and bourn, and shall bear no more.'

The trick is to think horizontally and vertically from each piece of evidence and to imagine every context, and, therefore, other sets of records. To work horizontally means to attempt to imagine everything immediately related to the document and, from that, what other manuscripts and administrative categories of papers need to be examined. For instance, with Defoe's arrest for seditious libel, I needed to identify other people and systems involved. Because this was a state offence, the office of the Secretary of State was involved, and there was new information in the State Papers and in the Secretary's Entry and Treasury Books. Because Defoe printed the libel, the Undersecretary of State charged with monitoring the press left notes about it. Defoe appeared before the Queen, and Privy Council minutes about that survive. His business, and everyone with whom he had contracts, was affected and I was able to track the failure of his brickworks and import–export business. What he wrote and where he published it changed. His family was greatly affected, and, by analysing that aspect carefully, I was the first biographer to notice that Mary Defoe was pregnant. The manic behaviour during a four-month period that biographers had attempted to explain suddenly made sense.

To think vertically is to move backward and forward in time, to search for the things, both historical, social, and personal, that motivated the action and event and then to identify the effects, again personal, community, and, perhaps, national and historical. Defoe took a terrible risk, for instance, when he left his family and thriving businesses to fight in Monmouth's rebellion against the king. As I worked, especially with letters and personal documents preserved in places such as the Dr Williams Library, a special treasury of Nonconformist records, what the years of prejudice and persecution meant to ordinary people became clear. The realities and the fears about James II and the brilliant patriotic, military career of the Duke of Monmouth as he fought on the continent for his father, King Charles II, brought to life the conversations and assessments being made in Defoe's intimate circle. I located information about several of Defoe's schoolmates and followed them through the rebellion and beyond, and how typical—and how fortunate—Defoe was could be told.

Every good biographer works to develop what Clifford Geertz, the pioneering cultural anthropologist, called 'thick description'. Every incident and action has multiple contexts, and, with the tools of the anthropologist and especially cultural studies specialists, we have grown more adept at recognizing them and finding material about them. While literary scholar-biographers have not forgotten how to relate a publication to the rest of the author's work and to literary history, they now look carefully at 'the literary market-place', what the author earned, how he or she got access to print, the reputation and list of the publisher, and what happened to the copyright. They now consider the reputation of the genre, not in the century but in the immediately relevant years, and the cultural acceptability of various themes, subjects, and genres and even of, for instance, women or working-class publishing. Serialization, circulating library selection, and inclusion in collections and anthologies over many years matter. Evidence from education, religion, politics, law, economics, and medicine is now considered as useful as the more traditional historical and philosophical sources. Biographers are now expected to be able to argue persuasively how conservative, original, or uninformed their subjects were. Today Richard Westfall's account of Isaac Newton's contribution to contemporary thinking about the laws of motion and the direction the new science took, Margaret Doody's of Frances Burney's medical treatment for breast cancer, and David McCullough's and others' accounts of Truman's part in the decision to drop the atomic bomb on two cities, for instance, are evaluated by the authors' abilities to bring evidence from many diverse sources to bear on their interpretations.

The search for new evidence and the long, patient work of developing rich contexts and thick description consume the majority of the time working on a biography. Many biographers have noted that no life has been definitively treated. Some highlight the fact that there is always more to find; Richard Altick writes, 'There is not a single figure in the history of English or American literature whose biography may be sealed up and labeled "Completed"'.[15] Recently biographers have become aware of how the time in which the biography is written influences it and also how each era has new questions and needs. Some are brave enough to say, even about their subjects, that a new biography is warranted every twenty or twenty-five years for 'all important and controversial figures in our civilization'.[16]

At some point, evidence begins to reinforce what the biographer has already concluded, and the missing pieces of puzzles begin to seem either improbable finds or not worth the candle. I am sure, for instance, that Defoe belonged to a Society for the Reformation of Manners in London, and I would hate to see the cost in hours in obscure record offices and archives and in dollars for extra days in London for this search. Had I been able to find it, I would have had two paragraphs, a page, at most to add to the biography and little to add to what I already knew about his activities during the moral reform years in London and from the full record of his participation in a founding Society in Edinburgh. At least I think that. Who knows who might have been in his

Society? or what they did? and was he a Mason? if so, his ability to work with important men such as Robert Harley, Secretary of State, and the Duke of Hamilton, a major player in Scottish politics while Defoe lived in Edinburgh, would be more completely explained. Such lingering reflections explain why many of us admire and envy Ronald Paulson for his stimulating re-working of his biography of William Hogarth.[17]

★

A lot of time has to be spent seeking trivia—asking for and searching out things that make polite people laugh at you. These same people, of course, want to 'see' the subject in a room, 'moving about and talking'. For the biographer, this means reaching the point Edel describes: 'He has heard the voice and seen the gesture' (*Literary Biography*, 19). Scraps of information about what the subject wore, drawings, portraits, photographs become treasures. Perhaps the purest guide to the individuality of a biographer can be found in his or her identification of unusual or even eccentric quests. For instance, we know that the way people speak matters, and yet few biographers seem seriously concerned with it. In one of the few discussions of the topic, Catherine Drinker Bowen gives examples and explains why the voice matters to her (*Biography*, 86–90). She ingeniously shows what we can learn about kinds of people, about influence in public places, about relationships in a family circle, and more. We know that accents and dialects not only identify sections of the country but socio-economic class; that habitual and characteristic tones of voice are keys to, for instance, thoughtfulness, charm, and the assumption of privilege. Indeed, the person with a resonant or musical voice and laugh has social advantages. Knowledge of Queen Elizabeth I's clear, lovely voice with its refined accents and pronunciation adds a dimension to numerous scenes in biographies about her. That Benjamin Franklin said that the Boston accent, described by an English traveller as 'a whining cadence', 'seem to revive and refresh me' (*Biography*, 87) tells us something about how people sounded and what it meant to feel American in the first years of our nation.

Biographers must be perpetually alert to anything that gives access to how the subject looked, acted, spoke, related to different kinds of people and to characteristic mannerisms and conduct. Paul Horgan captured Edmund Wilson's 'reluctant' handshake: 'He pressed his arm close to his ribs, extended the forearm as little as possible, and offered his inert hand as it retreated within his cuff.'[18] John Neale included the suggestive information that Queen Elizabeth I tickled Dudley's neck as he knelt before her to receive an earldom.[19] Scrapbooks, commonplace books, surviving objects—only the imagination limits what ingenious biographers can seek and make speak. Some biographers collect photographs of the rooms in which the subject lived and worked and are careful to include the views from windows. Whatever can be learned about the formation of the mind and its affinities, interests, and ways of thinking must be mastered; many biographers attempt to reconstruct lists of the subjects' schoolbooks and camp or summer activities. The goal is resonant knowledge about the material, social, artistic, emotional, and intellectual experience—the 'sense of life as she knew, felt, and lived it or worked within it'.[20] With apparently effortless economy, the biographer must be able to explain that the 'touchy' Mrs Thomas Carlyle was not 'making a good deal of unnecessary fuss' when she reacted with resentment and tears to the surprise gift of a silk dress, because it was the 'recognized gift for a housekeeper', not a great niece.[21]

La Rochefoucauld wrote that 'the accent and character of one's native region live in the mind and heart just as in one's speech'. For that reason, visiting the places that bred and mattered to the subject are essential. Coke's London, George Eliot's Chelsea, Truman's Missouri soaked into their souls. When Defoe finally had a large, pleasant house, he planted lime trees, and a man he admired and whose company he often happily shared had had a lime tree walk in Pennicuik, Scotland. His travel book tells the visitor how to approach various places, and, in almost every case, still today his advice gives a superior panoramic or historically rich view. His economic books can suddenly burst out in nearly poetic passages on what he has seen in his native country; Defoe is not known for his appreciation of beauty, but in these nonfiction works it is abundantly clear.

The biographer needs to know the significant houses, gardens, even rooms, the vacation spots, major trips, and favourite restaurants, front porches, and friends' entertainment spaces. Only by seeing them can the biographer write, as Leon Edel did about the Villa Bricheri, 'there is an umbrella pine at one end, as in a landscape by Claude', and thereby allowing us to visualize it.[22] Jeffrey Meyers describes the many places, beginning with Hemingway's childhood homes and including Michigan (where he swam a mile from shore to see a house from that perspective), Key West, St Mary's Hospital of the Mayo Clinic in Rochester, Minnesota (where Hemingway was a psychiatric patient), and Ketchum, Idaho, where he died and is buried (*Spirit of Biography*, 245–6). Richard Holmes came to refer to himself as a 'following shadow' as he described the gathering of such experience.[23] Edel refers to the 'certitudes' gained in such research (*Writing Lives*, 231), and, out of the mass of material that grows around what will become the book, he is right to single out places visited and seen. The places we live, the landscape we see each day, the weather that provides the rhythm of our year shape the soul and the sensibility.

This stage of research should serve another purpose. Changes in book production make it easier and less costly to have illustrations, and I think that every biography should have them. As a new biographer, I didn't think much about them, and that was a mistake. They should be collected throughout the entire period of research and writing, and information about permissions and reproduction fees carefully filed. To do otherwise can delay production of the biography by at least a year. The things that the biographer wants to see and is thrilled to find illustrated or photographed are the things readers want to see. Edel refers to the biographer as a 'four-eyed traveler', one who tries to see through the subject's eyes but also, necessarily, sees through his or her own and also must imagine at every moment converting what is seen into words that will transmit accurately and connotatively (*Writing Lives*, 236).

Ann Thwaite describes going through Edmund Gosse's house shortly before it was gutted, and the 'builders' foreman had never heard of Gosse, but he entered into the spirit of my quest. "Your chap would have touched that", he said, indicating a doorknob . . .'.[24] She remembers that Gosse had loved the view of Regents' Park from his windows, and she is careful to experience that—and readers would enjoy the framed view. Cynthia Ozick in a review of Quentin Bell's *Virginia Woolf: A Biography* argues that 'part of the special history of the Bloomsbury of mood [*sic*] is pictorial' and fills her review with images that transmit the seductive possibility of close, intellectual, intimate friends deep in good conversation and producing work that matters. She selects friends playing chequers 'on an old kitchen chair set out in the yard', friends and baby in the sand, a puppy held up to the camera, hands casually on books in very amateur shots of small groups, and Leonard Woolf and Adrian Stephen dressed alike in front of the Woolf villa in Sussex;[25] this hyper-reader brings cultural ideas of the Bloomsbury group and finds some reinforced in pictures but deepens and revises opinions as she 'reads' illustrations beside text. Descriptions that must be taken largely on faith become persuasive, memorable arguments with the right illustration. I could have told my readers that as the reputation of Sarah Siddons, the great eighteenth-century actress, changed, representations of her became distinctively masculine, but that point would never be fully credible without the harsh illustrations in *Spectacular Politics*.

Interviews, films, and tapes assume greater and greater importance if the subject is living or recently dead. 'Reading' these is a new craft, one historical and literary study poorly trains biographers to do. Interviewing in particular deserves more study and more analytical advice. The few books on writing biographies often take a pessimistic view of the accuracy of memory and are filled with accounts of unsuccessful or disappointing events. Doris Kearns Goodwin learned 'painfully', when she discovered that Lyndon Johnson's 'proud description of his great-great-grandfather's heroic death at the Battle of San Jacinto' was untrue; 'he was a real estate trader and had died at home in bed' (Pachter, *Telling Lives*, 98). My favourite anecdote is Jeffrey Meyers' interview with a friend of Katherine Mansfield: 'I peered through the window at the haggard profile of Ida, as she sat bent over in a deep chair, buried under a pile of old army blankets and surrounded by a ring of dirty tissues. My first thought, when she failed to answer the loud knocks, was that she was dead and that I was the first to find her.' Ida refuses to talk, and as he leaves he 'had to suppress a desire to pile a few more blankets on Ida and carefully go through her papers' (pp. 145–6). Meyers gives a number of helpful tips on interviewing, including pointing out that the elderly tire easily and the biographer must establish rapport quickly. The most candid interviewers shamefacedly admit how important charm is, and experienced biographers learn ways to make the tape recorder unobtrusive and to protect the privacy of the interviewed even as they get information they can use. The most successful seem to explain calmly that the tape recorder will be a way to assure that quotations are accurate and that information they are given 'off the record' is clearly labelled as such. The days of rushing out of an interview to some semi-public place and writing frantically are probably passing.

★

Having been told that a 'definitive' biographer had been chosen for Oliver Wendell Holmes, the subject in whom she had already invested years, and that she could not even use the letters she had already read and transcribed, Bowen, in her own words, 'began to think carefully about biographical evidence'. She asked, 'Were letters, after all, the best proof of fact, and must a thing be written down, to be true?' (*Adventures*, 63) She makes a list that parallels that of sceptical lawyers, and then collects physical evidence as well as creative interviews. Forced away from letters, the closest approximation to a diary or journals that most biographers have, she had to change not only her method but her relationship to her preconceived hierarchy of reliability.

The list of ways letters may be misleading, deadening, or worse is very long. Victoria Glendinning points out that reading the letters of Harold Nicolson and Vita Sackville-West would lead to the conclusion that the marriage 'was a miracle of sustained romance—as in a sense it was, except that Vita was writing love-letters of a different kind to other people as well, nearly all the time'.[26] As John Garraty observes, letters should not be confused with diaries and journals, regardless of how intimate the correspondents are; rather they should be seen first as showing a person 'in one form of interaction' with contemporaries, and thus offering insights into personality but not an unfiltered, clear window to it. He goes on to counsel,

One learns a great deal about a person from the way others handle him, and the way he responds to different approaches. Do flattery and subservience produce a favorable reaction in the subject? Do threats influence him more than reasoned argument? The character of each writer will affect his replies, but from a large group of letters certain generalizations can usually be made.[27]

Letters, like diaries, can give a fleeting mood. It can be impossible to reconstruct their context, and what survives is always to some extent an accident. Examples such as these are easy to find: 'One day [Henry James] heaped his correspondence of forty years upon a great roaring fire in his garden at Lamb House, in Sussex, and watched its progress from paper to ash'. He commented that he 'had been easier in mind since'. Charles Dickens, who did the same, said, 'Would to God every letter I have ever written were on that pile' (Edel, *Literary Biography*, 38).

Denied access to the Kennedy papers still held by the family and many interview subjects, Nigel Hamilton became increasingly creative in identifying alternative sources of information and evaluating them. Among them were revealingly annotated records at Choate, papers and publications from Harvard, medical records, painstakingly reconstructed descriptions of PT (Patrol Torpedo) boats, and interviews so ingenious as to include stewardesses on Joe, Sr.'s flights. Praised and condemned almost equally for his kinds, amount, and uses of evidence, Hamilton emerges as a biographer who nevertheless may put too much faith in documents and, tied a little too much to a popular form of Freudian psychology, cannot convey a wide enough range of possibilities to explain human complexity. Unlike Bowen, he insists, 'You must have the documents. To understand the moral dimension of a man you have to test the documents against the witnesses' (*NYT*, C10). In a generally good review, Alan Brinkley writes that the evidence is 'Disconcertingly skimpy for some of the book's most inflammatory passages' (*TLS*, 21 May 1993, 51). He recognizes that Hamilton 'is a prodigious researcher' and has 'trawled through enormous quantities' of material, and yet he feels Hamilton has lost control, letting the information 'cascade across the pages, numbingly and indiscriminately'.

M. R. Montgomery describes Hamilton's 'dogged search for the more lurid details' about Kennedy (*Boston Globe*, 7 October 1992, 73), and the review in the same paper says the great strength of *JFK* is the material from new sources that assures the 'vivid, readable, and dramatic' book will be 'the central and authoritative reference on Kennedy's early life' (22 November 1992, 36). Rhoda Koenig singles out some of the places that Hamilton is at his best and evaluates his technique; 'Hamilton's description of these boats—dangerous, unreliable craft requiring immense skill and daring—is one more example of the way his psychological portrait of Kennedy is drawn from fact rather than from speculation.'[28] In the early reviews such as these, however, 'repetitive' and 'gratuitous' begin to crop up.

Consider again the problem of Beckett's birth date. Which is more important? the documentary record or the 'felt fact', the meaning memory has assigned and the interpretation that has been integrated into identity? Victoria Glendinning once asked, 'Is the story of your life what happens to you, or what you feel happens to you, or what observers see happening to you?' ('Lies and Silences', 51). Unity may be found around a good but apocryphal story and important events encrusted in warring memories. Most biographers probably intend to write the life as it appeared to or was experienced by the subject. But Glendinning points out, 'are you going to take the perceptions and evidence of other people into account, which will change the picture a lot?' (p. 50). Biographers must; all their evidence cannot come from the subject alone.

What really happens is that the biographer gives readers the life as it appeared to be and to be experienced to the biographer,[29] not to the subject, and it is on this point that Hamilton is most vulnerable. Because of the way the biography is written, the reader does not sink into it, become absorbed in the narrative, but is distracted repeatedly in ways that trigger the testing and doubting of evidence. Nigel Hamilton's prejudices, glaringly against the Irish Catholics and 'old queens' (a particularly British phrase used for J. J. Maher, Kennedy's Choate master, p. 134), remind us that we are seeing Kennedy through alien eyes. We cannot imagine Kennedy thinking of 'jumped-up Boston Irish Catholic' (p. 103). As Virginia Woolf wrote to someone who had read her biography of Roger Fry as she hoped it would be read: 'It was an experiment in self suppression; a gamble in R's power to transmit himself. And so rich and to me alive and various and masterly was he that I was certain he would shine by his own light better than through any painted shade of mine. Lord! how I sweated! But to my amazement, its [sic] succeeded. . . . the public does see Roger plain' (Letters, 6: 417–18).

In the contested ground that Hamilton's biography became, conflicting judgements about evidence are instructive. It was no small thing to find so much evidence about what is always the most difficult part of a life to document and interpret, the first twenty-five years, and his methods and recognition of sources deserve imitation. For all the criticisms of Hamilton, his accomplishment outweighs them. Before this biography, the early life of Kennedy was as little known as that of most children of prominent parents, was often shied away from or characterized quickly as 'unpromising'; Hamilton has definitely documented the signs of great promise and also the recognition of them by people who knew him best or were thrown into his company in tense times.

Nigel Hamilton was rightly praised for candour, but he, like all biographers had to make countless decisions that can be seen as pitting the historian against the sensitive human being. It has been said that, finally, the biographer has nothing to offer but truth. Assuming truths can be known, should they all be told? Samuel Johnson answered ruthlessly, 'Yes'. He supported the decision of the author of the *Biographia Britannica* to note that Joseph Addison had loaned Richard Steele £100 and then taken legal action to secure repayment, and yet his own groundbreaking biography of Richard Savage is a fabric of wishes, speculations, and fantasies that put his friend and his most dubious actions in a favourable light.[30] Historians are trained to believe that they can be objective and that they have a nearly sacred duty to present their evidence, regardless of who will be hurt by it. 'Suppress' and 'withhold' are damning words; academic freedom and tenure exist to protect the telling of such truths. Biographers of long-dead subjects are far more sanguine and probably seem rather glib about this issue to those writing about contemporary subjects. Leon Edel, for instance, says that biography is 'truth seen' (*Writing Lives*, 213). Virginia Woolf adds a dimension to this conflict, 'How can one write the truth about friends whose families are alive? And Roger was the most scornful of untruths of any man' (*Letters*, 6: 169). Similarly engaged with the subject as well as survivors and the responsibility for 'truth', Diane Middlebrook considered Anne Sexton's relationship to harsh self-revelation and attempted to satisfy herself about what Sexton would have wanted or agreed to. In what has become a flash point for discussion of evidence and the contemporary practice of biography, Middlebrook, Sexton's psychiatrist, a few family friends, and Sexton's daughter and literary executor decided that Sexton would have approved of the release of tapes of her therapy sessions. Parameters that they worked out and that evolved guided Middlebrook's sensitive use of the material.[31]

Woolf also wrote of 'a sense of other people looking over one's shoulder' (6: 426). In the context in which she wrote this sentence, she was again comparing the freedom of fiction to the restraints of biography; living people can indeed contradict the biographer and may even come forward with solid evidence. The sane biographer thinks of such an event as advancing scholarship, is happy to see the evidence revealed, and knows that this risk is part of every publication—no one can find, know, understand everything. But the living can also look over the shoulder jealously and with the determination of protecting themselves or their image of reality, of a comfortable fiction they have erected with some effort. They certainly have the right to the first and may have considerable stake in maintaining the second.

The struggle over evidence about Sylvia Plath provides a sobering and instructive case. Which is more horrible? the fact that Plath's husband, the late Ted Hughes, destroyed the journal in which she wrote about the last weeks of her life or the deeply private Hughes's awareness that every biography about Plath would 'appropriate at least one chapter from the biography of Hughes'.[32] The poet Katha Politt recently described Hughes as 'with the possible exception of Xanthippe, the most notorious literary spouse in history' and observed snidely (and correctly) about his decision to destroy the manuscripts to protect the children 'as if they would never grow up and wish to make their own decision, and as if explosive but precious documents were not routinely sealed in vaults and archives for posterity' (*NYTBR*, 1 March 1998, 4). Linda Wagner-Martin describes being 'battered from dealings with the hostile estate' and 'bewildered and then amazed at the lambasting some British reviewers attempted to give *Sylvia Plath, A Biography*'.[33] Anne Stevenson, author of *Bitter Fame*, blamed flaws in her biography of Plath 'squarely on the Hugheses, who she says insisted on total control over everything that appeared in the book' and 'ordered her to delete any passages that sought to explore [Hughes's] role in the marriage's breakup'.[34] Hughes's sister Olwyn, who is accused of rewriting 'much of the book', summarizes what has happened with Plath biography: 'It seems that somebody always has to be crucified for Sylvia Plath. First it was Aurelia [Sylvia's mother], then Ted, and now it's me' (C-8). Hughes insisted that he was primarily motivated by the desire to prevent 'much new pain and bitterness into the lives of quite a few people' (quoted C-9). Ian Hamilton's sensitive review of Wagner-Martin's biography raises two very different but central issues. First he summarizes the amount of material available to Plath biographers and then questions what else we would know either about the life or the personality if we had the full, uncensored papers. Every biographer knows that a sign of having done the research well is the moment when conclusions, even conclusions about the interior life and character of the subject, are simply confirmed and confirmed again. Second, Ian Hamilton asks, 'How much more discomfiture should be required of [Hughes]?' and, by natural extension, goes on to 'what would Sylvia Plath have wished to preserve, if she had lived?'[35] Linda Sexton, Anne's daughter, freely admits, 'Reading in the transcripts about how much she hated me was devastating. I sat and sobbed.' These tapes cover 1960–4, and Sexton committed suicide in 1974; the journal that Hughes destroyed covered the time immediately before Plath's death. Himself a biographer of a troubled, erratic, difficult poet with many living friends and relatives (Robert Lowell) and of J. D. Salinger who sued Hamilton successfully for invasion of privacy and forced debilitating revisions of Hamilton's biography of him, Ian Hamilton offers little guidance but demands that these considerations be factored into any equation used to judge Hughes's management of Plath's estate. When she committed suicide, Plath opened her children's window and left them milk. It is hard to say with assurance that she would have handed that journal over to them.

What Hamilton does not address, which is a major consideration and acts as a particularly volatile element in the compound, is what might be better understood about Plath's creative processes and the relationship between artist and artefact. This is no small part of a literary biography; indeed, the most respected biographers of writers universally cite it as *the* major endeavour and the *raison d'être* for the genre. The journal Plath kept during the autumn of 1962, the period during which she wrote most of her *Ariel* poems, the poems that probably clinched the Pulitzer Prize, and the draft of her last novel are both missing. This fact coupled with the editorial oversight that seems to characterize all relations the Hughes have with biographers imposes difficulties few biographers face. Perhaps under the circumstances in which they have been written, the fact that biographies of Plath have been judged 'thin' is no surprise.

Middlebrook's work offers an instructive contrast. She establishes the link Sexton made between her psychotherapy and her writing and argues that Sexton invented a poetic form out of the associative methods of the kind of psychotherapy she experienced. Her therapist's tapes and notes firmly become a means of analysing the creative process, but they are far less important than interviews, reconstructions of the workshops and courses she attended, and even sensitive literary readings of Sexton's poetry. In Middlebrook's account, that Sexton knew and worked with poets important to the development of the 'confessional' mode of modern poetry is factored into every description of her developing art, her identity as a poet, and the relationship between her writing and her mental health.

Again, there are high stakes as well as personal considerations at work in these struggles and reactions. For many feminists, and sociology and history contribute much to the validity of their perspective, the neurotic woman is a threat to the cultural image of 'woman' that is needed for advancement in the public sphere. Cases of victims of patriarchy and the double standard can be used to discourage constricting behaviour. More generally, Plath is part of a generation of women poets who changed not only women's poetry but American poetry. Her *Bell Jar* describes the anomie that intelligent women often feel even today; expressing an inability to fit in metonymically and unforgettably through the heroine's cultivation of bizarre clothes and hairstyles; elevating a subject that was rocking poetry arbitrators, women's blood, to a place of great symbolic power by dramatizing excessive bleeding after first intercourse; and describing both intense suicidal longings and recovery as adolescent rites of passage, Plath produced a classic that still speaks intimately to the secret experiences of many women.

Too many of the women poets of her generation committed suicide, and the interpretation of alienation and rejection provides a mythic, acceptable story for many; to conclude that she was a bitter, neurotic, tedious, petty harpie whose suicide was a sad, psychotic act asks that we do what Anglo-American readers have never been able to do: separate the work from the moral being we decide the writer was. To discredit the woman will be a major step towards disqualifying her poetry from serious study and from general interest anthologies; they will become 'negative, sick, death-oriented'—not valuable or healthy reading, not artistic achievement that we can admire or allow to be influential.[36] In Middlebrook's portrait of an entire group of women poets— Sexton, Plath, Adrienne Rich, Maxine Kumin—struggling to balance their art with marriages and children, and the time's expectations for women with their energy and ambition, we see what was common if not 'normal' about Sexton's feelings and choices.

Anne Sexton suggests what we may be missing because we lack so many of Plath's personal papers, and it also shows in a quite reassuring way how tastefully such documents can be used. Perhaps the day will come when others in Hughes's situation trust a biographer to do what Middlebrook does over and over. An example is her important discussion of the creation of the poem 'Her Kind' that became the poem Sexton used to begin every public reading. She has already used the phrase with gentle emphasis to mark moments when Sexton escaped her feelings of singularity and wrote, 'These are my people'. After multiple revisions, Sexton wrote, 'I have gone out, a possessed witch, | haunting the black air, braver at night . . . lonely thing, twelve-fingered, out of mind. | A woman like that is not a woman, quite. | I have been her kind.' Middlebrook explains that Sexton told audiences that the poem 'would show them what kind of woman she was, and what kind of poet'. And then she makes the interpretative move that Plath deserves: 'The subjectivity of the poem insists on a separation between a kind of woman (mad) and a kind of poet (a woman with a magic craft): a doubleness that expressed the paradox of Sexton's creativity' (pp. 114–15). This insight, this carefully crafted argument, could not have been achieved without her access to so much of Sexton's inner musing and desperate participation in her own therapy.

Biographers grapple with evidence, and it is often a fierce struggle. Plath's biographers, like Nigel Hamilton, insist that if they had just been given all of the documents, they could have produced a fair, 'truthful' life. What is evidence anyway? and what makes 'good' evidence? Some biographers advise that if you can't find any words by your subject about an experience use someone else's, matching as closely as possible time and situation. But can you ever match personality? or individual circumstances? Does such matching give good evidence? These are not simple questions; indeed, in addition to other complications, the answers are surprisingly culture and time bound.

Until the fifteenth century, the jury members' personal knowledge of the accused's character and hearsay were given more weight than witnesses or documents; after that, witnesses, who were regarded as replacing the kind of knowledge jurors in a small community might have, and sworn documents gained importance but were soon superseded by written and physical evidence, the evidence of 'things' and of sense data. In 1680, for instance, a jury was instructed, 'where there are two men that positively tell you anything that lies within their own knowledge and swear it is true, it is scarce any improbability that should weigh against such evidence'.[37] The use of 'two'—a number still often cited as giving credence to testimony—is a holdover from Romano-canon procedure, a legal system that relied heavily on assigning set values to kinds of pre-defined evidence.[38] As late as the eighteenth century, the jury was still expected to use personal and common knowledge as well as common sense in evaluating all kinds of evidence, including sworn testimony. Lord Chief Justice Francis North powerfully captured the ideal:

> God forbid that the worst Villains should have it in their power, by positive swearing, to take away a man's life or estate. . . .
>
> it is the proper business of peers and juries to try not the grammatical construction of words . . . but the credibility of persons and things; which require collation of circumstances and a right judgement thereupon   (quoted in Shapiro, *Probability*, 186)

Very slowly, the jury 'ceased to be witnesses as well as judges of matters of fact' (Shapiro, 183).

Later belief, however, that 'circumstances cannot lie' received greater trust than positive testimony, that is eye witnesses who might be mistaken or defending personal interests. Sworn witnesses became merely verbal evidence requiring careful evaluation.[39] Victoria Glendinning raises the following example:

> if you go with friends to a party, and all agree to write down afterwards what happened at the party, the accounts will all be quite different. Each person will have had his own encounters and experiences, besides which each person has different attitudes, perceptions and prejudices. Also, most importantly, not everyone will tell the truth about what happened or did not happen to them that evening.[40]

Catherine Drinker Bowen quotes what she calls the scholar's adage: 'if I don't read it, I don't believe it' and remarks that 'men prefer the authority of print' (p. 9). Her words record the triumph of a contract society over one of verbal honour.

As Barbara Shapiro says, 'Rules are drawn from the culture's general understanding of how we "know" things to be true.'[41] Many disciplines define evidence in special and narrow ways, and enough evidence to persuade one person leaves another deeply sceptical. Even most statements about 'empirical fact' cannot really be conclusively, finally established. Consider the statements, both 'true': 'Any metal object expands with rising temperature' or 'Some chemical compounds do not dissolve in any substance.' Evidence can be available on no more than a finite number of cases, 'a finite number of data concerning volume changes in metal pieces at rising temperature' and a finite number of records of these compounds being dropped in a finite number of liquids and other substances.[42]

These scientific examples involving properties of matter would be excluded from 'evidence' and classified as 'experiments' by many philosophers. Ian Hacking, a philosopher and historian of science, puts what he calls 'the test, the adventure, the diagnosis, and the dissection' into the category of experiment and insists that 'evidence' is different from them. The test is set up to refute or corroborate a hypothesis, and the adventure, its sister procedure, takes place in the absence of any good hypothesis and is undertaken without much sense of what the results will be. Dissection takes something apart in order to examine the interior; diagnosis, the closest to the biographical method, uses evidence of one thing to infer another. Hacking moves quickly beyond the evidence of the senses to 'inductive evidence', which he argues originated in the seventeenth century and is the foundation of the concept of probability, and, therefore, basic to our experience of degrees of certainty.[43]

'Evidence' conjures up the court of law and the jury, the ultimate fact evaluators. The charge to jurors—'beyond a reasonable doubt'—is vexed in our scientific age. Few remember the history of 'reasonable to conscience' or conscientious belief. In most cases, people knew that they could never have infallible proof and were being asked to decide if they strongly *believed*, rather than knew, the person to be guilty. Richard Sennet points out that truth has come to mean that 'no other explanation but the one advanced after a given process of investigation is feasible'.[44] He explains the problems:

This empiricism, based on exclusion by the exhaustion of evidence, is in my view opposed to any real notion of intellectual honesty. We arrive at intellectual honesty by admitting, precisely, the reality of contradiction, and eschewing all hope of arriving at an immutable statement. . . . Anesthetization of the intellect is the inevitable product of this form of proof, because it requires that no judgments be made until all the facts are in . . .
In qualitative research, 'proof', if that anxiety-laden word must be used at all, is a matter of the demonstration of logical relationship; the qualitative researcher has laid on him the burden of plausibility. . . . Empirical plausibility is a matter of showing the logical connections among phenomena which can be described concretely.   (p. 43)

Evidence, reason, experience, opinion work together with juries and with readers, who are the biographers' jury.

Not only have we all been influenced by legal conceptions of evidence and good evidence, but, at the time historians and others consider the beginning of the modern period, philosophers, theologians, rhetoricians, scientists, and legal theorists exhibited considerable mutual borrowing in their writings about evidence, credibility, and proof. Some, including the great legal theorist Matthew Hale, wrote about both scientific and legal proofs.[45] We have, then, inherited and been steeped in strong assumptions about evidence. Generally we believe that direct or 'inartificial proofs'—eye or ear witnesses, deeds, reports, even 'common fame'—are better than indirect or 'artificial' ones—circumstantial evidence, examples, arguments, and other things that are the result of an orator's or writer's art. And yet witnesses and reports can be mistaken or corrupt, deeds superseded by a missing or suppressed document, and circumstantial evidence can be of such quantity and quality that it rises 'so near to certainty' that it commands 'universal assent' and governs 'our thinking as absolutely as the most evident demonstration'.[46]

William Best, an important mid-nineteenth century legal theorist, argued that 'all judicial knowledge was presumptive. Direct evidence presumed the veracity of witnesses and the genuineness of documents. Indirect evidence simply involved a different form of presumption.' Citing Locke, he said that 'in all important transactions of life and in all "moral, and most of the physical sciences", we must rely almost exclusively "on probable presumptive reasoning"'. He insisted, however, that 'a chain of presumptive evidence may afford as convincing proof as one based on direct testimony'.[47]

Best's use of 'chain' serves as a good transition to the art of biography. The human mind in deciding if something is probable, beyond a reasonable doubt, or certain makes inferences from direct, or hard, evidence and links them, assigning such things as sequence, intention, and circumstances. Other sources of knowledge, some without full recognition, such as our understanding of the physical world or of human psychology, also provide or strengthen links. As Hayden White and others remind us, facts exist only as congeries of contiguously related fragments, and we string them together. Degrees of probability and certainty are the result of our apprehension of the relationship between an hypothesis and the evidence for it.[48] In fact, it seems that 'A concurrence of well authenticated circumstances composes a stronger ground of assurance . . . than positive testimony, unconfirmed by circumstances, usually affords.'[49] Almost reflexively readers submit evidence to 'the test of corroborating circumstance' (Welsh, 8) and a number of other rational, irrational, and cultural tests. Some cultures elevate opinion over probability and others the reverse. 'The credibility of witnesses [is] related to social and economic status as well as to the opportunity to observe firsthand the fact in question', thus 'the value system of the . . . era [is] incorporated into the system of proof' (Shapiro, 188). For instance, in times such as that of 'scientific revolutions', as in the seventeenth century and our own beginning in the 1940s and 1950s with the atomic bomb and the response to Sputnik, there is always an increase in epistemological thinking and in pressure on evidence and argument to conform to the ideal of demonstrable or logical proof that characterizes the physical and mathematical sciences.[50] In contrast, for other peoples and in other times, signs, omens, and dreams bear evidentiary weight. As Alexander Welsh points out, 'All evidence, in short, has to be read or interpreted as such' (p. 7). Regardless of the era, jurors and readers seek a plausible narrative, and as Welsh observes in *Strong Representations*, 'A plausible narrative is often persuasive by itself' (p. 25).

The persuasive power of narrative rides upon the rails of evidence and our varying degrees of faith in different kinds of evidence—indeed, our very perception of which statements are evidence—often operate below the level of consciousness. Like the rules of language, these perceptions lie well below the surface of reader awareness. Yet readers look for and believe they rely upon 'facts' and hard evidence. As Park Honan contends in his study of Richard Ellmann's work, authority arises primarily from 'an attitude to personal evidence'. He explains how it depends on the depth, range, and imaginative alertness to one's research; it seems to depend on one's prose style and tone, also on structure within a chapter and the structural sequence of chapters'— in other words, on *narrative* built upon a wealth of painstakingly gathered evidence (*Authors' Lives*, 67).

The very fact that so many reviewers, my 'hyper-readers', write about the evidence testifies to the distraction it can become. In the most successful biographies, evidence is completely unnoticed. Most readers pause over it in the text or search for it in the notes only when something has raised their scepticism or arrested their attention. Although 'Boswellian moments' are not unknown, the 'Boswellian biographer' who 'accumulates credit by . . . revealing how his work has been manufactured, by acquiring and co-existing with the biographical subject, by valuing and being valued by the biographical subject, by eliciting spontaneous praise, by acknowledging his debts to the assistance of others [in the narrative], . . . by correcting the misrepresentations of others, by exhibiting his diligent and ardent preservation' is no longer in fashion.[51] The modern biographer, however, is on trial and must be plausible, cogent, and conscientious about presenting evidence. Here's an example of the distraction a reviewer experienced as he caught Ray Monk out:

> Monk has decided, he says, to show [Bertrand] Russell's life by letting Russell speak for himself, but one might wonder whether he hasn't mostly shown the elaborate ways in which Russell could feel lonely, frustrated, bored and depressed—the states of mind in which he was most effusive as a correspondent, but perhaps not those in which most of the rest of his life was conducted.   (Alan Ryan, *TLS*, 21 June 1996, 6)

The effect must be such that the notes are consulted out of admiration or individual special curiosity, not because scepticism arises.

In fact, Ryan's observation quietly problematizes an entire category of evidence, one biographers discover with joy and often treat rather uncritically. Obviously to whom a letter is written and its purposes must be taken fully into account and are essential evidence revealing a great deal about character and performative selves, but Ryan, as a reader of this manuscript noted, is reminding us that the letters, no matter how many, how varied, and how widely addressed, give us the subject as nothing except letter writer, not a trustworthy picture of human beings in the fullness of their lives. Monk argues that Russell's primary mode of communication and relating to people was writing letters. A typical portayal is in the account of Russell's time in Brixton Prison for violating the Defence of the Realm Act in 1981: 'With a warder sitting close enough to hear everything that was said, conversation was stilted and difficult, and real communications was conducted as so often in Russell's life—by letter. Officially, he was allowed to write no more than one letter a week, which had to be read first by a prison official to see that it contained nothing seditious. . . . a limit . . . obviously intolerable' (p. 526).

Monk's biography, like Ronald Clark's, tends to create a Russell who is desperately seeking human contact and connection, ways to escape 'feeling like a ghost'. *Bertrand Russell: The Spirit of Solitude, 1872–1921* has at least one quotation from Russell's letters on almost every page. In his own book, *Bertrand Russell: A Political Life*, which quotes very few letters, Ryan finds engagement, 'exuberance, vitality and stamina'. But he is interested in Russell's life as a polemicist, agitator, and reformer, and he is stimulated, even excited by Russell's mind and ideas and does not see his book encompassing topics such as Monk's discussion of how for the first time in several busy years Russell realized he had 'neglected his inner life' and turned to reflective self-scrutiny without his usual guilt (pp. 527–38). These biographies are too different to bear much fruitful comparison, but Ryan's review and his different conception of Russell serve to reinforce an important truth: Letters *about* a person and descriptions of social actions and interactions must be sought as diligently and used as fully as those by the subject.

There is a great deal of art in the presentation of evidence, and a fine line exists between too much and too little—either distracts the reader. Reviewers can be savage:

perhaps he believes that his book doesn't need footnotes because the common reader doesn't care who said what or where. (Samuel Hynes on Martin Seymour-Smith's *Hardy*, *TLS*, 18 March 1994, 3–4)

in spite of 'encyclopedic footnotes' his account of Garbo's mundane youth never quite becomes vivid. (Patrick McGilligan on Barry Paris's *Garbo: A Biography*, *NYT BR*, 2 April 1995, 3)

those thousand-page tomes heaped with tedious detail. (Robert Kanigel on a biography of B. F. Skinner, *NYT*, 3 October 1993, 26)

the factual information is presented in indigestible chunks, and the book is . . . badly researched. (Peter Thomas on Jeremy Black's *Pitt the Elder*, *TLS*, 24 May 1993, 28)

Coping constantly with the balance between too much and too little, the biographer must be the most ruthless of writers. Bowen remarks tartly that 'A biography is not an encyclopedia, it is the story of a life.'[52] 'To write accurate biography, one has to acquire vast amounts of collateral historical knowledge and then to *know* that 90% of it *is* collateral, and be ready to jettison it', Jay Martin attests.[53] He gives an example of a detailed argument that was important to establishing the canon of Henry Miller's work but of the type that would have drawn the book out to thousands of pages. Biographers agree that what they never use or cut actually gives them confidence, which translates into accurate presentations and an authoritative voice—or at least it prevents embarrassing statements and conclusions. As Antony Alpers, biographer of Katherine Mansfield, emphasizes, 'Get the facts . . . and get them right, or ludicrous conclusions may result. . . . This means collecting every trivial fact . . . and much detective work; and later, sacrificing precious discoveries' ('Biography—The Scarlet Experiment', 17). Some of my new Defoe material had to be published outside of the biography for the same reasons. Wherever an especially original, complex argument had to be made, as about Defoe's first arrest for seditious libel, the consequences of interrupting the story of the life for an extended period had to be carefully weighed. Readers and reviewers, like members of the jury, assess the manner of delivery as well as the content, and they use a variety of personal ways to decide on each segment's intrinsic probability.

There comes a moment when the collected evidence seems chaotic, overwhelming, miscellaneous, intractable, and somehow *wrong*. Virginia Woolf lamented, 'How can one make a life out of Six Cardboard boxes full of tailor's bills love letters and old picture postcards?' Later she writes, 'such a mass of odds and ends out of which to make a whole.'[54] Assembling, arranging, and interpreting evidence is an exercise in close work that can turn frustrating quickly. At some point, every biographer concludes, 'I just don't know.' Victoria Glendinning says that biographers do not have much choice about 'lies and silences' in the writing of biography.[55] We just try to have as few as possible. And we and our motives are often obscure to ourselves; how can those of another human being be any less? Sometimes a key piece of evidence is missing—lost in a library fire, destroyed by an over-zealous archivist,[56] never written down, lost in the dust of a hundred years. Sometimes the evidence could be laid out in several ways with differing inferences and significances as the result.

Iris Origo, author of *Leopardi: A Biography*, *The World of San Bernardino*, and many essays on biography, economically and bluntly summarizes the special dark night of the biographer's soul: 'Three insidious temptations assail the biographer: to suppress, to invent, and to sit in judgment, and of these the earliest and most frequent is suppression.'[57] The temptation to suppress can be very great. Virginia Woolf began to see the possibility of 'a long painstaking literal book' instead of a good narrative and wrote, 'How can one cut loose from facts, when there they are, contradicting my theories?'[58] I once seriously considered pretending I had never found a set of letters because they were so difficult to decipher. The most common watchword, however, is one that Park Honan extracts from Richard Ellmann's work: biographers 'may combine, assimilate, extract, and abstract, but not create' (p. 67).

And so we combine, assimilate, extract—arrange, draw inferences, and build chains. Crucial to the arrangement of evidence as the foundation of narrative are two concepts, the 'fertile fact' and 'emotional centres'. The first is Virginia Woolf's term and the second will be an important part of the next chapter. Woolf wrote,

But almost any biographer, if he respects facts, can give us much more than another fact to add to our collection. He can give us the creative fact; the fertile fact; the fact that suggests and engenders. Of this, too, there is certain proof. For how often, when a biography is read and tossed aside, some scene remains bright, some figure lives on in the depths of the mind, and causes us, when we read a poem or a novel, to feel a start of recognition, as if we remembered something that we had known before.[59]

She puts emphasis on what the biographer can do with a fact and instinctively trusts that the novelist in her will recognize and exploit it. 'Fertile facts' point beyond themselves and lead to productive, persuasive inferences. Sometimes these are so obvious that the biographer recognizes them with elation, as I did when I found the Exchequer court decision that explained why Defoe had sold his hard-earned, spacious house, left his beloved wife, and died in hiding on Rope-makers Alley. Sometimes their promise is obvious, but further difficult research will be needed to realize fully their potential in a narrative. At times, all biographers press a fact, making it into a 'creative fact', getting it to work in a way that a lesser writer or intellect would not find possible.

James Breslin, for instance, recognizes sign after sign that Mark Rothko was feeling pressured, depressed, destroyed over the gradual sale of his paintings and his inability to control the style of their exhibition. In a chapter central to the development of this theme, he quotes Robert Motherwell, another painter, recalling, 'Rothko remained "surrounded" by these dark paintings, hovering inside the space created by his works as if they were "shields"' (p. 525). In this remarkable chapter, Breslin describes how different these paintings were from any of those from the periods that had gone before and quotes Rothko himself as having 'wondered aloud' if he were 'making a Rothko painting by taking the color out' (p. 525). Breslin marshals one piece of evidence after another—interview, medical and pharmacological, document, physical—to show the paintings and Rothko's life being 'emptied out'.

In another powerful use of using hard evidence to draw what appear to be inevitable, organic inferences and gripping conclusions, Robert Massie develops a picture of Peter the Great of Russia that not only explains the building of a great city in a marshland with workers so deprived that they carried the earth in their shirts because they had no wheelbarrows but that also forges an impression of Peter's personality, character, and magnetism that cannot be forgotten. A combination of ruthless vision, democratic endurance, and theatrical gesture, Peter seems to be making everything over in his image. Imagining a capital on that bog and while it was still in the territory held by a powerful, undefeated enemy, a fortified city that would be designed so well that neither Charles XII of Sweden, Napoleon, nor Hitler,[60] becomes less impressive than the unlikely achievement. This vision could be actualized only with the reality of Peter's presence and, probably, with his use of the theatrical spectacles of power. He lived in a log cabin that lacked a stove or fireplace, but he had latticed mica windows and had it painted to appear to be brick; thus, he lived in the muck in hard conditions with his workmen and soldiers, but he carefully set himself apart. He led his men in battle against the Swedes. After personally exploring the harbour, he had an entire island built so a fort could be put on top of it; men dragged boxes of rocks across the now frozen channel, then sunk them to form the island. Banners in his procession read, 'We have not taken the land of others, but the inheritance of our fathers' (p. 353). He served as pilot to bring the first commercial ship into port, a task obviously belonging to a professional seaman, but then gave a banquet for the captain, exempted the ship from tolls forever, and presided over the renaming of the ship as the 'St Petersburg' (p. 358). Again, he showed his unstinting enthusiasm for the project, his willingness to work with the men, and his attention to detail even as he capped each effort with a spectacular, symbolic display of his power.

Evidence shapes the rhythms and patterns of these chapters and makes persuasive the narrative, and therefore the interpretation that makes meaning. Done well, biography helps us to understand human beings and even human nature and the texture of real lives; inevitably it also shapes our idea of reality, of human nature, and of predictable human action. It is in the patterns that the evidence forms that the most important truths are usually found. The difference between a list or a chronology is this flesh and blood, this emotional power, that actually arranges facts and clothes them in meaning. Whether the biographer selects a factual pattern based on chronology, an interpretative pattern based on a sense of the inner life of the subject,[61] a spiralling pattern that produces multiple, intermingled story lines,[62] or another pattern, the evidence must be presented in ways that make this arrangement seem to have arisen almost irresistibly from it. Sometimes the biographer must be flexible about life patterns, for the power of an experience and especially of memory's work upon it can rearrange the order of events. Something the subject knows or is experiencing in another domain of life can utterly transform the experience and the order in which even individual bits of information are told.

These are times when biographers feel they *know*, and there are also times when there is no evidence to prove a conviction, not even enough circumstantial and contextual evidence to allow a speculation to be presented. I became convinced, for instance, that Defoe had a romantic relationship in 1722 with a Colchester woman named Mary Newton. I found documents that the two of them had both signed and half a dozen pieces of circumstantial evidence, but so few Essex records survive that I could never find either a single piece of hard enough evidence or forge a chain strong enough to bear what would be a controversial assertion. Had I similar suspicions about Defoe's years in Scotland, I might have been more willing to put it forward as a pattern, possibly characteristic behaviour, and as something other biographers of Defoe might prove later. Because biographers' most common experience is to feel an enormous pride in the honourable carrying out of the contract with the reader and the subject that comes from the scrupulous effort—no matter how time-consuming or expensive—to locate evidence, interpret it carefully, and present it without flinching, speculations of this type are usually resisted.

It is with evidence that the biographer must, through graphic scenes, the telling quotation, the revealing detail, through character development and the depiction of interpersonal relationships, the power of suggestion, and dramatic narrative sweep, bring someone else's life into focus.[63] As Richard Altick said in ironic understatement, searching for evidence is 'not a profession for a lazy man', and it does indeed provide 'the test of a vocation [which] is a love of the drudgery it involves' (*The Scholar Adventurers*, 104–5). The next chapter takes up 'emotional centres' and a group of the most far-reaching decisions the biographer makes—those about personality, life shape, and organizing structures.

4. Perspective, Personality, and Life Shapes

Another bloody monkey mind! Can't you keep your grubby paws off of
our lives. You don't know anything and you can't guess right so shut up.
Katherine Anne Porter (marginal note in a biography of her)

Imagine yourself a modern Anglo-American biographer of a living subject who
firmly believes in reincarnation and remembers past lives. Imagine entering
into this person's mind. Imagine presenting aspects and periods of this
subject's life in ways that will be acceptable to your reader—and to your living
subject. If you are anything like me, a few moments reflection will bring you
to a grinding halt before the challenges and uncertainties, for biography carries
with it certain assumptions about what a person is,[1] about the parameters of
consciousness, motivation, and memory, and about the understanding, interpretation, and restructuring of experience.

Of all the choices biographers make, those regarding the treatment of
personality are most often tainted with unconscious cultural assumptions.
Cultural expectations and judgements are as powerful for readers as for biographers, and editors, if not biographers, are well aware of that fact. As my
opening paragraph implies, the biographers' perspective, interpretative categories, and moral judgements are so deeply embedded as to be unrecognized
or, even when recognized, impossible to break free from. Because reading is an
act of absorption not self-analysis, readers are even less likely to take into
account their own ingrained opinions.

This chapter was once two—one on personality and life shape, and one on
the perspectives chosen by biographers; the two topics are, however, inseparable. By the perspective of the biographer I mean the movement in and out of
the mind of the subject, the freedom assumed to interpret the subject's actions
and thoughts, the degree of the commitment to let the subjects speak for themselves, and the extent to which biographers are willing to insert their own voices
and sensibilities into the narrative. After all, on one hand, the perspective of
the biographer determines to a great extent the theory of personality encountered in the book and the readers' experience. And, on the other, many biographers have come to the unsettling truth that writing a biography is 'more
than a discovery of another person. It is a matter of self-discovery.'[2] Richard
Westfall, who participated in an experiment in which biographers were paired
with psychoanalysts concluded, 'It is impossible to portray another human
being without displaying oneself.'[3] He went on to say, 'It had not seriously
occurred to me that the Puritan ethic was also furnishing the set of categories
I used in constructing my picture of Newton.'[4] Near the end of her career,

Catherine Drinker Bowen came to believe that 'seduction in English prose', one of the qualities she believed essential for success as a biographer, was 'a reflection of the author's personality, his outlook on life . . .'. She remarked, 'The balance between historical facts and the biographer's personality . . . is an interesting phenomenon to observe upon the printed page.'[5] These statements, like the contemplation of writing the life of a reincarnated person, are to be conjured with—they open the curtain to give a glimpse of how limited biographers are, how imprisoned within their own experiences, societies, educations, and philosophies.

A pressure point where we can see the biographers' uncomfortable situation is in the intriguing idea that we need the death to measure the life. Not until death (and sometimes not even then) is the life complete, the individual's story closed. It is not only that we can then tally up accomplishments and evaluate the person, but we take how the person died as important evidence that can be used to test our portrait of character and personality—death is, perhaps, concrete expression of what the person and his or her philosophy 'really' were. This opinion is, of course, why biographies sometimes begin with the subject's death. We also, however, measure this death by the meanings and values our culture has assigned to dying and kinds of deaths. The suicide of a military man, a writer, and a religious figure, for instance, are judged in very different ways. In fact, the differences in the ways we discuss and judge the suicides of Ernest Hemingway and of Sylvia Plath and Anne Sexton are worth brooding upon. Stoic Roman, tortured poet, cowardly sinner with clay feet, violent sensualist, neurotic woman are not only stories, plot lines, and explanations, but they carry moral judgements.

In many settings I have been told how important 'a good death' is. In dialogue with students of all ages, lecture audiences, and NEH (National Endowment for the Humanities) seminar members, I've determined that that means both a satisfying sense of closure, of 'it was his time to die', and a narrative of courage in the face of the unknown and, preferably, some physical suffering as well. In a half-joking listing of characteristics of a successful biography, an NEH group insisted that biographers should be sure there was a good death before they undertook writing the life: 'Readers want it and demand it.' Above all, the death must be *explained* and dressed in momentous trappings.

Reading the concluding chapters for dozens and dozens of biographies, the prize winners and others, turned up a huge majority of 'good deaths', often revealed the 'magisterial' voice, but also seemed to require luck not all biographers could count on. Some had unusual effectiveness and true artistic achievement. Who could fail to admire Richard Westfall's carefully constructed final paragraph in *Never at Rest: A Biography of Isaac Newton*? He moves from the tribute of the often-maligned, lowly periodical, *Political State of Great Britain*, to the inscription on the Westminster Abbey monument, one located in a place 'often refused . . . to the greatest noblemen'. The author of the

Political State, Abel Boyer, had the wit to call Sir Isaac Newton 'the Glory of the British Nation' and the monument adorned with a weeping Astronomy, 'the Queen of the Sciences,' reads in part, 'Let Mortals rejoice That there has existed such and so great an Ornament to the Human Race.' Here 'the reality of the man' is captured in his achievements, which obliterate his personal characteristics and complexities. Each generation after Newton's would concur with this assessment. Equally lucky are the biographers with subjects about whom equally complex, equally compelling people have made arresting statements. Christopher Hill concludes *God's Englishman: Oliver Cromwell and the English Revolution* with a passage from Andrew Marvell's 'The First Anniversary of the Government under O.C.':

> And well he therefore does, and well has guessed,
> Who in his age has always forward pressed:
> And, knowing not where heaven's choice may light,
> Girds yet his sword, and ready stands to fight. . . .
> If these the times, then this must be the man.[6]

And who wouldn't want to be able to use the line Antonia Fraser quotes from Cromwell's servant as her final sentence: 'A larger soul hath seldom dwelt in a house of clay'?[7]

Elizabeth Frank, like many other biographers, traces the 'deterioration' of her subject in old age, chronicles the episodes of illness, falling, and failing senses and health, and tries to set the perimeters of interpretation. Frank states firmly, 'in the course of all of Louise Bogan's severe depressions—in 1931, 1933, and 1965—and in the course of the numerous milder ones which plagued her life, she never once seriously contemplated suicide' (p. 413). No Sylvia Plath or Ann Sexton here! Although Bogan is depicted as falling down drunk repeatedly and being 'besieged by fears' and appears to have fallen on the night of her death and then pounded on the floor trying to summon help, Frank concludes, 'She had come long ago to the realization that maturity meant the capacity to give full consent to necessity, to choose what fate ordained' (p. 415). Because of the smooth, masterful way in which the entire life is written and the presentation of evidence of Bogan's courage and ability to carry on during episodes of depression, the conclusion is not jarring; it is only in calling attention to Frank's language, to the ways she controls interpretation in order to give a familiar, somewhat sad story of a woman growing old, frail, and bearing the signs of imminent death do we see both the perimeters being set and the usefulness of cultural expectations.

In this chapter, I want to look first at more of the demands that readers make—desires that can batter or inspire the biography—and then at some of the decisions biographers make. In this section, the pitiful tools and the signs of struggle are all too clear. Finally, I offer some speculative conclusions.

READERS

Biographers recognize external demands with varying degrees of agreement and despair. What critics and readers state with easy confidence, biographers often call 'myths'. Perhaps the most consistent requirement, stated in the words of a critic is this one: 'What unites and synthesizes biography, however, what equates its performance with the desires of its readers, is the belief that biography *"can* deliver the essential person and that there is a core personality, the 'real Me', which we will find if only we dig deep and long enough." Biographers and readers believe in this myth . . .' (Nadel, *Biography: Fiction, Fact, and Form*, 180). Fewer biographers than he might think believe that, but they know they must deliver it or the reviews will read, 'Miss O'Brien has not delivered to us the presence of Willa Cather' or '[He] provides the quotation; what he fails to give us is any sense that Frost deserves it', and the readers murmur, 'I *still* don't understand his relationship to his suicidal son.'[8] Because they fear this response and because they are proud, they risk dishonest 'answers'. 'But as a biographer, I feel oddly inadequate at not being able to tell you who she was', John Worthen writes, 'I feel obliged to speculate: to wrap her in narrative phrases which will turn her from someone I am actually ignorant about into someone whose significance might be assessed.'[9] Dangerous. Fatal.

What is this 'real Me'? could we explain it about ourselves? What, in fact, is personality? The most famous definition is Gordon Allport's: 'Personality is the dynamic organization within the individual of those psychophysical systems that determine his unique adjustments to his environment' (*Handbook of Personality*, 4). An analogy probably explains it better and also reminds us of how sturdy and yet how delicate is personality, 'the psychological equivalent of the body's biological system of structures and functions'.

The human body as a whole comprises a well-organized yet open system of relatively stable structures that interconnect functionally as they process a wide range of both internal and external events in a coherent and efficient manner. The diversity of functions carried out by the body is awesome in its complexity and efficacy, as is the internal organization of structures impressively elaborate in its intricacy and articulation. The distinctive configuration of structures and functions that have evolved ensures that the system as a whole remains both viable and stable. This is achieved by processes that maintain internal cohesion and by actions that utilize, control, or adapt to external forces. The construct 'personality' may be conceived as a psychic system of structures and functions paralleling those of the body. (*Handbook of Personality*, 339)

How do we identify the 'real Me' in order to paint a detailed picture and yet sum up the 'essential' person? Underlying the belief in this possibility is a complex matrix of assumptions, more 'myths'. The strongest is that there is a core, an identity. Michael Neve senses the fantastic hope this desire is and says of two biographies of Mick Jagger, 'Take the case of someone passing under the name of "Mick Jagger", the object of two of the current spate of rock biographies.' 'In the cracks between these reactions a thought begins to take shape: that the hunt for "Jagger" is the hunt for someone who does not exist' (*TLS* 9 July 1993, 9). Another desire is that there is a unity and coherence to personality. In our culture there is the strong assumption that 'the child is father of the man'. Indeed, many believe that 'the apple doesn't fall far from the tree', and, therefore, careful, textured work with genealogy is essential. Regardless of how strong the opinion is that 'actions speak louder than words' or even that actions are all we know for certain, our culture leads us to feel that motives are readable, and, when we understand 'the real Me', we can discern motive. All of these beliefs assume an internal life and the crucial— even primary—importance of that interior. Few would deny Robert Frost's experience:

> Tree at my window, window tree,
> My sash is lowered when night comes on;
> But let there never be curtain drawn
> Between you and me.
>
> .   .   .   .
>
> But, tree, I have seen you taken and tossed,
> And if you have seen me when I slept,
> You have seen me when I was taken and swept
> And all but lost.
>
> That day she put our heads together,
> Fate had her imagination about her,
> Your head so much concerned with outer,
> Mine with inner, weather.[10]

And certainly we look to the biographer to open the mind of the subject to us and to 'make sense of it'.

The fact that I can draw so easily on familiar clichés testifies to the power of these readerly demands and the conscious and unconscious drives within the biographer. We make sense of lives by connecting things, by identifying (or creating) patterns, and by recognizing things. We want both linear and horizontal relationships. Join me in the mire of 'what formed the person' and the swamp of motive.

Readers like tight connections between child and 'man', what Edith Wharton described as 'my own growth and history' (quoted by Lewis, xii). Readers want to do what Nigel Hamilton explains as his goal: to 'enter into' the subject's life, 'its colour . . . its dilemmas, and its *development*'.[11] Many respond with deep pleasure to descriptions of ancestors, parents, homelife, and the distinctive features of the climate and homeland, all of which give 'colour' and lay a foundation for both development and dilemmas. In chapters that contrast Harriet Beecher's father and his world with her mother and her largely female family, Hedrick draws upon Harriet Beecher Stowe's writings and observes that she inherited her father's 'prophetic intensity' and her mother's creative, artistic, and literary bent. Ann Thwaite carefully and convincingly creates A. A. Milne's childhood home with his proud, loving mother and his funny, quick-witted, gentle father. Milne's father, an extraordinary teacher, emerges as a dedicated, attentive man who awakened his son to see an eclipse, encouraged him to walk to the summit of a peak at age 2 ½, and read *Uncle Remus* with unforgettable suspense and verve. The reader can delight in the fostering of the personal and literary characteristics of the man described with equal narrative skill and masterful command of detail in the later chapters. Thwaite makes Milne's outdoors a place in which to have adventures but one without natural beauty and detail; in contrast, Joan Hedrick plays Litchfield, 'emphatically a New England town,' where 'the tall chimneys of the stately Georgian houses march in procession toward the green.... built around shared values that included a godly hierarchy', against Nutplains, where 'every juniperbush, every wild sweetbrier, every barren sandy hillside, every stony pasture, spoke of bright hours of love, when we were welcomed ... as to our mother's heart' (p. 15).

For every ten biographers who are able to relate family and homeplace to the adult the child became, there is one who admits that the connections seem tenuous. Ola Elizabeth Winslow begins candidly, 'It would be easier to derive Jonathan Edwards from his posterity than from his ancestors' (p. 15). In fact, biographers typically derive the subjects' parents' salient characteristics and experiences by working backwards. Others try to discover which actions and qualities—real or imagined—in the parents and ancestors had particular importance for the subject. When such an argument is done well, as it is for A. A. Milne, the reading experience is smooth and persuasive; when it is inadequately developed and supported by other similar anecdotes, it jars the reader into a moment of scepticism or even into offering other interpretations. Joan Hedrick, for instance, says that Harriet Beecher chopped wood with her brothers in an attempt to gain 'her father's coveted attention' (p. 19). Earlier, however, Hedrick had presented convincing evidence that Harriet, like many younger children, struggled to be included in her brothers' activities and had given examples of her taking pleasure in physical, outdoor work. Because of Hedrick's own presentation of the evidence, either desire at that moment seems as probable as the one Hedrick gives. In the quotation Hedrick gives about chopping wood and pointedly in Forrest Wilson's biography of Stowe, the lesser value of female children, and Harriet's recognition of it, seem poignant to me. Harriet quotes her father as saying that he 'wished Harriet was a boy, she would do more than any of them' and, *in the next sentence*, Harriet says that she wore a little black coat 'which I thought looked more like the boys' (p. 19).

In the attempt to understand the parent–child relationship, the shaping relationship with the earliest world and with the givers—or withholders—of love, security, and confidence, we slide effortlessly into attempts to assign motive and then use it to gain access to inner feelings and the core of the person that makes them what we see and see them do. Motive, that cause of action for which we instinctively search and by which we judge others, like 'character', temperament, and values seems to be to a large degree the result of heritage and upbringing, of parental example and stated values. We decide which motives are acute, momentary and circumstantial, or chronic, habitual desires for praise, adventure, security, excitement—those that are components of personality. We speculate on motive within perimeters we construct from our apprehension of human nature but most especially from connections we believe exist with the subjects' formative years.

Perhaps nothing is more speculative than assigning motive. Judith Thurman writes, 'The poles Isak Dinesen knew as Dinesen/Westenholz . . . organized her ways of feeling and her stock of images like a magnetic field, sorting its contents. . . . In an earlier age such a pattern would unabashedly have been called Destiny. The modern biographer more cautiously says that hers is a "readable" life. Events seem to fall into place, and even small details are conserved, to appear later at some dramatic moment. They are like those birthmarks by which, in the old tales, one recognized the lost royal child' (p. 8). In the chapters that follow we can expect to find not just the life and its decisions (to be emaciated; to wish to shoot her dogs and horses and 'disappear') but Dinesen's literary works explained by these 'poles' ('Alkamene' with its tale of the child struggling to understand and express her rich, imaginative soul in a rigid, constraining bourgeois household). Even a fellowship Dinesen won was for a woman 'of liberal persuasion with a slightly conservative tendency' (p. 289). Rather than being simplistic or repetitious, the effect is to bring to reality a complex woman who created an exotic existence wherever she was and sustained an artistic career on her craving for experience and her sense of conflicting values.

Richard Ellmann, however, observes with the common sense that so characterized his analysis of biography:

As we push back into the mind of a writer, we are apt to lose sight of his conscious direction, of all that gives shape to what might otherwise be his run-of-the-mill phobias or obsessions and distinguishes his grand paranoia from our own squirmy one. It is relevant, though already suspiciously pat, to point out the existence of an Oedipal situation in childhood, but in the works of a writer's maturity this is usually so overlaid with more recent and impinging intricacies that we run the danger of being too simple about the complexes. We may reduce all achievement to a web of causation until we cannot see the Ego for the Id.   (*Golden Codgers*, 4)

One day my sister got a very sharp pair of scissors and cut half of her beautiful, shiny, nearly-to-her-waist hair off. The right half seemed perfectly even at a length of an inch below her ear lobe, and she had cut from the front to what appeared the exact centre of the back of her head. She was about 8 years old. Both psychology and literature have offered 'interpretations' for such actions, and they have done persuasive jobs using a variety of well-developed, even reliable methodologies. But the truth is, her motive cannot be known. Was she tired of the tangles that were so painful to comb out? Was she tired of the heat trapped by her long hair (it was a late, hot spring in the South)? Did she want to 'mutilate' herself, perhaps because the person who had taken care of and loved her most consistently had recently died? Or 'mutilate' herself because everyone she knew seemed to see only her beauty and value her only for that beauty? Did she envy my short, curly, easy-to-care-for hair as I envied her beautiful, straight, dark hair? Was this an act of rebellion of monstrous proportions (she did it a day or so before the 'big' spring piano recital, thereby thwarting my parents' public display of her and her beauty)? She *was* neglected, did she want attention, any kind of attention, even negative? Did she feel that she was inscribing her status as a freak, feeling that she was a freak as I myself felt, partly because my mother drank, partly because we were 'intellectually gifted' in a Southern town that judged that a handicap for women, and partly because we were so constantly reminded that we did not conform to the good ways to look? Was this a powerful symbol of a feeling of division, one of appearance and reality, internal and external truths, that children of alcoholics often feel so strongly?

The result was family chaos. The only answer I can remember her giving to interrogations of her motive was, 'Wanted to'. I was 11; surely my memory is not trustworthy. Perhaps she was too afraid at the time to answer truthfully; perhaps it was an impulse with the feelings behind it too deeply buried; perhaps she lacked the language to explain. Surely her memory is also untrustworthy, that day obscured in hundreds of other experiences and in the things an adult learns about interpreting experience but also learns to hide or use. Certainly her answers in subsequent years can be seen as unenlightening, unhelpful in pinning down the exact motive, intriguing as they are. She remembers, for instance, 'going into the bathroom with the scissors, taking hold of the hair over one ear—the right one, I think—and cutting it off.' (Since she is left-handed, cutting the right side first would make sense.) 'I do recall throwing the hair, long bunches of it, into the bathtub, of all places', she told me.

At the time, the question was why she did it. The more interesting question to me now seems why she did it that way. She was not interrupted. Why did she stop in the middle? Why was it so perfectly even and such a perfect half?

Surely the uninterpretability of that incident highlights the uninterpretability of every 'real' incident the biographer has to work with and the audacity with which we assign motive in order to present narrative. But it also argues the importance of attention to evidence and especially to repetition and pattern. If enough material can be collected on her experiences and behaviour in the months surrounding this incident, some possibilities can be eliminated and new ones admitted. But, I would argue, the exact motive can never be identified, only surmised with varying degrees of certainty (and satisfaction) on the part of the biographer and reader. Not only will it be impossible to eliminate all but one of her possible motives but there are possibilities that the biographer has not thought of, and the motive could be one (or more) of those.

When she read this passage, she wondered if she stopped cutting because her hair 'didn't look the way she hoped'. I can see a very simple explanation here. Partly because of inertia and partly because of isolation, my mother took me to get a hair cut once a year—late every spring—even though everyone acknowledged that my hair looked better short. Gayle was never allowed to think of short hair. It was common for us to cut the split ends off her hair; even I, a child, did it now and then. To this day, both my sister and I often cut our own hair with varying aesthetic results. Hair appointments aren't something we think of making regularly, and we grew up thinking women could cut their own hair. She also wrote, 'Lots of kids cut their hair . . . maybe it's a kid thing.' Did she just have scissors and nothing to cut? The beautiful simplicity of her answers confounds the elaborate explanations regardless of how grounded they are in scientific explanations of behaviour and the particulars of the larger experiences in her life. But the evidence is gone; had she done this in the year Dorothy Hamill won the Olympic medal or had someone remembered that she had on her dresser a magazine folded open to a model with her hair fashionably and somewhat bizarrely cut in the manner popular in the early 1990s with the top full and the nape and an inch or two above it shaved, speculations might be laid to rest.

It must occur to all biographers that they cannot possibly think of all the possible motives for an action, trivial or great. Gayle added a postscript to her letter that is hard to say better: 'Maybe biographers can't hit the mark because many times our own motives are so convoluted that they are mysterious to us as well.' And we cannot even be sure that the most simple and obvious motives have not eluded us.

The biographer, of course, could imbue the haircutting incident with great, long-lasting significance or could omit it as an unreadable, accidentally surviving but unimportant childhood event. Toni Morrison distinguishes between 'nest' (the 'safe harbor' and the 'inn') and 'adventure' (the 'ship' and the 'trail').[12] The chopped hair by setting and Gayle's age might signal 'nest', but parental and piano teacher response made it 'adventure'. Unfortunately bewildering 'adventure' incidents, and especially those at the heart of a career, cannot be omitted. Theodore Roosevelt wrote to a friend about his decision to join the Rough Riders, 'I know perfectly well that one never is able to analyze with entire accuracy all of one's motives.'[13] Accused of recklessness and lack of seriousness, of joining 'a cowboy regiment', or giving up 'the chance of his life' by leaving the Navy Department, Roosevelt offered a series of idealistic explanations that survive in letters at the same time he denied other motives, including 'I shall not go for my own pleasure' (Morris, 609). His biographers conclude that 'adolescence was behind his desire to become a soldier' (Pringle, 182) and that he needed to prove himself, 'once and for all, a man of his word' (Morris, 613) as well as contribute to his expansionist vision of America. Both biographers give us a picture of a man who revelled in 'gore' and yet knew the name of every soldier who served under him and could be maudlinly senti-mental about them. Morris, a canny handler of national heroes, concludes this section of his book: 'Eleven more times before his stenographer reached the end of her first page, he proudly repeated the words, *I*, *my*, and *me* [in his war memoirs, *The Rough Riders*]' (p. 687).

It is true, of course, that each of these explanations is based on the biogra-phers' long experience and analysis of Roosevelt. Each one has mapped dozens of decisions, contemplated—perhaps even listed or charted—the reasons Roosevelt gave for an array of actions. Good, meticulous, intelligent biogra-phers do know their subjects well enough to explain motives reliably. But the explanation is always to some extent coloured, perhaps even partly determined, by what the biographers' experience and culture have taught them about *human* motivation. Specifically, they believe in a fairly restricted range of motives common to human beings, and some of these, they also believe, are more likely because of 'national' behaviour. Moreover, they probably accept the idea that region of the country, family traditions (to fight in wars, 'to serve the nation' that way), education, age, ambition, and other such factors can be used reli-ably to understand motivation—and surely, to some extent, they can. Which ones, however, are given precedence—*or even noticed*—may depend on the biographers' own cultural and personal valuations and blindnesses. Readers can see the possibility of Pringle's mild anti-war sentiments in the conclusions reached about Roosevelt's motives. Unless the biographer bungles, that is, calls the reader's attention away from the story to the biographers' machinations, they are unlikely to notice the arbitrariness of the assignment of motive.

These little-noticed decisions have crucial power. They create the person that the biographical subject becomes in the writers' hands, and they are the rails upon which moral judgement rides. They not only lead the reader to select motives but also to come to a conclusion about the character and personality of the man. By quoting 'for my own pleasure' and by inserting personal judge-ments such as 'Roosevelt was not a coldly calculating person' (Pringle, 182), biographers attempt to develop and control the readers' perception of the subject, but they may also and inadvertently spark the reader to ponder the interpretation. What politician, especially one as committed to having the USA declare war on Spain as Roosevelt was, is not calculating? Could Roosevelt have succeeded in getting the assignment to the Rough Riders were he not calculating? Many readers are prejudiced against 'calculating', and 'calculators' are usually assumed to be doing so for personal rather than national gain. If not 'coldly', how was Roosevelt (and how do others go about) calculating? This incident, like many more, offers the careful construction of Roosevelt as the active, restless, idealistic man which is offered instead of an explanation for the master politician, whose personal engagement, whose 'frontline' mentality, made him the kind of president he was.

CHOICES AND TOOLS

'How do you decide among thirteen different (published) explanations of why Van Gogh cut off his ear?' This question, posed by Alan C. Elms in *Uncovering Lives: The Uneasy Alliance of Biography and Psychology*, is followed by two 'inventories of "the principal identifiers of salience"' that he located (pp. 245–7). By salience is meant criteria for evaluating data and evidence and deciding which are most reliable and important. Among them are items most of us see as having a high degree of reliability: 'consistency with the full range of available relevant evidence' and frequency/repetition. But others, such as 'logical soundness' trigger the question 'how subjective is "logical soundness"?' And frequency/repetition can be 'methinks the lady doth protest too much'.

Biography writing is not a career for the indecisive, and as I have written this chapter I have been surprised and somewhat intimidated by the number and kinds of decisions that we make. We decide what kind of person we are writing about and assign motive over and over, we construct a shape and a trajectory for the life out of actions and our surmises about decisions and motives. And as we do it, we think nervously about our readers' desires and are at least partly oblivious to our own biases, propensities, and limitations.

Even worse, many of these decisions can be placed within major, unresolved debates. For instance, biographers tend to cast their vote for nurture over nature, but we split into camps—or at least along a continuum—on made versus self-made. Our opinions about how much even a great person can resist what the world will allow him or her to be, what external forces will do to 'construct' or shape the person and their success and failure, are something of a constant, regardless of how different our subjects are. As American psychology has become more empirical, the view of the individual as an active agent has diminished in the face of a science that identifies individual actions as the product of independently observable, environmental inputs.[14] The extent to which an individual can be independent of impinging environments is seriously questioned; biography, in fact, has a stake in opposing this trend, for its appeal is its dedication to the special individual, the person who makes something of life. At the same time, it is accepted that 'temperament and early experience simultaneously affect the development and nature of several emerging psychological structures and functions; that is, a wide range of behaviors, attitudes, affects, and mechanisms can be traced to the same origins'.[15]

The degree to which we believe the unconscious and the subconscious influential and the weight we give cultural versus personal experiences in our everyday lives is translated into perimeters bounding our presentation and interpretation of our subjects—again, to some extent, regardless of the differences among our subjects and the strength of the evidence about each one's existence. The biographer who believes strongly in the unconscious will look for themes, for repeated metaphors in speech and writing, for patterns that seem to reveal this deep, inner life, while others will just as confidently assign these themes and metaphors to a sense of nationhood, to the influence of a parent, or to the subject's self-conscious attempts to present himself as, for instance, the ideal man to be governor of New York.

Just as we hold a range of opinions about the truth of 'the child is father of the man', so we do about the relationship between other domains and dimensions of life. How, for instance, do we link what we know about the inner life to actions? the private to the public life? the subject within the circle of the family and within the circle of the closest working associates? 'Black women seem to be able to combine the nest and the adventure', Toni Morrison once wrote (Heilbrun, 61). Would that the biographer could, and could solve the riddle of what binds each subject's adventures and nest to each other and of how they can be combined and integrated with fairness to both. Biographers know that the adventures somehow come out of the nest. Both the commitments and the adventurous spirit are born and nurtured there. What exactly has the nest contributed and how to know and express that? And was the nest the family? the boarding school? a circle of friends made in young adulthood? the first home created with an extraordinary spouse? How many nests, and are we capable of recognizing them? How can the nest and the adventure be combined and integrated, and how can the biographer be fair to both? And how to make the nest interesting . . .

We also have ingrained ideas about how fixed personality is. Some believe it is largely formed and almost impossible to change after the 'formative years' (and some push those formative years back to birth to 5 years old). As Paul T. Costa, jun., and Robert R. McCrae say, 'The belief that character or personality is set for life by the time the individual reaches adulthood has always been dominant.'[16] Many believe that personality is highly stable and becomes more inflexible decade by decade. For the first half of this statement, psychologists have amassed evidence. High correlations, for instance, between the coping styles of youth and those of old age have been verified, and conclusions such as the following are consistently reached: 'The anxious person, who is afraid of rejection in high school and of economic recession in adulthood, will probably be afraid of illness and death in old age' (Costa and McCrae, *Emerging Lives*, 90). Other researchers, however, as summarized by Kenneth Gergen, have found 'little in the way of adult behavior pattern [*sic*] that is compellingly fashioned by early experience. And, with respect to ordered change accounts, we find their applicability limited largely to early periods of physiological maturation' (p. 37). Rather, these psychologists find personality traits and changes, and this includes the diminution or increased expression of characteristics, to be most closely related to 'the accidental composite' of circumstances and events. It is well accepted that individuals differ in the degree to which they change and in how limited the number of attributes are that are resistant to change and how many are readily modified.[17] Fascinating recent research suggests that we force our personality to be stable by making our environment stable—sometimes at considerable cost and effort.

Related to these controversial personality issues are conceptions of the characteristics of what is sometimes called 'the life cycle'. Just as how self-conscious a biographer is about cultural theories of personality varies, so does consciousness of conceptions of the life cycle. And the degree to which biographers depend upon and draw attention to single theories falls along a continuum in both cases. Embedded in this conception of human life are assumptions about experiences and about normality as well as some scientific guidance to recognizing the personally significant and humanly remarkable and aberrant within the context of the statistically predictable.

Theories of life cycle tend to emphasize the person's relationship to self—how he or she feels about himself or herself—relationship to community opinion, or relationship to external choices. Some of the most familiar are seldom critiqued. Many Americans—perhaps too many—see life as infancy and early childhood, education, work, and retirement. Greek medicine tied the ages of life to the seasons and the elements, or humours: childhood, youth, maturity, and old age. The Roman stages of Puerita (0–15), Adolescentia (15–25), de Juventus (25–40), de Virilitas (40–55, 'second maturity'), de Praesenium (55–65), and Senium are our familiar Seven Ages of Man and can be correlated to many familiar descriptions of the phases of human life.[18] Other models have always been available. Some of the most dramatically contrasting are Far Eastern. The Hindu life pattern is dharma (socialization, the learning of norms, values, duties, rules, recognition of life task determined by previous lives as well as by choices and experiences; self-realization within a communal order); artha (acquisition, achieving material security); kama (pleasure, enjoyment, emotional passion), and moksha (liberation and wisdom).

Every culture has strong expectations for each of the 'ages of man'—'youthful vigour', 'forgetfulness' in old age, 'mature leadership', and 'grandmotherly wisdom' all capture the sense of lifespan expectations. The ideal trajectory of the life has been a smooth, pleasant, gradual rise to a pinnacle of success with a stay there for a long time. There may be momentary set-backs and obstacles (personal, physical, external), but these will be mapped as fascinating small, jagged blips rather than changes of direction or defeat. References to the 'straight way' and the 'straight and narrow' formerly led straight into Heaven and brought to mind the path to a goal within a strong moral framework, what has been called the 'doctrine of pursuits'.[19] The most common whole-life expectation in our society for ordinary people is curvilinear, an inverted U, in which people rise to power, success, and, perhaps, happiness and fulfilment, peaking at about age 40, and then begin a slow but depressingly complete decline. Some accounts even refer to old age as a second childhood, and the destructive effects of this mindset linger in the often condescending and insulting way elderly people are treated and their legal rights ignored. Some research concludes that society plays 'a substantial role in age-related cognitive decline'. In our culture, 'older adults are expected to be powerless and to think in a plodding, if not childish fashion . . . and social pressure may force older adults into powerless roles that encourage them to give up potent thought'.[20] The work of psychologists on lifespan and adult development theory more often confirms the power of age-norms and expectations than their reality.[21] In contrast, many biographies describe what Joseph Campbell has called the 'monomyth', in which youth is a preparatory period, early and middle adulthood induction and struggle to attain specific, individual goals, and mature adulthood and old age as full achievement and later consolidation and appreciation of success.[22]

The scientific investigation of adult development is a relatively new field, springing like so much of modern psychology from Freud's work. Many credit Elsa Frendel-Brunswik, a Viennese, with being the first psychologist to conceive of the life 'cycle' in stages. She attempted to take into account both external events and subjective, personal experiences and emotional responses. Erik Erikson's work made adult development and life stages a familiar idea. In *Childhood and Society* (1950) and then in two influential biographies, he described an eight-stage model. His theory was shaped around 'crises', a word he used as literary people do. A crisis is a moment of heightened tension, a turning point, during which the person is both more at risk and presented with more opportunities than usual. In that situation people make crucial choices and may regress or grow. Using his words for adult phases, they may develop an identity then seek intimacy, achieve generativity, and finally reach integrity or consolidation.[23] Some are arrested at a stage and others may even withdraw to an earlier phase.

For the biographer, these ideas are a mixed blessing. On the one hand, like other demands and expectations that readers have, they force the biographer into considerations of what will be credible. On the other, their plurality allows the biographer the freedom to inscribe a trajectory, a life shape that does not conform to the cultural norm. This freedom is not as great, however, as it might seem, because the reader also has favourites and genre expectations. Until very recently[24] readers of biographies seemed to have strong preferences, most notably the quest, the marked ambition and achievement of same, the adventures of a hero or dedicated public servant, 'the man of destiny', and the difficult, misunderstood often impoverished life of the great literary artist whom we now appreciate more than his contemporaries did.

In my study of prize-winning biographies, I was surprised at the number of literary biographies. Although I imagine the professions and academic backgrounds of the judges contribute to their over-representation, the modern fascination with the inner life is surely part of their appeal. Because writers are believed to have secret, creative, even fantasy-rich imaginations, they seem to offer unusual opportunities to understand the interior, subjective life. Also believed to feel free to explore and express emotions, they provide an acceptable way to indulge feelings in our culture, which demands control and restraint, even denial of emotion, especially from men. As Richard Ellmann points out, writers are 'so secretive about their intentions and sources that we look at their lives with even keener interest' (*Diogenes*, 75). In contemplating the possible relationships between source and published work, we see a fascinating variant on the flow from experience to interior life back to the life as it is lived and expressed. Because the literary life 'seeks always to illuminate the mysterious and magical process of creation', it has the potential of revealing, in Leon Edel's words, the 'deeper springs of our being where the gathered memories of our lives merge and in some cases are distilled into transcendent art' (*Writing Lives*, 35).

Many things in our national heritage prepare readers to believe that they can profit from knowledge of the life of a person who tries to maintain or to develop an admirable character, someone who struggles to remain kind, generous, and patient in the face of persecution, unusual misfortune, or great suffering. The person caught in the crucible of time captures our sympathy and imagination. Because of conscience, position, or even sex, race, or religion such a person faces almost unimaginable trials and difficult decisions. Such a person may turn out to be one of genius or even of destiny. Their lives reveal history and depict human struggle.

Another way to explain these examples is that they are popular stories or myths and that they can be classified into those that spotlight the individual and those that reinforce the positive, national self-image. Some biographers believe that subjects are more or less constructed, and more or less constructed at different moments in their lives. These biographers will often bring to the readers' attention times when the subject had the luxury of creative individualism and times when the person was the expression of constructing, determining forces. On the continuum that runs from biographers' belief in the unique individual to the strictly constructed citizen, the biographer of the former type sees the life as the text and the biographer of the latter type presents society as the text. Biographers quickly signal which they want readers to read. David Kennedy, for instance, explains in the preface that his aim is to illuminate a part of the life of American society through Margaret Sanger's work on behalf of birth control (p. ix), and his chapters have titles such as 'The Debate on Morality' and 'Birth Control and American Medicine'. In the first type of biography attention is on the individual as an individual and in the second, as with Kennedy's, on the subject as a cultural example. Readers judge the individual and learn from his or her experiences in the first case and study an era and judge a culture in the second. In a sense biographers choose to write about the individual as a rare, unusual person or about the person as a cultural icon or even conduit, thereby representing a unique time in a nation's history or identifying characteristics and values associated with a nation. Many of the prize-winning biographies single out qualities associated with the New England 'mentality' that were important in building the USA; others, such as Garrow's *Bearing the Cross: Martin Luther King, Jr.*, emphasize the American ideals that shaped the subject's vision.

William Epstein has located the demand for the 'myth' of the 'straight line' in the nineteenth century and associated it with the modern conception of a career, 'an organized trajectory of individual advancement' (p. 140). In the last fifteen years feminist and women's studies specialists have pointed out how different the shapes of many women's lives are from those of most men. They have created, at the least, a greater tolerance for unusual trajectories and life shapes and, at best, considerable interest in such biographies. In fact, the older my sources, the more I perceived the strength of 'man' as the norm, the fact that much description seemed to fit the life of men and demands of manhood, and a larger and larger gap between this work and the lives of women and the recent biographies about women. It was not just in the now-familiar differences in life shapes and story lines that have been described as multiple and recursive. The expectations and measures applied to men and women contrasted greatly, and in large and small ways they matter. Women have so many more choices in ways to dress than men, and what Mary McCarthy chose to wear to a *Partisan Review* meeting matters in a different way from what Theodore Roosevelt chose to wear to campaign for the governorship of New York in 1898. Although both were exercising a theatrical flair and making a statement, she could miscalculate in more ways than he, and her fashion as well as political and social acumen were on trial. Whether her Vassar slinky black dress brought her joy or trouble is, in Brightman's account, very much in doubt, but Roosevelt's military hat surely served him well. Because women have so many choices in dress, it is not unreasonable that women, McCarthy's colleagues, and Edmund Wilson 'read' her clothing, and their readings are valid material for the biography. What might have been a somewhat insecure assuming of her uniform as a Vassar intelligent woman spells 'vamp' for most of us, and later McCarthy described it as 'more suited to a wedding reception than to a business meeting in the offices of a radical magazine' (p. 151). Insights such as these have softened my feminist response: 'but we don't read what Mr. X wore and weighed in the morning papers'.[25]

I also became more conscious of where biographers get their life course trajectories. I see that a book could be written that maps the trajectories of the lives in each generation's most-respected and popular biographies against those of their fictional, heroic characters. Those trajectories would mirror each other very closely. The dominant genre, which for us had been the novel, establishes an expected 'type . . . of reading from an infinite series of trajectories or possible courses' and 'plays the role of order's principle'.[26] The *Bildungsroman* with its progressive story of a life begun in difficult, constraining circumstances, marked by obstacles overcome and the true self actualized or revealed, and concluded with the triumphant, confident overcoming of new challenges and difficulties that consolidates the self shapes many biographies. Repeatedly, reviewers invoke the great nineteenth-century novel form: 'Ms. Brombert . . . paints a broad canvas full of vivid characterizations; at times her biography reads like a substantial and detailed 19th-century novel. . . . engrossing, smartly written.'[27] The tones and conventions of the novel creep into even the best and most original biographies. In the 1962 volume of the life of Henry James, Leon Edel includes sentences that today sound strikingly sentimental: 'She [his mother] seemed unchanged by death; there was much life—unendurably much—in her lifeless face.' 'His mother still seemed to be there, in the house in which she had lived so long . . .'. In the 1985 single volume life, he omits these sentences and 'only' from this sentence: 'In life he had had to share her . . . Now . . . she belonged *only* to him.'[28] As strong as the influences of fictional forms, psychoanalytical models, cultural myths such as the Seven Ages of Man, the straight line, and adult development theory are, the best biographers win the struggle to be open to the shape of the subject's life. Richard Ellman's 'facing the task of getting the evidence to yield what information it will' extends to experiencing the 'subject's life as forcing its coherence upon' the biographer's mind.[29]

Erikson's *Gandhi's Truth* carries the potential of a clash between the theorist's strong belief and investment in his theoretical model and the Eastern conception of life and its stages. Another overdetermining factor is that Erikson begins the book confident that he understands charismatic, world-changing religious leaders (he refers to his *Young Man Luther* and Martin Luther numerous times at the beginning). Especially in the second half of the book, however, Erikson is admirably open to the implications of a sensibility formed by dharma and asrama (life style proper to one's biological age, an indispensable foundation for the next step). In fact, Erikson finds the Hindu model liberating and can write about what he calls Gandhi as 'householder' in South Africa with a broader perspective than other biographers had. Not only does he understand the importance of the phase in Gandhi's life but he feels no need to make it wholly consistent with the rest of the life. Erikson points out that the Hindu life course allows a person to 'get established in one stage in all sincerity and thoroughness—and then disestablish oneself in order to enter another stage' (p. 177).

Reflection on the book, however, suggests that Erikson may not have freed himself enough from his own and Western cultural models; he does not, for instance, make any attempt to apply Hindu views of sexuality in late life to Gandhi. At some level he also seems to be adapting the Hindu pattern to his own; he says, for instance, 'I find it very congenial that this whole scheme allows for a succession of pointedly different life styles' (p. 37). His own model with its stages and crises also contrasts with what he calls 'the almost vindictive monotony of Judeo-Christian strictures by which we gain or forfeit salvation by the formation of one consistently virtuous character almost from the cradle to the grave' (p. 37). And this is my point: perhaps no degree of self-consciousness can free us from the ideas we have imbibed and decided upon.

Leon Edel lists as his fourth principle of writing biography: 'Every life takes its own form and a biographer must find the ideal and unique literary form that will express it. In structure a biographer need no longer be strictly chronological, like a calendar or datebook' (*Writing Lives*, 30). Here he easily admits the connection between literary form and life shape and implicitly argues the primacy of the individual. Reed Whittemore cautions against excluding what he calls the 'biographee's final, controlling role' and admonishes, 'If [the biographer] cannot accept from the start that the venture is just not wholly his—or, rather, that the whole he is struggling to create is not his—he is a threat to his particular subject and to the model principle [that guides biography].'[30]

In reflecting on life-span models, I have begun to believe, first, that part of the appeal of many biographical subjects is their apparent departure from the 'normal' curve. Achievements that break our opinion about what people can do at a specific age, an extraordinarily high peak of achievement, an unusually long stay at the peak—a plateau rather than a peak, and a life marked by decline and then recovery of the peak appeal to readers, as does the life that seems to turn itself around—the criminal who becomes an effective social worker, the respected professional or parent who becomes a murderer. Part of the 'specialness' of biographical subjects, then, is their defiance of, or at least nonconformity to, the inverted U life span and the fixedness of personality traits, both sources of anxiety and fascination to most people.

The subjects of the prize-winning biographies do, however, conform very closely to the much-desired rise to a pinnacle of success with an 'abnormally' long tenure there followed by an old age experienced as benediction. Some biographies create the tableau of a monarch receiving friends and family, a long, ceremonial drinking at the fountain, receiving due respect, and farewell. A sentimental variant on this ending is Forrest Wilson's double ending of his life of

Harriet Beecher Stowe. He lingers not unduly on her dotage and quotes enough to show us that she recognized her state: 'My mind wanders like a running brook' (p. 633). His 'P.S.' covers the burial and ceremony, to which the 'Negroes of Boston' sent flowers with a card inscribed, 'The Children of Uncle Tom' and concludes with Paul Laurence Dunbar's poem 'Harriet Beecher Stowe':

> She told the story, and the whole world wept
> At wrongs and cruelties it had not known
> But for this fearless woman's voice alone.
> She spoke to consciences that long had slept.
> (ll. 640–1)

Wilson's ending records Stowe's loss of respect after she alleged in an *Atlantic Monthly* article that Byron had committed incest and especially later after several senile public acts, but it finally puts her back in her place of honour and has African-Americans, including an important literary figure, pay tribute.

In fact, in recent years psychologists within the field of adult development have argued that 'human developmental trajectories may be virtually infinite in their variegation' (Gergen, 37). Therefore, Edel's use of 'unique' becomes a possibility for biographers, and the need to go beyond the restrictions of cultural models and narrative expectations seems compelling.

At this point, I want to explore some of the things biographers do and can use to understand personality and make the connections that they need to forge, for instance, between interior and exterior, child and man, and nest and adventure. The bedrock truth is that our most important tools are the ones we use every day to understand people. The magnitude of effort is enormously different, however. Biographers live with their subjects as parasites and barnacles, attempt to follow them day by day, study their relationships with everyone, pore over their letters and diaries, pounce upon all descriptions of them, if possible sit in their chairs and handle their crockery. Even the obsession young lovers have with each other pales in comparison. No wonder living subjects sometimes initiate legal action against their biographers. The ways we all 'study' and understand people serve biographers well, and there is resonant truth to Joseph Lichtenberg's observation that

The great biographies [before Freud] . . . share with Freud's psychoanalytic discoveries a hallmark of genius: an uncommon insight into man's conflicts and his motivations.

The old concept expressed in a term little used today—'the mysteries of the soul'—remains the core of what great biography *conveys*. . . . To the extent that a profound enigma of man was penetrable, the great biographers 'knew': the virtues of political leadership that inspire; the mystic quality of religion that leads to and flows from a conversion; the inspiration and push of creative artistry; and the awesome force of enormous learning and penetrating, moralizing wit.[31]

But he goes on to point out, 'How the insight is presented depends on the view of man prevalent during the epoch for which each writer remains an outstanding spokesman.' And David Bromwich devastatingly observes, 'the successful biographies of an age have as much in common as their biographers *rather than as little as their heroes*'.[32] So, too, perhaps the heroes' motives. Although these quotations capture the restricting fetters each biographer wears, they also hint at the fact that very, very few people can imagine even their own conflicts and motivations outside those provided by the culture of their own times. As Robert Browning wrote, 'So free we seem, so fettered fast we are!'(*Andrea Del Sarto*, l. 51). And Freud closed the door, 'It is impossible to understand the past with certainty, because we cannot divine men's motives and the essence of their minds and so cannot interpret their actions.'[33]

Reflection also reveals how important preconceived generalizations about words, actions, and human nature and motivations are. Most of us do believe that 'actions speak louder than words', but we look for extenuating circumstances and unusual motives, even if less often than biographers. Thinking about how we evaluate and are influenced by others' comments and judgements highlights the more scientific methods of the biographer. It is crucial that friends, enemies, rivals, co-investors, lovers, and ex-lovers be sorted out, and the source carefully taken into account. Biographers, like all people, need to guard against unfounded predispositions to respect or believe one source over another.

Although intimates may have access to each other's introspective observations, such sharing is rare; biographers make the search for them an obsession. The sentence embedded in a letter, the unguarded answer to a question in an interview, a stark passage in a personal journal, a contemporary's recollection of a searching, late-night conversation—these are the biographer's private treasures. 'When I am with anyone in whom I am specially and sincerely interested, the hardest subject for me to broach is just that which is nearest my heart. An unfortunate disposition indeed! I hope to overcome it in time. I can at least speak plainly in writing. It isn't pleasant or convenient to have strong passions. . . . I have an uncomfortable feeling that I am carrying a volcano about with me', Woodrow Wilson wrote.[34] This quotation offers a glimpse at both how rarely introspective thoughts are shared and what a fragile, valuable dimension they can add to a biography. In an unsent letter, Mary McCarthy reveals the insecurity, defensiveness, and her distinctive kind of aggression on the occasion of having nowhere to go for Christmas: 'it was as if this popularity was an illusion or a deceit practiced on me . . . Could I have written *The Group* to show them?' (quoted in Brightman, 91). Some of these gemlike sentences, many apparently wrenched from the deepest levels of the mind, can be impossible to comprehend fully. Upon the death of his mother, Henry James wrote, 'she was the house . . . the keystone of the arch'.[35] The first part is a rich, moving image, one the imagination easily fleshes out; the second teases—what made this visual, architectural image come to his mind? why 'arch'? and, with its acknowledgement of the delicacy of the structure, what a compliment to be 'keystone'.

Myths, folklore, and suspect anecdotes about the subject might seem especially untrustworthy as keys to personality, but I can see more reasons to include than exclude them. Nietzsche once wrote that it took only three anecdotes to 'paint the picture of a man'; sometimes a myth, a fabricated anecdote, captures the subject brilliantly. There must be reasons that an anecdote survives, is repeated, and regardless of how its veracity is questioned continues to be a compelling portrait of a person. Related to this phenomenon but also adding to the pressures on the biographer is the fact that readers demand the myths; they enjoy them and also want to find something they already know in books. One of the myths associated with Daniel Defoe is that he appeared in the British parliament dressed as a woman and delivered a petition demanding the release of five citizens from Kent who had exercised their constitutional right to present a petition of their own to the House of Commons. According to the myth, Defoe, like his character Moll Flanders, cross-dressed and delivered the petition in person to the Speaker of the House as he stood before Commons. That would have been a dramatic and daring deed, and it can be fitted into common opinions of Defoe—that he was a reckless defender of civil rights; that he was basically a sneaking, snivelling spy; and also that he was cheap, for men had to give security (make bond) to deliver a petition. The first printed account was George Chalmers's in 1790. His papers survive, and his source was a letter from the son of one of the imprisoned petitioners. That might seem like a good source, but contemporaries of Defoe said that the petition was left in the MP's letterbox and such verifiable things as increased security at the House argue against the cross-dressing story. In the *History of the Kentish Petition*, Defoe himself acknowledges the rumour but denies it, and he and contemporaries say that he was accompanied to the House by sixteen gentlemen. Chalmers probably received a family story, a good story made a little better, especially in the wake of *Moll Flanders*. An aside here is the observation that this research took an inordinate amount of ingenuity, travel, and time, perhaps, for its results. Not only do I think myths about a person are important enough to merit such effort, but questions about Defoe and the dress were among the top four questions asked me by university lecture audiences.

Two questions related to including myths are ones all writers face—how can truth best be told and how can a truth be written to attract the reader's attention and assure the comprehension and the impact the writer wants? Some of the tactics available to creative writers are not acceptable in biography—satire, fictional conversations, parody, digressive essays, allegory, exaggeration, for instance. Myth, however, if presented with integrity is acceptable. From at least the Romantic period myth has been considered as 'a superior mode of knowing and expressing essential realities which could not be expressed literally or directly'.[36] Because myth is often used to express the 'true nature' of people and their aspirations, the fact that myths surround great national heroes and have both usefulness and a kind of accuracy is not surprising. Does it matter if Sir Walter Raleigh really said, 'What matter how the head lie so the heart be right?' Catherine Drinker Bowen smoothly writes, 'the stories were endless'.[37] But her admission is forgotten, because what we believe of Raleigh's life makes the quotation fully credible, and it is more 'accurate' because Bowen surrounds this quotation with an account of how the populace knew he died for hating Spain—as most of them did—and includes references to their ballads, 'Great Heart, who taught thee so to die?' (p. 417).

By something like the method of mathematical approximation, biographers can use anecdotes to illustrate the core attributes of a personality and define them quite precisely. In an essay on Samuel Johnson, B. L. Reid, winner of the 1969 Pulitzer for *The Man from New York: John Quinn and his Friends*, gives a series of anecdotes, some with comments on them by Johnson that delineate the kinds of courage Johnson had and approved of and the fears he believed became a man, and then Reid offers a probing reading of Johnson's brave, calm behaviour after a stroke, behaviour that Reid shows portrays his courage *and* his fear.[38] Not only do the anecdotes take us deep into Johnson's mind but they show both a maturing, less hot-headed Johnson and a pleasingly consistent, admirably stalwart strain in his personality. That at least two of the anecdotes have never been conclusively removed from the category of legend hardly matters, partly because of the quantity and quality of substantiated evidence Reid has and partly because they are so seamlessly consistent with what is known about Johnson.

Even more controversial means of access to the personality of the subject are handwriting analysis and such things as the Busemann–Boder Action Quotient (AQ) and the Dollard–Mowrer Discomfort-Relief Quotient (DRQ). Even though handwriting analysis is considered to have enough scientific validity to be used by some employers, beyond a few cautious observations such as speculating that the writing at a specific moment showed 'tension' or had 'a brave flourish' or asserting that the handwriting expresses an already-decided upon dominant character ('neat and painstaking' or 'bold'), biographers avoid using it.[39] Graphologists work with the slant, pressure, 'rhythm', margins and space, size, letter loop, specifics (how t's are crossed and i's dotted), and signatures (Arthur, 113). For approximately $300, a biographer could have the subject's writing analysed by a trained, certified member of a respected consulting firm. Frankly, at best that would be merely one more piece of evidence about personality—evidence that would confirm conclusions reached by analysing as many kinds of evidence as possible, evidence that might send the biographer back to re-evaluate or even look for additional evidence to uphold (or negate) an opinion about the subject, or evidence that when evaluated in the larger context would be judged too weak or invalid to include. There is some evidence that autobiographical content and language features are what graphologists 'read' most accurately, because judgements made with scripts correlated less well with personality tests and employer experience than conclusions reached with typed copies—in other words, the handwriting was distracting or misleading.[40] Would readers be interested in such an analysis? probably, if it could be fitted smoothly into the biography.

Truly useful, however, it seems to me, is constant alertness to handwriting, to signatures, and to changes that can possibly be related to stress, emotional conflict, unusual self-conscious caution, or bold, joyous confidence.[41] Defoe's absolutely clear, controlled, precise handwriting on his petition asking Queen Anne for mercy is worth contemplating. He is surely copying what he laboriously and carefully wrote. The ornate 'd's' and 'p's', precisely dotted 'i's' and crossed 't's', and mix of secretarial, italic, and modern cursive letters invite speculations about persistent personality characteristics. Would it not be interesting to compare the signatures of men ordering armies into battle? writing farewell letters to wives? Within quite conservative limits, what we see in the difference between, for instance, the writing of a person before and after the death of a child seems as good evidence about mood and response to events as many of the other kinds of evidence we use without much thought. The same tests used to attempt to demonstrate the reliability and validity of graphology have yielded results that should give biographers some confidence. For instance, 'naïve' control groups identify the sex of the writer over 70 per cent of the time and show high accuracy in some other categories, including 'psychotic' and general surmises about what are called Factor V characteristics, the depth and fullness of a person's mental life.

The Busemann–Boder and Dollard–Mowrer Quotients are probably unknown to most biographers.[42] When I have had biographers in my National Endowment seminars experiment with them, we have discovered high correlations with conclusions drawn in a variety of other ways and found some insights worth using. Briefly, the Busemann–Boder method purports to judge emotional 'instability' by calculating the ratio of adjectivals to verbs. In fact, it can be used to reveal periods when the subject's emotional or interior life is more important or active than other times and, perhaps, the degree of intimacy with various correspondents. In my experience, the most useful and intriguing results come from applying an expanded Dollard–Mowrer method to texts and recorded interviews. The biographer records and classifies all expressions of tension, unhappiness, and discomfort (the D factor), and records and categorizes all expressions of relief, satisfaction, ease (the R factor). When these results are analysed by familiar literary methods or other means of value-analysis, previously unnoticed sources of satisfaction or even lifelong anxieties have emerged. Ralph White, for instance, picked up Richard Wright's fears about personal safety this way and was even able to explain actions and tendencies such as aggression with more acumen.

When I experimented with the method on Jonathan Swift's 10 January 1721 letter to his friend Alexander Pope, I saw new things and could develop others. In this letter, Swift reflects on his London years during the tempestuous and dangerous conclusion of Queen Anne's reign. In some ways, it is an apologia for his life; intermingled with the reflections are numerous comments on his present writing. Swift's obsession with the fall of the Tory ministry, his feelings of helplessness, and his lingering anger, frustration, and disappointment have long been recognized by biographers and scholars. What the DRQ brings out is the level of his fear. Although he is safe in Ireland, all but forgotten by the English powers, he mentions the possibility of arrest, seizure of his papers,[43] and political retribution at least nine times. Even as he expresses this fear, the *only* expressions of relief and reward are associated with his writing. DRQ analysis of this letter shows that Swift's writing, regardless of its satisfactions, was always accompanied by high anxiety and fear. He uses phrases such as 'chains and dungeons to every person whose face a Minister [government official] thinks fit to dislike' and 'I have known an innocent man seized and imprisoned, and forced to lie several months in chains, while the Ministers were not at leisure to hear his petition.'[44] In a summary Swift writes, 'I have neither been so ill a Subject nor so stupid an Author . . . by fathering dangerous principles in government . . . and insipid productions' (p. 374). This letter includes a rather triumphant account of the trial of the printer of Swift's *A Proposal for the Universal Use of Irish Manufactures* and the verdict of *noli prosequi*; Swift was in no danger, but his references are to his past and others' present publications about England, not Ireland, and his thoughts put him in another setting. Swift's biographer Irvin Ehrenpreis questions the popularity of *A Proposal* (a double 'reward' entry in this single letter) and writes the episode as Swift's rescue of the printer: 'The whole spectrum of British politics, from Jacobite peer to Whig republican, had joined to rescue an Irish printer for the sake of an Anglican dean.'[45] What is missing from this account is what the DRQ reveals, an attractive psychological dimension showing that Swift's publication and his re-entry into political intrigue were more stressful and courageous than they appear.

All biographers use psychology to understand and discuss personality, and psychology can be as distracting and controversial as handwriting analysis. Sometimes biographers have such well-developed theories of personality that readers perceive them; at that point, the readers' opinion of that theory becomes an element in the judgement of the credibility and quality of the biography. Things once fashionable or thrillingly experimental such as the search for what Jean-Paul Sartre called 'the primal episode' or 'fatal instant' can strike another generation as intriguing or just plain unconvincing. Sartre, it may be remembered, located in the primal episode the moment in which 'identity, essence' is created and re-created it for readers in poetic language that seamlessly integrates into the events in the life his theory of the birth of a person's knowledge of separate identity. Jean Genet's, he argued, is the moment when 'a child dies of shame; a hoodlum rises up in his place; the hoodlum will be haunted by the child'.[46] Overt psychologizing often makes readers uncomfortable and is the butt of parody: 'In "psychobiography" the large deeds of great individuals are "explained" with reference to some hitherto unsuspected sexual inclination or incapacity, which in turn is "explained" by some slight the individual suffered at a tender age—say, 7, when his mother took away a lollipop.'[47] Victoria Glendinning, author of two of the prize-winning biographies, says, 'I believe only the most doggedly psychoanalytical biographers still want to explain the "because" all the time, and they seem curiously dated, following their own free associations as often as not rather than the irretrievable associations of their subject' ('Lies and Silences', 49). Alan Elms writes that 'psychoanalysts and pseudoanalysts have applied Freud to biography with such abandon that the term "Freudian biography" is now an even more derogatory term than "psychobiography"' (p. 4).

Regardless of how successful critiques of Freud and his methods are and how his stock has fallen, his influence lingers. To some extent all biography is still marked by the influence of Freud and of Erikson, and readers as well as biographers share what has been called a national language of psychology. Peter Gay, Richard Ellmann, and others have pointed out how facilely everyone in our culture, biographers included, use 'ego, superego, id', 'pleasure principle', 'repression', 'projection', 'defence mechanism', 'death wish', 'wish fulfilment', 'Œdipus complex' and dozens more Freudian terms.[48] It is hard to find a biography in which the subject is not assumed to have an internal life that is often separate from the manifestations of speech and actions and especially of the public life. In many, serious attempts to reveal the subconscious and the unconscious are made. But about others I would agree with the biographers who argue that the ideas and concepts from psychoanalysis 'have become so incorporated into intellectual discourse that biographers automatically employ them without always realizing whence they came'.[49]

Biographers come to writing with varying degrees of previous, educated knowledge of these specialized fields and with varying ideas of how valuable knowledge of them is and, therefore, how important concerted, additional education is. Rather than attempting to treat this vast subject in depth, I want to point out just a few possibilities on which biographers and readers of biography might brood.

Psychology can give us more places to look for evidence, more ways to analyse our subjects. For instance, psychologists tell us that personality can be analysed through five factors: 'intellect, character, temperament, disposition, and temper'. And they agree that 'each of these is highly complex and comprises many variables'.[50] In thinking and writing about people, how systematically do we think about each of these factors? Especially as we plot them over time and assess how they affect the subject's relationships with other people, the allies and enemies they determine, and the opportunities they help create, attention to these factors deepens our understanding of the life and sharpens our explanations. Models, such as the Big Five, provide ways to talk about personality and about individual difference. Validated by many scales and accepted as the best system of describing personality, the Big Five is a descriptive model of the dimensions of personality, derived from analyses of the natural language terms people use to describe themselves and others. Numbered according to the relative size of the adjectives in each factor, I and II capture interpersonal traits such as assertiveness, reserve, sympathy, and introversion; Factor III describes task and social behaviour, such as dependability and will to achieve; Factor IV describes temperament and, for instance, contrasts calm confidence with nervous tension; Factor V, the most elusive and variously defined, describes the 'depth, complexity, and quality of a person's mental and experiential life'.[51]

Attention to them and plotting apparent changes offer insights into how serious various experiences were for subjects as well as into what kind of persons they were. What came easily or 'naturally' can be separated out more precisely from what things were done with great difficulty or were highly uncharacteristic actions. Rudimentary knowledge of trait theory can contribute to recognizing these things and can also lead to new insights and clearer explanations. Traits are enduring propensities and dispositions. As early as Samuel Johnson, biographers have used them to characterize their subjects:

To his domestics [Jonathan Swift] was naturally rough: and a man of rigorous temper, with that vigilance of minute attention which his works discover, must have been a master that few could bear. That he was disposed to do his servants good, on important occasions, is no great mitigation: benefaction can be but rare, and tyrannic peevishness is perpetual.[52]

Because their traits cause people to seek out certain kinds of situations and experiences, they can offer another means of identifying and articulating what is consistent in a personality and of explaining motivation. There is some evidence that they are genetic, and that offers intriguing ways of considering the influence of ancestors unknown to the subject and 'family traditions' of, for instance, seeking risky occupations.

With some understanding of the power of socially constructed expectations such as age norms and gender profiles, biographers are also in the position to classify behaviour as conformist, brave, risky, or well within the period's social mores. All such judgements need to factor in the historical and intellectual period—today's religious fanatic might be the exemplary person of another era. It is obviously possible to map many of the subject's expectations and aspirations beside such pertinent things as the time's perceptions of the superior life pattern, age norms, and conceptions of the interior life. Thus, more of the pressures and enabling circumstances surrounding the subject can be recognized.

To some extent this chapter is about fashion. The influence of Freud, Erikson, and theories of personality can be discerned as can the river of such things as the nation's conception of 'hero' and the power of preferred narrative shapes. As a culture absorbs scientific insights, they appear in biography. Among the most interesting recent developments in biography, for instance, is the appearance of meaningful, some even profound, experiments in recording and interpreting a human personality that changes over time. Such biographies contribute to our understanding of how changes occur—what developmental and circumstantial events precipitate change, how much people can adapt, and how successfully they can strive for an ideal of selfhood. Even as the assumption of an internal life is constant, the demand for a 'unified personality' has changed. Errol Trzebinski called her biography *The Lives of Beryl Markham*, and Jenny Uglow was praised for capturing the 'great number of [Elizabeth Gaskell's] "me's"'. Gillian Avery, the reviewer, concludes, 'It is one of the many merits of this biography that it does just this, presenting a rounded portrait of a woman who had achieved much . . . and whom it would clearly have been a delight to know'.[53] 'Rounded personality' has come to mean, as Avery uses it, a recognition of the complexity of personality rather than a display of a unified personality acting in a variety of circumstances and domains.

Some biographers feel a new scepticism all around them; George Moraitis, a faculty member and training analyst at the Institute for Psychoanalysis in Chicago and one of the most analytic scholars of biography in our time writes, 'In this contemporary, post-positivistic period of intellectual history, the concept of interpretation and the search for meaning have been advocated as an alternative to the pursuit of knowledge, as a result of which "to doubt" and "to wonder" are more respectable than "to know". To blur is more acceptable than to define. Ambiguity has become a more reliable indicator, and often an acceptable point of arrival.'[54] I think him wrong. I think the readers of biography today are more sophisticated and also come to biography for things different from what other readers seek. Perhaps Norman Holland captures best the hopes for subtlety and unity: 'We look forward and see the life in its totality, recognizing "the human being as playing infinite variations upon a continuing, central identity theme"' (quoted in Nadel, *Biography: Fiction, Fact, and Form*, 188).

Knowledge of clinical psychiatry can be extremely helpful. By being aware of the differences among personality disorders, clinical syndromes, and adjustment reactions, the biographer has an advantage in recognizing themes and lifelong, unifying tendencies and traits and in interpreting the effects of events on the subject and understanding underlying motives. Especially interesting are syndromes, which are similar to adjustment reactions in that they are

set in motion by external events, but 'their close connection to inner personality traits results in the intrusion of memories and affects that complicate
what might otherwise be a simple response to the environment' (Millon,
343). Therefore, they can appear extreme or irrational or bizarre. The biographer can then see that an event that might have required no adjustment
or a minimal, predictable one from some people has triggered usually hidden
emotions. Theodore Millon describes what happens: 'The upsurge of deeply
rooted feelings presses to the surface, overrides present realities, and becomes
the prime stimulus to which the individual responds.' The biographer now has
access to what has been called the 'flooding into the present of the reactivated
past'.[55] The subject who displays syndromes far more often and more powerfully than adjustments may have overcome difficulties and experiences more
heroically than has previously been recognized. Such analyses offer new ways
to check hypotheses and understand subjects more profoundly. Biographers
know that there is something important beneath the surface when an encounter
or an event from which most people would recover in a few days or pass off
easily triggers deep grief or frenetic activity, but we probably do not spend
enough time looking for common denominators and tying incidents together
and then to the traumas or repeated experiences that elevated them from
adjustment reactions to syndromes or even into the realm of disorders.

We can use the clinical domains of personality as a checklist of possible
sources of additional evidence and as ways to find richer possibilities for interpretation. These domains are

(1) expressive acts [physical and verbal behaviour; for instance, contemporaries
    reporting repeatedly that the person habitually assumed a position at the
    head of a table and occupied more space than others];
(2) interpersonal conduct;
(3) cognitive style [the way the subject's mind processes, organizes, and works
    with information];
(4) regulatory mechanisms [need gratification, self-protection, coping style];
(5) mood/temperament;
(6) self-image;
(7) object representation [the nature and content of the inner world, often
    described with terms such as 'shallow' and 'undifferentiated'];
(8) morphologic organization [functional efficiency of the personality
    system].[56]

Expressive acts occur from inner momentum and with minimal provocation
and are, therefore, highly reliable guides to personality and aspects such as
temperament. One of the most neglected of these domains may be self-image,
especially as it may change with marriage, parenthood, career advancement,
illness, and the time in life when numerous friends and acquaintances die.[57]
As good as James Burns's account is of the effects of polio on Franklin
Roosevelt, he does not consider if the self-image of the man who went boating,

helped put out a forest fire, swam, jogged a mile and a half, and then swam again the day before he was taken ill changed.[58] Some biographers focus considerable attention on one or two of these domains with excellent, pleasing results. For instance, James Gleick's biography gives us a fascinating look at Feynman's cognitive processes, and John E. Mack keeps a steady gaze on T. E. Lawrence's self-image as a person of destiny, marked for a special life. The section of *Isak Dinesen* in which Thurman recounts the loss of the African land and Dinesen's adjustment to her return to her mother's home is a fine case study of morphologic organization, and readers who have some awareness of the concept probably gain additional pleasure from reading it.

Thinking about these domains can highlight important common denominators that bridge or even unify aspects of personality and observed behaviour. 'The way a person performs a common behavior is sometimes quite revealing', Kenneth S. Bowers writes. 'One person ordinarily eats and makes love fastidiously; another person is given to gluttony in both circumstances. The more idiosyncratically expressive a common behavior is . . . [the more it is] attributable to a relatively stable personality and behavioral organization.'[59] In some cases, a person's fastidious side can explain something previously unaccountable, such as an interpersonal reaction to a co-worker or neighbour who is slovenly and unclean or an action or manner of dress that seems unusually time-consuming or obsessive.

Some biographical subjects have recognizable personality disorders, and biographers need to recognize them and do serious research. Had Judith Thurman known more about anorexia, we would understand more about Isak Dinesen and be able to sort out the effects of syphilis. The disorder in rare cases can even be a major factor in the subject's most notable achievements. Sometimes specific disorders have come to be associated with occupations, and readers almost expect them. Anthony Storr has pointed out, 'Writers are so notoriously prone to recurrent depression and to manic-depressive illness that every aspiring literary biographer ought to know something about these conditions.'[60] The poet Robert Lowell once wrote, 'There's a strange fact about the poets of roughly our age . . . It's this, that to write we seem to have to go at it with such single-minded intensity that we are always on the point of drowning . . . it's . . . some flaw in the motor.' Lowell, Randall Jarrell, Theodore Roethke, Delmore Schwartz, Elizabeth Bishop, John Berryman, and more are listed in Diane Middlebrook's portrait of Ann Sexton's consciousness of 'her kind' (p. 109 *et passim*).

THROUGH THE EYES OF——?

This chapter has made clear the presence of the writer in every biography. Whether we are reading the works of those who try to disappear behind the voice of neutral objectivity, those who want to let the subject 'speak', or those who make themselves a character or even the hero of their biographies, we are affected by the writer's choice. Some biographers choose Olympian detachment and leave the reader to discover where they stand while others may address the question directly, sharing with the readers their philosophy of personality.

The biographer is explorer, inquirer, hypothesizer, compiler, researcher, selector, and writer; none of these is a neutral act. The best biographers know that they are inventing and psychologizing through their selection and arrangement of materials; they are establishing cause–effect and other relationships, and they are determining what was most formative and important for someone else, someone they do not know. They must choose what to include, leave out, emphasize, and subordinate, and when they do, they have constructed a narrative that, whether they are aware of it or not, partakes of cultural stories with expectations for resolutions and interpretations built in. That narrative becomes the life and the basis for the judgements that will be rendered about the subject's character, life course, and personality.

Perspective is not established and maintained without struggle. How psychoanalytical to be is not a decision made once, but one made thematically and then repeatedly as the biographer moves through the life and the evidence. Traces of the most sophisticated theory, of hard-line constructionist tenets, and of 'pop psych' can be found within a single segment of a book. Smoothly or with some audible sounds of gear-grinding, the biographer stages major scenes and moves the reader into the perspective that the biographer finds most comfortable. That comfort may be based on the biographers' subconscious feelings about the scene, on their identification with a perspective, or on the tone of neutrality or intimacy they are trying to establish as well as on the available evidence. Bowen gives an example using a state wedding: 'Is the writer in the hero's mind or in the public mind? It can be done through the eyes of the bride's mother in the front row—from inside the scene. It can be told from reported rumors among the crowd waiting outside or through news sheets next day—the public mind' (Bowen, *Biography*, 106). Victoria Glendinning poses the question more pointedly: 'Is the story of your life what happens to you, or what you feel happens to you, or what observers see happening to you?'[61] Or, I would ask, all of these. How the biographer relates to the material, conceives of his or her authorial presence, and participates in the narrative, while a global decision, is also one that often wavers in practice and can differ widely and wildly within a single chapter. Sometimes readers discern the signs of struggle, and sometimes biographers make their decisions part of the content of their books.

Biographies in which these struggles are unusually clear offer fascinating, influential examples of the intersections of perspective and the presentation of personality. When Carol Ascher interrupted her life of Simone de Beauvoir with a letter to her, she made her frustration clear. Words such as 'rancor' reoccur, and she complains of what she cannot understand and what she is not getting from de Beauvoir.[62] She admits the struggle explicitly and later reflects, '[Other biographers] must have come to impasses such as I was experiencing . . . Yet they have covered their tracks.'[63]

Many reviewers reacted with outrage, and Ascher seems to have some regrets about her decision: 'Why couldn't I have written a book whose clean, sleek surface lay unbroken, invulnerable, unruffled by the squirms of a conflicted "I"?' (*Between Women*, 102). But Ascher had a venerable predecessor: Erik Erikson's letter to Gandhi in the centre of *Gandhi's Truth*.[64] The first time I encountered this letter, I was surprised by its anger, its personal, judgemental tone, and its psychoanalytic invasiveness. Some of the stories about Gandhi with his wife and with his female students were shocking, and the fact that Erikson seemed to offer them for psychoanalysis but did not fully interpret them made them more suggestive and shocking. Erikson had set out to write what might be called a meta-biography.[65] The first chapter, and many subsequent segments, are specifically about Erikson's experiences, reactions, and thoughts. Parts I and II are about the people he interviewed, about his sources, and about Gandhi's autobiographical writings. It is not until the third section of the book that Erikson begins a standard biographical narrative, and it is that section that begins with the letter. In some ways, it is fascinating to read a biography in which the biographer is also a subject of it, and Erikson knows minds. That is, rather than assuming he knows his own mind, he often tells us what he thinks he thinks and why he thinks he thinks it, but then concludes 'whether because . . . or because . . .'.

Erikson began this book after the success and heady attention accorded *Young Man Luther*; his letter to Gandhi shows that he walks in the same uncomfortable shoes as the rest of us biographers. The letter records the struggle that occurs when the persona Erikson has assumed and feels he is crashes into the contradictory, inevitably impenetrable individual that a biographical subject is. Over and over, like a chorus, Erikson writes, 'I cannot accept . . .', 'but neither can I interpret . . .' and soon he accuses Gandhi of dishonesty and sadism (pp. 231, 235–6). The letter concludes, 'Having told you all this, I can now simply narrate, without argument or discussion . . .' (p. 254). And, indeed the last two hundred pages of the book flow and even use different kinds of sources. Erikson's voice and intelligence are there, but his clinical presence has been subordinated to the voice of the historian and human observer. Although he continues to call his 'a clinician's book', he treats with restraint what he calls Gandhi's maternalism and bisexuality (p. 403). Although he does not say so, he has accepted his limits as a student of Gandhi's psyche and as a biographer.

Sometimes the struggle can be found in the sense that the biographer has retreated from the subject, has broken the even tone of the book by withdrawing just a bit and looking at the subject in a way that seems more objective but may, in fact, be more distant. At other times, the struggle is revealed when interpretation seems to be dependent on things other than familiar kinds of evidence. In 'Breakdown and Despair', the chapter on the years when the young Johnson was in 'an appalling state of mind', Walter Jackson Bate appears to struggle. Sentences present ambiguities ('The next two years, to some extent the next five . . .', p. 115), and masses of evidence from various periods of Johnson's life, such as a long string of Johnson's journal entries stretching into his seventies, mostly exhortations to combat sloth, break the narrative. Rather than presenting a divided mind, some paragraphs seem to present the vacillating of the biographer more than of the subject: 'a part of him could seem to have sabotaged . . .', 'True, that magical world . . . had at first seemed possible to enter', 'But inwardly a part of him had, in self-protection, held back', 'He may not have wanted . . .', 'But more than half of him desperately wanted . . .' (p. 120). These phrases in a mere fourteen lines make the case for neither state of mind. Above all the chapter depends upon the readers' acceptance of 'the fierce and exacting', 'punishing' 'super-ego'. This argument, often put in strangely general and abstract sentences that contrast with the voice of most of the narrative, vies with speculations about his reaction to his material circumstances (the 'humiliations' of 'extreme poverty') and with admissions of lack of concrete evidence ('If we know very little about the external details of Johnson's life during the first two years after he left Oxford . . .') (pp. 126, 127). Every biographer faces years about which they know little, and these are fascinating places for the reader to watch struggle, creativity, and compensation. Few biographers dare to claim, as Bate does here, that they know more about the internal state than external events.

CONCLUSIONS

I began this chapter believing that I would conclude that biographers ought to have a theory of personality, one that included scientific truths about adult developmental psychology and about gaining insights into the inner thoughts of the long-studied person. Now that I've surveyed the contradictory and very-much-in-progress research in the field of psychology and read and reflected upon the essays of many biographers, at one end of the scale psychoanalysts and psychiatrists and at the other those hostile to what they call derisively 'psychobiography' and sceptical about any reliable insights into the interior lives of another,[66] my conclusions are different. First, biography is an art; exactly what combination of research skills, insights into human nature, and dynamic relationship between biographer and subject brings about a portrait of interior life, makes a persuasive connection between actions and thoughts/feelings/motives, cannot be defined and certainly does not depend on any single theory of personality. Second, human beings' lives take so many trajectories, exhibit 'development' or 'regression' in so many ways, and assume (probably not attain) coherence in so many ways that no developmental or personality theory will ever be adequate to the larger purposes of biography.

Above all, I believe even more strongly that 'identity' is the meeting point between what biological characteristics a person has, who a person wants to be, and what the world will allow him or her to be. For some, biological characteristics (exceptional intelligence, unusual athletic ability, schizophrenia) are strong determinants; for some people, Martin Luther King or Margaret Sanger, for instance, the kind of person or the specific achievement that the person wants, will be strong enough to decrease the influence of the other two; for others, 'what the world will allow'—a war that denies a man the opportunity for an education, a prejudice that shuts a woman out of the highest positions in her field—is the strongest determinant. The meeting point of these three factors, the meeting point that produces the identity that the biographer strives to communicate by the end of the book, although usually falling within a sphere within a three dimensional space, can be anywhere within that sphere and, indeed, occasionally outside that normative sphere. 'The *capability* of performing deeds of heroic character is a product of the biological gifts that the child possessed and the nature of his upbringing, especially of the parental investment in his development and future. The *opportunity* to play a heroic part in actual events requires a wedding of the capability with historical circumstances. His acceptance or *espousal* as an authentic hero by the culture is the product of the coming together of the actuality of great accomplishment, the myth-making that accompanies them . . .', John Mack explains.[67]

Fourth, biographers must recognize that they have strong conceptions of personality and aspects of personality and must do as much as they can to project other models and other categories for their subjects' lives. Only then can they test them against the subject's life and thought and be open to the shape, the trajectory of a life whose similarities to their own may be more illusionary than they think. They may go back to their original model, but they will have chosen it rather than fallen comfortably into it. Fifth, biographers benefit from the broad field of psychology in concrete ways. At the least, knowledge of psychology's findings function somewhat analogously to historical knowledge. For instance, they help a biographer determine what is sociocultural. As they try to sort out when their subjects are displaying average behaviours and when they are engaging in risky, unusual, and even unique conduct, biographers, for example, need to know what age norms and expectations are, how powerful they were at a given time, and how they might have influenced the subject or others' reactions to the subject.

Psychology can consistently contribute techniques of evaluation and analysis that will bring new aspects of the material to the fore and even bring to attention overlooked aspects of the evidence. It offers data that allows the subject to be compared rather objectively to 'most people'. Questions that psychologists ask can turn our usual methods on their heads and suggest exciting new lines of inquiry; for instance, suppose we look, not for 'the mechanisms by which personality changes with age' but 'for the means by which stability is maintained'. In a life of arrests, travel, and turmoil, what did Defoe fight to keep stable? 'Do individuals choose or create environments that sustain the behavior that characterizes them?'[68] Whenever Defoe could, he created a job for himself that entailed travel and danger. Pondering such questions and answers calls into question the portrait of Defoe as hapless victim and powerless economic slave. Most biographers who apply psychological tools find that apparent contradictions can be reconciled at a deeper level of the subject's consciousness.[69] And there will always be biographers who find high-order psychoanaltyic tools useful. Jay Martin employs this methodology and research on 'replacement children' (those who replace a dead sibling, even to the extent of being given the same name) in a speculative, intriguing essay on John Dewey.[70] The even tone of a good biography comes in large part from the firmness of the biographer's philosophy and degree of comfort with the methods and interpretation of personality. In this circumstance, judgements on personality sound appropriate and are accepted at face value. The biographer who addresses the issue of personality and motive only at moments of interpretation tends to divorce the philosophy from the narrative and to make the psychologizing inorganic. It has been said that 'all biography can hope to do is reanimate its subject through patterns of tropes, narrative technique or form' (Nadel, *Biography: Fiction, Fact, and Form*, 178). Not so; biography can illuminate human nature and potential. Park Honan praises Richard Ellmann for integrating emotional growth or psychological change into chapters so that 'The Joyce at the end of an Ellmann chapter is usually different from the Joyce at the start of it, and, perhaps more important, our view of Joyce through the chapter has taken on a new dimension' (p. 65). Ellmann produces, we are told, a satisfying, well-planned development and display of a personality. No wonder Ellmann is the most imitated of all literary biographers.

Part of the appeal of biography surely comes from the failure of theories of personality. We want to believe that we are unique individuals, that we have some control of our 'destiny' and what kind of people we are. Biographers by seeking that meeting point reinforce not only what we want to know about human life—how others have coped with it and the three meeting point factors that shape it—but what we want to believe about ourselves, that we are unique, that a meeting point is ours alone, not one shared by the masses but attained at least in part by our biological selves and by our will. What Oliver Sacks calls 'the play of [the mind's] sensations and feelings and drives and intentions' and the capacity for development and adaptation create the complexity and density that we recognize as human.[71]

What the best biographies deliver, then, is a narrative of the life trajectory plotted with what Freud called 'the traces of his life's struggle with inner and outer resistances' that culminates in a summary or the feeling of a summary that describes that point, thereby *measuring* the person's achievement by where that point is and, because it is a description of a *point*, delivering unity and coherence. What we hope to see is greater than the story of the way society 'moulds' the person, more than a portrait of the subject as the 'spirit of the age'; it is the emergence of an individual who has, in Erik Erikson's words, managed to 'transform instinctual energy into patterns of action, into character, into style—in short, into an identity with a core of integrity'.[72] And readers want to get inside that.

II

EXPANSIONS

5. *Feminist Pressures*

A woman's heart and brain and dreams must be of such size and no larger, else they must be pressed small, like Chinese feet . . .

George Eliot

The list of books that are the authoritative standard of judgement for a form, the 'canon', for biography, unlike that for any other genre, is largely composed of biographies that broke the mould, that redefined our conception of the genre's contributions, possibilities, and perimeters. Most familiar are Plutarch's *Lives of the Noble Grecians and Romans*, John Aubrey's *Brief Lives*, Izaak Walton's *Lives*, Samuel Johnson's *Life of Savage*, James Boswell's *Life of Johnson*, and Lytton Strachey's biographies, especially *Eminent Victorians*. Like most lastingly canonical books, each was born within powerful cultural movements and drew upon but excelled existing literary and social methods. For example, as John Garraty says, Plutarch 'represented the blending of Greek and Roman culture at the apex of its development'.[1] Plutarch began the pairing of subjects, such as Dion and Brutus or Alexander and Caesar, that remained popular until modern times; eighteenth-century biography, for instance, is filled with virtuoso moments that readers approach with heightened excitement, as happens in the many comparisons of Dryden and Pope. Thus, his work contributed to the development of biography as an apparently *objective* genre characterized by moral and cultural judgements of the highest order.

Both Johnson and Boswell wrote their lives in the shadow of the influential injunction: 'The proper study of mankind is man.' In quite contrasting ways, they used the artistic and revelatory strategies of novelists and dramatists to raise the stylistic bar even as they developed the form's dual purposes of interpreting a unique individual and of making generalizations about human nature. Inscribed in Strachey's biographies are the impact of Freud, the cynicism and disillusionment of the World War I generation, and a particular kind of pervading scepticism characteristic of modernism. His iconoclasm extends from labelling nursing and taking Anglican orders as careerism to a broader, systematic dismantling of his culture's sacred myths, a dismantling that often substitutes one life story (often sacred) for another quite different one (usually shockingly secular).

Out of great cultural movements, then, new forms, questions, responsibilities, issues, and possibilities arise. These cultural movements, the people and societies caught up in them, and the literary strategies created to participate in the immediate hegemonic processes not only bring sets of choices to the foreground but also force new decisions on biographers. The premier cultural movement of our time is, of course, feminism, and something of a feminist canon is being appended to the canon (or offered as a counter or rival line of biographies). Linda Wagner-Martin, for instance, offers, among others, Nancy Milford's *Zelda* and Judith Thurman's *Isak Dinesen*, and discussions of a line of biographies going back through Woolf, Elizabeth Gaskell, and Lucy Hutchinson, to the autobiographies of medieval women are proliferating. Bill Epstein has recognized the appearance of a number of new types of life stories and paradigms, and points out that biographies such as *Zelda* are deconstructing the language and enterprises of earlier biography.[2] By doing so, he, like Wagner-Martin, implicitly posits a new, developing lineage.

This chapter is a reflection on the ways feminism has permeated biography, beginning with some attention to a series of *differences* some centred on the special challenges in writing the lives of women and some centred on what I see as some lingering, discernible differences among biographies of and by men, those of women by men, and those of and by women. Then I shall return briefly to some of the topics of other chapters, especially evidence, voice, and the relationships between biographer and subject.

The most speculative part of this book, this discussion of the influences of feminism on biography takes up some familiar questions and opens subjects on which entire books could be written, and I admit freely that I have not tried to make a clear division between what might be identified as women's concerns and what is specifically feminist. Partly this is because my own feminist approach colours the entire chapter and partly because my subject is women as subjects of biography and their male and female biographers. Moreover, even though feminism has been one of the most pervasive causes for change, has been 'in the air' for more than twenty years, affecting everything from workplace demeanour and hiring to the use of pronouns, and is manifest in dozens of forms, its influence cannot be definitively identified. In a literary form so subject to its historical shapes and purposes, to its culture, which, for instance, constantly negotiates such terms as 'hero' and even 'ideal man', to the individual philosophies and practices of biographers, and to the market forces transmitted by editors and publishers, feminism's impact is especially hard to isolate. This book, however, is not about certainty but about choices and their implications, and feminismS and the vast amount of recent attention to women's lives have undoubtedly made biographers aware of new decisions, demands, and opportunities.

But first: what I mean by 'feminism'. There is no single definition for 'feminist', of course, and people now routinely speak of 'feminismS'. And there are traditions of female thought, women's culture, and female consciousness that are not feminist.[3] Many women never think about feminism while others resist the label and positions associated with it. I would say that, at the minimum, feminists are aware of women's special circumstances within the larger culture and resist the idea that man equals human/normal/the standard of measurement. Liberal feminists are concerned with advocating 'women's rights' and 'equal rights', especially economic, legal, and political. Some feminists are persuaded that a 'patriarchy', which, although it spans all classes and races to some extent, is usually perceived as middle class, white, and male, has an interest in and often operates to prevent women from sharing, establishing, and asserting their equally real, valid, and somewhat different frame of reference, which is the outcome of different experiences. Feminism is usually recognized as a political interpretation of experience and a struggle aimed at raising cultural awareness of the impact and implications of conceptions of gender and the treatment of women and at improving the situation of women. It engenders new ways of thinking about the family, culture, language, art, experience, and social institutions.

'Feminist biographer' is a term with many potential meanings and positions along a continuum and, even when two biographers share a definition, an ideological position, and degree of overt feminist advocacy, their books can appear very different because one may, for instance, believe that critical alignment and vocabulary should be smoothed into a perspective and language that cannot be dated or identified in distracting ways while the other feminist biographer may openly invoke the terminology and methodology of a strain of current feminism. Being a feminist biographer influences the way the biography of a man is written. For instance, my feminism meant that I cared intensely about Defoe's wife, Mary Tuffley Foe, and his many daughters. I wanted to know what happened to them, how they felt, and how members of the family related to each other. I also wanted to be alert to every woman who was important to Defoe, and some of the work I still consider unfinished concerns them. There were Mary Deering and Jane Foe, who were arrested with him; he may have been apprenticed to Jane. I wanted to identify the women, rescue them from obscurity, portray their importance in Defoe's life, and give a little insight into women's lives.

As I have written this book with gender differences as one of my themes, I have been outraged, amused, and also impressed by what men do with women subjects. Few women, I think, would write that Katherine Mansfield was the 'perfect subject' because she 'came from an exotic background; was extremely attractive; had an adventurous bisexual life and a bizarre marriage to the critic and editor, Middleton Murry . . .'. Jeffrey Meyers, the writer of these remarks, also notes she is 'a good writer', wrote a journal and letters that survive, and 'fought bravely against tuberculosis, which killed her at the age of thirty-four'. The gallant death of a young, attractive woman is high on everyone's list of 'good deaths'. He also notes that he was especially fortunate because 'she lived in the period I knew most about' (*Spirit of Biography*, 137–8). This does not mean that I think Meyers was not, indeed, a lucky person, that his research methods, which he describes helpfully, were not excellent, and that his biography of Mansfield was not useful and entertaining—he was and they were. I just think most women contemplating a biography of Mansfield would not lead with, or perhaps even include, many items on his list of perfections.

Nigel Nicolson, the biographer of Mary Curzon, was the son of Vita Sackville-West, author of *Knole and the Sackvilles*, and Harold Nicolson, author of biographies of Tennyson, Benjamin Constant, Swinburne, and King George V and of many essays on biography. Before he wrote *Mary Curzon* (1977), he had edited Virginia Woolf's letters (6 vols., 1975), his father's diary (3 vols., 1966), and written *Portrait of a Marriage* (1973) about his parents and *Alex: The Life of Field Marshall Earl Alexander of Tunis* (1973). There is much in *Mary Curzon* that a feminist would treat differently, and yet Nicolson's lineage and close study of both sexes serve him well. He captures admirably what marriage entailed for a woman of her time and position, emphasizes her readiness for adventure and her intelligent, engaged responses to experience, and makes judgements that more than give her her due. 'How little did *he* [her husband George, emphasis mine] understand that by always taking his side, she was doing him no service, and by always speaking with his voice she was throwing away her gifts and influence', Nicolson writes (p. 171). Although here and elsewhere the book occasionally wavers into privileging her husband's mind, he never fails to keep her the centre and important subject of the book. He quotes richly from her private writings and thereby expands our impression of the depth and breadth of her mind rather than selecting carefully in order to reinforce a predetermined portrait image.

If he romanticizes Curzon and repeatedly makes her the object of the male gaze, he also consistently depicts her, in her words, 'standing side by side looking over the battlements' with her husband (p. 136). Nicolson shows them facing disappointments and tragedies together, effectively illustrates and argues what she contributed to her husband's career, and occasionally makes her an individual, as he does when he describes her on hunting expeditions with George. Once she alone noticed a tiger's deadly attack on a guide (p. 134), and that incident is as vividly realized as the reactions of 'the little Maharajah who hovered near' and begged her to ride with him: 'He could not understand a woman who walked all day behind guns' (p. 188). Nicolson is also constantly aware of the position of women within various societies; he remarks, for instance, 'In a society [Washington's] more masculine even than Chicago's, a rich and unknown woman would find it very difficult to make her way' (p. 21).

Nicolson takes on a number of challenges that today's biographers often shy away from. How, for instance, to write about the fact that women's bodies are often the objects of scrutiny, comment, and evaluation? Are we prepared to write about Mary Curzon's body? She was one of Dana Gibson's first models and her poses in portrait after portrait, decade after decade are designed to exhibit such Gibson Girl requirements as an almost impossibly small waist.

3. Mary Curzon as Gibson Girl

4. Mary Curzon in her 'peacock gown',
designed for the State Ball on the
last day of Durbar, the celebration
acclaiming King Edward Emperor of
India; it shows she knew the peacock
throne of the Moghul kings once stood
in the ballroom

Biographers are hearing the message that they must not commit the old sins
and gaffes but that they must find ways to write about the importance of the
subject's body and the culture's reactions to it. In a culture in which women
know their bodies are scrutinized and judged, there is something false about
not writing explicitly and candidly about the body, and yet can we manage it
more smoothly than Nigel Nicolson? Can we do it without distracting the
reader with our ineptitude, ideology, discomfort, or axes to grind?

Another challenge Nicolson accepted is writing smoothly about women's
intelligence and the cultural contexts and responses. 'One who knew [Mary
Curzon] well as a girl', Margaret Terry Chanler, wrote that 'she could be
tiresome when she "unpacked her library" and tried to talk books and ideas' (p.
28). He discusses frankly what the comment might have meant. He finally
concludes, however, that she was quite intelligent but 'preferred to be told things
more than to discover them for herself' (p. 33). This topic fascinates because it
deals obliquely with a woman's self-fashioning and admits that intelligence is
a much more mixed blessing than beauty. Every smart woman knows it—'A
gangly, difficult girl whose father praised her for thinking like a man, Simone
de Beauvoir struggled with the legacy of that equivocal flattery all her life', Gail
Caldwell summarizes such women's relation to the world.[4]

Many of the prize-winning biographies by women began with the writers' fascination with how another woman had coped with her brilliance, always the impetus for 'equivocal flattery'. Elizabeth Minnich, for example, feels herself especially engaged with Hannah Arendt and her biographer Elisabeth Young-Bruehl, for she studied with Arendt for more than ten years and was Young-Bruehl's teacher: 'I see them as very much alike—breathtakingly brilliant . . . Both as young women struggled with the impact, the force, of their personalities on the world around them. But neither . . . gave in to the possibility, or even the temptation, of being an acceptable exception or being difficult for its own sake' ('Friendship Between Women,' 297). There is much to contemplate here; in differing degrees, the woman perceived to be intelligent 'struggles with the impact' on others and 'gives in' or accepts or resists one of the not-very-attractive poses the culture provides. We could, for instance, read Mary McCarthy's public persona through this lens, and any interpretation of Curzon without an awareness of responses to her beauty, presentation, intelligence, and position would fail.

In truth, writing the lives of men and women *is* different. The reasons that the lives of, for instance, male social reformers matter are not absolutely identical to the reasons those of female social reformers do. The reasons (and perhaps the reformers) are more similar than different, but there are differences. Women's conflicts are likely to be different, and a moderate or modest achievement may be truly remarkable. Shari Benstock offers a list of women's concerns, some unknown to most men and most varying greatly in intensity for the sexes: 'women situated within conflicting and mutually constricting roles (wife, mother, daughter, sister, lover); women placed in societies that make rigid distinctions . . . between the public sector and the domestic; . . . middle-class women seeking freedom from bourgeois definitions of women's intellectual and imaginative abilities; public women defying professional and personal experiences for women; women who find . . . a means to survive childbirth, illness, the deaths of spouses and children, loss of cultural identity and personal regard, fear of failure, aging, death, loss of beauty and physical strength . . .' (*Private Self*, 5). What is acceptable, what is possible, what is imagined and attempted often differ. Women may be seen as eccentric rather than exceptional, and the world she is perceived to live in and be destined for may be markedly different, especially in earlier times. Every biographer works with a model of contexts which, at some point, gives way to one of levels of consciousness, to surmises about the layers of the subject's interior life. Thinking in terms of one of these models underscores the differences between men and women and the problems biographers face.

The first context, the most distant concentric circle from the person to penetrate and recreate is the national, historical, social context. This first circle is always a challenge, for an almost infinite number of contexts and details could be selected, and, since they must be used in the very beginning of the book, identifying the most pertinent and necessary is especially hard. Yet how intelligently the elements from the national, historical, and social events are selected greatly influences the success and significance of all biographies, and we are surely not as adept at identifying some as we are others. As Carol Brightman wrote in *Writing Dangerously*, 'McCarthy's 1940s were not Koestler's. Nor were they Phillips's, Barrett's, Howe's . . .' (p. 303). And they were certainly not Churchill's or Truman's or Abraham Robinson's.

It is always something of a challenge to determine what the Events, the major, life-changing moments, as opposed to just small-e events were in another person's life—the bombing of Pearl Harbor might pass without a ripple while the person dealt with the loss of a job, the birth of twins, or even the death of a favourite horse. In the midst of the Great Plague of London, Samuel Pepys noted, 'I do end this month with the greatest content, and may say that these last three months, for joy, health, and profit, have been much the greatest that ever I received in all my life' (entry for 30 September 1665, the month 35,027 people died,[5] including several people he knew personally). He was fretting a little about a minor falling out between his wife and a servant and scheming to get at least £100 as his share of two captured ships recently declared a 'prize' (18 September). Biography needs to speak from a sense of Event, which things were Events to the subject and what they meant to them. Blanche Wiesen Cook points out that the Great Depression that moved Eleanor Roosevelt deeply had little practical reality to Franklin Roosevelt by, among other things, documenting his November and December notes about shopping at galleries and an auction of 'Chinese things' (p. 418). Perhaps roots of the 'cheerful strength' of his first Inaugural speech, which was made in the deep centre of the Depression, can be related to his own largely untouched life and personal circumstances.

Women's Events may be harder to recognize and less acceptable to readers. Erik Erikson explained that a historical moment 'is determined by the complementarity of what witnesses, for all manner of motivation, have considered momentous enough to remember and to record and what later reviewers have considered momentous enough to review and re-record in such a way that the factuality of the event is confirmed . . .'.[6] Notice that there are two sinkholes here. In writing about women, we must look for different groups of witnesses, especially for female witnesses. Second, women's writings and opinions have been obscured and lost, and, therefore, the Events for women have not been found 'momentous enough to review and re-record'. For instance, the years in which states voted on ratifying the Equal Rights Amendment seem to have slid into history with scarcely a ripple, but for the women who worked for it and listened to the idiocy of threats of unisex bathrooms as a serious reason to vote against it, the scars remain and symbolize a deep desire to 'keep women in their places'.

Biographers working with the past face another, general difficulty. Hayden White has pointed out that the events that history has singled out as turning points or of monumental significance may not have been the ones that contemporaries recognized as such or even noticed. White gives an example selected by many modern commentators: *The Annals of Saint Gall* records the Battle of Poitiers in 732 but does not mention the Battle of Tours, fought in the same year and 'which, as every schoolboy knows, was one of "the ten great battles of world history"'. White asks, 'What principle or rule of meaning would have required him to record it?' (*Content of the Form*, 9) This is, in fact, the biographer's problem. 'Principles' and rules of inclusion, if not meaning, come from the subjects' lives and the events and contemporary currents that the biographer judges were of most significance and notice to the subject; they come from the biographers' sense of what readers know and will need to know, and they also come from the biographers' often un-examined judgements about the most important events and contexts—from the 'principle or rule of meaning' that has been inculcated in or absorbed by the biographer.

The second context with which biographers work is the 'shared space'.[7] This very public space is intensely immediate to the subject, and it certainly points up the fact that disproportionate amounts of research have been done on various aspects of every era. The importance of New England church politics and Jonathan Edwards's intense interest in it is obvious and a great deal is known about it; key players were studied, correspondence was saved, minutes of meetings kept and preserved, and files and records systematically set up from the beginning of the settlement of the continent. In contrast to this centuries' old research, a group of diligent and impressively trained women historians have been working for a few decades to reconstruct the social movements and networks in which women such as Dorothea Dix, Mary Heaton Vorse, and Lucy Sprague Mitchell worked and moved. Thus, Ola Winslow, the biographer of Edwards in 1940, and David Kennedy, of Margaret Sanger in 1970, were still working in strikingly different vine-yards; only today, after twenty years of (mostly) women historians' work, can we say that John E. Smith (*Jonathan Edwards: Puritan, Preacher, Philosopher*, 1992) and Ellen Chesler (*Woman of Valor: Margaret Sanger and the Birth Control Movement in America*, 1992) have anything like a level playing field.

Often it is difficult to find and piece together the kinds of evidence that allow us to make good surmises about reactions and motives. While Carolyn Heilbrun can assume that Gloria Steinum had most of the same information published or transmitted by radio and television that men had and Deirdre Bair can assume that Simone de Beauvoir was in the same privileged situation, to what information Harriet Beecher Stowe or Jane Austen had access is a difficult question. And we know that even today within this public, shared space, men have sources and access that are still largely closed to, perhaps, all women, even those in the inner circles and positions of power.

The third context is the social space occupied by the public person, the 'face we see', the person in the most impersonal, largest setting. For most biographical subjects, evidence about this circle is readily available. For instance, Nicolson has no trouble quoting from newspapers and bystanders unknown to Mary Curzon. Descriptions of Curzon as she 'came out', successively, in Washington, New York, and London, and continued coverage of her during her married life help us to understand the way she presented herself and how people responded to her. There were consistent comments on her 'winning smiles and irresistible graces' (p. 85) and to her entrances, when her height, athletic body, and carriage led observers to remark that she seemed to 'float' and draw all eyes to her (see also pp. 27–30, 112, 119, 120–1).

At this point, the biographer begins to turn inward towards the subject, rather than looking outward from the subject towards contexts. Nicolson is admirably aware of the performative self and describes Curzon preparing her trousseau to pay tribute to India without borrowing so much as to be offensive or ridiculous (p. 138) and often '*performing*' her duty well by playing a part, telegraphing a state of mind. Over and over biographers explore their subjects in this way: how does the person act in public? what did someone see when they saw him or her hail a cab or order a meal in a restaurant? how did Roosevelt make political speeches? how did Harriet Beecher Stowe act at large abolitionist meetings?

The fourth context is that of 'social privacy', a place where all kinds of intimate thoughts, intellectual and political as well as emotional, are shared. Here Defoe appeared in public settings or in private settings with groups of people he knew well. Here Nicolson describes Mary Curzon adapting to her husband's circle of classmates and friends, 'the Souls'. At this point, biographers of women may encounter two problems: that the very categories of evidence are harder to recognize and aspects of women's lives may be less accepted as good subjects for detailed treatment. Certainly portrayals of the *Partisan Review* meetings whether 'about' Mary McCarthy or Delmore Schwartz hold considerable promise and interest in this category, but some readers may feel differently about, for instance, McCarthy's 1955 miscarriage. What Carol Brightman chooses to emphasize about *Partisan Review* meetings might be another example, for they often seem a series of sexual escapades among the participants, often with McCarthy in some humiliating position (a lover who made her do all the housework describes her as having 'no tits'). Were McCarthy's pursuits, pursuings, domestic arrangements, and break-ups that central even to her experience of the meetings? This example is indicative of a problem— the present feminist era has raised a demand for more. We want to know about the intellectual, political, and editorial discussions, want to know about the affairs, *and* we also want to know how McCarthy felt as she crossed the 'Turkish Divide', Irving Howe's phrase for the barrier that allowed no women except those recognized as a certain kind of writer to join certain conversations (Brightman, *Writing Dangerously*, 301).

At this point the concept of concentric circles of contexts and that of layers of interiority clearly work together productively. For instance, nearer to the core of the person is the domestic space, the world of the immediate family; for many people at many times in history, that would include extended family. To describe Mary Curzon's mother as 'sucking the titles like lollipops' as she recorded guests in her diary after social events is to sketch clearly an aspect of Mary's homelife and upbringing (p. 48). Linda Wagner-Martin, something of a pioneer in identifying evidence about women's lives, points out the information in Gertrude Stein's mother's spare journal, Sylvia Plath's meals, and Eleanor Roosevelt's visits to Clover Adams's grave (*Telling Women's Lives*).

The evidence about the domestic can be quite diverse, disorganized, and even contradictory. Jean Strouse uses it to especially good effect in her life of Alice James. Because the James family seemed to have personal writing bred in their bones, she can draw on a rich selection of diaries, journals, letters, and pedagogical essays to reconstruct such domestic settings as family dinners and depict Alice within them. The very things that made her like her brothers often decidedly emphasized the differences between men and women. Sometimes apparently silenced by her brothers, sometimes appreciated for her intelligence and insight, sometimes basking in their love and attention, sometimes suspecting that enough love didn't 'trickle down' to the youngest, Alice also imbibed the theories constantly being discussed, worked out, and propagated around her. As Strouse says, 'The impact of these ideas on Alice was direct and indirect, overt and covert, affecting her deepest feelings about herself, other women, and men throughout her life' (p. 46). Some of these ideas were about gendered behaviour and women's possibilities, but others were about the family unit; Strouse describes a 'Jamesian notion about a constant level of family health and pleasure. One member, when sick, might feel that he or she was making a sacrifice so that the others could remain healthy' (pp. 111–12).

Fifth is the personal space where only a very few, perhaps not even all members of the nuclear family are admitted. Nicolson's story of the increasing mutual intimacy and dependence that developed between George and Mary Curzon is a fine example. Nicolson is alert enough to see the change in the marriage from George's neglect and imperceptiveness about Mary to an effective working partnership that manifested itself in Mary's balancing George's personality and power with warmth and caring gestures and in great alertness to each other, as illustrated by Mary's knack for finding a way to allow the couple to be seated at formal events when George's back began to hurt badly

(p. 139). The political observations and planning, the discussion of the roles they played, the nicknames, and the frequent expressions of loneliness when separated all re-create persuasively this elusive space. 'I . . . rebel against this separation.' 'I do feel in my heart that in our life there is a sense of comradeship almost as great as love', she wrote (p. 145).

Another aspect of the personal space, perhaps especially for women is the aura of the place in which the subject lives. 'A woman's life is built largely of tangible matters; the furniture of her house is part of the furniture of her spirit', Catherine Drinker Bowen counsels, and mentions that Mrs Oliver Wendell Holmes had a white fur rug beside her bed that she must have enjoyed greatly (*Adventures of a Biographer*, 69). Victoria Glendinning finds and shares the place—physical and mental—where Vita Sackville-West lived:

In the deserted tower room everything has remained just as Vita had left it . . . The walls . . . lined with books. On her worm-eaten oak writing-table are photographs . . . a reproduction of the Brontë sisters . . . small engravings of Knole. In a rack at right angles . . . her reference books. Only the lamp is different; the utilitarian one that she used has been replaced by something prettier. There are flowers on her writing table, as there always were when she was there. One thing is missing: the small pink marble sarcophagus that had held her two ink-wells. . . . It contains her ashes.   (pp. 405–6)

In fact, Glendinning's biography is especially rich in re-creations of what places meant to Vita Sackville-West. The fact that she could not inherit her beloved home opens the book, and Knole's significance for her seems to grow as she ages, as Glendinning demonstrates by, for instance, pointing out how it figures into the plots of her novels and how she tried to 'tear Knole out of my heart' (p. 329). She quotes 'Knole gets in the way always' and relates this to Sissinghurst, but she also shows the absolute centrality of Sissinghurst, not Knole, to Vita's daily life. The gardens that made Sackville-West one of the most famous women in England and the tower room where she wrote become tangible, one changing with waves of plantings and war, one remaining so much the same that the tattered tapestry, embroidery, and fringed velvet are never removed. Joy Hooten in 'Autobiography and Gender' explains, 'Whereas men record external events, geographical features and climatic conditions, discoveries, feats of endurance or skill, observations on native flora and fauna, women concentrate on the minutiae of daily life, the pleasures and discomforts of ordinary relationships, the personal aura of the place that is the new or familiar home, the anxieties, griefs, loneliness, and achieved enjoyments of early settlement life.'[8] Showing Vita working in her garden and her tower study at odd hours of the day and night, recording that her best days were those 'when nothing happens . . . When no one comes to disturb my inward peace' (p. 280), Glendinning creates a woman for whom places are perhaps more important to her happiness and emotional balance than her family.

'The pleasures and discomforts', 'the personal aura'—scenes and characteristics of settings infused with experiences with people, with a remembered or hoped for way of living, and with deeply personal responses to environment—describe well Mary Curzon's relationship to places. Her beautiful room at the top of Blaine House in Washington and her memory, 'I had lived in fondness and affection at home' (Nicolson, 49), and her joy at eating luxuriously outdoors in India are but two examples.

The evidence of such unions of person and setting, of the desires and feelings that lead people to work hard to create or re-create especially harmonious, renewing living spaces is, perhaps, all around the biographer but often overlooked. This evidence is often of poignant, even deeply painful memories and it need not be within the walls of living spaces. Defoe, who had found caring friends and the kinds of conversation he most enjoyed in Scotland, planted a walkway of lime trees reminiscent of those he remembered there when he settled down in Newington. Unlike London before and after the Scottish interlude, there he was respected, part of the most desirable men's groups, and prosperous. Isak Dinesen wrote that she had trouble 'seeing anything at all as reality' in the first months back in Denmark after she had been forced to sell her African farm, 'I had been part of [the landscape], and the drought had been to me like a fever, and the flowering of the plain like a new frock' and 'The landscapes, the beasts and the human beings of that existence could not possibly mean more to my surroundings in Denmark than did the landscapes, beasts and human beings of my dreams at night.' Thurman comments, 'There was no one at home [in Denmark] who could gauge her loss' (pp. 241, 258–9).

Finally the biographer reaches for the individual personality and the interior life of the subject, the space of aspirations, fears, thoughts, and conflicts, and of the unconscious, that secret spring of some associations, actions, and reactions. Finding evidence about this realm requires an alert understanding of the many aspects and domains of life from which it can come. Surely deeply revealing of Mary Curzon's love of beauty and physicality were her preference for clothing that rustled or was made of 'slithering materials which changed colour as she walked' (p. 138) and her spontaneous expressions of happiness: 'I can live [in Simla] on views for five years' (p. 123). Her letters about loneliness, her constant coping with the inconveniences of homes without indoor plumbing, electricity, or practical floor plans, and her delight in the often impressive, ridiculous, touching, and funny receptions of the common people give us unusual access to her interior life.

Because the distance between the public person and the interior life is so interesting and because women often perceive their own inner lives as creative and powerful, yet also freakish, unacceptable, and perhaps even monstrous but still 'the real Me', women often are compelling biographical subjects. From an early age and throughout her life, one of Louise Bogan's favourite poems was Louise Guiney's 'The Talisman':

> Take temperance to thy breast,
>
> .   .   .   .
>
> For better than fortune's best
> Is mastery in the using.
> And sweeter than any thing sweet
> The art to lay it aside.
>
> (Elizabeth Frank,
> *Louise Bogan*, 33–4)

This poem is part of the 'how to live and be happy' admonitions popular at the beginning of the twentieth century and captures the need women writers have felt to mask the intensity of their desire to write and the degree of their ambition.[9] Bogan once wrote, 'The poet represses the outright narrative of his life. He absorbs it, along with life itself. The repressed becomes the poem. Actually, I have written down my experience in the closest detail. But the rough and vulgar facts are not there' (p. 55). This kind of statement is quite frustrating to a biographer, because it forces what some call 'pressing material out' of literary works harder and more ingeniously than they will bear—or at least bear with good accuracy. The biographer's model of contexts and interior richness is obvious here; Bogan regarded the events in her life as often 'rough and vulgar' at the same time she was living with intriguing lovers in New York and Vienna and writing poems for a collection she published as *Body of this Death*.

These 'circles' that biographers use provide ways to peel the performative selves and roles away as one removes successive petals of a flower to reach the seeds and pistil; in fact, they provide a way to recognize the performative selves, the roles that are available, natural, accepted, attempted, and forced upon a person. The fact that people, but especially women, often experience clear, dramatic breaks in their lives and sometimes have to reinvent themselves is underscored. For instance, George Eliot spent fourteen years caring for her father. His death and her freedom surely brought more changes than it would to most men. The death of a spouse, the departure of the youngest child, the relocation of a family, all of these events and more usually affect women more than men. Eleanor Roosevelt's trepidation about the move to Washington is presented by her biographers as one of those events where the surface is smooth, a story of a wife sharing her husband's success, but beneath is definitely trauma. In fact in 1933 Eleanor Roosevelt saw her life as a teacher at the Todhunter School in Manhattan and her political activities (director of the Bureau of Women's Activities of the Democratic National Committee and head of a Women's Advisory Committee to develop Al Smith's presidential campaign organization, 'the most powerful positions ever held by a woman in party politics' [Cook, 366]) at an end because of her husband's election.

The circles also highlight the permeable, nebulous borders between the public and private spheres. Ruth Crocker, author of an in-progress biography of Margaret Olivia Sage, explains that women like Sage politicize the kinds of spaces women use. She gives as examples fashionable restaurants, book clubs, and even card parties, and in describing the kinds of meetings, often for huge groups, that Sage held in her home, she locates sites of influential, quite élite political gatherings.

Most women, like Frank and Bogan, are acutely conscious of the way the public and private spheres feed each other but also create tensions between the public and private selves. Where they intersect in most people's lives they sometimes grate or at least chafe. Many times, the evidence about this intersection can be contradictory, but revealing in its contradictions. During the time that Mary Curzon was campaigning for her husband's election to parliament, he described her as extremely happy, the press represented her as highly effective and smiling, but she wrote to her father that she loathed George's district and the people in it and often found the experience 'miserable' (Nicolson, 85). Not only do we see the differences inherent in three of the parts of the model, but we see how different perceptions from various perspectives can be and how they create pressures.

It matters. It matters. It matters being a woman

~ 'What price a woman-child in 1811?' (*Crusader in Crinoline*, 21)

~ 'I hope its [*sic*] beautiful and a fool—a beautiful little fool' (Zelda Fitzgerald wishing for happiness for her new-born baby daughter, *Zelda*, 84).

~ 'I pray in these same words every day: "May she bear a child to thy honour and glory and to the good of thy kingdom, and may it be a male child."' 'Darling, I felt how miserable you would be, and though of course I too was somewhat disappointed [that it was a girl], I really felt it much more for you . . .' (from George Curzon's letters, *Mary Curzon*, 172).

~ 'The first great sorrow of her life was that, by accident of gender, Knole could never be hers' (*Vita*, xvii).

~ 'I can't come to any other conclusion but that you mustn't go through with a child at this time. It is a disappointment because we'd counted on having one but, after all, we can always have one' (from Edmund Wilson's letters urging Mary McCarthy to have an abortion, *Writing Dangerously*, 173).

~ 'At other times, she talked more intimately [in her diary] with an imaginary "other"—and then stepped back to note with irony her assumption that the gender of posterity was masculine' (*Alice James*, 275).

~ 'Her face was swollen, she had a black eye, and her arms were bruised. "Of course I wouldn't tell [the doctor] what had happened. You don't. You cover up"'

(Mary McCarthy after being abused by Edmund Wilson, *Writing Dangerously*, 174).

~ 'There is one career all females have in common whether they like it or not—being a woman' (Bette Davis as Margot Channing in *All About Eve*).

As I have written this chapter, I have often felt that the 'differences' between biographies about men and women and also between the practices of male and female biographers, even when the biographers are feminists, are much smaller than the similarities—in some cases even insignificant. There are differences, however, many coming from the different lives men and women lived, especially marked in the past but by no means erased today, and the different expectations held for them. Michelene Wandor refers to 'the imperative of gender' and points out that sex 'defines not only his or her biological sexual characteristics, but also implies imaginative and social assumptions about her/his personality, power and place in the world'. She goes on to speculate on how 'familial, political, and sexual relationships' are affected by gender and what they are perceived to be and supposed to be because of sex and gender.[10]

The lives women live and conceptions of Woman force a number of demands and, therefore, choices on biographers. It is often said that men are supposed to be individuals and women are supposed to be women. Just as readers can become aware of the way evidence, narration, and interpretation are smoothly interwoven and the degrees of subjectivity among them obscured, readers can begin to notice variegated judgements in biographies and reviews of them. Presentations and verdicts may be composed of elements mingling the conception of 'eternal Woman', cultural notions of women, perceptions of what was individual about this woman, or some combination of the three—Woman, women, woman. In a review of a biography of the playwright Lillian Hellman, Maureen Quilligan quotes: 'Only a handful of American dramatists of her period . . . are revived as frequently' and 'Her three-decade bond with that brilliant writer and enigmatic man Dashiell Hammett would, in itself, have assured her a place in the period's literary lore.'[11] In other words, Hellman passes both tests—she wrote plays of lasting regard, and she sustained a long relationship with an admired man. She excelled as an individual and she was true to woman's most desirable destiny. Most people read this with interest and approval, but we would be jarred if there were a similar paragraph congratulating F. Scott Fitzgerald or Franklin Roosevelt on his long marriage to a remarkable woman and noting that alone would have assured his place in history.

The biographer must determine how important sex and gender were and convey a balanced view, and readers have strong expectations and daunting 'thou shalt not's. Generally, they want the woman subject treated as that great individual, but they want her evaluated as a woman and within the standards and expectations they and their culture have for women. Most readers do not want a condemnation of their culture; they do not want the story of discrimination and internalized limits crushing a promising person—they call that melodrama or sentimental fiction. And yet, for men and women, but especially for women, 'One of those elements of an individual's identity which at the very minimum comprise *what one is never not* [is] membership in one of the two sexes or in a given race. What one is never not establishes the life space within which one may hope to become uniquely and affirmatively what one is—and then to transcend that uniqueness by way of a more inclusive humanity' (Erikson, *Gandhi*, 266). As Susan Friedman says, 'The emphasis on individualism does not take into account the importance of a culturally imposed group identity for women and minorities [and] . . . the differences in socialization in the construction of male and female gender identity . . . From both an ideological and psychological perspective, in other words, individualistic paradigms of the self ignore the role of collective and relational identities in the individuation process of women and minorities.'[12] Women know that and biographers are beginning to recognize when their subjects are especially conscious of gender. Sometimes integrating consciousness of gender is an essential part of the story they have to tell.

Phyllis Rose, for instance, describes coming to understand that 'this obvious thing I was going to write about' in her biography of Virginia Woolf was an exciting, even electrifying discovery: 'the fact that being a woman was important to the way she thought about her life' (*Life into Art*, 101, 107). One of the special challenges for biographers is to decide how important being a woman was for an individual, and individual is a key word. Some women encounter insurmountable barriers because of their sex; some women seem to have a talent for swimming smoothly by the obstacles or making their gender enabling. Some women glory in their femininity, some find it a bad-fitting cape, some scarcely think about it. What is almost certainly true, however, is that women are often reminded that they are women. 'A white man has the luxury of forgetting his skin color and sex', but a woman is often reminded that she is being defined as a woman, a member of a group whose group nature and identity are very frequently perceived to be determining, or at least stronger and more important than almost any individual characteristics.[13]

During this golden age of women's biography-writing, new subjects, neglected key moments in women's lives, are discovered periodically. For example, as I read the lives of women, I realized what a defining moment the realization of financial independence is for women. Comparable to the defining leap of independence and act of rebellion that Frances Burney's late-life marriage to the Frenchman D'Arblay was in the eighteenth century is for many women the recognition that, for instance, freelance writing provides an adequate income and can be expanded to provide true prosperity. The narration of Eleanor Roosevelt's discovery of Franklin's affair and of his neglect to pay for household expenses reaches a turning point with, 'Eventually she set out to earn her own money from lectures, magazine articles, and guest appearances on radio shows. During the 1920s, financial independence enabled ER to pursue the interests and causes she believed in, and to manage her own life' (Cook, 318). The key moment of recognition, however, is not reached until 1928 when 'ER decided to become personally independent and financially solvent. Within two years, she earned thousands of dollars . . .' (p. 332).

Cook's biography does not make as much of this process as it could, and most biographies, even feminist ones, do not even recognize it. From their earliest childhood, boys are expected to 'earn a living', become financially independent, and strive for wealth. Girls, however, are bred to believe that they have a choice about working or even that they have few if any ways to support themselves. Women often make dramatic, even traumatic choices about earning money several times during their lives. Suppose Franklin had lost his family money in the Depression and Eleanor could have made more money than Franklin? A professional woman once told my husband that, at middle age, she had discovered to her amazement that she was 'very good at making money'. Her surprise reveals again the need to look for the story of a woman's realization of economic independence and to tell it in the biographies of women.

Such awareness allows biographers to recognize when the 'unchanging' 'nature' of women and the culture's explanations for her behaviour may have obliterated the individual. Adrienne Rich treats lightly the images of Emily Dickinson as 'girl', recluse, lovelorn poetess, and neurotic, and ridicules the poem chosen to accompany the commemorative stamp issued in 1971. 'More than any other poet, Emily Dickinson seemed to tell me that the intense inner event, the personal and psychological, was inseparable from the universal; that there was a range for psychological poetry beyond mere self-expression', Rich writes.[14] She finds Dickinson to be an artist, ruthlessly protecting herself from distractions and demands that would diminish her poetry.

What has often been seen as a puzzling, or timid, or feminine, pattern of advance and retreat is now sometimes presented as far more complicated in terms of the individual and also inseparable from what social roles and work force on human beings. An example is Isak Dinesen's tyrannical treatment of her mother after her return from Africa, which we can now recognize as her attempt to carve out a space within the socially regulated domestic sphere that would allow her to be a writer—an individual creative mind with uninterrupted time and space. Her biographer points out the gender ramifications: 'it was an effort to dramatize the urgency and seriousness of her work, to resist the family's well-meaning attempts to repossess her, and to assert what had been a uniquely masculine privilege in that household:

associability, exemption from the duty to be emotionally accountable at all times to others' (p. 259).

In an interview about his decision to leave the Clinton cabinet, Robert Reich talked of the 'constant choices, constant guilt' for the person who 'loves his work and loves his family'. For women, 'the imperative of gender' charges the choices and the guilt with additional power. Thurman tells us that late in her life 'in a speech to a feminist congress, [Dinesen] spoke of woman's business as "charm" and confessed that if she were a man, "it would be out of the question for me to fall in love with a woman writer"' (p. 259). What Dinesen is describing is the loss of cultural identity and personal regard, a price paid routinely and repeatedly by women who achieve in the public sphere. Paradoxically, in the understanding that women's personal and psychological individuality is important is feminism born and in the realization that it can be encompassingly human is feminism nurtured and revisionary biography written.

Biographical subjects, or, put another way, women in order to be worthy subjects of biographies, must marry into, fall into, or fashion a worthwhile role in life. Little boys are taught that they *must* have a worthwhile position in adult life; they choose or create at least as often as they fall into or fashion a role. Rather too typical is Clara Shortridge Foltz, the first woman lawyer in California, who felt she had to fabricate a justification (false widowhood), a need, for her being a lawyer, and part of the importance and interest in her life is the way she did it—the way she got her education, worked within the male legal system, and chose and argued cases. Nicolson uses the fascinating phrase, 'marrying for a worthwhile role in life' (p. 75), and that is an option—or a fortunate accident—that is not often specifically narrated. Today a biographer of Mary Curzon would make much of her desire to start a school for poor children in London and her successful establishment of scholarships to train nurses, midwives, and female doctors in India years later, but Nicolson's portrayal of the way Curzon's marriage gave her a fulfilling, important role and how she made it more important seems true to Curzon's time and to many women's lives today.

Although it is becoming an overstatement, all women feel pressure to marry, marry well, have children, and be good mothers (whatever those things mean), and they are judged on these grounds. Developmental psychologists tell us how girls are always measuring themselves against the plot of attractiveness/dating, courtship, marriage, motherhood, how painful these measurements are, and how long it takes for women to free themselves. Mary Russell Mitford, Romantic era author of *Our Village*, the five-volume collection of 'rural sketches', humorously invoked the standard when asked if she would not have liked to have been married: 'No, I never wanted a full, normal life' (quoted in Heilbrun, *Writing a Woman's Life*, 76). With cultural pressures so great, is it any wonder that biographers assume that the subject wanted to marry, that it is the be-all in her—or women's—lives? Heilbrun points out, 'Marriage is the most persistent of myths imprisoning women, and misleading those who write of women's lives' (p. 77). She reminds us that not marrying may not be 'failure' but choice, conscious or unconscious. She asks that attention be given to 'the life of the unmarried woman who, consciously or not, has avoided marriage with an assiduousness little remarked but no less powerful for being, often, unknown to the woman herself' (p. 28). Jane Austen may be an example, and books on women writers often include long lists of those who were not married.

One way to avoid marriage, one probably not often consciously chosen, is to be stigmatized as unfit for marriage and a conventional life. 'In our own time of many possible life patterns', Heilbrun writes, 'it is difficult to grasp how absolutely women of an earlier age could expel themselves from conventional society . . . The lives of women who died before the middle of the twentieth century should always be carefully examined for such an act, which would usually (but not always) occur in a woman's late twenties or thirties' (p. 49). This sentence reverberates as we read the biographies of women. Sometimes such a casting out is empowering, liberating, the secret of the reason the woman became a candidate for a biography. Sometimes it determines a life of frustration, ineffectual striving, and social exile. Many of the women seem to swing between simulations of 'normal' domestic arrangements and acts that set them apart dramatically from the conventional and even acceptable. The prize-winning lives of Isak Dinesen, Louise Bogan, and Mary McCarthy can all be read this way. Too often the inability or unwillingness to deliver an acceptable image of a woman, at least part-time, has horrifying consequences, as it did for the sculptor Camille Claudel. She once remarked that it was her desire to live alone that got her locked up.

Described as able to 'beat the breathing bronze into the softest lines and capture the fleeting movement, drawing forth from marble the features of life, in an almost expressionist manner', Claudel was inspired but also destroyed by being the student, mistress, and competitor of August Rodin and the sister of Paul Claudel, who had her confined in a madhouse for the last thirty years of her life.[15] Treated as a footnote, inferior, or love-interest in most biographies of Rodin, often called Rodin's 'gifted pupil', Claudel has become a troubling presence, a living example of Woolf's image of the fate of 'Shakespeare's sister'. The woman who in her youth struck people as a proud genius, a 'tremendous personality', incisive, and even 'tyrannical' created work before her study with Rodin that other sculptors recognized as 'reality exploding in every detail, revealed, explained, monumental' (Delbée, 81). Before she met Rodin, she began a sculpting school for girls and later taught a servant maid to rough out her marble blocks. Her determination, skill, and creativity left a lasting impression on everyone who met her. Rodin once observed, 'You've become sculpture itself' (Delbée, 157), but, in fact, he and her brother

Paul made her the subject of their arts, remaking her, effacing all but the qualities that served their ends and allowed them to do whatever they wanted to her.[16]

Women who understand and are able to maintain a conformist image while striving for their individual successes often do well. Although her biographer Dee Garrison 'felt a shock so strong it was like a physical blow to the chest' when she saw Mary Vorse on film, we can understand why Vorse was careful to look like this: 'I saw a genteel New England lady . . . such a beautiful upper-class accent, her hair combed into a stylish bun, her clothes so carefully chosen and gracefully worn. She was eighty-seven then . . . my wonderful bohemian, sexual radical, and political deviant—looked and spoke like a respectable, wealthy matron.'[17]

If marriage is a morass, motherhood is a swamp. Its power in defining women and success is everywhere. 'I wish I were dead. Pause. But why am I feeling this? Let me watch the wave rise. I watch. Vanessa. Children. Failure. Yes; I detect that', Virginia Woolf wrote in her diary at the height of her fame.[18] Finding issues of motherhood is easy in comparison to interpreting them fully, and they lead biographers into the greatest swamp of all—a place where they guess at points of pressure, thoughts, and how much agency and how much self-knowledge a person can have. Sometimes—rarely—the evidence plays right into the feminist biographers' hands. When Mary McCarthy's letter about wanting the baby crosses with Edmund Wilson's don't 'go through' with having a baby now, and then his later recitation of the inconveniences supposedly in store for *her*, the ways her life is 'like a man's' *and* distinctly female are writ large. She is a working critic, essayist, and fiction-writer and having a baby will indeed, as Wilson says, 'badly tie her down' (Brightman, 177).

In *The Politics of Motherhood*, Toni Bowers points out that men throughout history have assumed authority over women's pregnant bodies and conduct as mothers, even as they have, when convenient—as it was not with Wilson at this moment—insisted that women had a unique mothering instinct and greater need and even affection for the child. They have made mothering something to be controlled and, contradictorily, an enormous responsibility which few women can live up to rather than the historically changing, political institution it really is.[19] Wilson's letters accuse McCarthy of being 'confused' and express anxiety that a baby would 'ruin your relationship with me'. 'I think, too, that you and I will get along better with this question out of the way' (p. 177), he writes, but she, not Wilson, is carrying 'this question' and that child cannot be replaced by another child conceived at some later, more convenient date. Later during divorce discussions, Wilson wrote, 'Of course, I shan't insist on having [the child Reuel] for the whole of my six months if I'm not in a position to give him a proper home or I think it's undesirable for other reasons. I decide all matters of his education' (p. 279). He takes for granted his culture's assumption that Reuel is her responsibility, creating a home natural for her, and yet that he has ultimate authority.

Mothering somehow always becomes a measure of womanhood and female success. Brightman is careful to cite babysitters and famous guests who left an abundance of descriptions of McCarthy as mother, descriptions that Brightman compares to good single mothers today: 'including him in conversations, treating his opinions with . . . consideration' (p. 285). Very much a part of her life and a matter of her interest and concern, Reuel is a minor but happy part of the story. Even Brightman, however, can write, 'She was married to Edmund Wilson, and she was Reuel Wilson's mother. These were positions of consequence, more difficult to sustain than that of critic, fiction writer, or bohemian girl' (p. 263). Brenda Maddox takes pains to point out that Frieda Lawrence had been a 'merry and indulgent mother' and played games, 'splashed beside them in the surf', and let Monty wear his new boots to bed (*D. H. Lawrence*, 163), and that, after she was separated from them, she couldn't sleep and huddled under the window or 'lay on the floor and cried' (p. 140). She did some bizarre things to see them, and rather than being strongly depicted as choosing Lawrence Maddox emphasizes how 'determined' she was to see them whenever opportunity arose (see pp. 155, 327).

The morass that biographers of women enter is, of course, partly because something like standards exist for judging a presidential term, a military campaign, canonical poetry, and even demagoguery. The *raison d'être* for writing a man's biography is often that he was a great president or general, and that position becomes to a large extent his identity. To some degree, George Washington, Horatio Nelson, and John Keats personify and set the standard for their occupations. No matter what else a woman is, if she is a mother that is seen as an important occupation. What are the standards for judging motherhood? It may be true that most women are still judged heavily by their private lives and men almost exclusively by their public. Mary Gergen in 'The Social Construction of Personal Histories' discusses Lee Iacocca's published comments on his wife Mary: 'According to Iacocca, each of her heart attacks followed a crisis period in his career. He concluded, "Above all, a person with diabetes has to avoid stress. Unfortunately, with the path I had chosen to follow this was virtually impossible . . ." The statement in reverse, a woman writing about her husband or child, would sound quite monstrous. It is acceptable in a man's story.'[20]

Biographers of women who must write about mothering frequently grapple with a lack of anything like 'objective' or reliable evidence, with their own cultural conditioning and a fear of their readers' judgements, and an awareness of how the conduct of an adult child may be a very poor way to measure the quality of mothering. Two biographies of Margaret Sanger show these signs of ambivalence and warring imperatives. Sanger's daughter Peggy died less than a month after Sanger returned from a year in Europe. David Kennedy, whose biography won the Bancroft prize, quoted from her autobiography, 'The joy in the fullness of life went out of it then and has never quite returned. Deep in the hidden realm of my consciousness my little girl has continued to live . . .' (p. 77). Without giving evidence, he says that she 'brooded on the possibility' that her absence caused the death and depicts her returning to her work on the cause of birth control with increased daring and purpose. Finding her puzzling, he writes, 'Whatever the peculiar blend of self-justification [for going abroad], stubbornness, ambition . . .', (p. 79). He and Ellen Chesler, her later biographer, give plenty of evidence that her work competed with her children. Chesler tells us that Sanger was 'strangely indifferent to the responsibilities of mothering', 'always burned the cocoa', found cooking a 'loathsome burden', and bickered incessantly with her husband over childcare and housework responsibilities (*Woman of Valor*, 53–4). Chesler tells us that Sanger neglected to have Peggy fitted with a brace after she had polio and spent summer holidays abandoning the children to do research.

These biographies expose a gap in current biographies: treating the subjects' parenthood in a sustained, systematic way. That would mean, of course, making hard—and revisionary—decisions. We spend countless hours collecting evidence and building cases about how people felt about important co-workers or positions, about what kind of, for instance, Secretary of the Navy, they were, and about their relationships and professional and personal experiences as, for example, part of the editorial inner circle at the *Partisan Review*. We know what questions to ask, what judgements need to be made, and have useful models to guide us in writing such sections. I cannot name a biography that treats parenthood, even when a family business is a theme in the work, in a direct, organized manner.[21]

At the very least, the biographer should treat the topic as important in the life of the person and, in most cases, should gather evidence for times when the subject's life and that of the child's intersected in major ways. The lengthy struggle between Defoe and his youngest daughter over her desire to marry Henry Baker is an example (Backscheider, *Defoe*, 500–3), as are Sanger's times of conflict over her son Stuart's education.[22] What the biographies of Sanger fail to do is develop the tensions between her satisfactions in mothering and her passion for her work. We simply cannot tell if there is anything like a balance in joy, the 'constant choices, constant guilt', 'love for work, love for family'. The evidence we are given confuses rather than sets the height of the balance pans on a scale. In one passage Chesler can quote from her response to Peggy's death: 'Dear Peggy, I could weep from loneliness for you—just to touch your soft chubby hands—' (p. 104). Immediately after this section, however, Chesler gives us truly heart-rending incidents such as one of Sanger's children walking 20 miles to meet a train his mother forgot to tell him she was not taking, or quotations from letters: 'Am I coming home Easter? Write and tell me so, please' (son Grant, p. 137).

Biographers such as those of Sanger often force the reader to read between the lines, to notice the painful conflicts Sanger experienced, and to imagine the complicated woman and mother she was. Chesler supplies evidence that must have been hard to gather but often presents it almost as scrapbook clippings. She argues convincingly that Sanger suffered greatly, went through a rather irrational period when she became a Rosicrucian in the hope of communicating with Peggy, and finally 'shaped' her grief into something she could endure and renewed her determination. In the letter to Peggy quoted above, she wrote, 'but work is to be done dear—work to make your path easier . . .'. In contrast, we are told not only about Sanger frolicking at the beach with the boys but abandoning them to do research, and we have no idea how that felt to her and what the imperatives were that drove her day to day. Sometimes possible motives are left unconnected to descriptions of behaviour. For instance, Chesler does remark in passing that Sanger feared giving the children the tuberculosis she had, and that could be an explanation for her 'distance' from the children.

Feminism, as it so often does, here reveals not only issues about gender and culture but an area of *men's and women's* lives that is still treated in culturally determined, unreflective ways. Readers of biographies of men would probably not pause at incidents that catch the attention and may even distract the reader as those in the Sanger biographies do. Constance Reid mentions the strain the mental illness of David Hilbert's only son put on his working life—both his time to work and the lack of distractions he needed—but she does not investigate at all whatever personal anguish Hilbert felt, and the narrative opens no space for such wondering. A recent biography of Robert Frost by Jeffrey Meyers does not develop the part the suicide of his son and the mental instability of his daughter played in Frost's life. As a female reviewer notes, 'The impact . . . cannot be understood if nothing is shown of Frost's relationship to these people until the actual moment of their decline' (*NYTBR*, 8 May 1996, 8). Attention to evidence shows that no case needs to be made that parenting is a critical issue for fathers as well as mothers; letters written by Albert Einstein and recently made public include the agonizing sentence: 'The worst is that Eduard is there alone [in a Swiss mental institution] without a caring hand, in his wretched condition. If only I had known, he would never have come into this world.'[23] We are accustomed to male subjects being judged all but exclusively on their public or professional success and, to some extent, by the ambition of their undertakings. Would it not be interesting to read about their ambitions as parents?

★

Plutarch wrote, 'It was for the sake of others that I first commenced writing biographies . . . but I find myself proceeding and attaching myself to it for my own; the virtues of these great men serving me as a sort of looking-glass, in which I may see how to adjust and adorn my own life.'[24] In contrast to biography novels, memoirs, letters, autobiographies—these, not biographies, have been women's forms, their places for seeking answers and models and expressing the self. Traditionally biography treats the exceptional human being, but casts that exceptionality as role model, admirable product/exemplar of a nation, or important agent in history. Until recently, rather than useful 'looking glasses', biographies of women have too often treated their exceptionality as accidental (queens whose fathers were unlucky enough not to have sons), as homilies on the nature and fate of Woman (exceptionally beautiful women such as Cleopatra and Marilyn Monroe), as sublimations of feminine desires (abandoned women becoming poets, motherless women becoming social workers), or cause for apology or rationalization. The roles male biographers assign to their subjects are routinely transformative, perhaps without conscious recognition while those of comparable women have shown the signs of traditional conceptions of the nature of Woman. Gandhi, Martin Luther, W. E. B. DuBois, Martin Luther King are cast as prophets and what gave them their power is a major subject of their biographies; although Forrest Wilson calls Harriet Beecher Stowe a 'major prophetess' and several female subjects of the prize-winning biographies might be treated as such, none is. Wilson seems to forget 'prophet' and depicts her 'dipping into her own maternal heart' (p. 275), Lady Bountiful (p. 301), organizer of 'Heaven's marines' (an ineffective effort to influence Congress, p. 400), and not recognizing the gathering war-clouds (p. 465). One comes away with the feeling that Stowe was a propagandist often feeding 'sectional hatred' (p. 297) and a sensation rather than a prophet.[25] Sewall explains that Emily Dickinson took as her 'vocation' communicating the 'central "dazzling" truth' about God and concludes, 'Such breathtaking authority becomes credible only in the light of the long, slow, hard pilgrimage, with every step honored and all honestly' (2: 725).

Although it may be accurate to say that birth control (especially in welfare politics) is a problem of the twentieth century tearing the country apart somewhat as race is, Margaret Sanger is a 'social reformer' while David Lewis shows us that W. E. B. DuBois was a prophet. The way quotations from speeches are used by Lewis are markedly effective and selected to resonate with our time rather than DuBois's:

Into the large cities will pour in increasing numbers the competent and the incompetent, the industrious and the lazy, the law abiding and the criminal. Moreover, the conditions under which these new immigrants are now received are of such a nature that very frequently the good are made bad and the bad made professional criminals. How can they stand it? The answer is clear . . . They do not stand it; they withdraw themselves as far as possible . . . shrink quickly and permanently from those rough edges where contact with the larger life of the city wounds and humiliates them.

Biographical writing often shows almost comic wrestling matches with our gendered language and expectations. For instance, Ellen Moers catalogued the ways people tried to describe George Sand: 'What a brave man she was, and what a good woman' (Turgenev); 'She has the main characteristics of a man; ergo, she is not a woman' (Balzac); 'Thou large-brained woman and large-hearted man' (Elizabeth Barrett Browning).[26] As Gerda Lerner, the ground-breaking feminist historian and author of *The Grimké Sisters*, and others point out, we still do not really know how to relate women who have been historical agents to the larger picture of historical change. Very recent biographers of Harriet Beecher Stowe, Margaret Sanger, and Pearl Buck among others see this positioning as an important part of their work, but we are surely still struggling to articulate women's exceptionality as we integrate the domains of their lives. These wrestling matches, and especially recent feminist work that calls attention to them, are changing biography and forcing difficult decisions about evidence, life course, and thematic emphases on biographers.

As this chapter has demonstrated, it is trivial to list major problems in writing the lives of women that are still to be solved or even addressed and to point out that they reveal gaps in the biographies of many men. It seems clear to me, however, that great progress has been made, and out of the dissatisfactions—the ways traditional biography does not fit women—have come major changes. I will conclude this chapter by briefly pointing out just four concrete differences that feminism has made and some of the additional decisions they encourage (or force) biographers to make.

First, over the past twenty years the study of women has finally become respectable, and, in fact, it has become unacceptable to ignore them. Gerda Lerner reports the exponential growth in women's history research in the last fifteen years. Among other things, she finds biography, 'which was very poorly represented' earlier, accounted for 48 of the 312 dissertations in women's history between 1980 and 1987.[27] Biographers now acknowledge, as Blanche Wiesen Cook does, that their books and approaches were 'made possible by a movement . . . that removed women from the margins of our culture and placed them in the center of their own lives, and our field of vision' (*Eleanor Roosevelt*, xi). In fact, feminism has transformed both the study of history and literature in universities. In the early years, the women who won prestigious prizes for biography had written biographies of men (the first Pulitzer on Julia Ward Howe is, of course, the exception); in the last fifteen years they have written the lives of women or of marriages twice as often as they have written about men.

We are still experiencing an opening up of biography to the lives of women and witnessing the loosening of gender stereotypes. Even ten years ago women chosen for biographies tended to be in roles seen as male (monarch, scientist) or who achieved things men were known for but were acceptable roles for women (writer, artist, social reformer) or had used their relationship to a man to exert power and achieve prominence (Susannah Wesley, Jacqueline Kennedy Onassis; Eleanor Roosevelt is still categorized with 'Noted Wives and Mothers' in the 'Childhood of Famous Americans' series). Now women in many other categories are the subjects of biographies, and queens, writers, and wives are being reconsidered and their lives written in quite different ways. In a carefully considered introduction to *The Macmillan Dictionary of Women's Biography*, Jenny Uglow includes as criteria for inclusion

Women whose role in history, or whose contribution to society or use of talent would be remarkable regardless of sex . . . [whose] life or work affected the position of women directly—by their breaking into new occupational fields, or by leading campaigns to alter women's opportunities and status . . . [who] have had an indirect effect—their embodying concepts of womanhood . . . (witches, domestic science writers, film stars) . . . [and who] are legendary figures, or because the imagination is caught by their courage, cruelty, gaiety, extravagance, or sheer eccentricity. (p. vii)

Historians and literary critics often observe that there is a basic opposition 'which places man inside history, and [presents women] as eternal and unchanging, except for modifications in terms of fashion . . .'.[28] At some level, women are often interpreted by a conception of woman's 'nature', some sort of unfading, imperishable gene. And what is seen as 'eternal woman' can be internalized without recognition. Stowe as fanatic mother and Dickinson as female mystic lightly tint the biographer's language. Joseph P. Lash's fine *Eleanor and Franklin: The Story of their Relationship, based on Eleanor Roosevelt's Private Papers* (1971) compared to the biographies by Cook and Goodwin illustrates my points. Lash is writing about Eleanor, but Franklin is in the title, and the narration can shift disconcertingly to judgements that seem unsupported with evidence. Especially telling contrasts are in the three books' chapters on the time when Franklin had polio and tried to recover the use of his legs. Lash tells us that Eleanor 'took her cue from Franklin's courage' and writes, 'Looking at his collapsed legs brought to mind Michelangelo's *Pietà*, that universal symbol of woman, the mother, grieving over the broken body of man . . .' (p. 268). This image that puts the man, 'the broken body', at the centre is mythologized and romanticized: Eleanor becomes the Virgin mother and Franklin Christ, the subject of the tragedy. Wiesen Cook's account is notable for its unsparing realism:

Eleanor slept on a couch in his room and, with Louis Howe or alone, managed to move him, bathe him, and turn him over at regular intervals. She administered catheters and enemas, massaged his back and his limbs, brushed his teeth, shaved his face . . . together they rallied for that extra effort to reassure each other: They bantered, laughed, and sought to conquer their gravest fears. (p. 309)

Wiesen Cook also describes the horrible struggle Eleanor waged with her mother-in-law, her brief breakdown, and the sacrifice of her space meaning that later she slept on a bed in one of the son's rooms and dressed in a bathroom.

Eleanor is kept at the centre, and the changes in her life and personality carefully drawn out. Although Doris Kearns Goodwin's book is subtitled in part 'Franklin and Eleanor Roosevelt', the account of Franklin's illness scarcely mentions Eleanor. Somewhat sentimental, it dwells on how much Franklin had loved to swim, hike, ride, and play tennis, on the pain he suffered in trying to regain movement and throughout life when he did such things as stand up, and concludes that his personality was permanently changed for the better: 'he reached out to know [people], to understand them, to pick up their emotions . . .' (p. 17). Eleanor appears once in the account, testifying to his new, exemplary moral character. Lash and Goodwin tell the familiar cultural story of the hero's trial and purification by fire, a resurrection to new purpose and higher cultural symbolic value. As with the *Pietà*, the admiring Maiden is sacrificed for 'purposes of male renewal'.[29] Wiesen Cook writes a revisionary story that moves a woman and a marriage to the centre of the stage already—and still— occupied by a man.

The second effect of feminism on biography is to assure that biographers will think about the significance and amount of space 'ordinary' aspects of life merit and that the importance of the private, domestic, or intimate sphere will be given attention. Anne Delbée writes at length about Camille Claudel's home and studio spaces and how they contributed to her happiness or her sense of alienation and struggle. Delbée pays some attention to her cooking and attempts to re-create as many nuances of her relationship with Rodin and her brother as possible. This attention has carried over into biographies of men. To some extent, however, it is a battle not yet won. In the 1989 edition of the *Oxford English Dictionary* biography is defined: 'The life course of a man or other living being: the life history of an animal or plant.' And feminist biographers, such as Linda Wagner-Martin, still describe frustrating efforts to explain their methods and the importance of the 'ordinary' to editors (*Telling Women's Lives*). Perhaps Laurel Thatcher Ulrich's *A Midwife's Tale* with its careful explication of material that might be described as social history or domestic trivia depending on the orientation of the critic gave an important boost to the use of such personal manuscripts and surely demonstrated ways of working with such material.

Just as we have different expectations today for the treatment of biographical subjects' sexuality than we did fifty years ago, so we are coming to have markedly different demands for the treatment of private life. It matters to us that Edmund Wilson hit Mary McCarthy, and we are now prepared to see the 'imperative of gender' and appreciate Brightman's use of a quotation from Louise Bogan, 'Any woman who has ever had her wrist twisted by a man recognizes a fact of nature as humbling as a cyclone to a frail tree branch' (p. 262). This kind of thing used to be hidden or down-played, and it was certainly not used as gender politics. The work linking the private to the public is often highly alert and creative. Alice Wexler recognized that Emma Goldman drew upon the conventions of popular fiction and the drama of her day to express the roles she played and the kind of heroine (romantic, sentimental, misunderstood) she felt she was. Wexler extends this insight: 'even this private self engaged in forms of role-playing and playacting . . . performances enacted for an audience of one'.[30] The connection made between adolescent reading and female self-fashioning and between the stories and moods available in the culture and the selves Goldman presented at the lectern and in her letters is a successful technique.

Quite a few topics are being treated with new candour, and biographers today are aware of pressures to make choices about these topics and their presentation. Among the most notable are the arresting power of women's deepest feelings, their comments about their own bodies, and the stark force of their drive to work. Isak Dinesen tells a friend that she is 'so full of untold stories that if you prick me they will flow out' near the time she wrote, 'I cannot walk two steps without support, nor stand and keep my equilibrium . . . I cannot get my weight above seventy pounds . . . The doctor tells me that I have all the symptoms of a concentration camp prisoner, one of them being that my legs swell so that they look like thick poles and feel like cannon balls . . . terribly unbecoming and for some reason very vulgar. Altogether I look like the most horrid old witch' (Thurman, 439, 442). Alice James at the end of her life calls her body 'a little rubbish heap' and 'a poor old carcass' yet needing an 'outlet to that geyser of emotions, sensations, speculations and reflections' (*Alice James*, 276, 274). The hold that Charlotte Brontë's *Jane Eyre* and *Villette* have on women comes from this rendering of the usually smooth, plain surface, the endurance of oppression and intellectual and economic poverty, with the sudden, fierce outbreaks that reveal the depths of feeling, thought, and longing. 'It is my spirit that addresses your spirit; just as if both had passed through the grave and we stood at God's feet, equal—as we are!' Jane Eyre, separated by class and sex from Rochester, cries out. Biographers are now learning to recognize the fierce, revelatory outbreaks that James's and Dinesen's words were, to interpret them as such, and to portray them unflinchingly and in all their complexity.

A heightened consciousness of gender and gendered judgements is everywhere. It can appear smoothly but revealingly, as it does in the conclusion of Diane Johnson's review of Bair's biography of de Beauvoir: 'De Beauvoir lived the often solitary, roistering, egotistical, hardworking, promiscuous, slightly alcoholic, affirmative life of a writer—but it was the life of a prototypical 20th-century male writer that she had the will to choose' (*NYTBR*, 15 April 1990, 24). It can appear with startling suddenness and sharpness as it does in Diane Wood Middlebrook's review of Paul Mariani's *Lost Puritan: A Life of Robert Lowell* or in Margaret Doody's review of Halperin's Austen biography.

Middlebrook: 'Maybe the problem is, after all, a guy thing. Mariani passed up an opportunity to engage with Lowell's grandiose sense of masculine entitlement, the character trait that informs both the heights of Lowell's risk-taking achievements and the sloughs of his betrayals. Looks as though the next biographer to take on Robert Lowell had better be a woman.'[31] Doody: 'This is as naive a piece of writing as ever appeared from an academic press—as totally naive in its antifeminism as in the author's schoolboyish desire for a romantic proposal scene' (*Nineteenth-Century Fiction*, 40: 227). Here are signs that new biographies are supposed to recognize and address these aspects.

The third major contribution of feminism, one important for the first two, is the recognition of new kinds of evidence. For instance, feminism has been enriched by representation, performance, and film theories, and an increasing number of biographies use photographs and portraits in original ways as evidence. Susan Ware is typical when she writes, 'Luckily I did not have to reconstruct the partnership [of Molly Dewson and Polly Porter] entirely through circumstantial evidence.' In this essay and in the biography, *Partner and I*, she adeptly interprets their 'photographic legacy' as 'all the proof I needed to document the love that bound these women's lives together for over five decades' (p. 56). In both publications, she reproduces a 1959 picture in which Dewson, in the kind of suit she wore as vice chair of the Democratic National Committee and a member of the Social Security Board, holds Porter's arm with both of her hands, and the women look warmly at each other. What is so remarkable is that the picture seems both posed and unposed, the women still and a little self-conscious and yet intimately connected, obviously long-, long-term friends. A striking set of photographs shows them consulting and laughing as they clear space for a garden, reading to each other in front of a fire with their bodies companionably close, posing with their car and dog before a trip, and entertaining many women friends.

Photographic evidence in biography can highlight themes that might be overlooked, suggest additional facets of the subject's life, or reinforce interpretations such as Elizabeth Frank's that writing was the centre of Louise Bogan's consciousness, one carried by her use of quotations from her poetry and personal writings on nearly every page. The pictures she selects to include, other than the obligatory childhood and family ones, reinforce this identity even during her unsettled early life. A group of literary friends—editors, writers, poets (W. H. Auden, Theodore Roethke)—provide silent commentary in the middle of a remarkable set of pictures of her as writer. She sits quietly at a typewriter on a cluttered desk, stands with a co-translator, and is portrayed at the writers' colonies Yaddo and MacDowell. Doris Kearns Goodwin includes pictures of Franklin and Eleanor together and provides numerous pictures of FDR with other women. More interesting are the unusual number that show Eleanor with African-Americans. An early and outspoken advocate of racial justice, Eleanor is at a segregated daycare centre and with 'Negro troops'. Vita Sackville-West as an old woman looking confidently into the camera and wearing a melange of comfortable clothes is clearly a different person from the sober woman whose poses seem drawn, like Goldman's verbal poses, from available characters of women (see the plates beginning with 'Portrait of Vita in 1910 by Philip de Laszlo' to 'Vita as a Young Married Woman', in Glendinning, *Vita*, pp. 106–7, and see p. 195 of this book).

The availability of such evidence, decisions to use it, knowing how to interpret it adequately and accurately, and ways of treating familiar kinds of evidence with new sensitivity undergird revisionary approaches. An example, one already apparent in this chapter, is the different kinds of attention given to the biographical subject's relationships. Certainly women's private lives, their relationships with people, *and* their public lives are all in play in the best biographies written today. Both men and women are writing more about marriages and treating family members as individuals worthy of serious study and fuller portrayals. For instance, Donald M. Thomas's *Alexander Solzhenitsyn: A Century in His Life* (1998) in contrast to Michael Scammell's 1984 *Solzhenitsyn: A Biography* gives full treatment to the struggle Solzhenitsyn and his first wife Natasha waged to preserve their marriage.

Feminists continue to criticize biography as a 'totalizing genre', one seeking the 'unique and autonomous subject', that will provide for men 'great stories of legitimation'.[32] As such, the subject is foregrounded and everyone else must fade into a supporting cast or a scenic background. Although some biographers have long talked about the way other people occasionally seem to *compete* with the subject, until recently it was rare to see serious explorations of the ways the subject might be portrayed in relation to others. What was singled out only a few years ago as a distinguishing mark of feminist biography or something feminist biographers had a responsibility to do has become a demand placed on all biographers. In 1990 Liz Stanley completed her list of important elements of a feminist biographical method with 'a rejection of the "spotlight" approach to a single individual' and a recognition of 'informal networks among feminists through friendships.'[33]

Some biographers have recognized other kinds of foreground/background possibilities. Nigel Hamilton, for instance, maintains that by writing the lives of Thomas and Heinrich in *The Brothers Mann* he brought out the idea 'that rivalries within a family inform the achievement of individual members' and allowed him to tell with unusual force the great crisis of Thomas Mann's life, which was also 'the crisis, or turning point, of modern German history: republicanism or fascism'.[34] Very experienced biographers such as Victoria Glendinning now write about their wrestlings with the traditional highlighting of the subject, while all others are 'cast in shadows'. In the preface to *Vita*, she worries, 'The people around Vita . . . are distorted or diminished' (p. xvii). This is certainly true. Her husband Harold Nicolson fades in and out of focus; just as Vita did not help him with his political campaigns and sometimes seemed to be a gap on a stage or at a dinner party, a person cut out of a photograph, Harold's public life and even personal feelings often seem cut out, not possible distractions or essentially unimportant to the biography but scissored out in a way that diminishes the picture. Even more often the children sometimes disconcertingly disappear, leaving us, for instance, to wonder why one of their relationships ended (and if Vita was partly responsible) or how they got from one place to another.

Many reviewers now castigate biographers for writing as if in men's lives it is still acceptable to cast others completely in shadows in order to reinforce the subject's individualism, that trait that has been admired in men and has been an essential part of most definitions of maturity. As Stanley observes, 'conventional biography sees the rich complexity of a person's life as an embarrassment, an obstacle to finding the real person . . . and, in writing biography, biographers have developed efficient ways of reducing complexity to manageable proportions' (*The Auto/Biographical I*, 163). No longer can the decision to handle a life this way be unrecognized and without awakening ambivalences and discomfort.

Women historians especially have devoted considerable time and energy to dense networks of women, women who were important to each other and worked together to effect social change. Many biographies today develop persuasive cases for the professional importance of friendships among women. 'When Eleanor Roosevelt', Goodwin writes, 'first came into contact with these bold and successful women, she found herself in awe of the professional status they had acquired. . . . Eleanor, encouraged by her friends, began to discover a range of abilities she never knew she had—remarkable organizing skills, superb judgment, practical insight . . .'.[35] These biographies have expanded our sense of the value of a variety of kinds of evidence. For example, the photographs in *Eleanor Roosevelt* seem selected by Cook to capture Roosevelt's happiness and the diversity of her warm relationships (see p. 158).

Finally, feminist biographers have focused new attention and, perhaps, problematized the relationship between biographer and subject. American feminism has always used personal experience as a valid kind of evidence, and it has insisted upon the relevance of the personal and the political, often demonstrating tellingly that the personal *is* the political. The movement in biographical voice in the twentieth century was away from the personal, away from the Bloomsbury men's position that the writer's voice should predominate. With the rise of New Criticism and the ascendency of 'objective' history presented in neutral tones, the biographer attempted to disappear. Feminism brought that presence back, and it is found often now in all kinds of biographies and especially in feminists' lives of men and of women. It gently permeates Deirdre Bair's *Samuel Beckett*, and not infrequently it breaks out with powerful immediacy, as it does at the conclusion of Brightman's *Writing Dangerously*. As Sara Alpern has said, many women biographers believe part of

5. Eleanor Roosevelt, with her hand on her bodyguard Earl Miller's knee

6. Eleanor Roosevelt holding hands with Hilda Smith, a dean at Bryn Mawr College

their job to be attachment and re-visioning, 'and, therefore an active, not a neutral voice, is appropriate' (*The Challenge of Feminist Biography*, 11). It seems to me that we are living in a formative moment for biography, a moment when we can see fashions changing and can wonder what style and form will prevail, what the prevailing perimeters of the genre's voice for the next decade or two will be.

A sense of the immediacy and fascination of the woman's life and experiences may give the biographical voice new energy. Women often bring an overt intensity to the writing of the lives of women that seems rather rare in male biographers. Most of the time, this particular kind of intensity is a great strength, one that fuels tireless research, resourcefulness, and unusual indifference to career considerations. Kathryn Sklar explains,

One reason historians of women have succeeded in transforming large areas of the discipline . . . is the missionary zeal with which they approach their work. They write for today, but they also write for the eternities. A group without a history is a group without an identity. By creating a history of women . . . they transform the possibilities in women's present and future.

Added to this responsibility for women's future . . . is the sheer fun of investigating women's past . . . [and] the ability of women's history to illuminate the interaction between women and social structures that are dominated by men.[36]

Sklar captures well both the 'sheer fun' of reading about and studying women and the 'missionary zeal', the *need* many women feel to contribute to a more complete version of women's history or to the rapidly unfolding revision of history that includes women's part in the larger story.

This intensity has many explanations. Perhaps because their own educations until very recently were almost barren of the study of women, women's writing, and women's achievements, there is a sense of urgency, curiosity, and dedication permeating the work. We have lacked the variety of stories, or even the stories at all, that are possible for women's lives. Bell Gale Chevigny, for example, writes of the 'urgency and fervor associated with the movement to redress historical and current injustice' and how women write 'to recover our history and ourselves, each at least partly in terms of the other'.[37] Maureen Quilligan sees herself part of a group who are refashioning history that has marginalized women or 'treated them in such a way as to make inaccessible to successive generations of women readers the historical lessons which the lines of such exemplary females might teach' ('Rewriting History,' 260).

Overcoming hardships that people writing about men seldom encounter—name changes, maiden names or even first names not even recorded, generations of lack of interest that allowed materials to be thrown away, to deteriorate in boxes, or to go uncatalogued, and persistent devaluation of 'domesticity' and women's 'interests'—biographers of women have to be ingenious and persistent. Until recently, they had to undergo additional hardships because of lack of institutional and fellowship support.

The relationship between these women biographers and their subjects is more overtly personal than the stances traditional biographers take. The *equality* of the relationship, the fact that the women subjects 'need' to be discovered, given their due, explained, gives a reciprocity to the enterprise that we encounter less frequently between biographers and male subjects. Sometimes, however, such engagement can be perilous, and books should carry warning labels for readers. Among the problems women biographers have admitted are identifying too closely, taking too much for granted, refusing to deal with things that are too personally charged (either because an 'ending' is resisted or the topic resonates in the writer's life), and refusing to include things that, in our opinions, reinforce debilitating stereotypes of women. Joan Givner, the biographer of Katherine Anne Porter, confesses to refusing to look at Porter's sexuality and marriage because of her personal situation (*Self-Portrait*, 74). 'When I first began to write a critical biography of Mary Wilkins Freeman, I thought I had a mission. Here was my chance to set the record straight, to redefine and reevaluate . . .', Leah Blatt Glasser explains, and then chronicles her need to find and portray in Freeman's work 'feminist rebellion'. It was, she concludes, probably 'a projection of my unfulfilled need to rebel' and confesses that she went through a period when she indulged in 'imaginary rewriting of her stories . . . remaking of her characters'.[38] Over and over the word 'need' appears in the essays by women biographers, and reviewers and biographers of male subjects are beginning to see the possibilities that the same kinds of relationships have often existed but have been unnoticed or masked in earlier biographies.

Even the most intellectual female biographers, even those who have grave reservations about their subjects, can be surprised by such affiliations. Jean Strouse describes herself as 'quite astonished' when she began to cry over Alice James's grave, which she had visited 'more or less as a lark'. She finds herself saying, 'I'll take care of you' and remembering Alice's poignant request of her brother, William, six months before she died: 'Pray don't think of me simply as a creature who might have been something else, had neurotic science been born' (Moraitis and Pollock, 69–71). Strouse's reaction to her thoughts and actions is complex and becomes more so. In the spirit of her initial opinion of James, she says that Alice had 'worked her powerful will on me, just the way she had done with the people who lived with her: there I was . . . taking care of Alice'. Alice, who spent almost her entire adult life as an invalid plagued by undiagnosable and incurable bouts of illness and ennui, a life Strouse described as 'limited and depressing', had come to feel different towards Strouse. She writes at length about her reluctance to end James's story as it really ended. Initially drawn to 'her spirit, her illness, her family, and her nineteenth-century milieu', she now wanted 'a happier ending' (pp. 68, 70). She had to accept an unhappy ending, as she called it, and recognize it not only as *the* story but as a worthy story.

Historical studies of literary genres prove over and over that when an old, established genre clashes with new ways of thinking, that genre changes or dies. It can transform itself; it can emphasize elements already within it and become a newly powerful version of its old self; or it can deconstruct itself. Indeed, the biographies listed as the canon share much with feminist biography. Each problematized and rethought the relationship between biographer and subject, and each has been greeted with some outrage. Most of them broke ground by reconsidering hallowed lives or by examining the life of what might be called an anti-model, Brutus, Richard Savage, or Strachey's Nightingale; thus, they expanded the subjects and purposes of biography. Each introduced new kinds of evidence and new uses of evidence even as they critiqued and problematized the methods and interpretations of other biographers.

Gerda Lerner cautions that we need to 'treat women as the majority', as Johnson in his strongly class-bound society treated Savage. To treat a person as part of the majority is to be free to discuss candidly the conflicts, 'scandalous conduct', and 'failures' of the subjects. The achieving woman who used to make her biographers uncomfortable because she was 'difficult' or even 'deviant' can now be described with real freedom and with completely different conclusions. When Nancy Milford wrote the story of the Fitzgeralds' marriage from Zelda's point of view, she illustrated the truth of Zelda's own description of herself and her novel as 'the story of myself versus myself' (p. 221), balanced the already-accepted story of Zelda's destructive influence on F. Scott, and represented an individual in a specific time and particular circumstances with mutually poisonous currents flowing in both directions. For instance, Scribner's lets Scott mutilate her novel and uses her royalties to pay his debts. After this biography, a line of biographers demanded reconsideration of female conduct labelled insane, aggressive, and destructive. Shari Benstock, for instance, depicts Edith Wharton as doing what writers do to protect their livelihoods—paying attention to and discussing royalties, publicity, and marketing with her Scribner's editors and making decisions about with whom to publish on rational rather than sentimental grounds. Carolyn Heilbrun, quoting Deborah Cameron's inspired choice of words, depicts the conflict as one between 'being unambiguously a woman' and the 'desire, or fate' of being 'something else' (*Writing a Woman's Life*, 20–1). Had Wharton been 'unambiguously woman', she would have been 'constant', loyal to 'her' publisher, and gentle and retiring—an oblique inquiry, a mumbled wish, a discreet retreat to her bedroom to write—the most private of the private sphere.

In 1973 Richard Ellmann wrote that the form of biography 'is countenancing experiments comparable to those of the novel and poem. It cannot be so mobile as those forms because it is associated with history, and must retain a chronological pattern, though not necessarily a simple one.' He continued, 'The attempt to connect disparate elements, to describe the movements within the mind as if they were movements within the atom, to label the most elusive particles, will become venturesome' (*Golden Codgers*, 15). In 1990 Diane Middlebrook discussed three biographies she described as postmodern and identified one as having created a new author position and a new relationship between biographer and subject in its first sentence: 'Josephine Herbst was dead four years before I heard of her, a handful of ash in an Iowa cemetery . . .'. Middlebrook explains, 'At the outset of the biography's time/space, neither one of them exists: one is dead, the other unborn as author. A profound sense of personal, womanly destiny enlivens this wonderful book. . . . a flexible position from which to coax us into interest in the subject's long life.'[39]

Ellmann was certainly prophetic, and Middlebrook is recognizing the conjunction of today's forces of feminism and postmodernism. Now, more than twenty years after Ellmann's prediction, we stand at a point when biographers are attempting to connect contexts and cultural forces—many long ignored or smoothed out—to personal action and interior life and, most revolutionary of all, to express what biography has always been—the dynamic interaction of lives, those of biographer, subject, and the reader.

6. *Pushing the Envelope*

> There are three rules for writing biography, but, unfortunately, no one knows what they are.
>
> Meryle Secret paraphrasing Somerset Maugham

This chapter begins to play again with the idea of a poetics of biography. In doing so, it takes for granted that every strong biography redefines our conception of the genre's perimeters and possibilities, uses experimental biographies in a novel way, and, in the next chapter, I look at two groups of biographers, British professionals and African-Americans, in order to make some predictions about the form's directions and challenges.

Readers and reviewers have strong opinions about what biography 'is' and should do. Recently I was on a committee to give a prize for the best biography of a Restoration/eighteenth-century figure, and it was nearly immobilized by discussions about whether biography 'had to be' whole life and how ideological it could be. N. John Hall discovered with wonder and outrage that beginning his biography in this way was controversial: 'Anthony Trollope was born on 24 April 1815 at 16 Keppel Street.' One reviewer wrote, 'not an auspicious beginning to a major new treatment of one of England's most prolific and popular novelists', while another wrote, '[how] reassuring it is to read the opening words. . . . That's how a biography should start.'[1] An almost unanimously accepted opinion is captured in this quotation: 'The full power of biography lies, I believe, in the biographer's ability to narrate and explain the subject's conflicts and choices against the backdrop of her [*sic*] own time and place and her specific emotional realities' (Joyce Antler in *The Nation*, 13 July 1992, 59).

Even the desired reading experience is often taken for granted: 'As the story of a life, it is difficult to put down. Written in a lively, accessible style, it moves almost as smoothly as a novel, imperceptibly drawing the reader in, lulling us into a comfortable suspension of disbelief' and 'If an important purpose of biography is to engage readers in the account of how another human being fashioned her life out of the advantages and disadvantages in her path, then [Weisen Cook's] *Eleanor Roosevelt* succeeds admirably' ('First-Ladylike Behavior', *TLS* 21 May 1993, 13). Surveys of readers consistently, even ubiquitously, emphasize that they want 'useful' and 'a good read'. 'Useful' can be historical knowledge, personal self-insight, better acquaintance with an admired, famous person, or understanding of a nation, a region, or an event—or a dozen other things. Elisabeth Young-Bruehl quotes Hannah Arendt's *In a Dark Time* to explain a secret hope many have for biography: 'In dark times we have a right to expect some illumination, and some lives cast a light upon the world' (Mandell, 190). 'Useful' and 'a good read' have been a contradiction for some time—as Puritanism, Victorianism, and modern hedonism have played out, enjoyment and improvement have separated. Yet they are demanded of biography, and lives are to give us inspiring, heartening examples, sturdy models, and escape—simultaneously.

The most basic and one of the most frustrating decisions biographers face is what the biographical form—or reviewers and readers of it—will allow. Distinguished biographers such as Virginia Woolf and Leon Edel have grumbled about the restrictions. Even today when quite experimental biographies have been well received, those who cross the line are often punished by reviewers and sales figures. At this point, I want to look at some extremely experimental biographies in a novel way with the hope of using them to illuminate some fundamental characteristics and purposes of 'biography'.

★

There are biographies that 'push the envelope'. Tom Wolfe made the phrase familiar, as he used it to refer to the limits of a particular aircraft's performance and the pilot's daredevil probing of these outer limits. Wolfe's book was titled *The Right Stuff* (1979), and biographers, like pilots, have to have the right stuff. The origin of 'pushing the envelope' is in nineteenth-century mathematics. In differential calculus, the envelope describes the locus of the ultimate intersections of a series of consecutive curves in a 'family' of curves or surfaces. The envelope of a system is touched by every curve in the system (see figure 1).

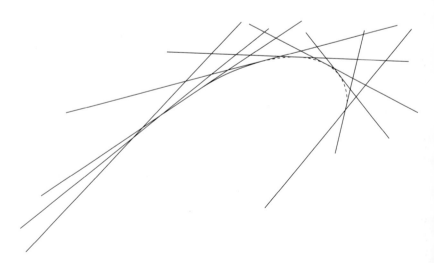

Fig. 1

This figure is a useful visual model for what is most interesting about extremely experimental biographies is the way they exist and to some extent are formed by the ways the 'surfaces' or 'curves' that are characteristics of conventional biographies touch them. Therefore, they often illuminate the most fundamental elements of traditional biography.

In my 'fair sample', the biographies that won major prizes, is an indisputably experimental book, *God: A Biography* by Jack Miles, which won the Pulitzer Prize. Some reviewers judged it 'dazzling', 'a scintillating work of literary scholarship', 'powerful, wide-ranging, thoughtful', and 'a brilliant, audacious book'.[2] I want to start with it and use it as something of a touchstone, for, like so many of the experimental biographies, Miles's book highlights basic aspects of—and, therefore, issues for—biographical practice. For example, Miles asks, 'How can an unbeliever enter the presence of God?' That is, of course, a biographer's question: how can I bring the reader into the presence of Defoe or Churchill or George Washington? And it is, after all, what readers of biography demand, and as many probably begin as pessimistic unbelievers as expecting-to-be-satisfied pilgrims. From the beginning, then, Miles takes on one of the basic requirements for practitioners of the form, and he is true to his promise to maintain steady attention to representations of God's presence.

He uses the Tanakh, the Hebrew Old Testament,[3] for chronological purposes, and, as each biblical character (or person) or group encounters God, Miles teases out what the encounter was like, what the relationship between God and humankind was, and adds components to God's 'personality'. Miles tells us at the beginning that we will discover, as he has, that 'God is . . . an amalgam of several personalities in one character' (p. 6). Quite often, as one might expect in a book that resolutely tries to block out the New Testament, God is judged to be vindictive, irascible, and even 'blood-chilling'.[4] At one point he concludes that the mood of the Bible, and therefore of God, is 'with impressive frequency . . . one of irritability, denunciation, and angry complaint' (p. 132). Near the end of the book he ties together some of his findings about God's personality: God is 'a menacing and, if for that reason alone, an overwhelmingly real figure' in Exodus and finally 'transferred to Ezra and Nehemiah [the prophets of the last two personal books of the Tanakh] and their associates his responsibility to make civil . . . provision for the Jews' (pp. 388–9). As this representative, Nehemiah cursed, flogged, and 'scalped' those who intermarried with other tribes (pp. 389–90).

Although this brutal enforcer seems to be the dominant strain in 'God's' character, the 'amalgam' of personalities has been demonstrated in the 'biography' even as Miles has developed several arguments. Among these are that, over time, God became the God of the Poor and Weak and, most notably for Miles, has developed a relationship with women (Miles carefully notes the first time God speaks directly to a woman) and taken on some feminine characteristics.

Miles began his book by proposing that 'the God of the Bible' is the 'mirror of the West', 'an ideal of human character that stands fast even though, for many, its foundation has been removed' (pp. 4–5). He reminds us that one story of creation has humankind created in God's image and that generations of people on half the globe have attempted to model themselves after and live up to an image of God. In his text, the image of the mirror has an unsettling way of shifting who is looking at whom. Nehemiah seems to be the image of the God of Exodus at one moment, looking in the mirror for his proper image, but at another place in the text God is presented as looking at humankind to see who he is and what he is like. As one reviewer noted, 'In the minds of most believers, [that God created humanity in his image] would be for humanity's sake. But in Miles [sic] biography, it seems, this is rather more for God's sake, that he might have a mirror in which he can . . . get to know himself' (Richard Harries, TLS, 8 December 1995, 26). In fact, Miles tries to have it both ways without developing either or distinguishing clearly which he is imagining at any moment.

Savvy reviewers called God a 'conceit',[5] probably meaning 'an ingenious or witty thought' but possibly 'an elaborate or exaggerated metaphor' (American Heritage Dictionary). Seen as the latter, a conceit of a biography, the objection that this is the obverse of a biography—a book that looks out at the subject rather than attempting to look out from the subject—fades somewhat. As conceit, God has things to reveal to biographers and readers of biography. Above all, Miles has reminded us of how little we can know of the 'person' and how subjective that knowledge is. For most readers, 'God' will probably become more opaque, not less, more the creation of those who report, represent, and interpret his actions and less an independent being whose consciousness, motivations, reactions, and subconscious can be confidently described. As human beings interact with God in each successive book of Miles's Old Testament, contradiction and difference, not coherence and agreement, emerge—just as they do in the notes of biographers interviewing the friends, colleagues, and family members of human biographical subjects.

'God' disappears in the cacophony of reports and interpretations, and the subject of the biography is lost, forgotten, in the attempts to understand and use the reports. The reports must be deployed to do at least one of two things: (1) form a narrative; (2) explain what (who) people have experienced. Miles constructs a narrative that is the shadow of a common Western life course: a young, talkative, involved, 'muscular' God experiences surprises, setbacks, and things beyond his control and becomes the 'ancient of days', silent, remote, and perhaps tired.[6] 'God speaks differently and reveals a different aspect of himself to each of the prophets, in speaking to each he is none the less addressing the same set of events in his own life and the same set of questions.' 'To read these responses is to pass through this crisis in the life of God in the company of the God who is suffering it' (p. 202). After what Miles styles as the mid-life crisis, there is the crisis with Job, and God 'never speaks' again but finally 'accepts' his divided nature, that he is the 'tender solicitous husband of Second Isaiah' *and* the 'sword-in-hand butcher of Joshua' (p. 408). Miles argues, and we feel the strain of the wheels and gears of that argument, that God's contacts with humankind have shaped his sense of himself, which produces the being we experience and have experienced. That every bit of evidence is mediated, transmitted, and the impossibility of getting inside another's mind and the ways biographers pretend to do it are laid bare.

Equally useful for those who would understand biography is thinking about his reference to mirrors. Just as Western people made God an ideal of charac-ter, nations have modelled themselves on and understood each other through the great, lasting subjects of their biographies: Confucius, Tsar Peter the Great, Richard the Lion Heart, and Simon Bolivar. They look in a mirror and see, or hope to see, themselves in the Queen Mother's or Jacqueline Onassis's image. In times of national crisis biographies are often commissioned—and what is commissioned is a way of reading a country's mood, aspirations, and ideal men and women. Many biographies are underwritten by grants or advances, and which are chosen is something of an index to the kinds and range of society's 'interests'—John Wilkes or Lord Bute? Lenin or Stalin? Andrew Jackson or Lyndon Johnson? Malcolm X or Martin Luther King? Madonna or James Levine? Fidel Castro or Che Guevara? In positing both that we cannot 'give our history away' and that we feel a 'tremor of self-recognition' when confronted with 'the protagonist of the Bible' (p. 4), Miles reminds us that biography has shaped us and that we look to it for models of what we might be, that we project qualities onto Montgomery or George Washington and we think, as Britons or Americans, we imitate him.

★

Miles's book resolutely develops the idea that God is an 'amalgam' of person-alities and makes obvious that a variety of people testify and disagree about God's nature and character. Therefore it exposes the contingent nature of biog-raphers' key decisions about the presentation of personality—who will be believed? whose experiences and interpretations privileged? how will contra-dictions and ambiguities be explained?

Equally contingent decisions are made about contexts and about the fullness with which the parts of the model of circles around and within the subject out-lined in chapter 6 are discussed. A classic experimental biography that uses the more common metaphor of collage rather than amalgam, which can mean alloy as well as combination, is Alethea Hayter's *A Sultry Month*.[7] She explains, 'My object—like that of the Pop Artist who combines scraps of Christmas cards, of cinema posters and of the Union Jack to make a picture—has been to create a pattern from a group of familiar objects' (p. 11), and reviewers have called it 'a sort of collage of anecdote, description, and quotation'. Hayter, author of *Mrs. Browning: A Poet's Work and its Setting*, which won the Royal Society of Literature Award for 1962, knows what a biography is and deploys the biographers' best tools and strategies. On one level, the book is a biography of Benjamin Robert Haydon, the painter and author of, among other things, *Lectures on Painting and Design*. On another, it is a portrait of a group of writers, politicians, intellectuals, and other public people and their activities and interactions—Robert Browning, the Thomas Carlyles, Elizabeth Barrett, William Wordsworth, the actors Fanny Kemble and William Macready, Sir Robert Peel, the Duke of Wellington, and others. Thus, an imaginative presentation of contexts and relationships, of related and also comparative lives, is economically and effectively accomplished.

The biography is 'about' 1846, and the central event is Haydon's grisly suicide in the sultry month. The narrative moves inevitably towards it, peaks with the event and the flurry of comment and fascination with news reports, and ends with the Brownings' marriage and a final chapter on Haydon, which lays him to rest by assessing his religious convictions and quotes his epitaph. In many ways, this is an extremely self-conscious and artful book. For instance, it begins with an account of Haydon taking three trunks of papers and five portraits to Elizabeth Barrett because he is afraid they will be seized for debt. Thus, the narrative begins and ends with Haydon and Barrett.

Among the paintings were those of Wordsworth, the Duke of Wellington, and Haydon's wife and son (p. 15). Hayter uses such details thematically, assuring that, for example, the central importance to Haydon of the people in the portraits emerges gradually and that they as well as he become known. Haydon notes at the time he delivered the portraits that he had kept Wellington's hat and boots; later we learn that he pestered the duke for money and more articles of his clothing and 'even got at the Duke's valet' (p. 43). The day after Haydon's suicide, the duke sent to his widow for the hat. Among the most moving details in the book is evidence of the relationship between Haydon and Wordsworth; in 1815, Wordsworth sent Haydon a sonnet which 'was a support and inspiration to him' for the rest of his life ('High is our calling, Friend!') (pp. 140–1). Of such contrasts are the human contexts of Haydon's life made.

Hayter makes her collage out of the strongest of the biographer's tools, but she uses them with flair and unusual freedom. She marshals documentary evidence and ideal witnesses: 'Nothing in this book is invented', she writes in the Foreword. 'Every incident, every sentence of dialogue, every gesture, the food, the flowers, the furniture all are taken from the contemporary letters, diaries, and reminiscences of the men and women concerned, nearly all of them professional writers with formidable memories and highly trained descriptive skills' (p. 11). Yet she combines them and frequently works by inference in, perhaps, the manner the National Trust brought together objects to re-create Paul MacCartney's recently opened boyhood terraced house. The result is a richness of detail, a wealth of textured objects, beyond anything strict adherence to concrete evidence of contents of rooms.

Hayter can set telling, large scenes as well, ones that economically document the tastes of the time and contextualize Haydon and his work in horrendously pointed ways. In the hope of patronage or royal appointment, Haydon rented a hall for exhibition of his greatest works, mostly 'grand', huge historical paintings, and his friends—like most of London—chose to go see General Tom Thumb, displayed by P. T. Barnum in another hall in the same building. Twelve thousand people went to see Thumb, while four people came to a reception to which Haydon had invited four hundred. Later he was described standing outside the door of his exhibit 'with a general air of dilapidated power. There was something fierce and bitter in the expression of his face, as he glanced across to the groups hurrying to see Tom Thumb' (p. 22). In spite of the cast of better-known characters whose own lives were filled with drama that summer, Hayter keeps Haydon in the foreground as the central presence, and readers come away with a coherent idea of what he and his life were like: 'a furious, hopeful, urgent, preposterous man, forever painting his huge, unsaleable historical-allegorical canvases while the bailiffs took their familiar place at the door'.[8]

The collage works. Because Haydon left letters written on the final day of his life and twenty-six diaries, Hayter can move smoothly into his thoughts and back out to external events and to his acquaintances' reactions. This does not mean that she closes doors with answers that simplify cause–effect. For instance, we are shown that Haydon writes as often about the anniversary of his first imprisonment for debt, the suicides of other people, and the need to provide for his family as he does about the intense embarrassment and disappointment of seeing Tom Thumb preferred to his painting. Therefore, the reader leaves with a sense of the converging of effects and, above all, of the complexity of the sad, violent act he committed. The scraps from other people's lives, activities, social gatherings, and writings re-create Haydon's world—both that to which he was admitted and that beyond him—and their knowledge of him and their avid sharing of information and reading of such things as the coroner's report fill out the biography and give a persuasive picture of how he looked, acted, and lived. The Brownings' happy saga provides a backdrop for his desperation, and brief comparisons with, for instance, Keats are part of the themes of death and of the artistic life. Rightly, *A Sultry Month* has been praised for 'kaleidoscopic resourcefulness', using 'contrasting' pieces of evidence that 'offset' each other and yet giving a fascinating, smooth pattern.[9] In miniature, it is a tour of some of the biographer's most useful contextualizing tools put in the service of explanation and interpretation.

★

Biographers and Truth. Does it matter that Hayter furnishes the Barrett home with the right but perhaps not the exact artefacts? How imaginatively is she allowed to move from letters and papers to create scenes between Barrett and Browning? Which is more important, truth or how you tell it? And what is truth—what happened or how it felt? A woman I know was writing her memoirs, and all was going well until she reached the point of telling how her mother died. 'Bumped' (or pushed), and not for the first time, by the proprietor of a group residence for elderly people, her hip was broken, and she died from complications during surgery. No matter that the daughters had begged the mother to live in any of their (distant) homes. No matter that the mother had many pleasures and happy pastimes in her last years and even on the day of her death. At this time, that chapter of the memoirs is written as fiction, as a story with the free use of the techniques of a story, and, since my friend can't know everything that happened, some of it is undoubtedly fiction. She insists that no other method allowed her to capture the right tone and to express the unbearable, to avoid the temptation to drown the memoir in rage, grief, outrage, or unremitting regret that would sabotage the tone of the whole. It also conveys what happened and in a peculiar way maintains the convincing, apparently objective narrative of external events that characterizes the rest of the memoirs and balances the description of the writer's thoughts and reactions.

Human beings habitually explain, clarify, communicate, and introduce the emotional dimension with analogy, anecdote, metaphor, example, and story. Sometimes unnatural means are needed for life. What are biographers allowed? Judith Chernaik, author of *The Lyrics of Shelley* wrote *Love's Children* as a reconstruction of sixteen months in the lives of Fanny Imlay, Mary Godwin, Jane (Claire) Clairmont, and Harriet Westbrook.[10] Using fiction and real journal entries and letters, she has each woman speak for herself and, as they write to each other, discover new information about their pasts, and reflect on events and others' actions, they piece together whole-life 'biographies'. These biographies conform to what we know about the women's lives, and the letters and other writings dramatize the temperaments usually associated with them. In fact, the portraits of Shelley, Byron, and William Godwin seem more subjective than those of the women, although the fiction is created around and for them. Like Hayter's book, a kaleidoscope of evidence sources re-creates the daily lives of the principals, and death provides the central moment in the book. Fanny Imlay's and Harriet Westbrook's suicides occur at the midpoint, one on 9 October and one on 9 November 1816, and in both cases the coroners' inquests returned the verdict, 'found dead'. Soon after Shelley and Mary Godwin marry. The subsequent narration of their lives uses recurrent memories and talk of Fanny and Harriet to develop and sustain the biographies up to the point in 1817 when the Shelleys, Claire, and the children are packing to return to Italy.

Chernaik's book blends fictional techniques, many used to depict complicated emotions felt by the women towards each other, and 'hard' biographical evidence. Titled in Great Britain after the poem for which Shelley was prosecuted, *Mab's Daughters: Shelley's Wives and Lovers*, it takes a step beyond the gossipy lives of, for instance, actresses that have been read by the educated general public throughout the twentieth century. Indeed, Chernaik comments that gossip about the four women 'provided material for a dozen novels'. Filled with 'good stories', myths, casual speculation, generalizations from the lives of others in the same time period and occupations, and racy narration, such books still entertain.

More commonly produced today than books like Chernaik's are texts that depart markedly from the historical and veridical. For example, Frances Sherwood's *Vindication* is based on the life of Fanny and Mary Godwin's mother, Mary Wollstonecraft. Although the plot outline follows Wollstonecraft's life quite closely and occasional passages from her writings are used, the sensibility of the heroine and the expressions of racial, sexual, and class tensions are twentieth, not eighteenth, century. Gilbert Imlay is described as 'brown as a Negro', Wollstonecraft is almost forced to perform oral sex in an alley, and a list of ways Imlay and Wollstonecraft made love is annotated with visual and aural images of the violence of the French Revolution taking place beneath their window. Later Wollstonecraft abuses their baby Fanny and confronts Imlay with this dialogue: 'Nice of you to come home, Gil.' Wollstonecraft's radical, unconventional, scandalous, path-breaking life is dressed in twentieth-century novelese and commodified.

Yet even these books illuminate the practices and purposes of biographers. That the plots highlight the sensational and that the descriptions of feelings and motives are blatantly imagined reminds us that biographers take advantage of dramatic moments, identify and spend more words on events and actions that have significance and special interest to the time in which they are written, and that they always speculate, always make reasoned guesses about the emotions and decisions of their subjects. Once again, the writer's theory of personality and the beliefs about human nature determine crucial interpretations—obviously in the fictions, often invisibly in traditional biographies.

Love's Children is also in the family of the popular group biographies. Collections of the lives of generals, inventors, explorers, etc., have long been published, but the feminist movement gave new interest and energy to the form. As Linda Wagner-Martin says, 'When writers view women as members of differently defined families, they change the category of "family biography" '. 'The larger notion of a community formed by women who share interests and work, or simply like each other, has influenced the choice of many recent women biographers.'[11] Books such as Gerda Lerner's *The Grimké Sisters from South Carolina* (1967), Margaret Marsh's *Anarchist Women* (1981), Shari Benstock's pioneering *Women of the Left Bank, Paris, 1910–1940* (1986), and Mary Ann Caw's *Women of Bloomsbury: Virginia, Vanessa, and Carrington* (1990) have been followed by a host of creative, stimulating groupings.

The Limits of Sisterhood: The Beecher Sisters on Women's Rights and Women's Sphere by Jeanne Boydston, Mary Kelley, and Anne Margolis (1988) and Antonia Fraser's *Wives of Henry VIII* (1993) suggest the myriad forms this kind of book can take. *The Limits of Sisterhood* is a mixed presentation biography. The authors use a chronology, summary essays, and carefully excerpted quotations from the letters, private papers, and publications of the sisters and other family members. The book opens with a strong and seamless essay on how the Beecher sisters were like the women of their time, why they are important, and how they 'generalized' from their experiences to the lot of American women as a group and how that inspired and shaped their work. From this point on, the stories of the women's lives are threaded with themes including variations of female power, the original and revisionary ways the sisters made the ideology of domesticity an influential entrée into the public sphere, and how they used print and education to take their place in the Beecher family honour roll of reformers. Many recent books, primarily by historians, such as this one limit biographical information in the interest of demonstrating women's entrance into new domains of society or their collective action and impact. Examples are Ellen Fitzpatrick's *Endless Crusade: Women Social Scientists and Progressive Reform* (1990), Carole Turbin's *Working Women of Collar City: Gender, Class, and Community in Troy, New York* (1991), and Nina Baym's *American Women Writers and the Work of History, 1790–1860* (1995). Collections of short lives such as Penina Migdal Glazer and Miriam Slater's *Unequal Colleagues: The Entrance of Women into the Professions, 1890–1940* with the same goals have also proliferated.[12]

Sometimes it seems that Carolyn Heilbrun's *Writing a Woman's Life* provided marching orders for women's biographers, and collections such as *Significant Others: Creativity and Intimate Partnerships* addresses her call for the stories of marriages between two people with extraordinary talent.[13] Extending the idea of 'marriage' and union as Wagner-Martin does allows the authors of the essays in *Significant Others* to include a variety of talented pairs—Vanessa Bell and Duncan Grant, Jasper Johns and Robert Rauschenberg, Anaïs Nin and Henry Miller, among others.

All of these biographies are experimental in their treatments of relationships and in the balances they try to strike between traditional biographical inquiries and the new issues and expectations of late twentieth-century biography. For example, Brenda Maddox followed the trajectory Heilbrun described by following *Nora* (1988), the life of James Joyce's wife, with *D. H. Lawrence: The Story of a Marriage* (1994), which won the 1994 Whitbread prize. She writes, 'I have chosen to examine [Lawrence's] life through the greatest contradiction in it: his marriage, taking it not as just another aspect of Lawrence but as the encompassing whole . . . I have tried to capture the living quality of this marriage . . .' (p. 10). She demonstrates that Frieda von Richthofen Weekley Lawrence saw herself as an achieving woman who desired intellectual accomplishment, which she saw as difficult because 'people try to keep us women away by force from everything "brainy"', and that her influence on Lawrence's work was pervasive. In Maddox's account of the strange, almost violent marriage that lasted nearly thirty-one years, the Lawrences fought horribly, said and wrote shocking things about each other, but found the other as necessary as air and food.

Maddox gives us a Lawrence who before he met Frieda was already showing signs of the health problems that would kill him and whose writings, 'savagely sexual and angry', (p. 49) mirrored his moods. He wrote to one woman, 'Some savage in me would like to taste your blood' (p. 66). He already feared that he had tuberculosis, the disease that would send him 'with half-eaten lungs, [to wander] the world, determined like Keats and Stevenson (of whose fates he was well aware), to live to the full a life he knew would be short' (p. 15). Once married, Maddox never separates the couple. Because Lawrence was a writer working at home, he and Frieda were always together. They took walks together, wrote joint letters,[14] painted bowls together, read Italian—did all of the things together that many couples do separately. In some ways, Frieda represents the problem that the less public-figure partner faces in a collaborative marriage. Regardless of her intelligence and her contributions to his art and to conversations, many people wanted to brush her aside and ridiculed or resented her for her 'tedious insistence that she was just as important as her husband' (p. 208). For instance, she annoyed his friends by answering questions they posed to him. Maddox writes about this strain while many other biographers treat it respectfully but extremely sparely as Field does when he records that Mrs Nabokov insisted to him that her life was separate from Vladimir's and interesting in its own right (Nabokov, *His Life in Part*, 180).

Such experiments recast biographical treatments of individuality, autonomy, and personal development. In Maddox's biography, one of the most important keys to understanding the Lawrences and their marriage is the desire to remain free, independent people. Before he met Frieda, Lawrence had once written, 'I *cannot* marry save where I am not held' (p. 73). In middle age, he gave a bridegroom the advice to 'keep the centre of himself always alone' and beat his wife should she cross him (p. 325). By 1907, while still married to Weekley, Frieda was described by her lover the psychoanalyst Otto Gross as 'the erotic partner of his dreams' (p. 99), one 'free from the code of chastity, from Christianity, from democracy and all that accumulated filth . . . *free through her own strength*' (p. 104). Over and over they demonstrate the strength of that element in their characters. Held together by the life of the mind and intense sexual attraction, Lawrence and Frieda seem to fascinate others as much as they fascinate themselves. Lawrence once wrote that 'a storm of desire for her . . . shook and swept him at varying intervals all his life long' (p. 118), and Frieda wrote, 'it's fearfully exciting when he writes and I watch while it comes and it is a thrill' (p. 135). Lawrence wrote unceasingly and they discussed his work unceasingly, he read her passages and they fought over them. As Frieda wrote after Lawrence's death: 'His life and his writing was one—and I say to everybody . . . hats off to our relationship! Bring off the same if you can!' (p. 510). This is the kind of thing that Heilbrun recognized and urged biographers to explore and portray, and it fundamentally changes the kinds of evidence privileged and the ways the narrative is structured. New issues are posed for readers such as whether a biography can be true and fair to two people and whether the fundamental questions that are brought to biography can even be addressed in such books. Do we, for instance, learn less or more about the genesis of Lawrence's greatest novels? Less or more about the stages of his life? Less or more about Frieda as an individual and as a woman of a specific historical context?

★

It is now quite fashionable to add the word 'biography' to the titles of books; in some cases the aim is obviously commercial gain but in many others it points to the usefulness of biographical methods, strategies, and inquiries. *Cod: A Biography of the Fish that Changed the World* is not, of course, a biography, but it carefully points out that it is taking up selected, specific biographical conventions and exploiting them in creative ways. The chapters on the early history of cod fishing (a novel kind of genealogy) and on the spawning, habitat, birth, feeding habits, behaviour, and lifespan (a 'life') come closest. However, Mark Kurlansky's book brings into focus the distinctive character of the writing of biography: it is interdisciplinarity in the extreme; it requires wide sources of evidence, awareness of all the contexts and the impacts each context had, both immediately and over the course of the subject's life. Among the disciplines Kurlansky has drawn upon intelligently are climatology, maritime commercial law, cookery, genetics, history, actuarial studies (the death rate of fishermen remains horrendous), ship building, the science of freezing food, and, of course, ichthyology. He is especially good at describing the importance of cod in various cultures at different time periods. With the kind of easy grace that only mastery of a subject and narrative skill gives, for instance, he describes the impact of cod shortages on modern British fish and chips shops and the importance of the protein and salt in imported cod to the West Indian slaves of the seventeenth century (15,000 slaves died between 1780 and 1787 when Great Britain barred the new United States from trade with their Caribbean colonies).

With a biographer's use of startling facts, intriguing speculations and well-narrated short chapters, Kurlansky moves the cod through history. As in good biographies, the categories of knowledge are impressive, even panoramic and kaleidoscopic. His prose is spare and clear whether he is explaining that cod produce a protein that 'functions like anti-freeze' when they are in freezing water but which causes them to 'instantly crystallize' when hauled out by fishermen, or that by 1550 sixty per cent of all fish eaten in Europe was cod, or that the carved wooden cod was moved to the new Massachusetts state house in 1895 wrapped in an American flag, carried on a bier by three representatives escorted by the sergeant-at-arms, and greeted by the legislators rising to their feet and applauding. He inserts cod recipes dating back to the Middle Ages and uses fairly lengthy quotations and epigraphs for chapters.

Biographies, of course, have themes, and biographers have strong opinions, some about historical events and the people who played key roles in them. Kurlansky's interpretative strategies, all common to biography, emphasize them in unusual ways. For instance, one of the most important stories is cod against man, and in the chapter in which Kurlansky explains the biological habits of the fish, including that they swim with their mouths open and eat anything and everything, he summarizes, 'If ever there was a fish made to endure, it is the Atlantic cod. . . . But it has among its predators man, an open-mouthed species greedier than cod' (p. 45). At intervals we are reminded that a 'middling sized' cod 'is amazingly prolific'; allegedly Leewenhoek counted 9,384,000 eggs in one (p. 109). The nature of its enemy unfolds. Chapter 5 opens with a quotation from Edmund Burke that describes the New England fishermen's industry and determination as unprecedented, never 'carried . . . to the extent which it has been pushed by this recent people' (p. 78). Near-worshipers of the fish, placing its image on coins, state seals, and public buildings, the New Englanders swell in the narrative in wealth and unruly independence. Kurlansky points out that human beings were an 'indispensable commodity in all this trade'. By that he means the slaves labouring on sugar plantations and in need of salt and protein to manage sixteen-hour work days in tropical heat. 'West India Cure' becomes the name for the inferior, quickly (and poorly) cured cod that anchored one of the corners of New England's own triangle trade, slaves became one of the commodities carried on American trading ships. Later he points out that cod created capitalists wherever it went and reinforces his story of the importance of the 'cod aristocrats' to the American Revolution with the often-hilarious, mock-analogous account of the three Cod Wars between Great Britain and Iceland.

Like all biography, this one moves inexorably towards death. Begun when cod were so numerous that weighted baskets lowered without bait would come up filled, defining what might be called the mid-life of cod when men could write, 'Harvey could see the glimmering cod below, swimming slowly in droves, biting as steadily as they swam' (p. 111), and concluding in a time when cod are the object of scientific study carried out in ways that tauntingly mimic the fisherman's former work, the book traces the life of the cod trade, personifying the fish as the trade. Perhaps the most original touch is the way the author uses recipes; there are many from all over the world and from many centuries, and cumulatively they make an absolutely persuasive case about how many people have loved preparing and eating it. Yet the scramble for cod, the devastating limitations on fishing grounds and size of catches, and the hard evidence of the dangerously shrinking size and numbers of cod provide the picture of an ageing fish (trade). Kurlansky provides us with a biographer's dramatic closing (a kind of death) scene. Fittingly, the requiem is a recipe from Newfoundland, one of the greatest cod fishing areas in history, with this introduction: 'Stella's is a popular, cozy little restaurant on the St. John's waterfront. Miraculously, one day the restaurant was able to buy enough large, thick, cod fillets . . . to put this old standard back on the menu for one night' (p. 275).

For quite different reasons, Virginia Woolf wrote the life of a non-human creature and created a minor classic in *Flush: A Biography* (1933). Woolf seems to revel in creating the limited point of view of a dog. Flush knows and understands less than the reader, and that triggers doubts about the near-omniscience biographers confer upon their human subjects and often on themselves, and certainly about the ability to imagine the sensibility of another. What we understand and how we explain decisions and actions are quite different from our knowledge and experience during the immediate situation. Flush's limited ability to remember, to contextualize, and to project the future is an important and delightful way for Woolf to create a dog's point of view. Sometimes biographers explain what their subjects could not know or were yet to discover, but thinking along these lines about what Flush reveals about biographical subjects might introduce new and rightly complicated expectations. I came to wish that David McCullough had given us more of the human condition of 'now I see through a glass darkly' as Truman pondered dropping the atomic bombs. Should we demand that biographers recognize 'the accidental life' more often? assess more carefully what information their subjects had at critical moments? search more diligently for evidence about how an imagination of the future, projections of the implications of various choices, influenced decisions? We have developed formidable skills in linking subjects' pasts to their decisions and states of mind: can we be more alert to and increase our ability to factor in the aspect of life that Samuel Johnson described as causing the most misery and the vainest hopes: imaginings of the future and the consequences of actions?

The point at which *Flush* is most gripping is when he is kidnapped, and his owner, Elizabeth Barrett, is trying to persuade those who love her that rescuing Flush is more important than refusing to enrich the kidnappers. Her decision to go to the dognappers herself is an emotional *tour de force*. The languid, near invalid largely ignores the dangers that such a trip into the social underworld held for a woman, but it emphasizes her fear for her dog, her frustration with her family, and her agonized sense of the calendar and the dognappers' deadline. The vividly rendered squalor in which Flush is being kept is in stark contrast to her world of luxury. The sensuous experience of both places—smells, light, fabrics, hellish noise versus decorous, subdued quiet—remind us of Virginia Woolf's power as a novelist and how infrequently biographers bring into play all five senses. Here, as in many biographies, we are reminded of the importance of setting, the pleasures of skilled descriptions of specific places, and the contributions they make to understanding the time period and the most significant themes and characterization in the book.

The notes to *Flush* give scholarly sources but also insight into Woolf's artistic decisions. She writes, 'As a matter of fact, Flush was stolen three times; but the unities seem to require that the three stealings shall be compressed into one. The total sum paid by Miss Barrett to the dog-stealer was £20' (p. 105). The tongue-in-cheek reference to the unities combined with the utter specificity of the biographer (three stealings, £20) captures a mood and method biographers often experience as they write. A few essayists in her own time played with reviewing the book as if it were a biography. David Garnett points out a few points vulnerable to carping over inaccuracies and names the size of Flush's first home and the kind of paving on the walks in Regent's Park.[15] He asks tongue-in-cheek for more evidence with a few incidents.

Woolf takes the most obvious licence with the account of Flush's death—he races through the Italian streets to leap on Barrett Browning's sofa where she is reading. Browning and he look at each other nose to nose, 'her face with its wide mouth and its great eyes and its heavy curls . . . still oddly like his' (p. 102). Here is a sudden variant on the rich suggestiveness of mirror images to biography. She thinks of her poem on him, she returns to reading, and he dies quietly at her feet. Woolf's note reads, 'It is certain that Flush died; but the date and manner . . . are unknown' (p. 111). Only here, perhaps, in the improbable run and the final communion does Woolf deliberately elevate the means of the fiction writer over the tools of the biographer. In doing so, however, she throws into relief some of the least confessed aspects of biography, its speculative nature and reliance on fictionality. Woolf began *Flush* as repartee with her friend Lytton Strachey, and, as Garnett points out, in the last lines she speaks 'in the unforgettable accents' of Strachey and re-creates his point of view and voice, one that is inside the subject's mind but with his own voice firmly inserted into the narrative. Flush becomes, Garnett says, 'the first animal to become an Eminent Victorian'. Woolf, who would publish the life of Roger Fry seven years later, was already taking a hard look at Strachey's large, masculine 'I' that could obscure letting biographical subjects speak for themselves.

★

Literary biography is always to some extent 'about' the individual creative intelligence, a topic in which readers are perennially interested but one consistently critiqued and even neglected today. As the idea of 'author' has become increasingly problematized, writers less a subject of study than 'texts' and language, as attacks on 'positivist' history and our ability to 'know' or even 'reconstruct' the past have gained widespread acceptance, literary biography and its contributions to human lives have become both more isolated and more precious. Another experimental biography that pushes the envelope can be read as a clandestine way to return the author to the study of literary works. *Biographies of Books* edited by James Barbour and Tom Quirk, takes as its 'conceit' studies of how ten American novels came to be what they are. As Quirk says in the introduction, historians and critics on the left and right have 'obscured' the fact that literature is the product of the human imagination, which 'is as notoriously variable and unpredictable as the products of its efforts'.[16]

Weaving nature and nurture together, each contributor puts together a story of the genesis, development, and mature personality of each book. If genealogy (literary roots and influences) is sketchy, what we learn about the authors, their compositional methods, and their engagements with events, editors, family, personal pasts, and other shaping forces more than compensates. The stories of Edith Wharton's *House of Mirth* and of John Steinbeck's *Grapes of Wrath* are very different but illustrate the benefits of this use of biographical practices. Candace Waid gives great attention to Wharton's methods of composition and revision, which, among other things, reveal her building confidence, the effect of serialization, and her increasing commitment to serious social commentary. In contrast to Wharton's painstaking revisions and growing seriousness of purpose, Steinbeck began his novel burning with fury over the plight of migrant workers and wrote in a white heat—all 200,000 words written in approximately 93 sittings. DeMott argues, 'What Steinbeck had witnessed . . . called forth every ounce of his moral indignation, social anger, and empathy . . . provided [the novel's] haunting spiritual urgency' (p. 217).

One of the greatest strengths of the biographical method is its reliance on mosaic—the use of evidence drawn from many domains and the assembling of it into coherent, even highly original patterns. Waid, for instance, points out that Wharton was translating a play at the same time as she was 'staging the scenes of her novel' (p. 167) and that Wordsworth's 'She Was a Phantom of Delight', a poem 'prominent' in her mother's commonplace book and often cited as a vision of the ideal woman to girls of her generation, was important at numerous stages of the composition of *House of Mirth* (pp. 172–5). DeMott brings into play the greater political activism of Steinbeck's wife, his interactions with editors and film-makers, the 'vicious', 'mean' book that was *Grapes of Wrath*'s forerunner and opposite face, and, most important, his experiences working in Visalia, California, where migrant families marooned by floods and abandoned by social services starved and died of smallpox and dysentery. The mosaic method of the biographer leads DeMott to some inspired insights. During the time Steinbeck was writing of the migrants' desire for land, he and his wife were negotiating for a ranch they wanted very much. 'I want that ranch', he wrote in his journal on 13 July, and he started a chapter that philosophizes 'the obsessive quest for a home' (pp. 215–16). By juxtaposing such evidence and putting pieces of evidence from various domains next to each other, he persuades us that much of Steinbeck's novel comes 'from a place far deeper than the intellect . . . from the visceral center of the writer's being'. Writers of literary biographies could learn much from this argument.

In a book devoted to creativity, it is not surprising that the editors and many contributors are deeply concerned with the way literature 'makes meaning'. A good example is Stephen Tanner's essay on Ken Kesey's *One Flew Over the Cuckoo's Nest*. He reminds us that Kesey was ahead of his time in expressing the oppositions that came to drive so many of the political and cultural movements of the late 1960s and early 1970s. Tapping into what were then 'the fears and desires that flow just beneath the level of articulation', Kesey brought to the surface, among other things, the longing for an endless West—an unexplored natural space with evergreens, sparkling rivers, and the promise of a fresh start for the strong and brave—and the fear of the Combine, the homogenizing, dulling forces of a technological society. As one of Kesey's friends wrote after reading part of the manuscript: 'the Combine. You're trying to give a name to something that has no name. It's an emotion, a complacency, and a dulling of the senses that we're fighting . . . Everyone that reads with any intelligence knows what you're writing about' (quoted p. 299).

Tanner does a convincing job of showing us how *One Flew Over the Cuckoo's Nest* came to be the 'personality' it is. Over and over he shows two influences coming together, sparking not an amalgamation but something dynamic, new and urgent. For instance, the Kesey family's westward migration, its American Protestant values, and Oregon landscape meet Kesey's experiences in San Francisco around the time the North Beach Beat poets and Jack Kerouac were ascending. Popular culture elements—cowboys, comic books, frontier humour, Batman and superhero movies—and his university education which included creative writing courses at Stanford with Malcolm Cowley, former editor of the *New Republic* and author of *Exile's Return*, are an equally dynamic pairing. Kesey's compassionate work in a mental hospital and his much-better known experimentation with mind-altering drugs (sometimes as a volunteer in a drug experiment) contribute powerful elements of the novel. This section of the essay is a good example of how complex the imagination and creative process are and how great the challenges of communicating them. Tanner tells us that Kesey has said he wrote the first three pages of *Cuckoo's Nest*, which remained almost unchanged, after swallowing eight little cactus plants: 'from this first spring I drew all the passion and perception the narrator spoke with during the ten months' writing that followed' (p. 310). Yet the 'passion and perception' was already there, Tanner shows us, in Kesey's earlier stories, in a first unpublished novel, in his work in the psychiatric hospital, and in his reactions to events, such as the building of a dam on Celilo Indian land. Rightly, he concludes the section with another Kesey quotation: '*drugs* didn't create those descriptions any more than Joyce's *eyeglasses* created *Ulysses*' (p. 311). What part drugs played, thus, has an important but not dominant, a verified but not specifically identifiable, place in the genesis and creation of the novel.

Some of these experimental biographies deliberately choose the methods of one discipline and pose the question: what happens to biography and what will we see when a single powerful lens is used? Waid, for instance, draws deeply on her skills as a literary critic to demonstrate Wharton's relationship to the biblical quotation from which she draws her title. Waid explains that Wharton refused to allow her publisher to print Ecclesiastes 7: 4 as an epigraph because she believed it would limit the resonance of the title (pp. 176–9). Using other writings by Wharton, she points out that Wharton came to connect her novel to immediate social forces: 'a frivolous society can acquire dramatic significance only through what its frivolity destroys. Its tragic implication lies in its power of debasing people and ideals' (quoted p. 168).

In contrast, Steinbeck wanted the entire text of Harriet Beecher Stowe's 'Battle Hymn of the Republic' printed before his novel. DeMott uses literary methods to weave its importance into his biography of *Grapes of Wrath*. For instance, Steinbeck's prose seems to feed off of and march to it; at one point, he wrote, 'There is a crime here that goes beyond denunciation. There is a sorrow that weeping cannot symbolize. . . . In the souls of the people the grapes of wrath are filling and growing heavy, growing heavy for the vintage' (p. 210 and see p. 189). In another place, he wrote, 'What some people find in religion a writer may find in his craft . . . a kind of breaking through to glory' (quoted p. 187).

God can be written, Miles says, because God can be treated as a literary character, and a number of biographers have tried to solve problems endemic to the form or to avoid hard decisions by falling back on that ploy or drawing upon strategies for literary analysis in other ways. Miles argues that the literary character most like God is Hamlet, surprised victim of the 'slings and arrows of outrageous fortune' (p. 327), a 'contradictory' character trapped 'within its contradictions' (p. 408), and prone to changing his mind and even failing to act. The Bible is often treated as literature, of course, and seeing each successive biblical figure and prophet as a 'reader of God' offering an interpretation might have made *God* a better book. After all, not all of them saw him as Hamlet. These 'readers', each a part of specific socio-historical moments and with desires, needs, and individual temperaments and personalities, not only create an image of God but are drawing upon images of deities and of humankind.[17] Because Miles is inadequately alert to this fact, many places in the text are jarring as they seem to be blatant imaginings of what God, 'his rhetorically constrained hero, has in his head' (Hamel, *Judaism*, 379). Of course, imagining what subjects have in their heads is the biographer's job, but those imaginings are best founded on evidence. The *actions* of people are notoriously untrustworthy guides to thinking and even motive, and many people believe more of the events and actions in the Old Testament are more mythic or symbolic than Miles admits (for instance, he argues that the exodus is based on a real event). The accounts of what others said, especially when those words were quickly used for political, religious, or legal purposes, are also considered suspicious sources.

Miles is, however, playing a game, and he has set the rules, just as Chernaik, Sherwood, and DeMott have. Among the rules is that we must pretend his departing from biographical methods to embrace old-fashioned literary ones creates a useful heuristic tool. Sometimes this happens, but more often, as in this case, there are delightful ironies. For instance, Miles acts as if there is an agreed-upon interpretation of Hamlet. Far from it. Shakespeare's Hamlet, David Garrick's Hamlet, and the Romantic period's Hamlet are as different from each other as the representations by Sir John Gielgud and Sir Richard Burton. No wonder the God of the centuries past in the Old Testament is found to have contradictory personality elements. God is more like Hamlet (and all literary characters) than Miles knows, and biographers to some extent always create their subjects into figures meaningful to themselves and their times, images that mirror both fears of what we are and aspirations of what we might be.

The 'surfaces' that these experimental biographers introduce into the 'family' of surfaces that is 'biography' highlight the situation of conventional biographers. The 'amalgam' of personalities and the 'collage' of what survives of a life and a time must be forged into 'a person' and a narrative. If the biographer's imagination and willingness to use the methods of playwrights and novelists are more obvious in these experimental biographies, it does not mean that the best conventional biographies are not as imaginative—or even more so because they must achieve the same effects while wearing heavier shackles. If the opinions, philosophies, and biases of these biographers are unusually obviously influential, that alerts readers to the need to seek those same infusions and influences beneath the surfaces of mainstream biography. Every strong biography pushes the envelope, and the surfaces each one adds as a possibility for the form and a tool for other biographers imaginatively expand the ways to work with amalgam and collage.

7. Eyeing the Future: British Professionals and African-American Academics

> We are a people. A people do not throw their geniuses away. If they do, it is our duty as witnesses for the future to collect them again for the sake of our children. If necessary, bone by bone.
>
> Alice Walker

Two groups of biographers seem to be signs of the future of biography, of the form's directions and challenges. The first are the British professionals, men and women commanding huge advances and headline-making marketing campaigns who are pushing the envelope by using pronounced narrative methods to write the lives of quite traditional subjects (Samuel Coleridge, Jonathan Swift, William Blake, Samuel Johnson, Charles Dickens). Among the most prominent of them are Richard Holmes, Peter Ackroyd, Victoria Glendinning, Andrew Motion, and Michael Holroyd.[1] The second is a small group of academics writing a new kind of biography of African-Americans, and it could be argued that they are standing where feminists were in the early 1970s—beginning to write important, revisionary biographies and poised to affect the form, content, and questions addressed by a large number of present and future writers of biographies, regardless of their subjects' and the authors' race, ethnicity, sex, and class. Arnold Rampersad has called them 'Black biographers', and that term is useful here to distinguish them as a group. Rampersad used the term in 1983 to mean 'the formal, detailed life story of a black individual as told by a fellow black' but in 1988 expanded the term to include biographies of 'black Americans by anyone' in recognition perhaps of the contributions of such biographers as Louis Harlan and Robert Hemenway.[2] Among the African-American biographers are David Levering Lewis, Arnold Rampersad, and perhaps a half dozen other academics.

I

Peter Ackroyd was given £650,000 to write biographies of Charles Dickens and William Blake; Victoria Glendinning got £200,000 for *Trollope*.[3] Before them, and therefore creating the category of superstar professional biographers, Michael Holroyd received an advance of £625,000, somewhat more than a million dollars, for his life of George Bernard Shaw.[4] A biographer might point out—realistically—that Holroyd's 'income' should be calculated at about

£52,000 a year and his research and other professional expenses deducted, since he spent twelve years writing before volume one of the three-volume life appeared. Many professional writers and university professors with successes as notable as his with his biographies of Lytton Strachey and Hugh Kingsmill have comparable incomes and subsidized research. That does not, however, decrease the remarkableness of the sums these biographers now command. Holmes won the Whitbread Book of the Year Prize in 1990 for *Coleridge: Early Visions*, Ackroyd won the Whitbread for Biography with *T. S. Eliot* in 1984, and Glendinning Whitbreads for *Trollope* and *Vita*. On both sides of the Atlantic, whatever they publish draws featured reviews.

What distinguishes many of these professionals is simple to explain and generally agreed upon: they push the envelope in mingling fact and authorial licence, between, if you will, fact and fiction. Michael Holroyd describes how he was 'shocked and delighted' when he was introduced at a biography conference as a 'fantasist'. He goes on to note that there are '843 reference notes' to his *Augustus John* but was thrilled that for once a biographer's 'inventive gifts and artistic talents' had been recognized as novelists' routinely are.[5] Peter Ackroyd says that novels and biography are just 'writing', and even insists that in fiction 'the vision [which he calls "the truth"] we understand that recurs behind any fiction is far more intense than in biography where you have to fabricate stuff technically more' (Onega, 213). Richard Holmes explains the 'genesis' of biography as, 'Invention formed a love-match with Truth', and throughout his essays he remarks on 'the fluid, imaginative powers of re-creation pull[ing] against the hard body of discoverable fact' ('Biography', 20). Unlike Virginia Woolf, he finds biography more fluid, more open to the imaginative powers of invention than fiction. Holroyd says combatively, 'Nonfiction is regarded by many critics as non-creative. They confuse invention with creation.'[6] His *Strachey* documents so unobtrusively and includes his opinions so freely that the reading experience is closer to fiction than to other rigorously researched biographies. The reader often needs to find the sources of Andrew Motion's quotations in *Keats* in earlier biographies of the poet. Yet it is tempting to argue that they practise the purest biographical art, for they begin in obsessive, boundless research, struggle to make their subjects live and connect to our time, and write as if biography were really *belles lettres*. Richard Holmes says outright, 'I have attempted to recapture [Coleridge's] fascination as a man and a writer, and above all to make him live, move, talk, and "have his being". If he does not leap out of these pages—brilliant, animated, endlessly provoking—and invade your imagination . . . then I have failed . . .' (*Coleridge*, xv). Hilary Spurling, herself a distinguished biographer and often mentioned with this group, sums up the method: 'You dig and dig and dig, and then you use it all without holding back' (Lubow, 236).

Their research is formidable—as formidable as that done by many academic biographers. Holroyd, for instance, read 30,000 of Strachey's letters and mastered British social, intellectual, and political history from the time of Victoria through Churchill for *Shaw*. He even read (and somewhat tediously summarized) a 70,000 word college essay and Strachey's doctoral thesis, 'Warren Hastings, Cheyt Sing, and the Begums of Oude'. Holmes can drop casually that Coleridge was married to Sara in the church where Chatterton's Rowley manuscripts were 'discovered' and that James Miller's *The Coffee-House*, a 1734 play, features Richard Savage, and he may be the best-informed and fairest portrayer of the little-known Eliza Haywood's place in Savage's life (some biographies of Savage do not even mention her although he lived with her for a time and they influenced each other's careers). Ackroyd explains that he 'immersed' himself in Wilde's writing and read nothing but books and newspapers of the period during the time he prepared to write *The Last Testament of Oscar Wilde*, and for *Chatterton* did the same with the eighteenth-century until 'I could write 18th-century prose as easily as I could write 20th-century prose' (Leivick, 31). For *Dickens*, he read all the novels, journalism, and correspondence three times.

Their 'hold nothing back' method translates into immersing themselves in the writings of and information about their subjects and the times in which they lived, then having (or making the effort to believe consistently that they have) absolute confidence in their understanding of their subjects, the ability to get inside them and do such things as assign motive or move from the private to the public from an assurance about the emotional and intellectual life. In sum, and this is crucial, they have intimate knowledge of their subjects, recognize it as such, and feel (most of the time) utter confidence in it. This intimacy gives them the ability to speak for and interpret the man about whom they are writing.[7] Like all biographers, their reading and research is directed in large part towards locating, transcribing, and even memorizing revealing passages from the person's letters, diaries, notebooks, essays, poems, marginalia, journals, etc., while keeping in mind and deepening a sturdy, detailed chronology of the life and its historical contexts.

This painstaking accretion of fact and of quotations leads in their work to a step few biographers take. They create a voice that is the blend of their own writing style and the quotations, the 'familiar voice'[8] they have come to recognize. Often called ventriloquists, impersonators, or mimics, they quote, paraphrase, and imitate, often without acknowledgement. By borrowing the style and syntax of their subjects, they release the 'inner man' and his characteristic public and private personae. After a while, no one can be sure if Wilde or Ackroyd wrote of James Whistler, who came to see Wilde 'only so that he could talk about himself', upon his death: 'now he is about to be enshrined among the Immortals. He will never leave them in peace' (*Last Testament of Oscar Wilde*, 46). Or when accused of stealing lines from other writers, 'Wilde' responds, 'I did not steal them. I rescued them' (p. 161). This ability is grounded in knowledge of the period and its languages, as is strikingly demonstrated in the obituary Holmes creates for Savage at the beginning of *Dr. Johnson and Mr. Savage*: 'Report has just reached us in the Bristol mails, of the Demise of Mr. Richard Savage . . .'. More important, however, is the way these biographers can make a quotation advance the narrative or smoothly prove a point. For example, Holroyd asserts that Strachey experienced 'a slowly reawakening interest in his fellow beings' in 1929, and then smoothly inserts Strachey's diary account of observing an intriguing solitary diner whom Strachey judges to be a 'thin-lipped intellectual epicure', an 'embittered eunuch' of the Civil Service, and one of 'that dreariest of classes, the cosmopolitan' (2: 691–2). The anecdote is pure Strachey and his special kind of 'interest in his fellow beings' is unmistakable.

They speak with active verbs: Holroyd describes 'plumbing' the inner life as taking 'a step on his own initiative' and responding to the desire for 'the spirit of truth' rather than 'the letter' (Fromm, 207). They are willing to push the envelope of interpretation and speculation and to admit that paying allegiance to 'the spirit' may require the creation of scenes or parts of scenes. Holroyd describes finding 'a personal style which grafts on to the original so that the narrative can seamlessly continue', and sorting out quotations and paraphrases from Shaw's and Strachey's own writing from Holroyd's prose is never easy.[9] That Harold Fromm does not separate Strachey from Holroyd's representation of him is telling (Fromm, 217), and Ackroyd has been called 'sometimes more Wildean than Wilde'.[10] Because they try to go where their subjects have been and literally walk in their footsteps over and over and over, their sense of place seeping into the consciousness and soul of their subjects is exceptionally powerful. Holmes titles a book '*Footsteps*' and begins, 'All that night I heard footsteps'. In trying to trace the walking tour of Robert Louis Stevenson, he becomes increasingly conscious of what a biographer can recover and how much remains beyond possibility, erased by time and other sensibilities, yet his illustrations in *Shelley: The Pursuit* are as likely to be of places as of people and he includes maps and uses them tellingly in *Coleridge*. Ackroyd's revealing interview with Laura Leivick begins with a long walk through the oldest London landmarks, Bunhill Fields, Spitalfields, Wren's churches. His biography of William Blake makes the small area bounded by the Strand, Holborn, and Oxford Street where Blake spent most of his life tangible— not confining but richly entertaining and variegated. Walking and images of walking permeate Anne Barton's review of *Dr. Johnson and Mr. Savage* (*NYRB*, 1995: 6–8).

These biographers tend to select writers as subjects, and, although they scrupulously study each subject's writing habits and relationship to writing, the fact that they see themselves as writers rather than biographers contributes to extraordinary personal investment, which raises the interest of their books. Holroyd's life of Strachey can be seen as the first of this group of biographies, and it is remarkable partly because we can observe Holroyd studying the art of biography and, in fact, find the map of Holroyd's career, which would lead to a biography of a highly experimental novelistic biographer, Hugh Kingsmill, now 'isolated and disregarded' who 'partially identified himself' with authors and searched for 'the personal impulse behind a creative work' (*Strachey*, 1: 12). Later he explains the appeal of the lives of writers, finding the opportunity to blend the 'scientific' ('documentary and factual') and 'literary' ('personal and imaginative') 'only' in such lives (2: 263). Here and elsewhere he is self-consciously contrasting his interests and methods with Strachey's. He argues neatly that *Eminent Victorians* is 'caricature' (2: 267) and that the biographies of Queen Victoria and Queen Elizabeth are 'most elegant tapestries depicting scenes of historical pageantry [that] seldom . . . pierce far enough below the surface to present an imaginative reconstruction of reality' (1: 11)—obviously unacceptable in a post-Freudian world.

Holroyd has brief sections in which he does quick evaluative comparisons among, for instance, Harold Nicolson, Strachey, Boswell, and Lockhart. He is often concerned with perspective, point of view, and the biographer's place in the narrative, especially as they shift the balance between biography as art and as polemics, the poles he often mentions. At one point, he describes Boswell's feelings playing 'like a warm luminous glow about their subjects' and condemns biography as 'higher journalism' (2: 266). From a rather awkward reference to himself as 'this author' in volume 1 (compare pp. 63, 102), Holroyd comes to write passages such as the above that tell us something about himself, his opinions, and his principles while also making judgements about Strachey and his biographies and contributing to an incremental assessment of Strachey as revisionary biographer and as human being. In this biography he also tries out a number of the fictional strategies he and the group of biographers would continue to use and improve; for instance, he moves into his subject's subconscious and uses a variety of techniques such as staged conversations. At this stage, some of these are quite jarring. How, for instance, can he possibly know that Strachey 'felt as though he had heart diseases. His pulse . . . rocked him to the very spine like the recurrent vibration of a pneumatic road drill' when he found out that Duncan Grant and Duckworth 'had fallen in love' (1: 286)? It is not even convincing that Strachey 'most desired in life, lust and power, love and humanity. He wanted to be a superman' (1: 86). The 'conversations' between Strachey and Carrington written almost like a play strike the habitual reader of biographies as strange and dubious (2: 222–3, 225). Yet Holroyd is clearly reaching for a full portrait of the man, his social presence, his private self, his interior rivers, and his creative springs.

All of them work at rendering vividly a writer's life and what might be its governing principle, stated acutely by Holroyd: 'Amid all the talk of literary technique, of influences, effects and tendencies, the real character and impulse behind any poem or novel [is] the fruit of certain individuals' experiences within those times . . . the quintessential quality of all literature' (*Strachey*, 2: 37). Those experiences are personal as well as social, historical, and national and, notably, imbued with technical experimentation and, usually, increasing expertise. Holmes explains that he has attempted to trace, to make the fabric of his biography of Shelley how the 'great poetic themes were gradually conceived and progressively executed' (meaning not chronologically but technically, p. xiii). Even more explicitly, Andrew Motion contends, 'Accounts of [Keats's] reading, his friendships, his psychological imperatives, his poetic "axioms", his politics, and his context can never completely explain this marvellous achievement. The story of his life must also allow for other things— things which have become embarrassing or doubtful for many critics in the late twentieth century, but which are still, as they always were, actual and undeniable: inspiration, accident, genius' (*Keats*, xxvi).

Ackroyd is absolutely right that 'the development of a novelist can really best be understood, not in terms of his "moods" or even of his "themes", but rather in that slow process of experimentation and self-education which changes the techniques of his prose' (*Dickens*, 674). Subtle; absolutely true. And the biographies, then, come closer to tracing the literary imagination and intense relationship between writer and writing than most biographies, which focus on the 'development' or 'subject-matter' displayed in individual works treated chronologically. John Updike, significantly another writer, is struck by the 'detailed impression of Eliot's hardworking worldliness' and comes away with 'renewed appreciation of the immense difficulty with which Eliot pulled his few poems out of himself . . . utterance achieved out of a desert dryness' (p. 128). And no one will forget Dickens compulsively arranging his furniture before he can work or Holroyd's account of Strachey's struggle to use his new understanding of psychoanalysis in *Elizabeth and Essex* (pp. 2: 586–9). At their best, they produce literary analysis of a high order. Holroyd, for instance, begins a chapter by categorizing the characters in Strachey's *Queen Victoria* with the clean economy of a good surgeon's first cut and then discusses with subtlety the 'two Victorias' Strachey gives us, one who 'engages his intellectual attention' and one 'to whom he responds emotionally' (2: 410–11). He goes on to use this insight to explain the sympathetic responses readers have to his harshly delineated, silly and mediocre Victoria.

This intimate knowledge, however, is definitely not to be confused with identification, which Holmes calls 'the first crime in biography'. Michael Holroyd describes how the biographer 'must continually lead two separate but overlapping lives—his own and that of the person about whom he is currently writing'.[11] Each one of them constantly strives to do this, and it is an important part of their ability to make the lives they write meaningful today. Self-conscious about their writing of biography, they understand, as Ackroyd once said, that 'every biography is a prisoner of its time'. But it is also a voice of its time, selecting and re-creating notable people whose lives speak meaningfully to us. Holmes notes that he is fascinated by 'the power of certain lives to draw endlessly repeated reassessments', which 'suggests that they hold particular mirrors up to each succeeding generation of biographers . . . Each generation sees itself anew in its chosen subjects' ('Biography', 19). And each biographer has an acute sense of foregrounding parts of his subjects' personalities or even of choosing *an* Eliot, Dickens, Coleridge, or Shaw from a number of possibilities. They tend to take on huge subjects—men who wrote prolifically, lived prodigiously, and are now seen to have been essential weaves in the tapestry of their times. As Ackroyd says of Dickens, he 'was such a large figure, such an amorphous figure, he takes whatever shape you want him to take' (quoted Finney, 260). What they really want to do is create for the reader *one* of the Dickenses (or whomever), and they believe in the truth of that representation. They never completely lose the moorings of the evidence and the probable; that is, they never succumb to fictional desire even as they use fictional techniques and even fictions to make this Dickens live.

Several of them identify with Samuel Johnson, whose biography of Richard Savage is truly the patriarch of theirs. Holroyd describes himself belonging to the 'Johnsonian branch' of biography (Bostock, 4), and Holmes has written *Dr. Johnson and Mr. Savage* (1993). In Johnson they find the distinguishing and distinguished combination of confident, masterful understanding of the subject and apparently detached, even Olympian judgement that goes beyond evaluating the subject and his/her decisions and actions to casting a critical and discerning eye over the contexts in the broadest sense. As Holroyd says, involving himself 'utterly' and yet remaining 'quite detached' (Bostock, 4), or, in Holmes's words, 'setting the love of a friend against the judgement of a moralist', taking 'scandalous materials—an adultery case among the aristocracy, a birthright claim, a blackmail campaign, a murder trial, an obscenity charge . . . and a prison death . . . and [turning] them into a meditation on virtue' ('Biography', 21). In Johnson's view, Savage is destroyed by the breakdown of values that creates monstrous, neglectful mothers and a heartless culture indifferent to artists, but in Holmes's *the evidence* is on trial and the subjects are the men's friendship during a period of extreme hardship and the fragility of the fabric that becomes Johnson's life of Savage. In Holmes's book and in the biographies they write, all of these authors ascribe to what they feel Johnson introduced into biography, the 'ideal of finding private motives behind actions' (Holroyd quoted, Lubow, 236).

This remarkable double voice (that which presents the subject's life, which combines the interior and exterior, motive and context, and that of the critic-biographer) gives the biography double authority—the first for interpreting the subject and the second for the biographer as magisterial presence. As Holmes says, something in Johnson 'became Savage, and lived him out with the force of fiction' ('Biography', 22). And yet in a grieving, magisterial final judgement, Johnson wrote, 'Nothing will supply the want of prudence;

and . . . negligence and irregularity long continued will make knowledge useless, wit ridiculous, and genius contemptible'. The detachment is always judicial in both connotations of that word, judging and exercising wisdom, and assumes considerable, overarching perspective.

Both voices are warm, assured in their presentation of the subject and of their opinions, and in Richard Ellmann, their other guiding star, the clarity and distinctiveness of the two voices is high art. Ira Nadel among others has discussed Ellmann and Holroyd together and praises them for combining 'the detached, objective style with the interpretative, creating a biography that is both factual and critical' (*Biography: Fiction, Fact, and Form*, 173), but this is somewhat too simple. Ellmann represents the expansion of subject-matter to include the full range of human experience and desire, the authoritative mastery of life and works, and the clear, polished, beautiful prose style that this group of biographers desire. As Holroyd says, it brought new standards to biography as it was 'scholarly and researched, but also written with great imagination and the kind of psychological acuity unavailable to Victorian biographers' (quoted Atlas, 59). Ellmann's research and phenomenal memory allowed him to marshal details as few had, and his writing style gave them novelistic persuasiveness. In understated triumph, he tells us, for instance, that Wilde fell from 190 to 168 pounds very rapidly and his hair was cut in humiliating, bizarre ways throughout his prison term. Similarly from Ackroyd we 'see' Dickens's loud, tacky, brightly coloured clothes and his compulsive, rapid walking, often with a victim-companion panting along beside or, more likely, behind.

Ellmann, like Johnson, felt free to judge his subjects, their times, and history's treatment of them. In his harshest judgements, as in most of Johnson's, there is the tone of sorrowful regret and consciousness of broad, social and human implications. He can do it in Wilde's voice, as when he quotes Wilde as saying of prison: 'I could be patient . . . for patience is a virtue. It is not patience, it is apathy you want here and apathy is a vice' (p. 485). And he can do it in the other voice, that of the biographer: 'Wooldridge's crime was appalling, but so was his execution, and, like Wilde's punishment, inhuman for a crime that was human' (p. 504).

It is telling that these biographers' work began with Michael Holroyd's *Lytton Strachey* and *Hugh Kingsmill*, for in some ways they are the heirs of the 'novelistic' biographers of the early twentieth century, Strachey, Kingsmill, David Cecil, Harold Nicolson, and even Aldous Huxley, yet their break in tone, style, and world view is as complete as was Strachey's from the Victorians' practice of biography. They continue the particularly English tradition of conceiving the biographer as moral authority, but, by celebrating Johnson and Ellmann rather than Strachey and especially Kingsmill, they construct a new relationship to culture and Englishness. As Jon Stallworthy wrote of this group, 'Once upon a time there were heroes. Some time later, some of those who recounted the lives of heroes were themselves accorded heroic status: Homer and Shakespeare became heroes of the second order. And in our own century, some who have recounted the lives of second-order heroes seem themselves to be emerging as heroes of a third order: Lytton Strachey, Richard Ellmann, Michael Holroyd' (Batchelor, 27). Reviewers chorus 'confidence', 'boldness', even 'arrogance'. These biographers are drawn to difficult personalities that achieved great things but, even more important to them, also embodied the spirit of an age or at least some of an age's central *Angst* and striving as T. S. Eliot and Lord Byron did. Eliot, for instance, it has been said, 'reflected the chaos of his own life and shaped it into that of modern existence'.[12] Swept into Ackroyd's *Dickens*, the usually temperate Hermione Lee writes, 'He shows us that the early Pickwickian benignity answered to a new sense of national identity, a middle-class surge in self-confidence that Dickens was peculiarly in tune with' and he had 'a personality that had the forces of the time running powerfully through it' ('Man Who Didn't Sleep', 37). Holmes begins *Coleridge: Early Visions* with the reminder that the poems by Coleridge that we know best 'have become part of the folklore of Romanticism, and entered proverbially into the language—"an albatross . . ." ' (p. xvi). Very often their allusions weave a dense web of associations, an invoking of English history of a particular kind. Holroyd, for instance, tells us on the first page of his biography of Strachey that an ancestor was part of the 1609 Virginia Company expedition and wrote an account that Shakespeare saw and used in *The Tempest* (pp. 3–4).

These British professionals also take up the experimentation with voice and with the degree of the biographer's presence that characterizes the greatest English biographies. There is often a sense of a mind and a personality at work, one not afraid to reveal some biases and opinions. Holroyd describes homosexuality as 'the love which passes all Christian understanding' (1: 209), and the hostility towards religion revealed in phrases such as 'pompous mummery and faked emotions' (1: 70) can be read as his as well as Strachey's. Theirs is a self-conscious craft, always engaged with 'biography' as well as the subject's life. Holroyd begins the first volume of *Lytton Strachey* sounding this reflective note: 'With the majority of writers a survey and assessment of their antecedents is unnecessary. In the special case of Lytton Strachey some knowledge of his family and its inherited culture is fundamental to the understanding of his development and the individual nature of his contribution to critical and biographical literature' (1: 3). He has weighed other literary biographies and found them tradition-bound and with thoughtless superfluity. His own sentence, as heavy and balanced as any of Johnson's, carefully specifies to what this genealogical part will contribute; in fact, the attentive reader can see Holroyd setting his book up, beginning the aesthetic and thematic design that is as characteristic of his biographies as the design or 'composition' of any master painting. Shortly thereafter he pauses to use one of Strachey's remarks about his grandfather to contrast his own insight with Charles Sanders's in his earlier biography of Strachey (pp. 9–10).

No discussion of these biographers would be complete without some mention of what first brought them into public discussion: their attention to sexual and emotional life, especially as that emotional life is related to the subject's sexuality. Dale Salwak and others have insisted that they know of readers who know little or nothing about the subjects but go to the biographies 'in search of anything even remotely scandalous'.[13] As Holmes does in *Coleridge: Early Visions* when he lists in the preface 'Coleridge's opium addiction, his plagiarisms, his fecklessness in marriage . . . his sexual fantasies' (p. xv), they often put sex out front. Glendinning's *Vita* presents the parents' 'sexual idyll' with love-making in the library, the bath, the park, and on a fur rug, alludes to several instances when the adolescent Vita was nearly molested, and matter-of-factly narrates bisexual adventures, sometimes with somewhat presumptuous conclusions such as 'She and Rosamund shared a diffuse and sentimental sensuality, but never, then or later, did they technically "make love". They did not think of it' (p. 42). Sometimes the sex is more novelistic, and therefore more titillating, because it is left to the modern imagination. As Marjorie Garber describes bisexuality in biographies, 'it appears at first to be everywhere . . . is ultimately, not nowhere, but elsewhere'.[14] Volume 1 of Holroyd's *Strachey* is an account of extended adolescence, a time when Strachey was insecure, puerile, and frantically searching for sexual liaisons. As Holroyd summarizes, his 'continuous peregrinations . . . have about them an air of desperation' (1: 459).

Critics often argue that the centrality of sex to these biographers' narratives is their distinguishing characteristic and identify them with Strachey, who is now routinely described as transforming the genre so that it was 'more candid, more novelistic, more scurrilous, more psycho-analytical', and more an art form.[15] In a rather typical discussion, Harold Fromm notes 'the excitement produced . . . by Holroyd's candid accounts of the "amatory gyrations" . . . of Strachey's circle' (p. 202), and the revelation of Maynard Keynes's homosexuality in that biography was regarded as scandalous by many. Richard Jenkyns in *The New Republic* snipes, Holroyd's 'is a Shaw that Judith Krantz and Harold Robbins could write about' (p. 39). Michele Field in *Publisher's Weekly* says that revelations about Strachey's homosexuality sold books and portrays Holroyd as describing Shaw's sexuality as 'simply Shavian in its exuberance' (p. 46). Holmes, completely without evidence, gives Chatterton 'clap'. Again, we find the long shadow of Ellmann, who treated James Joyce's sexuality in pathbreaking and revisionary ways and who wrote in *Oscar Wilde*,

'Homosexuality fired his mind. It was the major stage in his discovery of himself' (p. 281).

Making sexuality the primary spring in the complex watch that is a personality has risks. Tellingly, *Strachey* has been found more convincing than *Shaw*. One reviewer remarked insightfully that 'the search for love' in *Bernard Shaw* is a 'thematic grid that the biographer employs' rather than 'powerfully present' as it is 'throughout most of the documents and events of Strachey's life' (Fromm, p. 217). The work of another member of the group illustrates another danger, that of letting sexual speculation substitute for an openness to a variety of motives and interpretations. Brenda Maddox says that Frieda Lawrence was convinced that 'her destiny was to be an erotic muse for the comfort and liberation of the creative male' (p. 113). She plumbs the depths of Lawrence's need for Frieda ('Do not leave me, or I shall break', 'If she left me, I do not think I should be alive six months hence') and Frieda's need to be needed by Lawrence ('he gives me his . . . love of life'). Frieda Weekley (Lawrence) is introduced to us 'dancing around her bedroom nude, draping herself with a shawl like the notorious Isadora Duncan' (p. 96) when she was in the middle of an affair while married to a Nottingham professor whom Maddox speculates had 'dark, and satisfying, sensuality'.

Both Lawrences remain in this account obsessed with sex. A cloud of homophobia, sometimes sensationalized, often settles over the book. D. H. Lawrence allegedly suffered from 'a terror that he might be homosexual' (p. 202), and in imagery reminiscent of John Donne's sexually explicit aubade, 'To His Mistress Going to Bed', he finds Frieda 'his new found-land'. He is, however, 'wanting' and begins to try to satisfy 'his real longing' with a place that would give him health and that special sense of the home of the soul. Maddox speculates that the couple had anal sex and makes it part of a power struggle; her language is allusive in ways that suggest she was disgusted and uncomfortable with the idea. Maddox writes of Frieda Lawrence, 'With her light hair and fair complexion, she radiated untroubled Teutonic sensuality' (p. 96) and 'Frieda suffered more than most from the low self-esteem of the middle child . . . ' (p. 97). This kind of sentence is typical of some of this group's writing—there is a breeziness, a comfort with stereotypes and social commonplaces, with 'pop psych', and an assumption of freedom of interpretation of evidence here. Holroyd speaks casually of 'Scottish love of argument and discussion' (*Strachey*, 1: 31). In *T. S. Eliot*, Peter Ackroyd writes, 'In late June 1906, Eliot passed his entrance examination to Harvard University. He was a tall, thin, rather handsome young man with that clean-cut listlessness which is characteristic of young and well-bred Americans' (p. 30). Read closely, this sentence is nearly meaningless (what kind of 'entrance examination' did Harvard have in 1906? did they even have one?), and 'clean-cut listlessness' is an obvious stereotype, the stuff of popular, general fiction. The conservatism or rigorous principles of documentation that would hold many biographers back from writing these sentences are deliberately set aside. And this is the interesting part: they are set aside only now and then and in limited ways.

Maddox is hindered by not using the full range of feminist tools,[16] and all of the biographers' work show at least some signs of strain when they are confronted by subjects for whom the 'private life was not the mainspring of his public being' (Jenkyns, 40). Foregrounding sexuality as they do spotlights the kinds of decisions biographers make and the dangers of attempting thematic rigour and of creating a unified personality, both major characteristics of their writing. Few would say with Carolyn Heilbrun that some of the lives read 'as easily, as inevitably as those of the Hardy boys' (*Writing a Woman's Life*, 38) as she does of *T. S. Eliot*, but even favourable critics can observe, as John Worthen does of *Dickens*, that the biography sanctions 'the vision of life seen as inevitable progress to that final point; it informs us that this life is to be comprehended in terms of its ironically achieved ambitions, and of the power of the father'.[17] Unified. Inevitable. Developed. Contradiction not admitted. In them, the power of this conception is everywhere: 'The biographer's art is patterned on Austen, Thackeray, and Eliot.' It is clear in the primacy of narrative and of character creation and even in moral lessons (or at least longings). Holmes once defended biography in exactly these terms: 'By reconstructing a life through narrative, it emphasises [*sic*] cause and consequences . . . the vivid story-line of individual responsibility and meaningful action' (quoted Atlas, 58).

It is easy to neglect the moral longing and commitment that is part of all of this group of biographers' writing, but Johnson and Ellmann point us to it. Holroyd remarks that Johnson was preoccupied with human nature, 'though devoted to piety' ('How I Fell', 98). Ackroyd insists that 'there has to be some ulterior or further vision' in the purpose of any biography: 'the man's or woman's life has to be like an allegory' (*Dickens* quoted Leivick, 36).

Anne Barton once observed that Holmes and the others believe in the 'integrity of human character' (*Over the Dark River*, 6) and that this is a source of the narrative power of their books. It is no accident, I think, that England not the USA produced these biographers. They have a level of comfort with writing for what British publishers call 'the educated general public', a category that US booksellers steadfastly refuse to admit exists, and see themselves as creative artists with an audience for 'serious literary entertainment'. Their educations included deep reading in the great eighteenth- and nineteenth-century novels by Defoe, Smollett, Austen, Dickens, Eliot, Hardy, and Conrad that their books somewhat resemble and occasionally specifically invoke. Glendinning, for instance, ends early chapters of *Vita*: 'He got hurt beyond healing, and then he began to hurt his wife in return' (p. 16) and 'And so, at last, to bed' (p. 63).

From the eighteenth-century novel, they learned the value of providing statements or summaries of what is going to happen and what the reader should watch unfold. The suspense or anticipation, then, becomes watching an inevitable event, such as a fall from respect, and the pleasure of studying how something comes about or what it determines in a person's life. Very early, Holroyd writes that Strachey fluctuated between 'impressionistic and analytical criticism' and explains, 'His immature emotions and wonderfully quick comprehensive mind were seldom harnessed satisfactorily together, so that only spasmodically did . . . his powers crystallize into a deep and imaginative penetration' (1.12). In almost all of Strachey's published work and even in his relationships, these insights are made to hold true. In chapter 4 Glendinning tells us, 'The cluster of characteristics that were always to be [Vita's] had already developed: a distaste for the idea of marriage; an apparent candour with her intimates that was not candour at all . . . her disinclination to let anyone who loved her go—keeping them on a string, rebuffing them if they asked too much of her, but drawing in the line sharply if they showed signs of straying' (p. 50). This summary happens to be part of a description of Vita's ambivalence about which relationship—with Harold, Lord Lascelles, or Rosamund Grosvenor—to choose and a revealing portrayal of the contrasts between what she said, what she did, and what she was thinking (as preserved in her diaries and notebooks). These biographers habitually choose a fairly small number of personality traits. The advantages are that the subject seems to be a coherent, predictable, even knowable person and the life has a pattern, which contributes to narrative shapeliness, for the patterned life makes an aesthetically unified biography.[18] The disadvantages are that some personality characteristics are over-emphasized and others ignored, that changes or development may be unnoticed, and that the subject can be identified with such a small number of behavioural patterns that, as Jamie Bush says, the biographer is reductive.[19]

These novels, as do their biographies, link character, action, context with results; the relationship between cause and effect is exceptionally strong and explicit for late twentieth-century biographies, but never is it simple. Unlike American biographers, they know and feel free to use the whole range of nineteenth-century narrative voices and perspectives. They can choose a variety of omniscient tones and stances and permeate their narratives with quite carefully chosen, distinctive *Weltanschauungen*. They can choose the degree to which their hands as puppet-master are visible—in small ways, as in the selection of words that convey the biographer's unique, even eccentric, personality, and in large ways, as in the deliberate setting and dramatizing of scenes. They can choose Jane Austen's ironic voice, a perspective that draws the reader to stand beside her and take pleasure in seeing the subject's limitations and limited self-awareness, in knowing that the self and even motives are different from what the subject believed. Their knowledge of and confidence

7. Vita Sackville-West in her favourite clothes. Photograph by Jane Bown

in these narrative controls, although different in each one, are a major explanation of why they are a group and why their biographies are different from others.

Are these biographers that good, transforming the whole field, as Spurling says? Sometimes. Ackroyd's narrative of Vivien Eliot's behaviour after Eliot left her as a 'woman who is tearing herself to pieces, and scattering those pieces in the sight of all those she had known' (p. 216) is. Holmes's weaving of life and art in his discussion of Coleridge's 'Frost at Midnight' with the apparently inevitable 'Any reader feels this [mysticism] intuitively' is. Glendinning's bringing together of the 'fierce, devious, defiant' person and the 'gentle, cheerful, modest' person that Vita could be into the unified, older woman who knew herself to be a 'patchwork' and controlled her environment, her every contact, and herself with self-protective, iron will is. Her choice of Bown's confident, forthright photograph of Vita as the final picture of her reinforces major themes and descriptions.

It seems clear that they see themselves if not transforming the field then practising a new, specific kind of biography. That they often choose subjects for whom there are already superb biographies testifies to this fact and allows culturally significant comparisons. For more than thirty years, Walter

8. Detail from Benjamin Robert Haydon's *Christ's Entry into Jerusalem*. The bowing figure is Wordsworth, and a passionate, engaged Keats is behind him. Beside Wordsworth are Voltaire and Newton.

Jackson Bate's *Keats* has stood like a monument; both it and Aileen Ward's biography won major prizes, and Andrew Motion's 1997 *Keats* begins by pointing out that Keats's 'posthumous existence' is uncommonly strong, deeply appealing, and emotionally important to readers, but that it has distorted not only the facts of his life but his achievement. Like most of these biographies, it establishes compelling themes that at their best tellingly portray the subject and also manage to make the present (the reader's sensibility and perspective) connect with the past (the subject's life and times). 'Posthumous existence', for instance, was a phrase Keats used on his death bed to describe his prolonged final stages of tuberculosis, but it also captures his longing for poetic immortality and Motion uses it in ways that remind the reader of all these resonances, especially that desire and of the permutations of his reputation after his death. In fact, the last chapters of his biography catalogue the immediate myth-making (such as Shelley's *Adonais*) and the feeble attempts by his friends to deny that he was, for instance, weak, gentle, and killed by bad reviews and also rehearse in more detail the quick neglect and then the mythologizing of Keats into the 'byword for the poetic identity' and the distressed, neglected genius.

The Keats Motion gives us is a passionate man, often torn between duty to his family and his longing for the time, setting, and peace of mind necessary to write the poetry he himself calls 'abstract' (p. 305) and consummately ambitious. An entire year or more goes into nursing his brother Tom, who probably infected him with tuberculosis and whose unpleasant death surely haunted Keats as he told his companion, Joseph Severn, what to expect in his own (dark blood, 'continued diarrhoea', chills, fever, p. 559). More frustrated with his own failures to live up to his 'Delphic task' than by the unsympathetic reviews, which Motion says Keats would have understood as politically motivated and part of a journalistic world he knew, this Keats feels he has betrayed his calling at the same moment an acquaintance writes, 'Keats I admire thine upward daring soul, | Thine eager grasp at Immortality' (Motion, 148–53).

In many ways the biography is inferior to Bate's, Ward's, and even Robert Gitting's, but for the last 300 pages it is compelling. Keats, the short man we all know will be dead within weeks after his twenty-fifth birthday, heroically takes care of his family, falls tragically in love, writes one great poem after another, and suffers incomparably more because of the opinions of his time (love was believed to make his illness worse, starvation and bleeding were treatments for tuberculosis). As in all of these biographies, the writings of the subject seem to be fresher, more accessible to them than to most biographers, and they are used to hammer home interpretations, both large and small. Motion uses a quotation from Keats on his deathbed describing his sister Fanny 'who walks about my imagination like a ghost—she is so like Tom' (p. 557). And it is painful to read, 'How astonishingly does the chance of leaving the world impress a sense of its natural beauties on us. . . . I muse with the greatest affection on every flower I have known from my infancy—their shapes and colours . . .' (p. 507). His love for spring and for flowers culminates in his sending his companion to see the place he will be buried and being pleased that early violets and daisies are already blooming there ('The spring was always enchantment to me . . . perhaps the only happiness I have had in the world— has been the . . . growth of flowers,' p. 564).

The *act* of writing becomes vivid, an action, as concrete and physical as it is mental and emotional. After Tom's death, Motion describes how Keats, so long frustrated by the lack of time to write, felt a 'sense of waste, guilt and desperation' that stood in the way of writing (p. 305). This combination—a new resonance to 'the writing is the life' and the admission of the complex feelings family obligations arouse regardless of how wholly felt and gladly assumed—is too seldom described in literary biographies. Motion also milks the romance between Keats and Fanny Brawne for as much sentiment as possible, telling us, for instance, that Keats could not bear to read the letters he received in Rome and asked to be buried with them. Hovering over the entire ending is the sense that Motion (and Keats and Fanny) believed his trip to Rome a hideous mistake, sometimes admitted in wrenching words, such as Fanny's 'he might have died here with so many friends to soothe him and me *me* with him' (p. 568).

Reading Ward's, Bate's, and Motion's biographies of Keats together highlights the choices biographers make, the necessary kinds of decisions and interpretations forced on them, and also how biographers' distinctive personalities, experiences, and educations animate biography. Ward and Bate are as novelistic as Motion, but Bate's primary interest is the poetry. Any comparison of Bate's literary criticism with Motion's exposes the latter's superficiality (for example, 'a pattern of possession and abandonment . . . runs throughout his poems', Motion 42). Although Bate and Motion use a rather surprising number of the same quotations, Bate is much more at home with the poetry, which he probably taught year after year; where Motion uses letters Bate draws upon the poetry. 'With shatter'd boat, oar snapt, and canvass rent, | I slowly sail, scarce knowing my intent; | Still scooping up the water with my fingers', Bate quotes when Keats was straining to find subjects worthy of his poetic ambitions (p. 70). In fact, Keats was such a powerful, expressive, moody letter-writer that Motion's familiarity with the letters adds dimensions unfound in Bate's biography.

Bate, the great humanist, gives Keats a philosophy and uses it to elevate his character and in an artful conclusion unites it with his artistic aspirations to create what is usually called a 'great soul'. Bate closes with Brown sending Benjamin Bailey Keats's beloved engraving of Shakespeare, which serves as a springboard for reflections on Keats's 'philosophic conception of what was to become his polar ideal of "disinterestedness" and to the creative use of the selfless potentialities of the moral imagination' and for a final quotation from a letter from Keats to Haydon: 'Is it too daring to fancy Shakespeare' the 'good Genius presiding over [me]?' (pp. 698–9). Bate is at pains to find this Keats in his final, horrible weeks when he was often wild, embittered, frantic, depressed, suicidal, and irrational. Motion, too, points out that Keats's 'exquisite sensibility for every one' survived, but it is much more a quality summoned than an easy expression of inner being. Bate writes a wonderful chapter about Keats's appearance, carefully arguing his 'peculiarly dauntless expression' and going on to make it inseparable from his character and actions; there is nothing quite like this section in Motion (Bate, 112–17). This kind of humanistic work may be dated, but it also lets us 'see' Keats living, moving, talking, thinking, and reacting, and by elevating Keats elevates humankind. It also leads to an evaluation of surviving portraits of Keats with unparalleled expertise—and we care what the subject of a biography looked like at each stage of life.

The most obvious differences between the two biographies are typical of the emphases and methods of these British biographers: Motion feels much more free to use evidence creatively and some stories and people hardly found in Bate's biography are given considerable emphasis in his. For instance, Bate uses the phrase 'posthumous life' repeatedly in his biography, too. He locates it correctly first in Keats's last letter to Charles Brown (p. 680) and has him ask Dr Clark 'searchingly', 'How long is this posthumous life of mine to last?' (p. 687) and then quietly repeat the question 'each time' Clark came (p. 693). His source is Severn's letters. Motion makes it a desperate, angry question asked of Dr

Clark (p. 558), gives no citation, and does not give us the St Keats that emerges from Bate's account. Bate assigns a very limited meaning while Motion makes the phrase widely emblematic. They give slightly different accounts of his last hours—Motion allows Severn to fall asleep and awaken still holding Keats's now-dead hand (p. 566). In both accounts, Clark orders daisies planted on Keats's grave, but Motion includes the outrage of Severn's return to their apartment to find the landlady waving her bill and having the furniture stacked for burning.

Similarly, Motion makes Keats's becoming a medical dresser and passing his medical exams a fascinating story while Bate handles it in a sketchy fashion—in fact, reducing some of the most interesting information to a footnote. From Motion's account, we learn to see Keats as more intelligent, sharper, a man with professional 'technical precision', who attracted notice both for his manner and his ability, and we learn more about medical education. We can delight in a bested schoolmate's musing that it was only because Keats was so good at Latin (p. 98). Motion's research is in some ways more ingenious than Bate's—in this section his study of medical education and the help given by Roy Porter, a generous resource to a great many of us, add dimensions we miss in Bate. And, of course, Motion gives full attention to Fanny Brawne and reads the relationship completely differently from Bate. In Motion's biography, Fanny shares centre stage with Keats for many chapters and the relationship is multi-dimensional, and, most significantly, mature. Motion argues that Keats and Brawne worked through their uncertainties and Keats, unlike Bate's representation, was no longer conflicted in the immature ways he had been about women. Neither 'grid' nor obsession, Keats's sexual love becomes but another source of acute regret and agonizing torture. Is this interpretation 'true'? It is certainly dramatic and interesting and possible, but it also pushes the evidence beyond where many biographers would be willing to go.

Are the British professionals good for biography? In some ways. Biography at its best should be *belles lettres*; it should strive for the highest order of imaginative re-creation of a life, and its writers should know why the life matters to living readers. It should be honest and it should be an honest craft. It should be practised by writers who love language, who take the time and have the wit to call Strachey 'a dangerous pedestrian' and then illustrate the perfection of the phrase or describe his family's house as 'afflicted with elephantiasis'. Because many of these biographers are pushing the envelope of Truth, embracing the spirit (as they apprehend it) as opposed to the letter of Truth, they are always on the edge of teetering into meltdown. Another biographer in a wonderful phrase wrote that biography 'strives for infinite complexity, hesitant before obscurity of motive where the subject stands in shadow'.[20] Some of the practices developed to push beyond the shadows, however, threaten both the complexity and even the nature of biographical truth. In an important essay, 'Biography: Inventing Truth', Holmes himself calls his group's practice of biography 'complicated, provisional, and to some degree perilous' (p. 20), and with impressive self-recognition he discusses ethics, authenticity, celebrity, and empathy. Every day all over again biographers face the choices embedded in these words, and the benefits and faults that this diverse group of experimenters lives out and illustrates make us confront central issues and the implications of biographical decisions.

II

Although 'Black biography' is youthful, like so many topics in *Reflections on Biography*, it deserves a book of its own. In fact, there is no topic raised in this book that is not tacitly commented upon or extended by Black biography, and several aspects of it are already obvious subjects for books. What interests me specifically are its potential to 'transform the whole field' to an even greater extent than feminist biographers and the British professionals and the way it brings to consciousness and forces on biographers new issues and decisions. This section is a reflection on a few central demands of Black biography with emphasis on those that are new or heightened by the special challenges in writing the lives of African-Americans. Throughout there are mentions of some of the topics of other chapters, especially voice and the relationships between biographer and subject.

★

What distinguishes this group is their commitment to representing simultaneously the complexity of African-American life, the immediacy of history, and individual, personal identity formation over time. In other words, they are starting over by taking each person as a unique individual and resisting as much as they can the conventional purposes of biographies of African-Americans: the panegyrical creation of a role model, the reinforcement of a flattering paradigm or myth, and the contribution of 'ammunition' for existing arguments about mainstream history.[21] The effort has often been to integrate African-American history into *American* history or make it a separate history of noble individuals. These biographers recognize that most African-Americans move through cultures that feel markedly different from each other and often sharply feel the contrasts and nuances. Their biographical subjects are more frequently in an intense and dynamic relationship with history, immediate events, and even the concept that is the USA than are white subjects. Issues of identity and presentation of context are inherent and, for these biographers, are not only essential but urgent.

One of the earliest of these biographies, Nellie Y. McKay's *Jean Toomer: Artist*, contends that 'Toomer's desire for a unified self was the most pronounced organizing principle of his life' (p. x). A man who could easily pass for white, indeed would be assumed white by most people, Toomer spent most of his childhood with his grandparents—a white grandmother and a grand-father who insisted that he was Black, although most people then and now were sceptical. As McKay says, 'his physical appearance belied that'. Toomer went to segregated, some Black and some white, schools and to integrated schools. When his first book, *Cane*, was published, he was 'upset that everyone around him considered him a "Negro" writer'; he wanted to be 'an American writer, whose work reflected one part of the American experience' (McKay, 6). Later he refused to let James Weldon Johnson reprint sections from *Cane* in *The Book of Negro Poetry* 'on the grounds that he was not a Negro' and answered a request for permission to translate *Cane* into German: 'The publication of my book several years ago gave rise to the impression that I was a Negro . . . In America there is forming a new race which, for the present, I will call the American race. In so far as I affiliate with any group less than the entire human group, I am a member of this race' (McKay, 198–9). He experienced many Americas, and his struggles to define himself are dramatic. As McKay says, he struggled 'with the issue of his right to individuality' (p. 22). As these Black biographies make clear, 'the right to individuality' is a complicated, illuminating topic—not just for people of colour in a white hegemony but one with the potential for making the practice of biography more adept, more profound, and more culturally significant.

Personality and Identity

From the chapter on feminism: 'One of those elements of an individual's identity which at the very minimum comprise *what one is never not*, [is] membership in one of the two sexes or in a given race. What one is never not establishes the life space within which one may hope to become uniquely and affirmatively what one is—and then to transcend that uniqueness by way of a more inclusive humanity' (Erikson, *Gandhi*, 266). Even more than sex, in the USA race is the dominant component of identity with all that means—shaping self-image, the perceptions and reactions of others, and the impression of the 'nature' and destiny of the person. On the immediate level, the African-American is almost always in the position of being recognized first as a member of a race and second as an individual. Arthur Ashe describes his learned ability, which he insists is necessary if African-Americans are to 'preserve their sanity', 'to live with reasonable freedom and dignity and yet also avoid insult, disappointment, and conflict rooted in racism,' that he calls 'not so much to turn the other cheek as to present . . . no cheek at all' (*Days of Grace*, 138).

There are the remarkable moments of entry and re-entry into US culture. Returning from Mexico, Langston Hughes delays this moment by speaking Spanish; just hours out of San Antonio, a man asks, 'You're a nigger, ain't you?' and moves to another seat (Rampersad, *Hughes*, 1: 35). DuBois records the shock of returning from Germany: 'I dropped suddenly back into "nigger"-hating America' (quoted Lewis, 149). Even Teresa de Lauretis recognizes the experience: 'I have never, before coming to this country, been conscious of being white', she writes (p. 8).

'What one is never not'—white. Writ large is the fact that the Black biographer must always write about race. The ways that race permeates are numerous and always contribute to identity and personality formation. Writing about them poses intimidating challenges because they are often invisible at worst and uncomprehended at best and often push the biographer into violating taboos. For example, it is not yet socially acceptable to reveal the full range of racist atrocities in US history during reconstruction, in the 1920s, or immediately after World War II, and there are privacy issues and racial risks. Biographers are forced to find ways to write about anger and about death.

It is hard to imagine the life of an African-American that did not call for some writing about the most threatening of human emotions: fear, rage, and powerlessness. These are unacceptable emotions in our culture. Black biographers, however, must fearlessly depict the moments when these emotions are apparent but also attempt to explain what part they played in the mosaic of total personality and meaningful action. For that reason, John Garraty's experimental revelations of Richard Wright's fear for his physical safety and lack of identification with African-Americans and Allison Davis's argument that DuBois's political activism was at heart aggression, not idealism, and an integral and comprehensible part of his mature personality are important and brave examples.[22] Biographies that admit powerlessness stress relationships and social context in new ways. They move another step away from the Great Man theory of biography by examining opportunities and the things that give or absolutely rule out possibilities.

Good biographies make these unacceptable emotions understandable, acceptable, even natural. As Toni Morrison once said, 'Aggression is not as new to black women as it is to white women' (Tate, *Black Women Writers at Work*, 122). Arthur Ashe said that 'being black is the greatest burden I've had to bear' and eloquently compared it to his AIDS: 'Racism . . . is entirely made by people, and therefore it hurts and inconveniences infinitely more . . . I sometimes think that this indeed may be one of those fates that are worse than death' (*Days of Grace*, 126–7). 'For most blacks in America, regardless of status, political persuasion, or accomplishments, the moment never arrives when race can be treated as a total irrelevancy', Ellis Cose concluded in *The Rage of a Privileged Class* (p. 28).

There is a need to provide the information to understand what the USA feels like to an African-American and a need to write about the key racial Events in the individual's life. Every Black biographer provides numerous, often ludicrous examples of the many, small, insulting reminders that convey what it is like to live always perpetually braced to endure, outwit, or resist being denied a good table (or a table at all) in a restaurant, ignored by a store clerk, or assumed stupid: men and women forced to walk around a train station and down tracks to get to a platform because they are not allowed even to cross a white waiting room, a cashier in a cafeteria going berserk and punching the keys wildly 'until the amount became ridiculous, "her face growing more and more belligerent, her skin turning red"' until the would-be diner leaves his tray and flees (Rampersad, *Hughes*, 1: 31); Martin and Coretta King spending their wedding night at a black funeral home, a frequent forced substitute for motels for African-Americans at that time. Like the sound of the man spitting on the ground just behind the African-American who has passed peacefully along the street, none is without insult and threat. Jesse Jackson's biographer Marshall Frady discusses 'the mortifications encountered at every turn', and, because so much of his biography is based on interviews with Jackson is able to depict the range of emotions they evoke—rage, fatigue, humiliation, resentment, shame, explosive combinations that led to Jackson's first act of civil disobedience and to his comparing white people to someone who hits you, knocks out a few teeth, then explains you aren't hurt and 'it's all over now' (p. 31).

Former Senator Bill Bradley describes his time in the National Basketball Association as living 'in a sort of a black world' and says that he learned from his teammates what it meant 'never to be able to relax, never to know where the next insult or slight would come from' (Cose, 40). Even so self-controlled and even privileged a man as Arthur Ashe writes of disciplining himself 'to walk away with what was left of my dignity, rather than lose it all in an explosion of rage' (p. 138). In the first meeting of the first class I taught at the University of Rochester, I introduced the syllabus and the material and then asked for questions. There was only one: 'Can women be great scholars?' This student wanted to be sure he was going to get his money's worth and a valuable name on his letter of recommendation. Twenty years later, I was asked to observe the teaching of an African-American colleague for a tenure review. The ways her students challenged and tested her amazed and saddened me; rather than the first day of class, this was mid-quarter. My student's question made me angry and cynical; I cannot imagine being insulted every day with challenges to my knowledge of the material on which I had received a Ph.D. and spent a lifetime studying.

There are the 'small' and all-too-frequent incidents that portray the special position of African-Americans that demand the re-creation of the *frisson* of recognition, the intense surge of adrenalin and gut-searing fear, what Arnold Rampersad describes as 'the thrill' at being called 'nigger'. Freeze, fight, flight the options. W. E. B. DuBois was almost sent to reform school for eating a few of a neighbour's grapes: 'It was the close call historically awaiting all black males in American society, putting Willie on notice of his fragility and isolation' (Lewis, 34). At age 55, Booker T. Washington was punched, clubbed, and chased by a man living with a woman not his wife and then arrested: 'in the atmosphere of American racism even Booker T. Washington was lynchable' (Harlan, 2: 404). Washington's assailant was given three years' probation (and ordered to pay child support to his wife, suggesting that his love life, not his assault offended the judges), and Washington was barred forever from the New York hotel where he customarily stayed. *Frisson*, then rage, fear, outrage, humiliation—what human being would not feel surges of these emotions?

If these emotions are unacceptable subjects, retaliation is even more so, a true taboo, and yet Black biographers are dealing with it in a forthright manner, often striking difficult balances. Lewis calls it 'bloody black retribution, the other element besides sex at dead center of the historic psychosis about race' (p. 541). One of Langston Hughes's seldom anthologized poems reads:

> For honest work
> You proffer me poor pay.
> For honest dreams
> Your spit is in my face,
> And so my fist is clenched
> Today—
> To strike your face.
>
> ('Pride')

Arthur Ashe records his surprise and disappointment as he sees the spirit of revenge, 'the idea of getting even', become 'the new order' (p. 144). In contrast, a Harvard faculty member of Ashe's generation observed reflectively, 'Retaliation may be your last possible way to express your humanity.' Lewis is right; the fear of retaliation is at least as great as the fear of sexuality but, until the most recent group of these biographies, almost never admitted.

When a new group comes to writing lives, they join what feminists call 'the quest for her own story'. As in modern biographies of women, plot lines, familiar key moments, and interpretative paradigms in identity and personality formation are discarded, reconsidered, or drastically revised by these biographers. The life courses of white men have often been written to seem inevitable (Heilbrun's 'Hardy boys') and those of women as 'unscripted' and 'accidental'. The lives of many African-Americans, in contrast, might be described as 'conscripted'. In other words, they often seem compulsorily enrolled in a group (their race) and enlisted into services in causes and struggles. Thus, we deal with a different paradigm and one largely unexplored but carrying enormous resonance in the lives of all who feel the weight of responsibility or conscience or group identity and respond—or struggle against responding. For African-Americans, however, it is more than resonant. Adam Clayton Powell, for instance, when a student at Colgate University was assumed to be white until the fraternity he was pledging did a background check. Ridiculed and ostracized by the other students, he emerged from the experience confirmed in his racial identity and militant. A major force in integrating businesses, buses, and even utility companies that served Harlem, he could take unusual ways of making his point. When John Rankin, a Mississippi congressman, used 'nigger' in his speech before the House, Powell walked to the rostrum and punched Rankin, knocking him down.[23] The moments of 'coming to consciousness', times of great importance in every biography, usually have additional elements in the lives of African-Americans. Often a powerful recognition of an 'authentic identity', one always shared and always to be shared with a group,[24] the experience can be comfortable, dangerous, or traumatically unpleasant.

An African-American psychiatrist explains that 'home' is often not where the Black person is living but where the 'homefolks', 'their people' are. He concludes that geography 'is thus part of the extended identity as is the extended family' (Grier and Cobbs, *Black Rage*, 103–4). A concrete example is the Auburn Avenue neighbourhood where Martin Luther King grew up, and one of the weaknesses of Garrow's book is his inability to evoke it and to use it to help explain King's sense of his people as a nation willing to fight and die together. Rampersad does much better with Hughes's Harlem, a space into which Hughes would periodically move, blend, draw strength, and find both a projection of his inner self and protection from pressures. Those to whom one belongs, expressed as tribe, clan, family, community, become more important—more of a psychic space, more of a sanctuary, and more of a burden that one is expected to assume whenever it calls. The understanding of individual people and the bonds between them become more adept when explored from this angle. For instance, Jesse Jackson is obviously in the mainline tradition of African-American social reform, both more free from and more related to Martin Luther King than he seems in most writings about him.

Coming to consciousness is often tied up with discovering new dimensions of the individuals' relationships with their race and, as it did for Powell, making decisions about 'taking up the burden of race'. Sometimes the first is a horrific insult, depressingly often in school. Langston Hughes runs out of a classroom and refuses to stop yelling that his new teacher has a 'Jim Crow row'; children like James Weldon Johnson discover that white children can go to high school but there are no provisions for Black children beyond the seventh or eighth grade. Incidents such as this often happen in the lower grades, and, strikingly early, many commit themselves to achievement that will 'reflect credit on the race'.[25] Each asks at some time, 'Does my black blood place upon me any more obligation to assert my nationality than German, or Irish or Italian blood would?' (quoted Lewis, 172). The answer, as Roy Wilkins explains it, is usually this: 'It was almost like it was dirty just to use your education to go out and earn money. You're supposed to go out and *serve* . . .' (Frady, 112). Some embrace this life as DuBois seems to, others seem to lose themselves in dedication to it as Washington does, and others, if we are to accept Garrow's account, find it a cross to bear with alternating weariness and unmatched satisfaction as King does. And it can be doubly deadly—as it was for King and as it was for Ann Sexton, whose recognition of belonging to a group of poets gave her an identity, made her a writer, but also delivered the message that madness and early death were her destiny.

In fact, death is another topic that sets these biographies apart. It appears in many forms and ways and springs as often from the African-American collective experience as from the individual. In Black biography the unusually frequent possibilities of reading about, witnessing, or suffering violent death are often written about sensitively and realistically with careful blending of the history of violence, current situations, and individual psychology. The *conscripted* individual must accept the risk, come to terms with death, along with whatever turning away from an earlier career costs. The physical daring that taking up certain callings or becoming involved in specific community or national causes is a story frequently told since so many African-American leaders have been killed, silenced, or driven into exile. The psychological dimensions of life lived in the shadow of death are yet to be fully presented. Rampersad in the life of Hughes and Garrow in that of King come closest to realizing the dimensions of the topic, but Rampersad tends to deal with it as a literary critic more than as a biographer and Garrow simply repeats how often and at each stage of his life that King expressed that he expected to die young.

Garrow's biography almost in spite of itself illustrates the complexity and importance of the topic. Garrow's quotations from King often include the preacher's reassurance to his flock and movement leader's assurance to his followers (and threat to his adversaries). Garrow does not appear to notice these identity-revealing elements or when and in what circumstances King chooses to invoke both or one rather than the other. Garrow tells us in stubbornly simple statements about the young King jumping out of his window twice. Although he puts them in the sections that deal with death, there is no real analysis, either psychological or contextual. Are they signs that he already knew his life was conscripted? Exactly what thoughts, life circumstances, and reactions might have been brought to bear on interpretation?

Literary critics spend more time writing about thoughts about death than do historians, and Rampersad quotes richly and intelligently from Hughes's writings on the topic. Now and then he observes something like this: 'most of his readers seldom notice this deadly undertow in his art; yet his fascination was certified throughout his career by many poems about melancholy, loneliness, and suicide' (1: 14). We do not know, however, what actions and moods at various points in his life the poetry might be related to. In fact, the wish for death, the ultimate removal of burdens or expression of weariness with a frustrating society must haunt these biographies, as it seems to glare in their authors' faces only to be dismissed or turned away from. Hughes's wandering life, his expressions of desire for rest need to be connected in a larger variety of ways to his writings. The richness and centrality of the issue resonates in Arthur Ashe's ruminations on race, in which he states firmly that he in no way wishes for death but 'the shadow [of racism] is always there; only death will free me, and blacks like me, from its pall' (*Days of Grace*, 128). In King, Hughes, and Ashe 'death' is deeply symbolic as well as real; it resonates in the Bible, which all of them knew intimately, and in the music and their own cultures. The ultimate 'rest for the weary' as well as the horrific end of the lynch mob's rope, allusions to death in the subject's writings and speeches are seldom given their full resonance. Although all biographers deal with death, few find it necessary to make it a major subject; in many Black biographies it is often strikingly present from at least their subjects' teenage years, and it brings together the personal and the historical, as Lewis does here: 'this northern city [East St Louis] of 59,000 had been the site of the first American pogrom' (Lewis, *DuBois*, 537).

Again from chapter 6: 'The emphasis on individualism does not take into account the importance of a culturally imposed group identity for women and minorities [and] . . . the differences in socialization in the construction of . . . identity . . . From both an ideological and psychological perspective, in other words, individualistic paradigms of the self ignore the role of collective and relational identities in the individuation process of women and minorities.' No biographer of a Western white person has ever had to write a sentence such as this: 'Now that the right had been won to die discriminated against in the war for world democracy, DuBois momentary stood back from the fray to write another synoptic piece . . .' (*DuBois*, 543). Lewis is speaking of Camp Des Moines, the training camp set up after an unpleasant struggle to graduate African-American officers for World War I, and the commissioning of its first group in October 1917, most of whom were assigned to labour and stevedore units.

The sentence ends, 'DuBois momentary stood back . . . to write another synoptic piece.' We are called back to the individual, to the intellectual, to the person who probably felt that his writing was his life. There is tremendous poignancy in what happened to the intellectual, scientific, pioneering sociologist, the man who published the methodologically ground-breaking *The Philadelphia Negro* at age 31, and who was being compared to Karl Marx and Herbert Spencer. His studies of Black Belt counties and his brilliantly designed and conducted model study of Lowndes County, Alabama, for the Bureau of Labor Statistics ended with the suppression and then destruction of the last because it 'touched on political matters' (Lewis, 355). The individual, his brilliant mind and talented pen, were soon conscripted, and except for a few pieces reminiscent of his scholarship and abstract thought he spent the rest of his life writing what he called propaganda. His research skills, sociological training, and scientific method are often apparent in his *Crisis* pieces, but publications such as his essays on World War I that anticipated Lenin's *Imperialism, The Highest Stage of Capitalism* became rare. That he wrote them at all given his schedule and other work reveals a key to his very being that biographers must struggle to keep before the reader.

That being African-American is a *psychological* state, race an all-penetrating fact of existence, a condition of the mind's being, presents another challenge for the biographer that has few if any true analogies.[26] DuBois wrote a statement in his autobiography, *Dusk of Dawn* (1940), words that reverberate in current titles (*Black Rage, The Rage of a Privileged Class*):

It is difficult to let others see the full *psychological* meaning of caste segregation. It is as though one, looking out from a dark cave in a side of an impending mountain, sees the world passing and speaks to it . . . but notices that the passing throng does not even turn its head, or if it does, glances curiously and walks on. It gradually penetrates the minds of the prisoners . . . that some thick sheet of invisible but horribly tangible plate glass is between them and the world. They get excited; they talk louder . . . They may scream and hurl themselves against the barriers . . . . They may even, here and there, break through in blood and disfigurement, and find themselves faced by a horrified, implacable, and quite overwhelming mob of people. (my emphasis, pp. 130–1)

'As biographers of blacks we should not forget the simple truth that being black in America is above all a psychological state', Rampersad writes ('Psychology', 18). In his novel, *Autobiography of an Ex-Coloured Man*, James Weldon Johnson writes of the aftermath of his character's discovery that he was 'a nigger' as a passage into another world:

From that time I looked out through other eyes, my thoughts were coloured, my words dictated, my actions limited by one dominating, all-pervading idea which constantly increased in force and weight . . . And this is the dwarfing, warping, distorting influence which operates upon each and every coloured man in the United States. He is forced to take his outlook on all things, not from the viewpoint of a citizen, or a man, or even a human being, but from the view-point of a *coloured* man. It is a difficult thing for a white man to learn what a coloured man really thinks . . . I have often watched with interest and sometimes with amazement even ignorant coloured men . . . maintain this dualism. (p. 403)

The complexity of interpreting personality is more difficult with African-Americans, and it foregrounds the performative self, the fact that each person *performs* a variety of roles, chooses to act a part in certain situations. Where is the line between self and performance? Harlan says that the complexity of Washington's personality 'probably had its origin in his being black in white America. He was forced from childhood to deceive, to simulate, to wear the mask. With each subgroup of blacks or whites that he confronted, he learned to play a different role, wear a different mask' (preface). Harlan's biography shows a ruthless control freak ('Power was his game') who could accommodate his behaviour to every group, an 'exemplar of humility, deference, and openness to suggestion' and was accepted by Northern whites 'on perhaps more equal terms than any other black man in American history' (preface).

Just as this constant interplay, alternation, or reversal, if you will, of experiencing the self as individual and as racial must be understood and portrayed, so the experience of whites as a race that is unpredictable and prone to unexpected, disloyal, or even cruel actions. Both are necessary for a full portrait and components in interpretation of actions and personality. For example, white *individuals* working with the National Association for the Advancement of Colored People (NAACP), the Southern Christian Leadership Conference (SCLC), or fund-raising suddenly seem to shift to behaving as the privileged race used to deciding and leading or suddenly begin representing and enforcing mainstream white opinions and conduct. A safe and happy haven such as DuBois's classroom can be the place the world changes, as another child refuses 'peremptorily' to accept a card from him. Langston Hughes once remarked on the Harlem Renaissance, 'I thought it wouldn't last long . . . how could a large and enthusiastic number of people be crazy about Negroes forever?' (Berry, 108). A Black military man tells of being stationed in rural Montana and going into a restaurant. The manager chatted with him and admitted that he was 'the first Negro he had ever laid eyes on'. Then he told him his restaurant had a policy against serving Negroes.[27] It is hard to understand why most African-Americans don't believe that white people are mean or crazy or both.

Part of the challenge is that white people are usually both individuals and a race to these biographical subjects, and part of a race first. Biographies of Martin Luther King suggest that he hated and feared white people from his youth and believed the South would never 'impose limits on itself'; they record among his last statements, 'America has been, and she continues to be, largely a racist society' (quoted Garrow, 568). His decision to work in the North and Midwest in his last years shows his universal distrust for the white nation. Langston Hughes is described as having a 'chronic if slight fear of all whites who could be now friendly, now needlessly cruel'. DuBois never thought whites were well-intentioned, and his combative style was sometimes described by other African-Americans as the 'eternal vigilance' required of him as a battler for the 'rights of his own people to a voice in their government' (quoted Lewis, 402). In *The Souls of Black Folk*, he laments the fading of his early feelings of contempt and the desire to 'beat my mates at examination time, or beat them at a foot-race, or even beat their stringy heads'. These examples suggest how taboo, how complex, and how motivating these feelings about whites are. For instance, DuBois, like Washington and King, was sometimes shy around powerful white people and at other times out of his fierce idealism excessively and unrealistically demanding.

In recognizing the challenges and new dimensions in Black biography, some surprising gaps in other biographies come to consciousness. The photographs more than the prose in Doris Goodwin's book show the intriguing centrality of Eleanor Roosevelt's interest in the Negro. Only in recent years have biographers of George Washington, Thomas Jefferson, Andrew Jackson, and others looked in any detail at the relationships between their subjects and people of other races, and when they have the biographers and scholars have been accused of political and scandalous motives. No biographer of an African-American has a choice; contact between the races must be a major topic. Harlan, for instance, points out how closely Booker T. Washington worked with whites and occasionally concludes a segment with observations such as this: 'He became the houseboy of General Lewis Ruffner . . . developing a closeness to upper-class whites' and learning the benefits of white 'paternalism' (pp. 39, 47, 52). Harlan certainly explains well this way that Washington learned to be such an effective fund-raiser and so adept at making white people comfortable with him; we do not, however, know what that *felt* like, how the double vision that DuBois describes so well finally reveals the person within and the person who acted. Johnson remarks that African-Americans' thoughts and actions 'are often influenced by considerations so delicate and subtle that it would be impossible for him to confess or explain them'. Ashe, and almost every African American, speaks matter-of-factly about their dual or double consciousness, 'seeing oneself through one's own eyes but also constantly through the eyes of the dominant group' (*Days of Grace*, 163). Thus, the dual vision of the subject, the 'reading' of the situation, and the complexity of motives for specific actions are added to the usual problems of interpreting and portraying personality, experience, and action.

Most biographers pride themselves on the ability to evoke history and to take it into account. Just as feminists showed how much could be done with sex and gender, Black biographers are showing us how much better history can be done. History is centre stage in Black biography. People are both rooted in it and shaped by immediate events and opinions. In contrast to the masterfully understated, confident invoking of Englishness in the British professionals' biographies, history is a major complication in Black biography. It requires rethinking and recasting to create new balances between how history and events divert and take over lives *and* how the individual influences historical events and outcomes. It requires re-educating readers and forces biographers to admit that most life courses are deeply contingent.

Black biographers know that they are writing about a member of a people, a concept that links identity and history. What makes African-Americans a people within a nation is their shared, inherited condition of life. DuBois's *The*

Souls of Black Folk captures that fact and retains the status it has because it does it so well. Slavery and the history of legal discrimination, tolerance of prejudices, and racism embedded in institutions such as education and government assured that African-Americans would become a people, a political community within a nation. Sadly, very shortly after slavery documents such as 'The Laws of the African Society' (1786, New York City; 1796, Boston) were more common than earlier formulations such as 'Constitution of the American Society of Free Persons of Colour' (1831). Orations and essays commemorating the Act abolishing the African slave trade (1 January 1808) use addresses such as 'My African brethren' and 'My beloved Africans'.[28] How a people is hailed tells a great deal about their perceived and accepted identities, and 'My beloved Africans' is decidedly different from 'My fellow Americans'. As Etienne Balibar theorizes, they have been brought 'mutually to recognize one another within a historical frontier which contained them all'.[29]

Anthropologists and political scientists tell us that dominant cultures generate 'the people' and also 'peoples' and that language and race are seen as the most 'natural' reasons for ethnicity. Toni Morrison has gone so far as to argue that the 'black community is a pariah community' (Tate, 129). Part of the double vision and double experience for most African-Americans is that they are asked to act like Americans when it is to the dominant culture's advantage and to accept that they are different and excluded when that is beneficial to whites. And it is true that 'No other racial group in America's history has endured as much rejection on the path to acceptance. No other group has stared so longingly and for so long at . . . "the final door". And no other group remains so uncertain of admittance' (Cose, 9). DuBois combined this insight with sharp historical observations such as this one about the end of the nineteenth century:

Here was a mass of black workmen of whom very few were by previous training fitted to become the mechanics and artisans of a new industrial development; but here, too, were an increasing mass of foreigners and native Americans who were unusually well fitted to take part in the new industries; finally, most people were willing and many eager that Negroes should be kept as menial servants rather than develop into industrial factors . . . The difference is that the ancestors of the English and the Irish and the Italians were felt to be worth educating, helping and guiding because they were men and brothers. (quoted Lewis, 204)

The relationship to the USA, their 'own country,' and to Americanness is different in degree and kind regardless of how important the relationship is to white subjects. Black biography attests over and over to 'the promise and mirage of America as the land of opportunity' (Rhiel and Suchoff, 80), of the fragility of being 'American', and the heritage of being African-American. Perhaps little can express it better than the image of DuBois singing 'America

the Beautiful' and 'Steal Away Jesus' on his birthday in 1894. Langston Hughes
wrote 'I, too, sing America', 'I am the Darker Brother', 'Here Again the
Christmas Story', and in 'One-Way Ticket':

> I am fed up
> With Jim Crow laws,
> People who are cruel
> Who are scared of me
> And me of them.

Martin Luther King's speeches ring with phrases such as, 'First and foremost
we are American citizens' (quoted Garrow, 24), and his life offers many
moments as symbolic and as dual as DuBois's songs. On the way to compete
in an oratorical contest with a speech entitled, 'The Negro and the Constitution', he had to stand for hours after being forced to give up his seat on a bus
to a white person.

Here and elsewhere the absolute necessity for a biographical ability
that Holmes assigned only to great biographers: the ability to 'see the far
intellectual horizons of biography, as well as the tiny pebbles scattered on its
foreshore'.[30] The remarkable thing is the extent to which the biographer of
an African-American deals with 'pebbles', individual insulting acts of racism,
and with a panoramic history of racism and its periodic socially symbolic
events. The contexts, the meanings, and the ironies complicate—or increase
the significance of—anecdotes such as this one: Dorie Miller, one of the
discriminated-against African-American sailors relegated to the mess shot
down four Japanese planes at Pearl Harbor. Ringing through every biography
of an African-American are idealistic statements about what it means to be an
American, longings to be awarded the rights, responsibilities, and respect of
full citizens, moments when skill, training, and desire like Miller's have their
opportunity, and times of profound disappointment and disillusionment. What
is surprising is how long before, if at all, disenchantment sets in.

These biographies stretch to argue the dynamic interactions among
historical processes, individual abilities, immediate socio-historical circumstances, and individual personality. 'Ideology', a word neither used nor evoked
in biographies, sometimes nears expression in Black biography. It is possible
to write the biography of many white people without consciousness of the
nation and its institutionalized ideology, but sooner or later African-Americans
bring to awareness that even after individuals are defeated, persuaded, or cir-
cumvented, 'the bureaucracy', the amorphous, ubiquitous, unreachable final
adversary can close a door forever. The medical care of even the most prominent and respected African-Americans illustrates the situation of people seen
as less affluent, powerful, and valuable; the death of DuBois's son in Atlanta,
the treatment of Langston Hughes in a New York hospital, and of rudeness
visited upon the wife of an African-American university vice-president last

year seem recurrent and always-possible events. Contingencies, 'luck', the vagaries of who is sitting at a desk seem to multiply endlessly. Just as African-Americans find severely limited opportunities in the foreign service today, so a legion of institutions have closed themselves to, slotted, or typecast African-Americans throughout the history of the USA. Few succeed as DuBois did when he confronted former president Rutherford B. Hayes over the cancellation of a scholarship, but, as Lewis shows us, DuBois still failed to receive his German Ph.D. because support for such an education was considered politically unwise 'in Booker T. Washington's America' (Lewis, 146). Conspiracies of silence, failure to act, disappearances of the individuals with power and authority defeat individuals and, in some cases, determine tragedy and injustice. As Theodore Roosevelt took a yacht trip to see the Panama Canal, his order was carried out to discharge 'without honor and with forfeiture of pension' 167 of the 170 men in the 25th Infantry Regiment (Colored), some of them 'with twenty-five years service, six of them Medal of Honor winners' who were alleged to have 'shot up' Brownsville, Texas (Lewis, 331–2). Ironically, this troop had been effective reinforcements at a critical moment in Roosevelt's charge up San Juan Hill. But it was politically exigent for Roosevelt to harden his racial position. Similarly, everyone was powerless against anonymity and unavailability as the machine retired Charles Young, the hero who should have been given command of Camp Des Moines.

These biographies are quite good at explaining the dynamic among history, historical processes, immediate socio-historical circumstances, and the individual, but they are yet to actualize the portrayal of the interior life. How aware was DuBois of the social currents that legislated against his obtaining support for one more semester of study in Germany? Was King of the climate that kept the FBI dogging his every movement? More essentially, when did Booker T. Washington become truly alarmed at the relentless disenfranchisement of African-Americans?

Even as they deal with the complex and troublesome ways African-Americans are born and live in a special relationship with history, more than most biographers, Black biographers struggle with ignorance, resistance, and disbelief as they try to initiate the average reader, Black or white, to a nearly unknown history and a cast of characters who have been footnotes or excluded from history. The Hardwick Act, the Plessy–Ferguson decision, the reallocation of money to public schools as they became segregated—this rapid, ruthless march collapsed post-slavery hopes and truncated the growth of an educated, socially active African-American middle class. Over and over DuBois writes about the lynching that occurred in Abraham Lincoln's birthplace on the one-hundredth anniversary of his death (see *Dusk of Dawn*, 223). How many readers know this history? How many know that African-

Americans began to celebrate Jubilation, or Freedom, Day because they were discouraged from joining in Fourth of July celebrations? That from 1880 to 1920 one Black person was lynched every two and a half days? How many, if they know of it, connect the violence of the summer of 1919 to the fact that little more than fifty years after the liberation of the slaves African-Americans were virtually excluded from 'meaningful participation and citizenship in American society'? (Lewis, 579). How many are prepared to understand the history that makes Roy Wilkins's remark at the 1963 March on Washington so appropriate: DuBois's 'was the voice calling you to gather here today in this cause'?

The intersection of little-known history and unknown, forgotten, or habitually misrepresented people confronts the biographer at almost every turn. There are invisible lineages. Rosa Parks's predecessor Ida B. Wells defended herself from ouster from a 'white' train car by, among other things, biting the conductor who laid violent hands on her. Her life and actions resonate in the lives and utterances of DuBois, Washington, Hughes, and even King. She, Philip Randolph, Charles Young, Mary McLeod Bethune, John Hope, Jessie Fauset, and a host of others deserve biographies of their own, but, as important characters in others' stories, they threaten to bring narrative to a halt while the biographer has to review their lives and importance.

There are important, invisible aristocracies that have been all but unknown to us, and, once deep into some of these lives, they show how ignorant and irrelevant familiar ways of thinking and classifying are. Based on military service in the Civil War or even the Revolutionary War, part of well-established and affluent families in northern cities, or honoured members of a civil rights movement as old as our country, these aristocracies often play important parts in the lives of individual biographical subjects but nowhere are they fully explored—they remain shadowy factors that suggest how incomplete our understanding is, not only of these aristocracies and subjects but also of our country. For example, Langston Hughes's mother was a member of one of the most politically prominent and well-educated African-American families of the nineteenth century and one of his grandfathers died fighting in the Civil War. His grandmother had a bullet-riddled shawl her husband had worn when he fought with John Brown at Harper's Ferry, habitually wore it, and sometimes covered Hughes with it. Other relatives included conductors on the underground railroad, recruiters of Black soldiers to fight in the Civil War, and the first Black American to hold office by popular vote.[31] DuBois's grandmother sued and won her freedom and 30 shillings in Massachusetts in 1783; DuBois wrote a biography of John Brown. Washington moved through the circles of clubwomen to good advantage. As Clayborne Carson, director of the Martin Luther King Papers Project, says, we recognize the limitations of present biographies and biographical methods when we confront the absence of taking into account in every published biography of King that 'No other black leader of his time was so firmly rooted, through family, religious, educational, and political experiences, in the rich soils of both Afro-American culture and American reform thought.'[32] This dual exposure, steeping, heritage, Afro-American and American is the 'far intellectual horizon', and it intersects with 'pebbles' of all kinds, such as King's Auburn Avenue neighbourhood. To how many aristocracies, white as well, are we blind? How many connections are we missing? There are groups like the huge network of African-American club-women who, were they white, would have been closely studied by now by the kind of historians who have written about groups such as the suffragettes, the settlement workers, and 'the London hanged'.

Resistance to revisionary interpretations is certainly not limited to Black biographers, but it comes from more directions. The preface to Louis R. Harlan's 1972 *Booker T. Washington: The Making of a Black Leader, 1856–1901*, winner of the Bancroft Prize, begins,

Booker T. Washington has been the schoolbook black hero for more than half a century. The white authors of the American national myth have made him the token Negro in the company of white heroes. . . . This has been because of his acceptance of segregation, his outward humility, and his opposition to black militancy, even more than because of his constructive achievements. . . . his methods were too compromising and unheroic to win him a place in the black pantheon. . . . As a public man, Washington was best known as the Negro spokesman who, in the Atlanta Compromise Address in 1895, accepted the Southern white demand for racial segregation. (no page)

Yet at a Jubilation Day event in 1896 Booker T. Washington prophesied, 'I make no empty statement when I say that we have . . . a cancer gnawing at the heart of the Republic, that shall one day prove as dangerous as an attack from an army' (Harlan, 1: 237), and he often financed court fights against the disenfranchisement of African-Americans. Both African-Americans and whites are discomforted by this fuller, more complex Washington.

This discomfort is a stark and accurate reminder of something else that continuously faces the biographer of an African-American; politics is everywhere, and, the race of the biographer doubles the politics. It is, for instance, probably true that 'black and white America are distinct cultures' (Rampersad, 'Biography', 12), but the way that statement is experienced depends to a considerable extent upon whether the writer is Black or white. It can sound angry and combative and it can be interpreted as everything from conciliatory to exclusionary. White people fear being called racist and, as African-American writers remind us, there are often costs extorted for telling unpopular racial truths. As the editor of a recent book on race noted, 'It is at present virtually impossible to write or say anything on the topic of race that is not in some way objectionable or embarrassing' (LaCapra, *The Bounds of Race*, 2).

Biography is not a neutral art; in fact, of all the major literary genres it is probably the most political—the one most likely to influence how a nation and its history are defined and to be forced into serving the dominant point of view. Western culture has been far more likely to set up dichotomies than continuums, and the less known the historical players the easier that is. For example, it is common to emphasize the 'competition' between Washington and DuBois and King and Malcolm X, but not to shine a spotlight on the fact that none is given a place in the American nation, granted full citizenship and protection, or that they express the dual life of the member of a nation and of a people. Schoolchildren are often presented with a *de facto* choice: admire King but not Malcolm X. As Michael Dyson, author of *Making Malcolm: The Myth and Meaning of Malcolm X*, says, Malcolm X's 'entire legacy until recently has been demonized and dismissed by the traditional academy'.[33] African-American biography and scholarship often calls attention to what these men shared, even which statements they made that sound like carbon copies, and which shared battles they fought (as Washington's and DuBois's against the disenfranchisement of Blacks), and, thus, begins revising not only conceptions of lives but of history. James Cone, for instance, argues rightly that King and Malcolm X 'began to embrace aspects of each other's viewpoints' and their thought and work was 'converging' at the time of their deaths (Dyson, 47).

Although the 250-year-old tradition of Black Nationalism is often minimized or even denied, it exists. Based on rejection of optimism, it takes for granted a 'black nation unassimilated alongside the American nation'.[34] Little is known of the all-Black communities, some started by philanthropists, and much effort has been spent in discrediting Marcus Garvey, Father Divine, Stokeley Carmichael, Bobby Seale, and even DuBois. In the West, Black people are 'socialized in the dominant form of national belonging' but also made aware of the ways they do not belong; this fact is well conveyed by existing biographies. When they are formed 'within a field of social values, norms of behaviour and collective symbols' (Balibar, 94–5), the meaning of these norms and symbols and the behaviour and identity that results are sometimes different from whites, and this fact has been less well developed, even unrecognized (many African-American scholars consider rap an expression of it), and are often unacceptable to most of the reading public. As Dyson says, the greater cultural visibility of King over Malcolm X has 'to do with the style, content, and aims of his leadership, which for most of his life were easily translatable and largely attractive to white America. On the other hand, Malcolm's complex leadership . . . which appealed especially to working and poor blacks, has invited derision, caricature and dismissal, forces which undermine . . . scholarly investigation' (p. 45).

All of these examples, both the nurturing, invisible aristocracies and the bi-polar portraits of African-American leaders, extends our understanding of the variety of ways history is recorded, transmitted, and, more significantly for biographers, felt. Horace Pippin's painting 'Mr. Prejudice' brings together a history and a set of images that illustrate this point. The Statue of Liberty, that great symbol of the USA is black, and to match the torch is the startlingly white Ku Klux Klan figure and parallel to Liberty's face that of a white man holding a lynching rope. White and black military figures mingle at the bottom, and the aviators clearly reach for each other,[35] but a worker is driving a wedge, breaking the familiar 'V for Victory' in half and separating the two workers, one black and one white, who might have joined together to increase the USA's industrial greatness. Like so many of these biographies, it captures both race and class antagonism. War and a few other experiences strip most class markers and create brief, artificial situations, and then, when they are over, the domi-nant society quickly works to restore prior social, economic, and political posi-tions. Painted in 1943, the painting is a journalistic report and horribly prophetic of widespread efforts to push African-Americans back 'into their place'. This history, too, is little known, often suppressed, denied, or diminished.

Feminists used to say that everything had to be done all over again, and that

9. Horace Pippin, 'Mr. Prejudice'

applied most profoundly to the most familiar, the most commonplace, and least questioned stories and opinions. Such things as women's needlework expressed their distinct culture but also proved to be far more complex than perceived, sometimes showing artistic sensibilities, sometimes revealing protest, sometimes carrying on traditions with subtly revisionary or stubbornly conventional meanings, always more available for interpretation than had been perceived. An example in African-American culture is music, certainly a place history has been recorded, transmitted, and felt. Just as DuBois sang 'Steal Away' to himself on his birthday, Martin Luther King's tombstone reads, 'Free at last, Free at Last, Great God Almighty . . .'. Spirituals, gospel, soul, and jazz in Black biography are often expressions of feelings, of shared feelings, and of a familiar history and responses to that history. The power and resonance of Lewis's prose occasionally comes from this music: 'He saw written across the faces deep in Wilson County the rebuked destinies of the black people who came . . . aspiring out of slavery' (*W. E. B. DuBois*, 70) and he 'raised such a couth ruckus' (p. 104). Some subjects stretch back to Africa hoping to make a connection to lost families and histories. DuBois insists that he heard the same rhythm and part singing in Monrovia that he had heard at Fisk (*Dusk of Dawn*, 119). Scraps of songs, lines of disconnected syllables, such as the one DuBois remembered as a 'West African' song as part of his babyhood, are carefully preserved but usually unidentifiable.

Langston Hughes deliberately married his poetry to it, and understanding that lifts him out of the stereotype of 'simple folk poet' to an innovator and deliberately experimental artist. As Henry Louis Gates summarizes, 'Hughes . . . demonstrated how to use black vernacular language and music—especially the blues and jazz—as a poetic diction, a formal language of poetry . . . [He] undertook the project of constructing an entire literary tradition upon the actual spoken language of the black working and rural classes.'[36] Some of his poetry captures the complex weave of grief and hope in the blues: 'Out of the dust of dreams, | . . . Out of the purple and rose of old memories, | They make purple wings.' Just as King's biographers have been called for not explicating fully his roots in African-American culture and US reform movements, almost all biographers can be chastised for not taking traditional African-American music seriously enough. It is a frustrating code, infinitely complex and as moody as race relations. We now know something of the ways spirituals provided means of secret communication in slave times, but few are explicating Black music as a form in which Black musicians 'have always sought to express something uniquely black and to express it in a way which leaves whites dumbfounded and excluded' (Grier and Cobbs, *Black Rage*, 125). Biographers are not yet asking at what moments and from what causes do new variations and new forms arise nor are they yet looking to see when revisions in the history they bear occur.

★

David Lewis's sentence is not neutral reportage: 'Now that the right had been won to die discriminated against in the war for world democracy, DuBois momentary stood back from the fray . . .'. Like Holroyd's 'the love which passes all Christian understanding', it is a harsh judgement, the mark of a biographer practising an art he has decided is moral, authoritative, and personal. Like the British biographers, Lewis assumes the right to use tone to comment and also seems to be unselfconscious about a harmony he feels between his mind, his perspective, and DuBois's. Here and elsewhere he draws upon his own identity as an intellectual and a social scientist to communicate the texture of DuBois's life.

In contrast to the British professionals, the Black biographers, like Lewis, are academics, trained in the most advanced methods of modern historiography and cultural studies. In cultural studies, paradoxically, knowledge and clarity are arrived at by exercises in endless complication, in 'thickening' description, working 'horizontally and vertically' to expand contexts, thickening each. Comfortable with manuscripts and primary documents, well-connected and confident enough to demand access to largely unaccessible archives, dedicated, and (thanks to their academic appointments) well-funded, they share the commitment of the British professionals to dig and dig, to achieve mastery and intimacy, and to write a compelling story, but they fear summaries and tightly unified portraits and know that they must be utterly convincing, that they must bring the full arsenal of academic strategies of fact finding and argument to their biographies. They can pick and choose among historical methods and the agendas of their field. They know they are revisionary, not only in the representation of their individual subjects but also in their insistence that each subject is more complex, more individual, even more intelligent and feeling than has been previously thought and rendered.

As Black biography evolves it is developing a new kind of biographical presence, one overtly and unapologetically collaborative, somehow both harmonious and academic and another rich variant on the double voice of the best biographies. Perhaps finding its roots in *The Autobiography of Malcolm X* 'with the assistance of Alex Haley', it is now somewhat common and with books such as *Days of Grace* in more self-conscious relationships to true biography. Variations on the form are multiplying. For instance, Sara Lawrence-Lightfoot calls herself a 'portraitist' in the opening sentence of *I've Known Rivers: Lives of Loss and Liberation* (p. xv), and her collection of biographies is based on extended interviews that often seem to turn lunch tables and offices into spaces as intimate as the topics being discussed. Her questions and implied reactions occasionally portray moments of intense agreement, even recognition and identification, yet each subject is separate from herself, individual, complex, and depicted over time. Heritage, early life, education, marriage, career, major decisions—all of these things are carefully recorded and linked not only in time but in an interpretation of the person.

A typical example is the life of Felton, 'Tony', Earls, a professor in the Harvard School of Public Health. Earls's life is one of dedicated work and high achievement. Lawrence-Lightfoot allows us to follow his decisions, which often lead to major, unpredictable changes. For instance, she connects to the lynching of Emmett Till his leaving a prestigious, pure research neurophysiology postdoctoral fellowship for an internship in paediatrics in East Harlem where he was always exhausted, sleep-deprived, and sick with the colds and illnesses of his patients. Immediate events resonate with history in all of the Black biographies. As DuBois had written much earlier, 'One could not be a calm, cool, and detached scientist while Negroes were lynched, murdered and starved' (*Dusk of Dawn*, 67). Again, this theme often begins in childhood, as it does with Jesse Jackson's efforts to know the news every day and Jean Toomer as president of his school's Current Events Club.

Shortly after going to Harlem, Earls resisted the draft and remembered, 'I realized once again that I'm not an American, I'm a black man.' Over and over, Lawrence-Lightfoot makes Earls's divided soul, his decisions, and their costs not only comprehensible but 'logical'. To refuse military service pitted him against his father and a 'parade of proud black veterans' (p. 367). Rather poignantly, she shows us a person who consistently longs for 'a life filled with the beauty, subtlety, and discipline' of science (or of playing the classical guitar) and an ideal family life but who cannot shut out the 'raw emotion' that personal and national events trigger. Race and several news stories including the Rodney King verdict and the subsequent riots draw the biographer and her subject together, but he is always her subject, not her spokesperson or alter ego. When he says that 'Retaliation may be your last possible way to express your humanity' (p. 341), we feel her draw back even as we understand the evolution of *his* thought, that *he* conceives much of his life in terms of 'stories of rage and hurt', and that his internal struggles are as intense at age 50 as they were in his youth. As late as 1984 Jesse Jackson preached in an attempt to convince: 'Sometimes we may have . . . may have *narrow* choices. But we *do* always have choices. We struggled long and paid in suffering to win the right to those choices, and we . . . *do* have choices now!' (Frady, 6).

Richard Newman, managing editor of the *Harvard Guide to African-American History*, describes Lawrence-Lightfoot's book as inventing a new literary genre out of biography, sociology, and oral history with an especially original 'controlled participation in the process'.[37] In fact, none of these things or the combination of them is original, but her self-consciousness about 'the developing relationship between me and the storytellers' and the way she begins with middle age, at the point of mid-life crisis for several of her subjects, are. She talks about the way she deliberately 'revealed' her voice, and her methods provide unusual and productive ways to deal sensitively with privacy issues without eliminating them from the biography. Collectively, her subjects reveal themselves as individuals, a people, and caught in the particular history, past and immediate, of the USA.

This collaborative presence is, again, an extension of common biographical practice and an expression of the ways all biographers work by inference, projection, empathy, and imagination. The fact that the reader can feel Lawrence-Lightfoot pulling away points out the potential the collaborative stance has for conflict with the duties and obligations traditionally assigned to biographers. Lawrence-Lightfoot pulls away from taboo emotions, and as an individual, a woman, and a social scientist she is making an honest and entirely appropriate gesture. What is unusual is the overt nature of her action, the clarity of her communication of her opinion. A much more serious conflict arises when the biographer shifts from this meaning of collaboration to the word's other meaning, 'to co-operate treasonably'.

Just as some of the British biographers are aware of issues of 'ethics, authenticity, celebrity, and empathy', Black biographers sometimes consider 'treason'. They see that they can commit treason against the biographical form and against their race, and sometimes they feel trapped into choosing one or the other. Should, for instance, the biographer decide that the subject's privacy be protected? Is it the biographer's duty to reveal what he knows about the actions and feelings of his subject? Arnold Rampersad wrote, 'Without an attempt to pursue the elusive and unattainable truth within recognizable rules of evidence . . . the biographer is a menace to literate society'. Yet the recognition that privacy and self-protection are important to African-Americans and that there is a high-level of insistence upon the inner self as a refuge of dignity has constrained him.[38] Even after uttering this challenge to biographers, he admits resonating to the special intersections of privacy and race. Sections of *Days of Grace*, Arthur Ashe's memoir which he co-authored and completed, however, discuss privacy eloquently and in subsequent interviews Rampersad admitted the constraints that left large, important issues untouched. 'I yearned for the majesty of biography', he once said.[39] And yet, statements like James Weldon Johnson's must make biographers pause, sensitive as they often are to privacy and image and especially as they recognize that for African-Americans privacy, performative selves, and race are inseparable: 'My inner life is mine, and I shall defend and maintain its integrity against all the powers of hell' (*Negro Americans, What Now?*)

Beyond considerations of the individual's desires and feelings, the inclination to protect the image of a race's hero or heroine and of the race itself and the fear of offending work strongly against the biographer's duty to give full, fair even unflinching accounts. Even if the reticence born of diplomacy can be overcome, the nexus of political considerations may be impossible to comprehend fully. Richard King's and Clayborne Carson's reviews of *Bearing the Cross* suggest just how difficult is the task. King points out that Ella Baker (and numerous others) were far from objective sources, and, for instance,

Baker's 'opposition to the emphasis upon the importance of the "great man" was political, not metahistorical', as she had broken with Martin Luther King over the competing theories of leadership exemplified by the SCLC and SNCC (Student Nonviolent Coordinating Committee).[40] Carson's evaluation of Garrow's portrayal of Martin Luther King's sex life and its place in fixing an aspect of King's character, making it part of 'historical reality', makes clear the seriousness of the biographer's responsibility and the power of the genre to create opinon. Carson, like so many African-American writers, immediately and simultaneoulsy sees the historical baggage that Hoover and others carried, the political climate in which they could exercise their obsession with 'Negro sexuality', and the political ramifications of Garrow's representations of King.[41] Reminders of these truths are all around us—in a discussion in 1998 of which African-Americans deserve to be on a US postage stamp, a Stillman College student said that W. E. B. DuBois should be disqualified because he had been a Communist.

One of the most striking things about the lives of African-Americans is the extent to which even youthful or ordinary individuals were intensely engaged with influencing or even recasting the image of their race and, by natural extension, of themselves. Black biographers may share this hope. The reviewer of Lewis's *W. E. B. DuBois* in *The Journal of Negro Education* highlights this theme and praises Lewis for reflecting 'upon how African-Americans prized the portrait of themselves served up by DuBois's writings'.[42] He continues to discuss the continued importance of biographies that champion 'the merits of a well-trained mind for people of color in their struggles against prejudice and discrimination' (p. 650). This theme is alive and important in the biographies of African-Americans by African-Americans; for instance, *Days of Grace* is full of evocations of it, and it is clear that Ashe revered Martin Luther King and found him a useful example because he demonstrated how 'the high moral ground' might be occupied and even 'commanded' 'splendidly' (p. 138 *et passim*). In 1998 so liberal a newspaper as the *New York Times* was still invoking race and individual responsibility for the race's image. In its coverage of the history of the US Open tennis tournament, Susan B. Adams writes, 'the articulate, introspective Ashe, who brought dignity to a sport and a race . . .' (*NYT*, 30 August 1998, Sports 36). An individual's awareness of his or her impact on the perception and even fate of a group is another important but neglected topic. How aware, for example, were Washington and King of their influence and to what extent did they feel it a burden which they took up and consciously honed? To what extent did Eleanor Roosevelt think of herself as remaking the image of women and then of presidents' wives? Have we treated the Jewish and Irish and Italian *Angst* adequately in any prominent person's life?

The stakes are great, of course, and even the lives of long-dead people such as Booker T. Washington still evoke the political issues that angered, frightened, and divided people in his lifetime. In 1969 I taught some of Langston Hughes's poetry in an eleventh-grade American literature survey. After I made the assignment, one of the best students in the class raised his hand and said, 'You know he's a Communist, don't you?' The day I taught the poems and for a week after that, the student's father and two other members of the John Birch Society sat in my classroom and watched me teach five periods of English a day. The class liked Hughes's poetry, and no one—not the department head, principal, or even John Birch Society observers—ever spoke to me about teaching Hughes.[43] This incident suggests just how easily African-American writers can be eradicated from the canon and how successfully accusations such as being Communist can discredit. Accusations regarding King's friendship with Stanley Levison, who was believed to be a Soviet agent, complicated his work and still, in some people's minds, tarnish his reputation. Ironically, it was the reason Izola Curry gave for stabbing King, and she was, in Taylor Branch's opinion, committed to a mental institution for insisting King was 'mixed up with the Communists' and being investigated by the FBI (*Parting the Waters*, 245). Performance at the McCarthy hearings is still a litmus test—Rampersad implies an apology for Hughes's performance, and Lewis quotes approvingly what someone said of DuBois's: 'They could not look at him and call me inferior' (p. 3). The McCarthy hearings, the Red Scare, and the treatment and response of African-Americans are fading memories, but the impact it has had on present reputations makes it an important 'far intellectual horizon'.

A number of topics that need to be dealt with sensitively in any biography are more immediate in the lives of most African-Americans, open issues of privacy and racial protectiveness, and are also deeply political. For instance, these biographies usually must deal with what is often called 'accommodation'. All people 'accommodate' themselves to power structures and social mores; they 'accommodate' for popularity, economic and social gain, and now and then for safety. The Anglo-American tradition is to demand the weight put on standing up for principles as opposed to conformity or retreating to fight again when the odds are better; this demand is especially strong in the USA, which teaches its schoolchildren to admire such speeches as Nathan Hale's 'I only regret that I have but one life to lose for my country.' Although we don't say so, we prefer martyrs to diplomats, warriors to those who choose to engage another day another way. Therefore, biographers of African-Americans cope in various ways with the ways their subjects have navigated the minefields of American society. Lewis writes a wonderful sentence, 'Booker T. Washington had not walked out of slavery and a West Virginia coal mine thirty-six years and multiple personalities ago to find welcome in Theodore Roosevelt's White House and the foyers of the rich by mistaking merit for reality' (p. 238). Harlan writes bluntly that Washington 'manipulated' people, that he 'acquiesced in segregation . . . repressed freedom of speech and press among his faculty, students, and graduates . . . and sought an identity of interest with . . . the dominant white leadership' (pp. 157–8). And Harlan feels he must say, 'He kept his dignity through it all.' How on earth could he have succeeded, or survived, had he not acquiesced?

The issue of accommodation runs through Martin Luther King's conflicts with SNCC and through the accounts of King's conduct at Selma. So far, however, biographers have allowed the subject to arise in the narrative without treating it seriously. Was King's conduct based in a philosophy of leadership, perhaps of his own Gandhi-like symbolic centrality, or was it a fundamental undemocratic distrust of the masses, or something else? Why did he secretly agree to turn the 2,000 protestors back as they approached a line of troopers when he was in the lead at the 'Tuesday turnaround'? Accommodation is a nascent issue in many biographies of white people, too, as is the fact that all successful people study human nature, but the opportunities for it, progress in it, behavioural adaptations, and concrete results are seldom major topics. In biographies of African-Americans they are and suggest that they ought to be in the lives of many people of all races. If we knew how Eleanor Roosevelt accommodated herself to the Democratic leadership, how Mary McCarthy compromised at the *Partisan Review*, and how Huey Long adapted his message to different Southern classes would not that be deeply interesting and important keys to understanding their personalities, their principles, their successes, and their understandings of society? We learn more about Theodore Roosevelt's accommodating himself to the growing anti-black feeling from lives of Washington and DuBois than we do from biographies of him, and this should not be.[44]

James Weldon Johnson describes the narrator of *Autobiography* watching a lynching and being overwhelmed with revulsion at the white people who were transformed into 'savage beasts' but also with shame with his own race, which 'could be so dealt with'. Here the complexity of a Black individual with a white nation, the individual with his 'own powerless people',[45] and the individual and the race's with concepts such as freedom, justice, and American become obvious even as issues of privacy and protectiveness are aroused. Perhaps this struggle is most clear in biographies of Richard Wright, whose race hatreds seem central to his personality. A good biography absolutely must express, explain, and make these things vivid; it is a pressing, essential demand on the form and is interwoven with major developmental themes such as 'coming to consciousness'. None of these relationships is easy to ferret out and harder yet to represent fully, fairly, and sensitively.

★

Embracing complexity and individualism, committing themselves to letting biographical subjects' lives reveal form, and accepting hills, valleys, curves, and straightaways in stories, Black biographers are practising the honest craft of the form. Coming to maturity at the nexus of pushing the envelope and traditional biography, they are beginning with individual lives and exploring how race and history permeated consciousness and enfolded the life. They are devising ways to narrate polyvalent relationships and reconceptualizing nationhood and community. Just as Langston Hughes's movement in and out of Mexico and DuBois's immersion in European and African countries changed them and the way the USA looked, so readers' conceptions of the subjects and the USA undergo revision. Over and over they illustrate the inseparable, dynamic relationship among history, historical processes, immediate socio-historical circumstances, and the individual, his or her actions and interior life. Asking new questions about relationships and contexts, they are breaking ground that may give biography new significance and profundity. With the British professionals, they are examples of something Marita Sturken once said, 'Biographies . . . mark the moment when personal stories are imbued with cultural meanings.'

Conclusion

> The biographer's art is patterned on Austen, Thackeray, and Eliot, not on Beckett, Faulkner, or DeLillo.
>
> Sharon O'Brien[1]

If biographers and their subjects are collaborators, biographers and readers are soul mates. They share the willingness, even desire, to be drawn into another life and look forward to being absorbed in it, sinking into it and a comfortable chair. No matter the critical fads and theory wars, they know there's a there there—a human life, a 'real person', emotions that still reverberate, meaningful actions, meaningful feelings. They may be celebrating, hoping to learn from, analysing, or gossiping about a life—just like the biographer. They may be seeking to understand the springs of a poet's consummate art, doing a close and careful study of a moment in history, or poking through a famous person's rubbish bin. They can be high-minded, seeking the 'objectivity', 'panoramic range', and 'epic thrust' that readers consistently find in Ellmann's *Joyce,* or they can enjoy what Phyllis Rose describes as the kinds of things 'real biographers' find: 'that X was hospitalized for depression in the 1950s, despite his public air of equanimity, or that Y couldn't face the day without drinking a half bottle of gin before noon' (Rhiel and Suchoff, *Seductions,* 133). More to the point, perhaps, just like the biographer, they have questions such as this: 'What brought an ordinary, likeable man into one of the ugliest businesses we have, the making of war, and what made him so damn good at it?' 'Can we render historical, meaningful, and interesting what has hitherto been hidden from history, this woman's life?' 'What was it about the men, their attitudes, the country, its institutions and above all the era which had allowed this tragedy to take place?'[2]

Readers ask biographers for honest things. They want integrity, judgement, interpretative skill, and a good read. They want what in a novel would be called a character whose outer life of work and activity and inner life of emotion and thought are depicted with the clarity of a novelist and the rigour of a scholar. In their words: They expect biographers to have good evidence in their possession and 'make sense' of it while being accurate. They want neither too much nor too little 'data' published. They hope that some of the evidence will yield 'vivid detail' that reveals something profound or characteristic or startling or 'human' or even 'encapsulating' about the subject. They want to 'follow' the life and not encounter repetition, unexplained actions, blatant moralizing, or unrestrained speculation. They find summaries of familiar exploits or of literary works 'pedestrian' but want them included in some imaginative guise.

Although critics and biographers can call it a 'synthetic genre' and say that what it is and should attempt 'has been and remains a contentious subject'[3] among themselves, readers are wiser. They know there will never be a poetics of biography, and yet there is a there there, too. Even an undergraduate student knows what biography is: 'Biography is written to capture a person's life or at least an aspect or aspects of it, so that it will be remembered and meaningful to later generations as well as the present. When one begins to read a biography he or she has certain expectations of the work including accurate facts about the life and a reason why the life is important. The reader also assumes that the person's life story will be told with as much fairness as possible' (student group). This non-expert, somewhat awkward definition captures the appeal and the importance of biography: its presentness—it is meaningful to the present, the life *is*, not just was, important.

Like music, biography will continue to exist in myriad forms, and, like the lovers of music, readers of biography will differ in their favourite kinds, enjoy several kinds, and, in tune with their moods and needs, select different kinds at different times. Although some people are devoted to only one or two kinds—perhaps biographies of military heroes and prime ministers—most are moody readers, ready to lose themselves in Ellmann's *James Joyce* and Joan Hedrick's *Harriet Beecher Stowe*, or find amusement in Barry Paris's *Garbo* and Kitty Kelley's *His Way* (on Frank Sinatra), or delight in an intellectual experiment such as Jerome Christensen's *Practicing Enlightenment* (on Hume) or Lloyd Kramer's *Lafayette*, or try out fictions about the art and its practitioners such as Henry James's *Aspern Papers*, A. S. Byatt's *Possession*, or Alison Lurie's *The Truth about Lorin Jones*.

But, just as they recognize music as music, so they seldom debate whether or not a book is a biography. Like the lines that make up my mathematical envelope, the characteristics of biography and demands on the form endure. The narrative of the life of a person told with honesty and interpreted with integrity and imagination will always speak to the human soul. Like the listeners who gathered around a bard or an American Indian storyteller, readers of biography enjoy interpretations of the world and humankind's—their own—place in it. Just as biographers bring themselves to biography and find personal meaning, so do readers, and what they bring and find validate truths about biography and about life and also expand and deepen the meaning of the life and the book. There is a three-way dynamic.

And so there is something of a poetics of biography, best described as functional ('I know it when I see it') but with elements of the prescriptive and controlling. Like 'prose fiction' or even 'novel', the genre it most resembles, 'biography' is an inclusive term, amenable to a variety of forms, comfortably encompassing and suggesting fluid rather than fixed shapes. Even better than the novel, biography can be discussed and defined by the 'work' it does in society. Just as every strong biography expands the possibilities of the form, so some biographies have the power to define how a person, a nation and its history will be judged, to contribute to maintaining, revising, or shaking its self-image.

Biography, like the novel, is not a static genre. Definitions of it capture that fact as well as its enduring characteristics. Harold Nicolson said that 'pure biography' should be 'written with a sense of history, should describe an individual character, and should be written with an adequate feeling for style'. Stephen B. Oates summarizes, 'Biographies . . . attempt to simulate a human life through the magic of language, through character development and the depiction of interpersonal relationships, through graphic scenes, the telling quotation, the revealing detail, the power of suggestion, and dramatic narrative sweep . . . illuminate universal truths about humankind through the sufferings and triumphs of a single human being.'[4] Jeffrey Meyers introduces a collection of essays on seven biographies by calling them 'works of art' and describes them as having the 'qualities of great works in this genre': 'original research that casts new light on the subject, a complete and accurate synthesis of both public and private life, an elegant yet lively style, a perceptive interpretation of character, a sound dramatic structure that brings the pattern of life into focus, an evocation of the subject's achievement—the real justification of the work' *(Biographer's Art, 1).*

As this book has shown, ideas of the form have softened or even moved past some of these ideas, especially Meyers's American masculine position. Readers and biographers are too wise to think that they ever get 'a complete and accurate synthesis of both public and private life' and too experienced not to pause over 'achievement' and 'real justification', first sensing its older meaning and second thinking with pleasure on how the subjects and the definition of 'achievement' have expanded in recent years. It can include Nelly Ternan, subject of Claire Tomalin's *Invisible Woman*, who Catherine Peters suggested opens a 'modern sub-genre: the biography of the forgotten servants and inspirers of literature', in this case, that of Charles Dickens (Batchelor, 47). In fact, biography is more interesting today because of the acknowledgement that the portrayal of an individual is not the only possible one.

For a long time, too, as an anonymous essayist wrote in 1962, we've known that 'objective truth . . . whether in large matters or small does not exist, that the multiplicity of incidents making up any social event are capable of such various interpretations that no single view of them can be finally "true", and that no life is ever written with definitive completeness' ('Portraits in Prose', 130). We distrust too much unity, too neat a pattern, and are more likely to be gripped by statements like this one: 'He was a complex, many-sided character. "He wore masks, and he was always changing". . . under one mask there is always another' (Eribon, *Michel Foucault*, xi). And this one: 'These selves of which we are built up, one on top of another, as plates are piled on a waiter's hand, have attachments elsewhere, sympathies, little constitutions and rights of their own . . . so that one will only come if it is raining, another in a room with green curtains, another when Mrs. Jones is not there . . .' (Woolf, *Orlando*, 277). We expect to get to know people and see them defined by their conflicts, their changing, mixed selves and their performative selves as well as by their projects and actions. We fear and resist paradigms—the idea that a group of lives of women might be formed (or written to form) the story of a woman 'with talent undeveloped and ability unused' seems reductive. Even though most biographers probably feel as Richard Sewall did when he wrote, 'I hate the thought of having *thinned* Emily Dickinson . . . I am appalled at what I left out' (1: xii), except for straight academic biographers who know that they are producing reference works as well as biographies, selectivity, telling anecdotes, symbolic moments, encapsulating scenes, and even self-conscious decisions about which personality aspects to emphasize and which to subordinate or even omit are today accepted as responsibilities of the biographer.

Readers expect more context, presented in far more sophisticated and wide-ranging ways. In an essay on Freud's biography of Leonardo da Vinci, Alan Elms began a list of what we would expect today in addition to a theory of personality: 'comprehensive knowledge . . . of art history, Italian culture of the fifteenth and sixteenth centuries, Roman Catholic religious history and tradition, the Italian language, paint chemistry, European Renaissance politics and several other fields' (*Uncovering Lives*, 39). In a full biography, readers expect that. 'Rollicking biography of an old-fashioned sort, all about politics and nothing but politics' (Gaddis Smith, *NYT*, 23 August 1993, 3) and other contextually or psychologically limited forms are labelled as just that, 'old-fashioned', sometimes enjoyable and useful but no longer a fully actualized example of the form. Readers can now choose among biographies that treat history, culture, relationships, and the individual's psyche with varying degrees of emphasis and development, but serious attention is given to all. How much weight family, experiences, society, history, and talent and ability are given in constructing the person differs, and readers expect that, too.

Readers are becoming more aware of the power of biography and the need to recognize when biographies are being deeply, even threateningly, revisionary or are powerful instruments of maintaining the status quo and received opinion. They recognize that certain stories and plot lines become a culture's myths and its ways of understanding the way society and the world are. These cultural stories teach people how to regard themselves, how to make themselves intelligible to each other, and how to conduct themselves; they affect relationships and a people's perceptions of themselves and their destiny (Gergen and Gergen, 193). More than any string of 'facts', the narratives create nationhood and historical consciousness. Many biographers are now self-conscious about these powers and willing to write about the complexity of a nation's life over time with reinterpretations of, for instance, how much class still determines in Great Britain and what part it, gender, and history played in shaping Margaret Thatcher and, in turn, her impact on Great Britain. Many are also aware that they decide to contribute to mainstream historical inquiries or break into new inquiries as David Lewis did when he introduced the great variety of leadership models confronting African-Americans and the white power structure at the beginning of the twentieth century in his biography of DuBois.

These things are certain.

The demand for narrative will not diminish. Indeed, even though some successful biographies have departed dramatically from chronological narration, the demand for it will not decrease. Reviewers blame lack of clarity or interest on 'scrambled time sequences'. What Maurois observed a long time ago still holds, that it is 'extremely difficult to interest a reader in facts which are not presented in their normal order'. As this book argues, narrative is far more than the engine that drives a gripping biography and makes a life story absorbing. Narrative is the chief means by which we understand a life, ours or anyone else's, and endow it with coherence and meaning over time. That argues for narrative and for arrangement that lets readers see the person become what they were. As Richard Holmes says, 'By reconstructing a life through narrative, [biography] emphasizes cause and consequence, the linked pattern of growth and change, the vivid story-line of individual responsibility and meaningful action' (Atlas, 'Holmes on the Case', 58). Cause–consequence, growth–change: chronological stories. In Holmes's terms, biography not only explains the subject's life but it teaches lessons. Often overlooked are such subversive powers of narrative as these and others—decisions biographers make. By dreaming and imagining, people create new possibilities; narrative is one of the means by which biographers can learn and then show readers how and how many ways human beings dream.

The cultural significance of biography will grow. With the infusion of methods and issues from cultural studies, feminism, social anthropology, and other disciplines in the human sciences, especially as they continue their slow advance in university history departments, biographers will be able to explain the greater importance of subjects' lives and the reciprocal significances of historical processes and individuals. With the continued entry of feminists and people of colour, new lives, new issues, and new methodologies will be developed, again raising the significance and, more importantly, the drama and sweep of narrative lives. Any art that becomes mass culture, as biography has with television, magazines, and numbers of new book series, carries heavy cultural weight and can perpetrate or create new myths about the men and women that a nation's people imitate or scorn.

Increasingly biographies will be judged by the quality of storytelling, by sensory fullness—and by willingness to use terrifying reportorial candour. New Journalism and the non-fiction novel, born during the Vietnam protest years in the USA, contributed to the methods of biographers, the expectations of readers, and the propagation of the pleasures of reading (or watching) biography. Journalistic biography is now firmly established, both in the short forms so popular in the mass media and in full-length books such as Robert Caro's *The Power Broker: Robert Moses and the Fall of New York*, one of the ground-breaking, strong biographies that expanded the possibilities of the form. As practised by the New Journalists beginning in the 1960s and 1970s, it combined investigative reporting with fictional techniques: 'Only through the most searching forms of reporting was it possible, in non-fiction, to use whole scenes, extended dialogue, point-of-view, and interior monologue . . . "entering people's minds". . . that was one more doorbell a reporter had to push',[5] as Tom Wolfe wrote. Some of their work was obsessive, as everyone describes Jimmy Breslin's to have been when he was a columnist for the New York *Herald Tribune*, and as Robert Caro's research rightly was for *The Power Broker* and *The Years of Lyndon Johnson*.

Often vilified in Great Britain as Humphrey Carpenter's life of Archbishop Runcie was (who did deserve better and is a far more important figure than Carpenter indicates), in the Americas it is encouraged, mature, and respected. The place for such lives is suggested by the nearly simultaneous publication of Claude Clegg's *An Original Man: The Life and Times of Elijah Muhammad* and Karl Evanzz's *The Messenger: The Rise . . . of Elijah Muhammad* and of Jorge Castañeda's *Compañero: The Life and Death of Che Guevara* and Paco Taibo's *Guevara, Also Known as Che*. Clegg and Castañeda are university faculty; Castañeda is one of Mexico's most distinguished political scientists, and Clegg, a history professor, has been working on his biography since his dissertation days. Evanzz works for the *Washington Post* and Taibo is a reporter and best-selling Mexican detective fiction-writer. The narratives are closer to each other than they would have been even two years ago, and Castañeda and Taibo exchanged notes, while Evanzz consulted Clegg's work. The pleasures are often similar, but the contrasts are part of their lineages. Castañeda does better portraying the mind of the revolutionary, who while surrounded by illiterate peasant-soldiers read or played chess in the midst of filthy camps and whose idealistic, theoretical politics were both ludicrous and mythic within the realities of the Congo and Bolivia. His explanation of the relationship between Castro and Guevara is also much better, because it provides a worldwide context, especially of the Soviet Union's presence in Cuba and South America. Taibo gives a much more sensory and dramatic account of Guevara's experiences in Castro's revolution; the trip to Cuba, life in the Sierra Maestras, and the battle of Santa Clara are especially full and vivid.

As Tom Wolfe explains, part of the journalists' work was to gather detail, and much of the detail the New Journalists recorded was 'novelistic', the stuff of the eighteenth- and nineteenth-century realist novel (gestures, individual facial and verbal expressions, observations on the environment such as clothing, furniture, carpeting, landscaping). Some critics see a trend in biography towards movement from scene to scene as opposed to more conventional alternation of action or event and interpretation or exposition. Scene-to-scene construction was typical of the earliest practisers of the New Journalism and, as part of their desire to communicate character and emotion and their need for compression, developed into a highly symbolic code. As Wolfe says, manners, customs, 'styles of traveling, eating, keeping house, modes of behaving toward children, servants, superiors, inferiors, peers, plus the various looks, glances, poses, styles of walking' are 'symbolic details . . . through which people express their position in the world or what they think it is or what they hope it to be' (pp. 31–2). Thus, they reveal both character and class, an increasing concern of biographers. This practice and his skill at it made Caro's biographies devastating exposés. Not only do scenes and details add interest and vividness, they also allow biographers to introduce social themes and provide another way to intrude in the narrative and pass judgement without drawing attention to their intrusion.

The connection between biography and popular culture may be especially strong with journalistic lives; certainly a Che Swatch and a Rage Against the Machine CD with his image, news and magazine stories with pictures of the geophysicists and forensic scientists shedding tears as they excavated Guevara's body in Vallegrande, Bolivia, are signs of the way some unforeseen need in society rises to visibility because of biography and may be explained or perpetuated by it. 'Short-form biography', as the kind of lives or 'profiles' that appear in magazines, the A&E and other TV biographies, and in book series such as 'Biography' are often called, introduces a very large number of living and dead subjects to the masses. History, literature, Drury Lane, the Highlands, Wembley, Hollywood, Madison Square Garden, the Grand Ol' Opry, and the Kremlin have been plundered for material, and most of the series, especially A&E, set high research and presentation standards.

The rewards for writing full biographies in universities will never be adequate to the years they consume. Although there will be a few cross-over biographers, like Diane Middlebrook, Arnold Rampersad, and the late Leon Edel, most academic biographers will choose to write biographical books, a distinct type that uses many of the biographer's methods for different purposes or for the exploration of an aspect of a life. Both Paula MacDowell's *The Women of Grub Street* and Richard Wendorf's *Sir Joshua Reynolds: The Painter in Society* are exemplary models of this form. Biography and especially its research methods are now enjoying new respectability and even trendiness on both sides of the Atlantic, and a number of important and highly readable books are published every month. These biographical books usually limit themselves to a key decade or experience or achievement in a person's life, as do John Herivel's *Joseph Fourier* and Bryan LeBeau's *Jonathan Dickinson and the Formative Years of American Presbyterianism*. Many of them, like the latter, are as interested in illuminating the subject's times and the forces that shaped them or contributing to or even opening in-depth, particular historical inquiries as in presenting the life and thought of the subject. Some, like Wendorf's, examine a part of a subject's life and explain how it illuminates character and achievements. The best of these books are meticulously researched, gracefully written, and ingeniously use biographical methods for purposes unimagined five years ago; among these is Elaine Breslaw's *Tituba: Reluctant Witch of Salem*, a reconstruction of the life of the American Indian slave woman whose confession led to the deaths of nineteen 'witches' (but not Tituba's) in Puritan Massachusetts.

As this book has suggested, biographies about different kinds of people and new kinds of biographies create new audiences, and the potential for increasing the numbers of *readers* of biographies of traditional, experimental, and new kinds of biographies and of biographical books has never been better. As the editors of *The Troubled Face of Biography* remarked in 1988, the lives of most people remain unwritten (Homberger, p. xii), and our growing awareness of the number of important, interesting women and people of colour for whom there are no biographies dramatically underscores that observation. And nothing has changed the fact that new biographies of controversial, important, and familiar lives are useful. As Holmes says, 'We get back the answers only to the questions we ask of a life' ('Inventing the Truth', 19), and each generation asks new questions. One of the most illuminating things about Lloyd Kramer's *Lafayette* is his demonstration of how the 'meaning of a particular life is always changing in conjunction with the evolving experiences and perspectives of other people' *over a very long period of time*. He shows that Lafayette, even in his own time, became a 'text', one which people 'read', sometimes with little or no real knowledge of Lafayette's actions and upon which people imposed meaning and significance, both in his own time and at varying times in the histories of France and the USA, including the present. His 'identity' and 'significance' have been disconcertingly malleable and detached from the human being who lived, dreamed, and suffered. Many viewers exposed to four different takes on John Wayne or Donald Trump or Anne Boleyn are seeking both full-length studies of the people who interest them and new intellectual experiences.

These things are possible.

Leon Edel once observed that centuries of biography writing 'has culminated in singularly few masterpieces' ('Biography and the Science of Man', 5). I would disagree. The masterpieces are there, but the books and the 'cultivated readers' are not. Readers today are conditioned to think of books as classics (best shelved in matching bindings and often unread) or ephemera. They are conditioned to be consumers of biography, not book collectors and reading connoisseurs and to consume art, to read to the ending and note the death and concluding judgements, not savour beautifully written passages and the way the narrative flows along—certainly not to take pleasure in the decisions the writer makes and the ways biographers make interpretations credible and emotionally persuasive. Modern biography is not regarded as a literary genre, and no biography has been firmly placed in the canon in more than half a century except Ellmann's *James Joyce*. Few biographers have any name-recognition even with lifelong readers of biographies; books are usually bought because of whom they are about—certainly not because of how well they are written, because they are literature, or because they are the epitome of or a landmark in the art of biography. Almost before readers know that a biography is especially good, the publisher has ripped the cover off to make a paperback and then remaindered it to save warehouse space. One of my editors said in frustration that the shelf life in today's bookstore chains was 'slightly shorter than that for cottage cheese'. Readers who are intrigued by the biographies mentioned in this book had better know where their nearest public library is.

But biographers are at fault, too. Rather than literary artists or even 'writers' they too often see themselves as slaves to documentary fact, 'the surviving evidence', or the subject. For all their rare bursts of bravado, most often they see themselves as handmaiden or curator. Artists, however, and especially narrative artists need to be aggressive, asserting a dominance over the content and control over the form—and imagination, labour, and creativity over the style. The quotations above about biography all mention writing style, all use intimidating phrases such as 'elegant', and that is the least studied aspect, the least likely to be commented upon in any specific, useful way in reviews. Most readers pay little attention to decisions biographers make about presentation, point of view, and style. Both groups, therefore, contribute to biographers' inadequate attention and mastery. In Chapter 7 I wrote of the 'daring of accepting a calling'. If biography is to come closer to reaching its potential either as art or as cultural force, then readers must demand art, collect the books, think in terms of canons and school courses, and biographers must have the daring to accept the calling, consider reaching for 'magisterial', and risk passion.

In fact, calling, magisterial, and passion are consistent demands on the form, and now and then books are so labelled and reviewers and readers make quite unusually risky statements—and therefore expand the possibilities of the form. For instance, quite recently both James Knowlson's *Damned to Fame: The Life of Samuel Beckett* and Nigel Saul's *Richard II* have deservedly been called 'magnificent biography' and 'magisterial biography', 'authoritative' and 'commanding' without 'ostentation'. Beyond aspiring towards these, biographers should also aspire towards wringing out praise such as this for, for instance, showing a poet's 'mysterious power that transmits the lusts of the earth into the passions of art' (F. D. Reeve's letter on a biography of Robert Frost, *NYTBR*, 23 June 1996, 4) or 'The Emerson who emerges in these pages is alive to his fingertips, blazing with the God within', (Jay Parini on Robert Richardson's *Emerson*, *TLS*, 21 July 1995, 6).

And perhaps, just perhaps, the time is coming when reviewers will think and write about how a biography is written. Rather than reciting the most exciting parts of the subject's life, they will tell us how well it is written and composed, how skilfully evidence is used and intelligently interpretation done, how decisions are made about personality and life shape, whether it is art, and whether a respectable or exemplary actualization of the form. They will do what reviewers of other kinds of books routinely do. And then perhaps the sub-genres of biography will begin to be recognized. And readers will do more often what they sometimes do now—buy biographies not only of people in whom they are interested but also biographies so well written that they are worth collecting and leaving as an inheritance—their own and their culture's.

Notes

1. Ira B. Nadel, 'Biography as Cultural Discourse', *Biography and Source Studies*, ed. Frederick Karl (New York: AMS, 1994), 73.
2. Quoted in Ruthellen Josselson and Amia Lieblich, ed., *The Narrative Study of Lives* (London: Sage Publications, 1993), 210.
3. I am grateful to the University of Rochester's *Research Frontiers* for permission to use material from my essay 'Biographer: Both Ally and Enemy' (Autumn, 1989), 20.
4. Mandell, *Life into Art* (Fayetteville: University of Arkansas Press, 1991), 18–19.
5. 'American Book Title Production', *The Bowker Annual: Library and Trade Almanac*, ed. Catherine Barr (New Providence, NJ: R. R. Bowker, 1995), 512.
6. Quoted in James Atlas, 'Holmes on the Case', *New Yorker*, 52 (19 Sept. 1994), 59.

1. Clayborne Carson, 'King Scholarship and Iconoclastic Myths', *Reviews in American History*, 16 (1988), 132–5.
2. Although using reviews as a means of testing this hypothesis has the fault of using 'hyper readers', the fact that reviews and biographical sketches before and after the biographies show differences consonant with these biographies is significant. A particularly obvious example: Northrop Frye has described Alexander Gilchrist's *Life of William Blake* (New York: Dodd, Mead and Company, 1906), the biography that established Blake's literary reputation, as having 'infected' almost every later study of Blake and skewing the critical estimate of Blake's poetry into the shape of a 'biographical stereotype', Aileen Ward, 'William Blake and the Hagiographers', *Biography and Source Studies* (New York: AMS, 1994), 2–3. David Bromwich argues that Bate made Keats resemble a marble bust more than the man who was 'morbid, uncertain, and congenial to decadence', 'The Uses of Biography', *Yale Review*, 73 (1984), 164.
3. Victor Nell, *Lost in a Book: The Psychology of Reading for Pleasure* (New Haven: Yale University Press, 1988), 73–8, 213–15. On physiological changes, which the author posits as motivational and sources of pleasure, see pp. 167–8 and 184–95.
4. Judith Mayne, *Private Novels, Public Films* (Athens: University of Georgia Press, 1988), 16.
5. Honan, *Author's Lives* (New York: St Martin's, 1990), xi, and Mandell, *Life into Art*, 19.
6. Bowen, *Biography: The Craft and the Calling* (Boston: Little, Brown, 1969), xiii–xiv.
7. Woolf, *The Waves* (1929; New York: Harcourt Brace and World, 1959), 259.
8. This debate over the possibility of tragedy in the modern world, smouldering at least since Joseph Wood Krutch's 1920 'The Tragic Fallacy', flared into public discussion shortly after the first production of *Death of a Salesman*. As Arthur Miller notes in 'Tragedy and the Common Man,' [*New York Times* (27 Feb. 1949) 2: 3], it was partly fanned by reviews of his play and his reactions to conversations with reviewers. John Gassner, then Sterling Professor of Playwriting at Yale, among others noted that definitions of genres must be fluid enough to absorb 'new knowledge, new awareness, and new issues', 'Tragic Perspectives: A Sequence of Queries', *Tulane Drama Review*, 2 (1958), 12–13 *et passim*. Representative articles in this debate are George de Schweinitz, '*Death of a Salesman*: A Note on Epic and Tragedy', *Western Humanities Review*, 14 (1960), 91–6, and Alan A. Stambusky, 'Arthur Miller: Aristotelian Canons in the Twentieth-Century Drama', in *Modern American Drama*, ed. William E. Taylor

(Deland, Fla.: Everett/ Edwards, Inc., 1968), 91–115. So pervasive was the controversy that it became a favourite undergraduate exam topic, and thousands of students were asked if a tragedy could be about a man as lacking in any noble characteristics as Willy Loman was perceived to be. It is easy to see the parallel between the weakening of the 'great man' tradition in biographical subject selection and the growing interest in the lives of ordinary people and in group or collective biography and the implications of questions about Miller's play. I am grateful to my research assistant, Amy Muse, for help with this note.

9. *New York Times*, 27 (11 Feb. 1949), 2; Gassner, 'Tragic Perspectives', 21–2, respectively. It is important to note that reviews often described the performance of Willy Loman's part thusly: 'tragic portrait', 'something of the grand manner in . . . the deep tone', 'grandeur', 'keeps it on the high plane of tragic acting—larger than the specific life it is describing', Brooks Atkinson, *New York Times*, 11 and 20 Feb. 1949. Atkinson's first review, published the day after the opening performance of *Death of a Salesman* and presumably written to a pressing deadline, is the most impressionistic and puts the most emphasis on the *feeling* of tragedy experienced. As the play came to be discussed as text, further and further removed from the memory of experienced performance, critics increasingly referred to 'the limitation of language' and to the sentimental and pathetic elements.

10. McKeon, *The Origins of the English Novel* (Baltimore: Johns Hopkins University Press, 1987), 22.

11. *The Imaginary Puritan* (Berkeley: University of California Press, 1992), 195–216; the quotations are from pp. 197 and 198.

12. Bakhtin says of Aristotle that his 'poetics . . . remains the stable foundation for the theory of genres', 'everything works as long as there is no mention of the novel', *The Dialogic Imagination*, trans. Caryl Emerson and Michael Holquist (Austin: University of Texas Press, 1981), 4.

13. Quoted in Colie, *The Resources of Kind* (Berkeley: University of California Press, 1973), 11. Colie later discusses a literary kind as 'a language full of idioms. But as in language, it is the idioms which we must learn in order not to be caught out' (p. 115). With a different point in mind, she also compares them to 'subcultures' (p. 116). She is interested in the way they 'melt into' other cultures while I am interested in the variants within a subculture.

14. J. A. Cuddon in *A Dictionary of Literary Terms* (Garden City, NY: Doubleday, 1977), s.v. 'Biography'. C. Hugh Holman defines biography as 'a written account of a person's life, a life history', *A Handbook to Literature* (Indianapolis and New York: Odyssey, 1972), s.v. 'Biography'. Holman goes on, however, to discuss biography for four more pages; his Aristotelian style sounds startlingly dated: 'It must be the life of a "particular" man focused clearly on that man. . . .' 'the life history from birth to death . . .' (p. 64).

15. *The Resources of Kind*, 76. John Gassner remarks that genre is useful in taking 'the height and width of some plays' and taking 'soundings', 'Tragic Perspectives', p. 12.

16. Epstein, *Recognizing Biography* (Philadelphia: University of Pennsylvania Press, 1987), 169.

17. Many of Strachey's chapter titles emphasize his greater empathy with the men: 'Lord Melbourne', 'Lord Palmerson', 'Mr Gladstone and Lord Beaconsfield'. Two chapters are centred on Prince Albert ('He was not in love with her'; she felt 'unqualified devotion' towards him, from 'Marriage'. 'Victoria . . . was all breathless attention . . . Sometimes Albert would actually ask her advice', 'Last Years of the Prince Consort').

18. *Writing a Woman's Life* (New York: Norton, 1988), 25 and 40, respectively; Heilbrun gives a number of interesting examples of modern critics analysing the limited 'voices' available to women and their inappropriateness to, for instance, Caroline Norton's struggle to change the nineteenth-century child custody laws (pp. 15, 35–8, 56).

19. Toril Moi, *Simone de Beauvoir* (Oxford: Blackwell, 1994), 34. Later Moi observes that in *The Second Sex*, trans. and ed. H. M. Parshley (New York: Bantam, 1961), 'she carries the polemical forcefulness of this style with her to great effect' (p. 66). Several chapters of this book analyse critical and popular reactions to her work.

20. Moi, *Simone de Beauvoir*, 31; the quotation is from a report on the examiners' comments on the examinations.

21. This biography, like many by men and women among the winners, might fail several 'tests of purity'. Written by Laura E. Richards and Maude Howe Elliott, 'assisted by Florence Howe Hall', the book is arguably part autobiography.

22. William H. McNeill won the 'History and Biography' category for *The Rise of the West* (Chicago: University of Chicago Press, 1963).

23. David Kennedy points out that before Margaret Sanger 'the now familiar phrase, [birth control], had not yet been coined', *Birth Control in America: The Career of Margaret Sanger* (New Haven: Yale University Press, 1970), 1 and 36. The number of words and phrases, such as sex-gender system, added to discourse by women anthropologists is another easy example to cite.

24. This is not to say one is superior to the other; I am describing contrasts.

25. Hugh Brogan writes, 'American biographers' custom of starting their books with a prologue set in the middle of things—an innovation which has become a deadly cliché', 'The Biographer's Chains,' *The Troubled Face of Biography*, ed. Eric C. Homberger and John Charmley (New York: St Martin's Press, 1988), 105.

26. See Diane Wood Middlebrook, 'Postmodernism and the Biographer', in Susan G. Bell and Marilyn Yalom, *Revealing Lives: Autobiography, Biography, and Gender* (Albany: SUNY University Press, 1990), 160–4. She argues, rightly I believe, that the author can no longer assume that ' "he" speaks from a secure center of culture, from the apex of the intellectual pyramid that provides the most trustworthy view of reality' (p. 164). The magisterial voice is obviously dependent on that kind of 'he'.

CHAPTER 2

1. Quoted in Leon Edel, *Writing Lives* (1959; New York: W. W. Norton, 1984), 228.

2. Capper, *Margaret Fuller: An American Romantic Life* (New York: Oxford University Press, 1992), ix–x.

3. The Perkins daughters, who had turned down other requests from would-be biographers, are cited by Thomas Congdon, whose words are quoted, 'Lives that Matter', *Humanities*, 5: 3 (1988), 4.

4. Thwaite, *A. A. Milne: The Man Behind Winnie-the-Pooh* (New York: Random House, 1990), xiv, and see the rest of this 'Introduction'.

5. Quoted in Mandell, *Life into Art*, 172–3; Elizabeth Kamarck Minnich, 'Friendship between Women: The Act of Feminist Biography', *Feminist Studies*, 11 (1985), 297, respectively.

6. I would like to note that I do not know if Professor Bate had a therapist at all, let alone one at the time he was writing this chapter. I offer this merely as a too-typical example of the speculation that results when readers and critics attempt to impose identification or similarity on biographers and their subjects.

7. Justin Kaplan, 'A Culture of Biography', *The Literary Biography*, ed. Dale Salwak (Iowa City: University of Iowa Press, 1996), 9.

8. It should be noted in warning that royalties seldom balance the cost of the research and the length of time required to write a good biography with new information. Jeffrey Meyers notes that he spent more than $6,000 in 1978–9 on such things as travel, postage, photocopies, and paper while working on his biography of Wyndham Lewis, *The Spirit of Biography* (Ann Arbor: UMI Research Press, 1989), 213. Thomas Congdon, publisher of many biographies, notes that, even for publishers, 'Biography is not often the route to big money in publishing; small-to-medium is more likely' and that it calls for an 'enormous overinvestment of time and energy', 'Lives that Matter', 4–5.

9. Kenneth Silverman, 'Mather, Poe, Houdini', in *The Literary Biography*, 115.

10. Lorna Sage, 'A Necessary Cruelty', *TLS* (20 August 1993), 3.

11. Three stimulating books on this subject are Howard Gardner, *Creating Minds* (New York: Basic Books, 1993), Desmond Shawe-Taylor, *Genial Company: The Theme of Genius in*

Eighteenth-Century British Portraiture (London: White Brothers, 1987), and Christine Battersby, *Gender and Genius* (Bloomington: Indiana University Press, 1989).

12. Quoted in Edel, *Literary Biography* (Toronto: University of Toronto Press, 1957), 49.
13. *Cardozo* is a life of Benjamin Nathan Cardozo, a US Supreme Court justice from February 1932 until his death in July 1938 (Cambridge: Harvard University Press, 1998).
14. Peter Monaghan, 'An Artist's Tortured Life', interview in the *Chronicle of Higher Education* (2 Feb. 1994), A6–7.
15. Quoted in Gail Mandell, *Life into Art*, 18–19.
16. Atlas, 'The Biographer and the Murderer', *New York Times Magazine* (15 Dec. 1993), 75.
17. Quoted in a review of Weimer's *Back Talk* by Sheila Rothman, *New York Times Book Review*, 16 Oct. 1994, 32. Weimer published 'Women Artists as Exiles in the Fiction of Constance Fenimore Woolson', in *Legacy: A Journal of Nineteenth-Century American Women Writers*, 3 (1986), 3–15, and edited *Women Artists, Women Exiles* (New Brunswick: Rutgers University Press, 1988), which includes another essay of hers on Woolson.
18. Bonny Vaught, 'Trying to Make Things Real', *Between Women*, ed. Carol Ascher, Louise DeSalvo, and Sara Ruddick (Boston: Beacon Press, 1984), 63–4, 67.
19. Linda Davis, 'The Red Room: Stephen Crane and Me', in *The Literary Biography*, 69.
20. See Christina M. Howells's and Catherine Civello's reviews of Moi's book, respectively *TLS*, 6 May 1994, 22, and *Southern Humanities Review*, 30 (1996), 87–90.
21. Ascher, *Simone de Beauvoir: A Life of Freedom* (Boston: Beacon Press, 1981), 107, 112, and 114, respectively. In this letter, Ascher traces her experience with de Beauvoir's writings and reveals her idealistic expectations, many of which seem to have been modified by close study of de Beauvoir's life and works.
22. See especially, Jean Gattégno, *Lewis Carroll*, trans. Rosemary Sheed (New York: Thomas Crowell, 1974), 45–61, 141–50, and 224.
23. See the chapter 'Gossip', *Portia: The World of Abigail Adams* (Bloomington: Indiana University Press, 1992).
24. The man is not identified except as 'an extraordinary and pathetically tragic man he had known in California', *Nabokov: His Life in Part* (New York: Viking Press, 1977), 31.
25. John Keats, 'O blush not so, O blush not so', *John Keats*, ed. Elizabeth Coole (Oxford: Oxford University Press, 1990), 169. I am grateful to my colleague David Haney for this identification.
26. I am aware of the sexist nature of these phrases, of the reasons that they may be appropriately applied to men alone, and of the fact that both are considered out of fashion; however, school and college curricula continue to inscribe them powerfully.
27. This summary is based on Antonia Fraser, *Cromwell: The Lord Protector* (New York: Knopf, 1974), and especially Christopher Hill, *God's Englishman* (1970; Harmondsworth: Penguin, 1983). Hill describes in detail the revolutionary way Cromwell recruited and organized his troops, the 'Ironsides', with men of 'middling rank' but consciences engaged in the struggle and he gives careful attention to Cromwell's committee experience, see especially pp. 59–70, and 155, 159 on Cromwell's foreign policy and Dutch respect for it.
28. Geertz points out that cultures are polyphonic, their citizens speaking with different and conflicting voices. We need to unpack events, working in concentric circles to discover how events came about and what they reveal about a culture, the different groups within it, and the processes that determine stability and change. Geertz's method is so stimulating partly because it allows movement backward and forward in time and also considers contemporary layers of meaning.
29. Catherine Drinker Bowen has written an entire chapter on the subject, *Biography: The Craft and the Calling*, 145–68.
30. Recounted in Gale Christianson, *Writing Lives is the Devil!* (Hamden, Conn.: Archon Books, 1993), 161.
31. Thomas Carlyle, *Life of Frederick II of Prussia*, 8 vols. (London: Chapman & Hall, 1897),

4: 3: 339. The footnote to this quotation in *Bartlett's Familiar Quotations* gives a number of similar statements by his contemporaries (Boston: Little, Brown, 1928), 584.

32. Edward Lytton, *Last Words of a Sensitive Second-Rate Poet* in *The Poetical Works of Owen Meredith (Robert, Lord Lytton)* (Boston: Houghton, [1900], l. 136, p. 403; the poem is pp. 400–4. The second quotation is from Bartlett's *Familiar Quotations*, q.v. 'James Russell Lowell'.

33. Dauben, *Georg Cantor* (Princeton: Princeton University Press, 1979), 2 and 'Epilogue'.

34. Alan Ryan, who has personal experience with the struggle as the author of *Bertrand Russell: A Political Life* (New York: Hill and Wang, 1988), 'Out of His Shell', *TLS* (21 June 1996), 6.

CHAPTER 3

1. Woolf, *The Letters of Virginia Woolf*, 6 vols., ed. Nigel Nicolson and Joanne Trautmann (New York: Harcourt, Brace, Jovanovich, 1975), 6: 426.

2. 'The Art of Biography' in *Collected Essays* (London: Harcourt, Brace and World, 1967), 221–8.

3. Woolf, *The Diary of Virginia Woolf*, 5 vols. (New York: Harcourt, Brace, Jovanovich, 1989), 5: 144 and 156, respectively.

4. Young-Bruehl in Mandell, *Life into Art*, 173.

5. A. E. Housman, 'The Application of Thought to Textual Criticism', quoted by F. W. Bateson, 'The Application of Thought to an 18th C. Text: The School for Scandal', in *Evidence in Literary Scholarship*, ed. René Wellek and Alvaro Ribeiro (Oxford: Clarendon Press, 1979), 332.

6. Aileen Ward, 'William Blake and the Hagiographers', in *Biography and Source Studies*, 14–15.

7. See Ward, 'William Blake and the Hagiographers', 18, and recent studies including E. P. Thompson, *Witness Against the Beast: William Blake and Moral Law* (New York: New Press, 1993) and John Mee, *Dangerous Enthusiasm* (Oxford: Oxford University Press, 1992).

8. James R. Sutherland, biographer of Defoe, quoted in Richard D. Altick, *The Scholar Adventurers* (New York: Free Press, 1950), 88.

9. Amusing discussions of filing are in Ann Thwaite, 'Writing Lives', in Eric Homberger and John Charmley, *The Troubled Face of Biography*, 25–6, and Gail Mandell, *Life into Art*, 183–5.

10. Thursday, 22 June 1786, *Boswell: The English Experiment, 1785–1789*, ed. Irma Lustig and Frederick A. Pottle (New York: McGraw-Hill, 1986), 74.

11. Jeffrey Meyers, *The Spirit of Biography* (Ann Arbor: UMI Research Press, 1989), 241.

12. Edel, *Writing Lives: Principia Biographica* (1959; New York: Norton, 1984), 224.

13. Edel, 'The Figure Under the Carpet', in *Telling Lives: The Biographer's Art*, ed. Mark Pachter (Washington, DC: New Republic Books, 1979), 23.

14. Altick, *The Scholar Adventurers*, 89–90. Jeffrey Meyers gives a good description of his process of collecting evidence in *The Spirit of Biography*, 138–48, as does John Garraty, *The Nature of Biography* (New York: Garland, 1985), 177–214.

15. Richard Altick, *The Scholar Adventurers*, 86.

16. 'Portraits in Prose', *TLS* (2 Mar. 1962), 130.

17. *Hogarth: His Life, Art, and Times* (New Haven: Yale University Press, 1971), and *Hogarth*, 3 vols. (New Brunswick: Rutgers University Press, 1991–3).

18. Quoted from Margot Peters's review of Paul Horgan's *Tracings: A Book of Partial Portraits* (New York: Farrar, Straus and Giroux, 1993), *NYTBR* (10 Oct. 1993), 11.

19. John E. Neale, *Queen Elizabeth* (New York: Harcourt, 1934), 126.

20. The quotation is from Honan, *Authors' Lives*, 6, in a discussion of the biographies of George Sand.

21. The example is from Iris Origo, 'Biography, True and False,' *Biography Past and Present*, ed. William Davenport and Ben Siegel (New York: Scribner's, 1965), 371–2.

22. Edel, *Writing Lives*, 229, and see his discussion of the importance of acquiring a sense of place, 227–36.

23. Richard Holmes, *Footsteps: Adventures of a Romantic Biographer* (London: Hodder and Stoughton, 1985), 67, quotation on p. 114.

24. Thwaite, 'Writing Lives', in *Troubled Face of Biography*, 19.

25. Cynthia Ozick, 'Mrs. Virginia Woolf: A Madwoman and Her Nurse', in *Art and Ardor* (New York: Knopf, 1983), 27–8, 36.

26. Glendinning, 'Lies and Silences', *Troubled Face of Biography*, 52.

27. John A. Garraty, *The Nature of Biography*, 195 and 202, respectively.

28. Rhoda Koenig, 'His Life as Boy', *New York* (16 Nov. 1992), 77.

29. An anonymous reviewer in a classic essay wrote, 'a biography is no more and no less than this, the interpenetration of one mind by another, the attempt to understand and assess the values of one who lived in the past, by one who lives in the present', quoted in David Novarr, *The Lines of Life: Theories of Biography, 1880–1970* (West Lafayette, Ind.: Purdue University Press, 1986), 136.

30. For the Addison discussion, see James Boswell, *The Life of Johnson*, ed. R. W. Chapman (Oxford: Oxford University Press, 1970), 1780–1. In spite of the fact that Johnson accepted his friend's anecdotes and interpretations too uncritically, his *Life of Savage* is as important for the modern history of biography as Boswell's *Life of Johnson*. For an original 'biography' of them, see Richard Holmes, *Dr. Johnson and Mr. Savage* (New York: Pantheon, 1994).

31. There are many discussions of this decision; two of the most informative are Linda Gray Sexton's 'A Daughter's Story: I Knew Her Best', *NYTBR* (18 Aug. 1991), 20, and a report of Middlebrook's talk at an American Psychological Association meeting, Shari Roan, 'Uncovering Secrets of a Very Public Poet', *Los Angeles Times* (13 Aug. 1991), E 1–2. Linda Sexton writes that the tapes were 'almost uniquely relevant to any searching analysis of her poetry', 20.

32. The phrase is Ian Hamilton's, *Keepers of the Flame: Literary Estates and the Rise of Biography* (London: Hutchinson, 1992), 298. His is a balanced discussion but more sympathetic to Hughes than many. For his account of his experience with J. D. Salinger, see Ian Hamilton, 'J. D. Salinger versus Random House, Inc.', *Granta*, 23 (1998), 199–218.

33. Linda Wagner-Martin, *Telling Women's Lives: The New Biography* (New Brunswick, NJ: Rutgers University Press, 1994), ix. She was denied permission to quote directly from Plath's writings and had to revise extensively to accomplish some of the things that quotations would have. For her restrained account of her negotiations with Ted Hughes and Olwyn Hughes and what has 'disappeared', see *Sylvia Plath: A Biography* (New York: Simon and Schuster, 1987), pp. 13–14 and 246–7.

34. Glenn Frankel, 'Reviving the Pain of Sylvia Plath', *Washington Post* (8 Nov. 1989), C8.

35. Ian Hamilton, 'The Tatty Wreckage of Her Life', *NYTBR* (25 Oct. 1987), 12–13. Hamilton was successfully sued by J. D. Salinger and forced to revise his biography extensively.

36. The adjectives—the expression of the stakes—are Janet Malcolm's in 'The Silent Woman', *The New Yorker* (23 and 30 Aug. 1993), 94.

37. Hacking, *The Emergence of Probability* (Cambridge: Cambridge University Press, 1975), 32–3; and for a fuller account see Barbara Shapiro, *Probability and Certainty in Seventeenth-Century England* (Princeton: Princeton University Press, 1983), 175–93. Shapiro discusses the development of the trial by jury as the alternative to the continental system.

38. The turn from trial by ordeal and by battle to what was called the 'Romano-canonist approach' or 'rational modes of proof' occurred in Europe in the late medieval period. Barbara Shapiro describes the process as 'a system of inquiry ... designed to obtain "full proof" defined by clearly established evidentiary standards' and explains the ' "rules" governing exclusions, the quality and quantity of proof, and the system's reliance on numerical calculations,' *Probability and Certainty in Seventeenth-Century England*, 173–4.

39. Shapiro gives an interesting list of tests to apply to witnesses, which she adapts from Locke, *'Beyond Reasonable Doubt' and 'Probable Cause': Historical Perspectives on the Anglo-American Law of Evidence* (Berkeley: University of California Press, 1991), 195–6.
40. Glendinning, 'Lies and Silences', in *The Troubled Face of Biography*, 50.
41. Barbara J. Shapiro, *Beyond Reasonable Doubt*, 3–6; quotation, p. 2; Alexander Welsh, *Strong Representations: Narrative and Circumstantial Evidence in England* (Baltimore: Johns Hopkins University Press, 1992), 16, 24; Susan Staves gives a history of the reception of sworn testimony in *Players' Scepters* (Lincoln: University of Nebraska Press, 1979), 220–34.
42. 'Confirmation: Qualitative Aspects', *The Encyclopedia of Philosophy*, ed. Paul Edwards, 8 vols. (New York: Macmillan, 1967) 2: 185.
43. Hacking, *The Emergence of Probability*, 31–7.
44. Richard Sennett, *The Fall of Public Man* (New York: A. A. Knopf, 1977), 43.
45. Shapiro, *Probability*, 171–3, 178–81, and 193. Neither she nor I are arguing causal relationships stemming from one discourse or another.
46. Shapiro summarizing a point in John Locke's *Essay Concerning Human Understanding, Beyond Reasonable Doubt*, 8.
47. Shapiro, *Beyond Reasonable Doubt*, 237, 240, and 239 respectively. See also Welsh, *Strong Representations*, 36–7.
48. Hacking discusses this idea briefly, *The Emergence of Probability*, 31–6.
49. William Paley quoted in Alexander Welsh, *Strong Representations*, 16.
50. Ian Hacking, *The Emergence of Probability*, 20–2, 34–7.
51. This apt term is defined by William Epstein, *Recognizing Biography*, 125–6.
52. *Biography*, 50–1. Many people use biographies as reference books; in fact, several librarians have told me they would prefer they be shelved together in the reference section so that the books would be convenient for answering telephone queries.
53. Jay Martin, 'Historical Truth and Narrative Reliability', in *Biography and Source Studies*, 43.
54. *Letters*, 3 Dec. 1939, 6: 374, and 15 Aug. 1940, 6: 416.
55. Glendinning, 'Lies and Silences', in *The Troubled Face of Biography*, 49. This rich phrase captures our limitations as well as the 'lies' we find in evidence and the 'silences', the gaps we cannot fill.
56. I experienced all of these things during the time I worked on the Defoe biography. Most amazing to the modern scholar is documents taken home. Several times Record Office staff and I would find cross references to more detailed documents and after great effort find a notation that someone had been allowed to borrow it. In a few cases, these documents were recovered—once in an unused desk.
57. Iris Origo, 'Biography, True and False', *Biography: Past and Present*, 372.
58. *The Diary of Virgina Woolf*, for 3 May 1938, 5: 138.
59. 'The Art of Biography', in *Collected Essays*, 228.
60. Massie, *Peter the Great* (New York: A. A. Knopf, 1980), 353–5.
61. Nadel, *Biography: Fiction, Fact and Form* (New York: St Martin's Press, 1984), 155.
62. This is the pattern identified in the lives of many women, Mary M. Gergen and Kenneth Gergen, 'Narratives of the Gendered Body in Popular Autobiography', ed. Ruthellen Josselson and Amia Lieblich, *The Narrative Study of Lives* (London: Sage Publications, 1993), 196.
63. Stephen B. Oates, 'Responses', *The Biographer's Gift*, ed. James Veninga (College Station: Texas A&M University Press, 1983), 32.

CHAPTER 4

1. This chapter has benefited from Lewis Langness and Gelya Frank, *Lives: An Anthropological Approach to Biography* (Novaro, Calif.: Chandler & Sharp, 1981), quotation, p. 101.
2. Andrew Sinclair, 'Vivat Alius Ergo Sum', in *The Troubled Face of Biography*, 123.

3. Samuel Baron, 'Psychological Dimensions of the Biographical Process', in *Introspection in Biography*, ed. Samuel H. Baron and Carl Pletsch (London: Analytic Press, 1985), 16.

4. Richard Westfall, 'Newton and his Biographer', in *Introspection in Biography*, 185.

5. Bowen, *Biography: The Craft and the Calling*, 94.

6. Hill, *God's Englishman*, 267.

7. Fraser, *Cromwell: The Lord Protector* (New York: A. A. Knopf, 1974), 706.

8. Quoted in Sharon O'Brien, 'Feminist Theory and Literary Biography', in *Contesting the Subject*, ed. William Epstein (W. Lafayette, Ind.: Purdue University Press, 1991), 125; and Miranda Seymour, 'Stopping by Woods for Seduction', review of Jeffrey Meyers, *Robert Frost: A Biography*, *NYTBR* (19 May 1996), 8, respectively.

9. John Worthen, 'The Necessary Ignorance of a Biographer', *The Art of Literary Biography*, ed. John Batchelor (Oxford: Clarendon Press, 1989), 228.

10. Robert Frost, 'Tree at My Window', *The Poetry of Robert Frost*, ed. Edward C. Lathem (New York: Holt, Rinehart and Winston, 1969), 251–2.

11. Nigel Hamilton, 'Thomas Mann', in *The Craft of Literary Biography*, ed. Jeffrey Meyers (New York: Schocken, 1985), 114.

12. Quoted in Carolyn Heilbrun, *Writing a Woman's Life*, 61.

13. Pringle, *Theodore Roosevelt* (New York: Harcourt Brace, 1931), 182. John E. Mack quotes a letter from T. E. Lawrence in which deeply personal, political, and psychological reasons for his actions are mingled; he lists friendship for an individual, furthering England's imperial ambitions, and desire for 'sensation' among others, 'T. E. Lawrence and the Psychology of Heroism', in *Introspection in Biography*, 278–9.

14. Kenneth Gergen, 'The Emerging Crisis in Life-Span Developmental Theory', *Life-Span Development and Behavior*, ed. Paul B. Baltes and Orville Brim (New York: Academic Press, 1980), 3: 38.

15. Theodore Millon, 'The Disorders of Personality', Lawrence A. Pervin, ed. *Handbook of Personality: Theory and Research* (New York: Guilford, 1990), 347.

16. 'Still Stable After All These Years: Personality as a Key to Some Issues in Adulthood and Old Age', *Life-Span Development and Behavior*, 66.

17. Theodore Millon, 'The Disorders of Personality', 352; Marilyn Bowman provides a helpful summary in 'Difficulties in Assessing Personality and Predicting Behavior', *The Write Stuff*, ed. Barry L. Beyerstein and Dale Beyerstein (Buffalo, NY: Prometheus Books, 1992), 205–8.

18. The Seven Ages of Man are attributed to Ptolemy and are based on astrology and the planets; Jaques's monologue about them in *As You Like It* is often given as the source.

19. See William Epstein, *Recognizing Biography*, 139. His discussion of the connection to 'how a man can live honestly' still has reverberations in our own time, pp. 140–71.

20. Lois Hoffman, Scott Paris, and Elizabeth Hall, *Developmental Psychology Today*, 6th edn., New York: McGraw Hill, 1994), 465.

21. Evidence is building that age-norms are even more powerful than gender, see Bernice L. Neugarten, 'Adult Personality: Toward a Psychology of the Life Cycle', *Middle Age and Aging* (Chicago: University of Chicago Press, 1968), 139–43.

22. Mary M. Gergen and Kenneth J. Gergen, 'Narratives of the Gendered Body in Popular Autobiography', *The Narrative Study of Lives*, 195.

23. Identity: to differentiate the self from others, especially parents; Intimacy: development of personal relationships with others, especially peers; Generativity: assuming responsibility for the growth, leadership, and well-being of others; Integrity: acceptance of one's life as having been appropriate and meaningful.

24. Biographies of women and couples do not conform to these 'stories' particularly well, and both now make up a significant number of the prize-winning and best-selling biographies.

25. A masculine exception is Gandhi in Erik Erikson's *Gandhi's Truth: On the Origins of Militant Nonviolence* (New York: Norton, 1969). By changing his costume, Gandhi forced those around him to deal with nationality, race, caste, and class. In some cases, as when he combined a lawyer's black frock coat and dress boots with a turban, he was ordered to

harmonize the pieces by removing a garment (p. 164). When he began to wear nothing but an impeccably folded loincloth to express the purity and simplicity of himself and his cause, he elicited outraged remarks from Winston Churchill and others (pp. 153, 447). Late in life, his followers wore a 'Gandhi cap', an imitation of prisoners' hats (p. 445).

26. Jacques Derrida quoted in Epstein, *Recognizing Biography*, 163.

27. James R. Mellow's review of Beth Brombert's *Edouard Manet: Rebel in a Frock Coat*, *NYTBR* (24 Mar. 1996), 13.

28. Leon Edel, *Henry James: The Middle Years* (Philadelphia: J. B. Lippincott Company, 1962), 34; *Henry James: A Life* (New York: Harper & Row, 1985), 274–5. While acknowledging Edel's need to cut, I do not think deletions are ever neutral, and the number that change the tone of the book when considered with popular novels seems significant.

29. Ellmann described by Park Honan, p. 68, and Jay Martin, 'Historical Truth and Narrative Reliability', *Biography and Source Studies*, 72.

30. Reed Whittemore, *Whole Lives: Shapers of Modern Biography* (Baltimore: Johns Hopkins University Press, 1989), 164.

31. Joseph Lichtenberg, 'Psychoanalysis and Biography', in *Introspection in Biography*, 42, 62.

32. David Bromwich, 'The Uses of Biography', *Yale Review*, 73 (1984), 167; emphasis mine.

33. Quoted in Anthony Storr, 'Psychiatry and Literary Biography', in Batchelor, *The Art of Literary Biography*, 73.

34. Quoted by John A. Garraty, *The Nature of Biography*, 216. This section has benefited from his chapter on 'The Problem of Personality'.

35. Quoted in *Henry James: A Life*, 11.

36. Ian Watt, *Myths of Modern Individualism* (Cambridge: Cambridge University Press, 1996), 191.

37. Catherine Drinker Bowen, *The Lion and the Throne: The Life and Times of Sir Edward Coke (1552–1634)* (Boston: Little, Brown and Company, 1957), 416.

38. B. L. Reid, *Necessary Lives: Biographical Reflections* (Columbia: University of Missouri Press, 1990), 31–44.

39. In some European countries, including Germany, France, and Sweden, graphology is taught in universities as a branch of psychology and is a well-respected corporate and clinical assessment tool. Approximately 80 per cent of all French companies use it to screen applicants and to consider people for teams and promotions. The Library of Congress classifies it as 'behavioral science'. More than 6,000 US employers, Ford, General Electric, H&R Block, the CIA, and Northwest Mutual Life Insurance among them, use graphology to some extent in personnel selection and assignment, see Mark A. Hopper and Karen Stanford, 'A Script for Screening', *Security Management*, 36 (1992), 72–5 and 77, 79, 81; Alessandra Bianchi, 'The Character-Revealing Handwriting Analysis', *Inc.*, 18 (1996), 77–9; David L. Kurtz, *et al.*, 'CEOs: A Handwriting Analysis, *Business Horizons*, 32 (1989), 41–3. Research on the accuracy of graphology compared with that of psychological tests has produced conflicting reports, see Hopper and Stanford, who note a favourable but uncited American Psychological Association study, pp. 72–3, and Diane Arthur, *Workplace Testing* (New York: American Management Association, 1994), 111–15. Arthur asserts, 'There is little empirical evidence regarding the validity or reliability of handwriting analysis', p. 114, and a conclusion shared by Marilyn Bowman in her overview and summary of the literature, 'Difficulties in Assessing Personality and Predicting Behavior', *The Write Stuff*, 225–7. Two studies which survey reliability and validity have an optimistic tone about graphology, and conclude by suggesting improvements that need to be made are Baruch Nevo, 'Reliability of Graphology: A Survey of the Literature' (pp. 253–61) and Elchanan I. Meir, 'Testing Graphology: Is Graphology a Test?' (pp. 311–14) in Baruch Nevo, ed., *Scientific Aspects of Graphology* (Springfield Ill.: Charles C. Thomas, 1986).

40. Marilyn Bowman, 'Difficulties in Assessing Personality and Predicting Behavior', 219.

41. Such efforts would require many precisely dated handwriting samples over the subject's lifetime. At least one carefully done study produced the results that graphologists were no better than a control group of non-graphologists in using handwriting to predict

job performance and that, in fact, psychologists working with handwriting did slightly better, Efrat Neter and Gershon Ben-Shakhar, 'The Predictive Validity of Graphological Inferences', *Personality and Individual Difference*, 10 (1989), 737–45. This study and others suggest that non-graphologists can draw useful material from handwriting; it is important to know that this study focused on predicting behaviour on the job rather than on describing personality. At this time research designed to collect information on changes in handwriting which might be related to different kinds of stress is needed; studies have not shown that graphologists as a group can identify individuals under stress, Giora Keinan, 'Can Graphologists Identify Individuals under Stress?', *Scientific Aspects of Graphology*, 141–50.

42. These techniques are described briefly but clearly in Garraty, *The Nature of Biography*, 224–37. His summary of what Ralph K. White discovered in Richard Wright's *Black Boy* is a good example of what this kind of text-analysis can yield.

43. At that time it was common for government officials responsible for what they called control of the press to seize writers' (and printers' and booksellers') papers, including books that might have notes or markers in them. *All* papers, even those obviously irrelevant to the case, were often taken and, as might be expected, many were damaged, lost, or never returned.

44. *The Correspondence of Jonathan Swift*, ed. Harold Williams (Oxford: Clarendon Press, 1963), 2: 373, 374.

45. Irvin Ehrenpreis, *Swift: The Man, His Works, and the Age* (Cambridge: Harvard University Press, 1983), 3: 130.

46. *Golden Codgers: Biographical Speculations* (New York: Oxford University Press, 1973), 6; see Jean-Paul Sartre, *Saint Genet: Actor and Martyr*, trans. Bernard Frechtman (New York: George Braziller, 1963), 2. Ellmann seems to have read it in French, for some words are translated differently.

47. Quoted from George Will in Alan C. Elms, *Uncovering Lives: The Uneasy Alliance of Biography and Psychology* (New York: Oxford University Press, 1994), 4.

48. Richard Ellmann, 'Freud and Literary Biography', *Diogenes*, 139 (1987), 70–1; and Peter Gay, *Freud for Historians* (New York: Oxford University Press, 1985), 17.

49. Anthony Storr, 'Psychiatry and Literary Biography', in Batchelor, *The Art of Literary Biography*, 73.

50. John M. Digman quoting William McDougall, 'Personality Structure: Emergence of the Five-Factor Model', in *Annual Review of Psychology*, ed. Mark Rosenzweig and Lyman Porter, 41 (1990), 418.

51. Oliver P. John, 'The "Big Five" Factor Taxonomy: Dimensions of Personality in the Natural Language and in Questionnaires', Lawrence A. Pervin, ed. *Handbook of Personality: Theory and Research*, 67 and 71; quotation from p. 71. The table of traits in each Factor is especially useful, p. 80. This model is accepted as capturing, 'at a broad level of abstraction, the commonalities among most of the existing systems of personality description, and provides an integrative descriptive model for personality research', p. 96.

52. Quoted in David Bromwich, 'The Uses of Biography', 175.

53. 'With Family and Friends', *TLS* (12 Feb. 1993), 8.

54. George Moraitis, 'The Psychoanalyst's Role in the Biographer's Quest for Self-Awareness', in *Introspection in Biography*, 351.

55. Theodore Millon, 'The Disorders of Personality'; Lawrence A. Pervin, *Handbook of Personality: Theory and Research*, 343.

56. Millon, 'The Disorders of Personality', 353–5.

57. This list is based partly on Bernice L. Neugarten, 'Adult Personality: Toward a Psychology of the Life Cycle', *Middle-Age and Aging*, 133, and see also pp. 139–41.

58. James Burns, *Roosevelt: The Lion and the Fox* (New York: Harcourt, Brace, Jovanovich, 1956), 86–91.

59. Kenneth S. Bowers, 'There's More to Iago than Meets the Eye: A Clinical Account of Personal Consistency', *Personality at the Crossroads*, ed. David Magnusson and N. S. Endler (Hillsdale, NJ: Erlbaum, 1977), 75. Quoted in Millon, p. 353.

60. Anthony Storr, 'Psychiatry and Literary Biography', in Batchelor, *The Art of Literary Biography*, 73. Storr concludes this essay with some other examples of psychiatric disorders useful to biographers.

61. Glendinning, 'Lies and Silences', in *The Troubled Face of Biography*, 51.

62. Ascher demands a personal, even nurturing relationship from de Beauvoir; this theme occurs in a number of feminist writings about biographies of women by women. Her letter is in *Simone de Beauvoir: A Life of Freedom* (Boston: Beacon Press, 1981), 107–22.

63. Carol Ascher, 'On "Clearing the Air": My Letter to Simone de Beauvoir', *Between Women*, 96.

64. Asher acknowledges Erikson as a model (p. 107), and there are some striking similarities in the two letters, Carol Asher, *Simone de Beauvoir: A Life of Freedom*, 107–22. Like him, she accuses her subject of dishonesty and says that, after writing the letter, she continued her book with 'more fluidity and joy', *Between Women*, 110. The letter is in Erik Erikson, *Gandhi's Truth*, 229–54.

65. Usually called a psychobiography, I believe that Erikson is too intent on analysing the process of writing biography—analysing himself and his relationship to Gandhi as well as Gandhi—for that to be an adequate description. For a clear explanation of the psychobiographical aspects of *Gandhi's Truth* and Erikson's contribution, see Ira Nadel, *Biography: Fiction, Fact and Form*, 187.

66. It is fairly easy to find statements such as Bernard De Voto's 'The interior of his subject's mind is forbidden him by the nature of reality', 'The Skeptical Biographer', *Biography Past and Present*, 287.

67. John E. Mack, 'T. E. Lawrence and Heroism', in *Introspection in Biography*, 285–6.

68. These questions are from Costa and McCrae, 'Still Stable after All These Years', in Baltes and Brim, *Life-Span Development and Behavior*, 81.

69. Some of these conclusions are the same as John A. Garraty's in *The Nature of Biography*; see especially pp. 237–40. I have benefited from his chapter on 'The Problem of Personality'.

70. Jay Martin, 'Historical Truth and Narrative Reliability: Three Biographical Stories', in Karl, *Biography and Source Studies*, 58–71.

71. Oliver Sacks, 'Making Up the Mind', *New York Review of Books* (8 Apr. 1993), 42.

72. Quoted in Reed Whittemore, 'Sigmund Freud and His Disciples', *Whole Lives*, 115.

CHAPTER 5

1. John Garraty, *The Nature of Biography*, 43.

2. William Epstein, 'Milford's *Zelda* and the Poetics of the New Feminist Biography', *Georgia Review*, 36 (1982), 335–50.

3. See Teresa de Lauretis, 'Feminist Studies/Critical Studies: Issues, Terms, and Contexts', and her quotations from Linda Gordon, de Lauretis, ed., *Feminist Studies/Critical Studies* (Bloomington: University of Indiana Press, 1986), 4–5. This introduction lucidly outlines the issues and problems in defining 'feminism' and 'feminist studies', pp. 1–19. And see also the special issue of *a/b: Auto/Biography Studies*, 8 (1993), 155–270, especially the introduction in which Janet Sharistanian raises a number of abiding questions about the nature and purpose of feminist biography.

4. Gail Caldwell, 'A Life of France's "sacred monster"', *Books*, *The Boston Globe* (15 Apr. 1990), A16.

5. From the Bills of Mortality, published in John Graunt, *Reflections on the Weekly Bills of Mortality* (London: 1665).

6. Erik Erikson, 'On the Nature of Psycho-Historical Evidence: In Search of Gandhi', *Daedalus*, 97 (1968), 722.

7. For most of his life, for Defoe that was the 1 square mile Old City of London with its important traditions, fraught relations with the monarch, and thriving modern commerce.

8. In Susan Magarey, ed. *Writing Lives: Feminist Biography and Autobiography* (Adelaide: Australian Feminist Studies Publications, 1992), 33.

9. I hope someday to return to the exploration I began in *Spectacular Politics* of the images of freakishness and addiction that early women writers used to describe their creativity and writing. See also Adrienne Rich, *On Lies, Secrets, and Silences* (New York: W. W. Norton, 1979) 175.

10. Michelene Wandor, *Look Back in Gender* (London: Methuen, 1987), xiii.

11. Maureen Quilligan on William Wright's *Lillian Hellman: The Image, the Woman*, 'Rewriting History: The Difference of Feminist Biography', *Yale Review*, 77 (1988), 263. She is quoting from the Preface, p. 12.

12. Susan Friedman, 'Women's Autobiographical Selves', in Shari Benstock, ed. *The Private Self* (Chapel Hill: University of North Carolina Press, 1988), 34–5.

13. See Charlotte Linde, *Life Stories: The Creation of Coherence* (New York: Oxford University Press, 1993), 102–3. The culture makes us conscious of what we are and are not. The quotation is from Susan Friedman's *The Private Self*. In a telling aside, Teresa de Lauretis notes, 'I have never, before coming to this country, been conscious of being white', *Feminist Studies/Critical Studies*, 8.

14. Adrienne Rich, *On Lies, Secrets, and Silence*, 168.

15. The quotation is from Rachel Gutiérrez, 'What is a Feminist Biography?' *All Sides of the Subject*, ed. Theresa Iles (New York: Teachers College Press, 1992), 53. See Ann Delbée, *Camille Claudel: Une Femme*, trans. Carol Cosman (San Francisco: Mercury House, 1992).

16. This is clear in Delbée's biography, perhaps especially in the telling quotations she uses from Paul Claudel's writings, and in other biographies such as Frederic Grunfeld's *Rodin: A Biography* (New York: Henry Holt, 1987), see especially pp. 211–43. Other biographies of Claudel are Reine-Marie Paris, *Camille Claudel: 1864–1943* (Paris: Gallimard, 1984), *Camille Claudel: The Life of Rodin's Muse* (New York: Seaver Books, 1988), and J. Adolf Eisenwerth, *Auguste Rodin and Camille Claudel*, trans. John Ormrod (Munich: Prestel-Verlag, 1994). The last is dedicated to Wilhelm Loth, 'sculptor of female torsos and idols', and takes every opportunity to depict Claudel as Rodin's imitator.

17. Dee Garrison, 'Writing the Biography of Mary Heaton Vorse', ed. Sara Alpern, *et al.*, *The Challenge of Feminist Biography* (Urbana: University of Illinois Press, 1992), 75.

18. Quoted in Nancy Walker, ' "Wider than the Sky": Public Presence and Private Self in Dickinson, James, and Woolf', Shari Benstock, ed. *The Private Self*, 285.

19. Adrienne Rich, Felicity Nussbaum, Toni Bowers, and cultural anthropologists lead us to see how many ways mothers have acted and been told to act.

20. Mary Gergen, 'The Social Construction of Personal Histories', in Theodore R. Sarbin and John I. Kitsuse, *Constructing the Social* (London: Sage Publications, 1994), 28.

21. Toni Bowers argues in several places that motherhood is undertheorized, and that seems absolutely accurate to me.

22. Kennedy tells us that she 'pitied' Stuart, who was in a Christian Science School, (pp. 27–8), and both biographers mention his education several times. In fact, Kennedy largely ignores the children as his stated intention not to deal in detail with her personal life allows (p. ix).

23. Quoted in 'Dark Side of Einstein Emerges in his Letters', *New York Times* (6 Nov. 1996), C15.

24. Quoted in William Davenport and Ben Siegel, eds. *Biography Past and Present*, 11–12.

25. In Wilson's book she definitely comes off better than her brother Henry, who is called the 'Adonis of the American pulpit'. Henry, Wilson tells us several times, knew how to wring the hearts of congregations for his personal, avaricious ends. In one scene, he inspires people to drop their rings and brooches in the collection plate while he rolls the rubies and emeralds in his pocket between his own fingers: 'He loved the feel of the precious stones and collected them passionately, carrying them in his pocket' (p. 413).

26. Quoted by Carolyn Heilbrun in a section of *Writing a Woman's Life* on gendered language, p. 35.

27. Gerda Lerner, 'Priorities and Challenges in Women's History', *Perspectives* (Apr. 1988), 19.
28. Claire Johnston, *Notes on Women's Cinema* (London: Society for Education in Film and Television, 1973), 24–5.
29. Phyllis Chesler describes this as the basis for a popular plot for biographies of women, *Women and Madness* (Garden City, NY: Doubleday, 1972), 25–31; quotation, p. 26.
30. Alice Wexler, 'Emma Goldman and the Anxiety of Biography', *The Challenge of Feminist Biography*, ed. Sara Alpern, *et al.*, 43.
31. Diane Wood Middlebrook, 'Robert Lowell's Life Again, Alas', *Boston Sunday Globe* (18 Sept. 1994), A17. I am grateful to Linda Merians for bringing this review to my attention.
32. Marlene Kadar brings these perceptions together in 'Write Down Everything Just as You Know It', forthcoming in a collection of essays edited by Elspeth Cameron. I appreciate their sharing this manuscript with me. See also Sharon O'Brien, 'Feminist Theory and Literary Biography', *Contesting the Subject*, 126–32.
33. Liz Stanley, 'Moments of Writing: Is There a Feminist Auto/biography?', *Gender and History*, 2 (1990), 62.
34. Respectively, interview with Hamilton, Frank J. Prial, 'At Lunch with Nigel Hamilton', *New York Times* (27 Jan. 1993), C10, and Nigel Hamilton, 'Thomas Mann', in Jeffrey Meyers, *The Craft of Literary Biography*, 108.
35. Goodwin, *No Ordinary Time: Franklin and Eleanor Roosevelt* (New York: Simon and Schuster, 1994), 208; and see Cook, *Eleanor Roosevelt* (New York: Viking Press, 1992), 119–23, 320–4.
36. Kathryn Sklar, 'Coming to Terms with Florence Kelley', ed. Sara Alpern, *et al.*, *The Challenge of Feminist Biography*, 21.
37. Bell Gale Chevigny, 'Daughters Writing: Toward a Theory of Women's Biography', *Feminist Studies*, 9 (1983), 81 and 99.
38. Leah Blatt Glasser, ' "She is the One you Call Sister" ', in *Between Women*, 187–211.
39. Diane Wood Middlebrook, 'Postmodernism and the Biographer', in *Revealing Lives*, ed. Susan Bell and Marilyn Yalom (New York: SUNY Press, 1990), 165.

CHAPTER 6

1. Quoted in N. John Hall, 'Those Wonderful Youths and Maidens, My Reviewers', *The Literary Biography*, 23–4. This somewhat impressionistic case study of the reviews of his biography is the only other close look at reviews of biographies that I have found.
2. Respectively, *NYT*, 28 Mar. 1995, C20; Gildas Hamel, 'Lives of God', in *Judaism*, 45 (1996), 377; and *Chicago Tribune*, quoted on book cover. I am grateful to my research assistant, Elizabeth Anne Cater, for help in collecting and evaluating reviews of *God*.
3. The order of the Tanakh: the Torah or Pentateuch (Genesis to Deuteronomy), the prophets, and the wisdom literature (Psalms, Proverbs, Job, Song of Solomon, Ruth, Lamentations, Ecclesiastes, Esther, Daniel, Ezra, Nehemiah, I and II Chronicles). The major difference between it and the Protestant and Catholic Old Testament is the location of the prophets.
4. I would argue that when Catholics or Protestants attempt to eliminate New Testament thought, they inadvertently devalue the characteristics that the lives, actions, and assigned personalities of Jesus and the disciples foreground. Miles says that Moses's description of God's curses on those who disobey God's laws is 'blood-chilling' and 'rises to an eloquence in the depiction of horror unmatched until Dante' (p. 145). Luke Johnson points out that the omission of the New Testament and 'Jewish intertestamental, rabbinic, and mystical literature' results in a literary abstraction, 'What a Character!' *Commonweal*, 122 (19 May 1995), 33.
5. Cf. Bruce Bawer, 'God on the Bestseller List', *Hudson Review*, 48 (Autumn 1995), 408, and *Wilson Quarterly*, 19 (Summer 1995), 91.
6. See Paul Johnson's description of this process in his review of *God*, 'Reading the Mystery,' *Commentary*, 100 (July 1995), 55–6.

7. First published in 1965 (London: Faber and Faber), the book was reprinted (London: R. Clark, 1992).

8. Naomi Lewis, 'A Camberwell Beauty', *Encounter*, 25 (1965), 79. I quote this review because it is, like many others, a remarkable testimony to Hayter's ability to create and communicate a unified yet detailed sense of her subject.

9. Cf. *The Economist*, 215 (17 Apr. 1965), 310; Lindsay Duguid, 'City Lights', *TLS* (21 Aug. 1992), 4; A. N. Wilson wrote in *The Spectator* that he had 'enjoyed it more than any book this year' (21 Nov. 1992), 39.

10. Many rather traditional biographies with similar groupings have been written in the last ten years; among them are Rebecca Fraser, *The Brontës: Charlotte Brontë and her Family* (New York: Crown Publishers, 1988), and Stanley Weintraub, *The Four Rosettis* (New York: Weybright and Talley, 1977).

11. Linda Wagner-Martin, *Telling Women's Lives*, 124, and see her chapter 11 for a stimulating discussion of some of these collections.

12. I am grateful to my colleague Ruth Crocker for sharing her knowledge of women's history.

13. So, of course, do the biographies centred on marriages. The path-breaking full-length biographies of the mid-1980s have become an apparently unending stream. Examples carry titles such as *Dared and Done: The Marriage of Elizabeth Barrett and Robert Browning* (Julia Markus, New York: A. A. Knopf, 1995), *Loss of Eden: A Biography of Charles and Anne Morrow Lindbergh* (Joyce Milton, New York: HarperCollins, 1993), and *Hellman and Hammett: The Legendary Passion of Lillian Hellman and Dashiell Hammett* (Joan Mellen, New York: HarperCollins, 1996). Brenda Maddox's *Nora: A Biography of Nora Joyce* (London: Hamish Hamilton, 1988) and *D. H. Lawrence: The Story of a Marriage* (New York: Simon and Schuster, 1994) could be used to show one biographer's contribution to the form. See Carolyn Heilbrun, *Writing a Woman's Life*, 81 and 80–95.

14. Some people, including E. M. Forster, were annoyed by the practice, p. 199.

15. David Garnett, 'Current Literature', *New Statesman and Nation* (7 Oct. 1933), 416. See all the *TLS* review 'Brown Beauty' (5 Oct. 1933), 667: "Here and there Mrs. Woolf has moulded facts to her fancy . . .". Woolf explains that the book began as 'a joke on Lytton [Strachey]', *Letters of Virginia Woolf*, 5: 161–2.

16. James Barbour and Tom Quirk, ed. *Biographies of Books* (Columbia: University of Missouri Press, 1996), 1–2. The overview of the relationship between various kinds of criticism and studies of the imagination is useful.

17. To some extent, Miles works with the influence of other Middle Eastern religions and gods on the definition of 'God'.

CHAPTER 7

1. Other writers whom I might have discussed are Hilary Spurling, Claire Tomalin, Ann Thwaite, and A. N. Wilson.

2. Arnold Rampersad, 'Biography, Autobiography, and Afro-American Culture', *Yale Review*, 73 (1983), 3, and 'Psychology and Afro-American Biography', *Yale Review*, 78 (1988), 6. Other African-American critics including John Hope Franklin point out that whites who have 'invested time, energy, and commitment' and are trained in the 'structures, moorings, and anchors' of African-American life and scholarship are making valuable contributions, see Nellie Y. McKay, 'Naming the Problem That Led to Question', *PMLA*, 113 (1998), 359–69.

3. I am grateful to my research assistant Elizabeth Anne Cater for her extraordinary work on this group of biographers.

4. Holroyd is being paid the money gradually, and it appears certain that Chatto and Windus will lose money on the deal. *Vanity Fair* reports that only 40,000 of volume I and 25,000 of volume II have sold, Arthur Lubow, 'Charms and the Man,' *Vanity Fair* (September 1991), 238.

5. Michael Holroyd, 'How I Fell into Biography', in *The Troubled Face of Biography*, 101.

6. Respectively, Richard Holmes, 'Biography: Inventing the Truth', in Batchelor, *The Art of Literary Biography*, 15, and quoted in Nadel, 152.

7. None of the men in this group has yet taken a woman as his subject. Peter Ackroyd explains that because he is not a woman, his subjects are men, and I think the group's biographical acts demand sexual and perhaps even gender harmony, 'Interview with Peter Ackroyd', conducted by Susana Onega, *Twentieth-Century Literature*, 42 (1996), 216.

8. Many biographers use the phrase not only to describe the characteristic style of a writer but even to attribute anonymous works, some as short as newspaper book reviews to authors. Almost all of them feel at least some of the time as Jeffrey Meyers describes, 'By the time I completed the book . . . I felt I knew not only Hemingway's tastes and habits but also how he would think and act *in any situation*', *The Spirit of Biography* (emphasis mine), 254.

9. Kate Bostock, 'Interview with Michael Holroyd', *Literature Matters*, 9 (1991), 4. Holroyd admits that he 'lived most vividly in the Strachey world', and that Shaw's voice was 'usually more dramatic and I am usually more oblique'. Perhaps unsurprisingly, Holroyd's biography of Shaw has been found far less seamless and persuasive than *Strachey*.

10. Roger Lewis, 'Review of *The Last Testament of Oscar Wilde*', *American Spectator*, 17 (1984), 40; Brian Finney, 'Ackroyd, Postmodernist Play and *Chatterton*', *Twentieth-Century Literature*, 38 (1992), 244.

11. Michael Holroyd, 'How I Fell into Biography', in *The Troubled Face of Biography*, 94.

12. William Phillips, 'Eliot and Kafka', *Partisan Review*, 52 (1985), 444–8.

13. Dale Salwak, 'Sketches from Life: Philip Larkin—An American View', *Biography*, 21 (1998), 197.

14. Marjorie Garber, 'Bisexuality and Celebrity', *The Seductions of Biography*, eds. Mary Rhiel and David Suchoff (New York: Routledge, 1996), 27.

15. For a typical description, see Ian Hamilton, *Keepers of the Flame* (London: Hutchinson, 1992), 238–9.

16. In a sympathetic analysis, Malcolm Bradbury, a true authority, remarks that these 'freelance' biographers do not use or are even in adversarial relationships with advanced critical methods, *The Troubled Face of Biography*, 136.

17. John Worthen, 'The Necessary Ignorance of a Biographer', in *The Art of Literary Biography*, 235.

18. Ruth Hoberman, *Modernizing Lives: Experiments in English Biography 1918–1939* (Carbondale: Southern Illinois University Press, 1987), 61.

19. Jamie Bush, 'Authorial Authority: Johnson's *Life of Savage* and Nabokov's *Nikolai Gogol*', *Biography*, 19 (1996), 29.

20. Lyndall Gordon, 'Women's Lives: The Unmapped Country', in Batchelor, *The Art of Literary Biography*, 97.

21. David Levering Lewis, 'From Eurocentrism to Polycentrism', *Historians and Race*, ed. Paul A. Cimbala and Robert Himmelberg (Bloomington: Indiana University Press, 1996), 84; this section has been influenced by his essay.

22. Respectively, John Garraty, *The Nature of Biography*, 226–9, and Allison Davis, *Leadership, Love, and Aggression* (Boston: Harcourt, Brace, Jovanovich, 1983).

23. Matthew McCann Fenton, 'Shaking Up the House', *Biography*, 21 (1998), 62.

24. See Joan W. Scott, 'The Evidence of Experience', *Critical Inquiry*, 17 (1991), 794. Her chief example is from Samuel Delaney's autobiography, *The Motion of Light in Water: Sex and Science Fiction Writing in the East Village* (New York: Arbor House, 1988); he is a gay, Black writer of science fiction.

25. The words are James Weldon Johnson's in *The Autobiography of an Ex-Coloured Man, Three Negro Classics*, introduction by John Hope Franklin (New York: Avon Books, 1965), 417.

26. It might be argued that some women are so conscious of their sex and its social implications or some men, for example, perhaps a Kennedy or a Roosevelt, of their lineage and expectations for them that analogies exist.

27. William H. Grier and Price M. Cobbs, *Black Rage* (New York: Basic Books, 1992), 33.

28. These documents are preserved in Dorothy Porter, ed., *Early Negro Writing, 1760–1837* (Boston: Beacon, 1971).

29. Etienne Balibar, 'The National Form: History and Ideology', in Etienne Balibar and Immanuel Wallerstein, ed. *Race, Nation, Class: Ambiguous Identities* (London: Verso, 1988), 94–5.

30. Richard Holmes, 'A Literary Obsession', *New York Times Magazine* (4 Jan. 1998), 43.

31. Faith Berry, *Langston Hughes, Before and Beyond Harlem* (Westport, Conn.: Lawrence Hill & Co., 1983), 1–4; Arnold Rampersad, *The Life of Langston Hughes: I, Too, Sing America* (New York: Oxford University Press, 1986), 1: 1–11.

32. Clayborne Carson, 'King Scholarship and Iconoclastic Myths', *Reviews in American History*, 16 (1988), 135. I would like to thank my research assistant Rod Andrews for his work collecting material for this section.

33. Michael Dyson, 'Inventing and Interpreting Malcolm X', in Rhiel and Suchoff, *The Seductions of Biography*, 46, and see his *Making Malcolm* (Oxford: Oxford University Press, 1994).

34. See Rodney Carlisle, *The Roots of Black Nationalism* for a brief introduction (Port Washington, NY: Kennikat Press, 1975), quotation, p. 3.

35. The Tuskegee airmen were excellent combat pilots and in 1944 such effective 'Close Support' escorts that white bomb squadrons began to ask for them.

36. Gates and the contributors to this collection see Hughes as a bold innovator who began a tradition of poetry by African-Americans, *Langston Hughes: Critical Perspectives, Past and Present*, ed. Henry Louis Gates, jun., and K. A. Appiah (New York: Amistad, 1993), quotation from pp. x–xi. See also essays on music and Hughes's poetry by Arnold Rampersad, especially pp. 54 and 66–7, and by Steven C. Tracy, pp. 69–103.

37. Richard Newman, 'Sara Lawrence-Lightfoot: "To Chart Different Journeys"', *Publisher's Weekly*, 241 (5 Sept. 1994), 80.

38. Arnold Rampersad finds this aspect of African-American life in direct conflict with the spirit and practice of modern biography, 'Biography, Autobiography, and Afro-American Culture', *Yale Review*, 73 (1983), 13–15.

39. Karen J. Winkler, 'Seduction of Biography', *Chronicle of Higher Education* (27 Oct. 1993), A14.

40. Richard H. King, 'Martin Luther King: Problems of History and Biography', *Southern Review*, 24 (1988), 983 *et passim*.

41. Clayborne Carson, 'King Scholarship and Iconoclastic Myths', *Reviews in American History*, 16 (1988), 132–5.

42. Hanes Walton, jun., review of *W. E. B. DuBois*, *Journal of Negro Education*, 63 (1994), 649.

43. On reading Rampersad's biography of Hughes, I learned of the firing of Jonathan Kozol for reading a Hughes poem in his Boston classroom and of the publicity that resulted, *The Life of Langston Hughes: I Dream a World*, (New York: Oxford University Press, 1988) 2: 391.

44. Although he does not treat the Brownsville incident in the context of Roosevelt's race relations, Henry Pringle is an exception with his rightly harsh treatment of the incident in *Theodore Roosevelt*; he points out the opposition to Roosevelt's action and that Roosevelt spent $15,000 in government money trying to obtain evidence to prove himself right and then omitted the incident from his autobiography, pp. 458–64.

45. The phrase is Arnold Rampersad's in 'Biography, Autobiography, and Afro-American Culture,' *Yale Review*, 73 (1983), 13; I have benefited substantially from his essays on Black biography. The quotation is from Johnson's *Autobiography*, 497; shortly after that, his character begins to pass for white.

CONCLUSION

1. Sharon O'Brien, 'Feminist Theory and Literary Biography', *Contesting the Subject*, ed. William Epstein (West Lafayette, Ind.: Purdue University Press, 1991), 125.

2. Respectively, William McFeely, 'Why Biography?', in *Seductions of Biography*, xi, and adapted from Joan Scott, 'Evidence of Experience', 775; and David Halberstam quoted in Steve Weinberg, *Telling the Untold Story: How Investigative Reporters Are Changing the Craft of Biography* (Columbia: University of Missouri Press, 1992), 15.

3. See, for example, Carl Rollyson, 'Biography as Genre', *Choice*, 35 (1997), 249–58, quotation from p. 249. Cf. William McFeely, 'Why Biography?', in which he calls 'a definitive statement of what biography is' 'unattainable,' *Seductions of Biography*, ix.

4. Quoted in 'Portraits in Prose', *TLS* (2 Mar. 1962), 130; Oates in Veninga, *The Biographer's Gift*, 32.

5. Tom Wolfe, *The New Journalism*, ed. Wolfe and E. W. Johnson (New York: Harper & Row, 1973), 21. And see Steve Weinberg, *Telling the Untold Story*, which has influenced this section of my book.

Bibliographies

BIOGRAPHIES

Ackroyd, Peter. *Blake*. London: Sinclair-Stevenson, 1995.
——. *Dickens*. London: Sinclair-Stevenson, 1990.
——. *T. S. Eliot: A Life*. London: Hamish Hamilton, 1984.
Alpers, Antony. *Katherine Mansfield: A Biography*. New York: A. A. Knopf, 1953.
Andersen, Christopher P. *Jagger Unauthorized*. New York: Delacourte Press, 1993.
Ascher, Carol. *Simone de Beauvoir: A Life of Freedom*. Boston: Beacon Press, 1981.
Ashe, Arthur, and Arnold Rampersad. *Days of Grace: A Memoir*. New York: A. A. Knopf, 1993.
Aubrey, John. *Brief Lives*. Edited by Oliver Lawson Dick. Foreword by Edmund Wilson. Ann Arbor: University of Michigan Press, 1962.
Backscheider, Paula. *Daniel Defoe: His Life*. Baltimore: Johns Hopkins University Press, 1989.
Bainton, Roland. *Here I Stand: A Life of Martin Luther*. New York: Abingdon-Cokesbury Press, 1950.
Bair, Deirdre. *Simone de Beauvoir: A Biography*. New York: Summit Books, 1990.
——. *Samuel Beckett A Biography*. New York: Harcourt, Brace, Jovanovich, 1978.
Barbour, James, and Tom Quirk, ed. *Biographies of Books: The Compositional Histories of Notable American Writings*. Columbia: University of Missouri Press, 1996.
Bass, Jack. *Taming the Storm: The Life and Times of Judge Frank M. Johnson and the South's Fight Over Civil Rights*. New York: Doubleday, 1993.
Bate, Walter Jackson. *Samuel Johnson*. New York: Harcourt, Brace, Jovanovich, 1977.
——. *John Keats*. Cambridge: Harvard University Press, 1963.
Bell, Ian. *Dreams of Exile: Robert Louis Stevenson; A Biography*. Edinburgh: Mainstream Publishing, 1992.
Bell, Quentin. *Virginia Woolf: A Biography*. London: Hogarth Press, 1972.
Benstock, Shari. *Women of the Left Bank, Paris: 1910–1940*. Austin: University of Texas Press, 1986.
Berg, Andrew Scott. *Max Perkins, Editor of Genius*. New York: Dutton, 1978.
Berry, Faith. *Langston Hughes: Before and Beyond Harlem*. Westport, Conn.: Lawrence Hill and Company, 1983.
Bjork, Daniel. *B. F. Skinner: A Life*. New York: Basic Books, 1993.
Black, Jeremy. *Pitt the Elder*. Cambridge: Cambridge University Press, 1992.
Bockris, Victor. *Keith Richards: The Biography*. New York: Poseidon Press, 1992.
Bonaparte, Felicia. *The Gypsy-Bachelor of Manchester: The Life of Mrs Gaskell's Demon*. Charlottesville: University Press of Virginia, 1992.
Boswell, James. *The Life of Johnson*. Edited by R.W. Chapman. Oxford: Oxford University Press, 1980.
Bowen, Catherine Drinker. *Yankee from Olympus: Justice Holmes and His Family*. Boston: Little, Brown and Company, 1994.

Bowen, Catherine Drinker. *The Lion and the Throne: The Life and Times of Sir Edward Coke (1552–1634)*. Boston: Little, Brown and Company, 1957.

——. *'Beloved Friend': The Story of Tchaikovsky and Nadejda von Meck*. Garden City: Garden City Press, 1941.

Boydston, Jeanne, Mary Kelley, and Anne Margolis. *The Limits of Sisterhood: The Beecher Sisters on Women's Rights and Woman's Sphere*. Chapel Hill: University of North Carolina Press, 1988.

Brabazon, James. *Dorothy L. Sayers: A Biography*. New York: Charles Scribner's Sons, 1981.

Breslaw, Elaine. *Tituba; Reluctant Witch of Salem: Devilish Indians and Puritan Fantasies*. New York: New York University Press, 1996.

Breslin, James. *Mark Rothko*. Chicago: University of Chicago Press, 1993.

Brightman, Carol. *Writing Dangerously: A Critical Biography of Mary McCarthy*. New York: Clarkson Potter, 1992.

Brombert, Beth. *Edouard Manet: Rebel in a Frock Coat*. Boston: Little, Brown and Company, 1996.

Brome, Vincent. *The Other Pepys*. London: Weidenfeld & Nicolson, 1992.

Brookhiser, Richard. *Founding Father: Rediscovering George Washington*. New York: Free Press, 1996.

Brown, Frederick. *Zola: A Life*. New York: Farrar, Strauss and Giroux, 1995.

Burns, James M. *Roosevelt: The Soldier of Freedom*. New York: Harcourt, Brace, Jovanovich, 1970.

——. *Roosevelt: The Lion and the Fox*. New York: Harcourt, Brace, Jovanovich, 1956.

Bush, Douglas. *John Milton: A Sketch of His Life and Writings*. New York: Macmillan, 1964.

Capper, Charles. *Margaret Fuller: An American Romantic Life*. I, *The Private Years*. New York: Oxford University Press, 1992.

Carlyle, Thomas. *Life of Frederick II of Prussia*, 8 vols. London: Chapman and Hall, 1897.

Caro, Robert. *The Years of Lyndon Johnson*. New York: A. A. Knopf, 1982.

——. *The Power Broker: Robert Moses and the Fall of New York*. New York: A. A. Knopf, 1974.

Carpenter, Humphrey. *Robert Runcie: The Reluctant Archbishop*. London: Hodder and Stoughton, 1996.

Castañeda, Jorge. *Compañero: The Life and Death of Che Guevara*. New York: A. A. Knopf, 1997.

Caw, Mary Ann. *Women of Bloomsbury: Virginia, Vanessa, and Carrington*. New York: Routledge, 1990.

Chabon, Michael. *Wonder Boys*. New York: Villard Books, 1995.

Chadwick, Whitney, and Isabelle De Courtivron ed. *Significant Others: Creativity and Intimate Partnerships*. London: Thames and Hudson, 1993.

Chalmers, George. *The Life of Daniel Defoe*. 1790; New York: Garland Publishing, 1970.

Charmley, John. *Churchill: The End of Glory*. San Diego: Harcourt Brace, 1994.

Chernaik, Judith. *Love's Children* (or *Mab's Daughters*). New York: A. A. Knopf, 1992.

Chesler, Ellen. *Woman of Valor: Margaret Sanger and the Birth Control Movement in America*. New York: Simon and Schuster, 1992.

Christensen, Jerome. *Practicing Enlightenment: Hume and the Formation of a Literary Career*. Madison: University of Wisconsin Press, 1987.

Clapp, Margaret. *Forgotten First Citizen: John Bigelow*. Boston: Little, Brown and Company, 1947.

Clark, E. Culpepper. *The Schoolhouse Door: Segregation's Last Stand at the University of Alabama*. New York: Oxford University Press, 1993.

Clark, Ronald William. *Bertrand Russell and His World*. New York: Thames and Hudson, 1981.

——. *Einstein: The Life and Times*. New York: World Publishing Company, 1971.

——. *The Huxleys*. New York: McGraw-Hill, 1968.

Clegg, Claude Andrew. *An Original Man: The Life and Times of Elijah Muhammad*. New York: St Martin's Press, 1997.

Coit, Margaret. *John C. Calhoun: American Portrait*. Boston: Houghton Mifflin, 1950.

Cook, Blanche Wiesen. *Eleanor Roosevelt*. New York: Viking Press, 1992.

Craveri, Benedetta. *Madame Du Deffand and Her World*. Translated by Teresa Waugh. Boston: D. R. Godine, 1994.

Dauben, Joseph W. *Abraham Robinson: The Creation of Nonstandard Analysis, A Personal and Mathematical Odyssey*. Princeton: Princeton University Press, 1995.

——. *Georg Cantor: His Mathematics and Philosophy of the Infinite*. Princeton: Princeton University Press, 1979.

Davis, Stephen. *Hammer of the Gods: The Led Zeppelin Saga*. New York: Ballantine Books, 1986.

Delbée, Ann. *Camille Claudel: Une Femme*. Translated by Carol Cosam. San Francisco: Mercury House, 1992.

DeMaria, Robert. *The Life of Samuel Johnson: A Critical Biography*. Oxford: Blackwell, 1993.

DeMott, Robert. "'A Truly American Book": Pressing *The Grapes of Wrath'*. In *Biographies of Books*, ed. James Barbour and Tom Quirk, 187–225. Columbia: University of Missouri Press, 1996.

Doody, Margaret Anne. *Frances Burney: The Life in the Works*. New Brunswick, NJ: Rutgers University Press, 1988.

Douglas, Hugh. *Flora MacDonald: The Most Loyal Rebel*. Dover, NH: Alan Sutton, 1993.

Dyson, Michael. *Making Malcolm: The Myth and Meaning of Malcolm X*. Oxford: Oxford University Press, 1994.

Edel, Leon. *Henry James: A Life*. New York: Harper & Row, 1985.

——. *Henry James*. 5 vols. Philadelphia: J. B. Lippincott Company, 1953.

Ehrenpreis, Irvin. *Swift: The Man, His Works, and the Age*. 3 vols. Cambridge: Harvard University Press, 1962-83.

Eisenwerth, J. Adolf. *Auguste Rodin and Camille Claudel*. Translated by John Ormrod. Munich: Prestel-Verlag, 1994.

Ellmann, Richard. *Oscar Wilde*. New York: A. A. Knopf, 1987.

——. *James Joyce*. Oxford: Oxford University Press, 1959.

Eribon, Didier. *Michel Foucault*. Cambridge: Harvard University Press, 1991.

Erikson, Erik. *Gandhi's Truth: On the Origins of Militant Nonviolence*. New York: Norton, 1969.

——. *Young Man Luther: A Study in Psychoanalysis and History*. New York: Norton, 1958.

Evanzz, Karl. *The Messenger: The Rise and Fall of Elijah Muhammad.* New York: Pantheon Books, 1999.

Field, Andrew. *Nabokov: His Life in Part.* New York: Viking Press, 1977.

———. *Nabokov: His Life in Art.* London: Hodder and Stoughton, 1967.

Fleming, Robert E. *James Weldon Johnson.* Boston: Twayne Publishers, 1987.

Forbes, Esther. *Paul Revere and the World he Lived in.* Boston: Houghton-Mifflin, 1942.

Francis, Charles E. *The Tuskegee Airmen: The Men Who Changed a Nation.* Boston: Branden Publishing, 1988.

Frank, Elizabeth. *Louise Bogan: A Portrait.* New York: A. A. Knopf, 1985.

Frady, Marshall. *Jesse: The Life and Pilgrimage of Jesse Jackson.* New York: Random House, 1996.

Fraser, Antonia. *Wives of Henry VIII.* New York: A. A. Knopf, 1993.

———. *Cromwell: The Lord Protector.* New York: A. A. Knopf, 1974.

Fraser, Rebecca. *The Brontës: Charlotte Brontë and Her Family.* New York: Crown Publishers, 1988.

Garrow, David J. *Bearing the Cross: Martin Luther King, Jr. and the Southern Christian Leadership Conference.* New York: William Morrow & Company, 1986.

Gattégno, Jean. *Lewis Carroll: Fragments of a Looking Glass.* Translated by Rosemary Sheed. New York: Thomas Crowell, 1974.

Gelles, Edith B. *Portia: The World of Abigail Adams.* Bloomington: Indiana University Press, 1992.

Gérin, Winifred. *Elizabeth Gaskell: A Biography.* Oxford: Clarendon Press, 1976.

Gilchrist, Alexander. *Life of William Blake.* New York: Dodd, Mead and Company, 1906.

Givner, Joan. *Katherine Anne Porter: A Life.* New York: Simon & Schuster, 1982.

Gleick, James. *Genius: The Life and Science of Richard Feynman.* New York: Pantheon, 1992.

Glendinning, Victoria. *Anthony Trollope.* New York: A. A. Knopf, 1993.

———. *Vita: A Life of V. Sackville-West.* London: Weidenfeld & Nicolson, 1983.

Goodwin, Doris Kearns. *No Ordinary Time: Franklin and Eleanor Roosevelt.* New York: Simon & Schuster, 1994.

———. *Lyndon Johnson and the American Dream.* New York: Harper & Row, 1976.

Grunfeld, Frederic. *Rodin: A Biography.* New York: Henry Holt, 1987.

Hall, N. John. *Trollope: A Biography.* Oxford: Clarendon Press, 1991.

Hall, Tord. *Carl Friedrich Gauss: A Biography.* Cambridge: MIT Press, 1970.

Halperin, John. *The Life of Jane Austen.* Baltimore: Johns Hopkins University Press, 1984.

Hamilton, Nigel. *JFK: Reckless Youth.* New York: Random House, 1992.

———. *Brothers Mann: The Lives of Heinrich and Thomas Mann, 1871–1950 and 1875–1955.* London: Secker & Warburg, 1978.

Harlan, Louis R. *Booker T. Washington.* II, *The Wizard of Tuskegee, 1901-1915.* Oxford: Oxford University Press, 1983.

———. *Booker T. Washington.* I, *The Making of a Black Leader, 1856-1901.* Oxford: Oxford University Press, 1972.

Hasse, John. *Beyond Category: The Life and Genius of Duke Ellington.* New York: Simon & Schuster, 1993.

Hayter, Alethea. *A Sultry Month: Scenes of London Literary Life in 1846.* 1965; London: R. Clark, 1992.

——. *Mrs. Browning: A Poet's Work and its Setting*. London: Faber & Faber, 1962.

Hedrick, Joan. *Harriet Beecher Stowe: A Life*. New York: Oxford University Press, 1994.

Heilbrun, Carolyn. *Education of a Woman: The Life of Gloria Steinem*. New York: Dial Press, 1995.

Herivel, John. *Joseph Fourier: The Man and the Physicist*. Oxford: Clarendon Press, 1975.

Herold, J. Christopher. *Mistress to an Age: A Life of Madame de Staël*. 1958; Alexandria, Va.: Time Life Books, 1981.

Herrara, Hayden. *Matisse: A Portrait*. New York: Harcourt Brace, 1993.

Hill, Christopher. *God's Englishman: Oliver Cromwell and the English Revolution*. 1970; Harmondsworth: Penguin, 1983.

Holmes, Richard. *Dr. Johnson and Mr. Savage*. New York: Pantheon, 1994.

——. *Coleridge: Early Visions*. New York: Viking Penguin, 1989.

——. *Shelley: The Pursuit*. London: Weidenfeld & Nicolson, 1974.

Holroyd, Michael. *Bernard Shaw*. 4 vols. New York: Random House, 1988–92.

——. *Augustus John: A Biography*. London: Book Club Associates, 1975.

——. *Hugh Kingsmill: A Critical Biography*. Introduction by Malcolm Muggeridge. London: Heinemann, 1971.

——. *Lytton Strachey: A Critical Biography*. II, *The Years of Achievement (1910–1932)*. New York: Holt, Rinehart and Winston, 1968.

——. *Lytton Strachey: A Critical Biography*. I, *The Unknown Years (1880–1910)*. New York: Holt, Rinehart and Winston, 1967.

Horgan, Paul. *Tracings: A Book of Partial Portraits*. New York: Farrar, Straus and Giroux, 1993.

Johnson, Samuel. *An Account of the Life of Richard Savage*. London: 1744.

Kanigel, Robert. *The Man Who Knew Infinity: A Life of the Genius Ramanujan*. New York: Charles Scribner's Sons, 1991.

Kaplan, Justin. *Mr. Clemens and Mark Twain: A Biography*. New York: Simon & Schuster, 1966.

Kates, Gary. *Monsieur d'Eon is a Woman: A Tale of Political Intrigue and Sexual Masquerade*. New York: Basic Books, 1995.

Kaufman, Andrew. *Cardozo*. Cambridge: Harvard University Press, 1998.

Kelley, Kitty. *His Way: The Unauthorized Biography of Frank Sinatra*. New York: Bantam Books, 1986.

Kennedy, David M. *Birth Control in America: The Career of Margaret Sanger*. New Haven: Yale University Press, 1970.

Knowlson, James. *Damned to Fame: The Life of Samuel Beckett*. New York: Simon & Schuster, 1996.

Koestenbaum, Wayne. *Jackie Under My Skin: Interpreting an Icon*. New York: Farrar, Straus, and Giroux, 1995.

Kramer, Lloyd. *Lafayette in Two Worlds*. Chapel Hill: University of North Carolina Press, 1996.

Kurlansky, Mark. *Cod: A Biography of the Fish That Changed the World*. New York: Walker and Company, 1997.

Lash, Joseph P. *Eleanor: The Years Alone*. New York: W. W. Norton, 1972.

——. *Eleanor and Franklin: The Story of Their Relationship, based on Eleanor Roosevelt's Private Papers*. New York: Norton, 1971.

Lawrence-Lightfoot, Sara. *I've Known Rivers: Lives of Loss and Liberation*. Reading, Mass.: Addison-Wesley Publishing Company, 1994.

Leaming, Barbara. *Katharine Hepburn*. New York: Crown Publishers, 1995.

LeBeau, Bryan. *Jonathan Dickinson and the Formative Years of American Presbyterianism*. Lexington: University Press of Kentucky, 1997.

Lerner, Gerda. *The Grimké Sisters from South Carolina*. Boston: Houghton-Mifflin, 1967.

Lewis, David L. *W. E. B. DuBois: A Biography of a Race, 1869–1919*. New York: H. Holt, 1993.

Lewis, R. W. B. *Edith Wharton: A Biography*. New York: Harper Colophon Books, 1975.

Levi, Peter. *Tennyson*. New York: Charles Scribner's Sons, 1993.

Limón, Graciela. *In Search of Bernabé*. Houston, Tex.: Arte Público Press, 1993.

McCullough, David G. *Truman*. New York: Simon & Schuster, 1992.

———. *Mornings on Horseback*. New York: Simon & Schuster, 1981.

MacDowell, Paula. *The Women of Grub Street: Press, Politics, and Gender in the London Literary Marketplace, 1678–1730*. Oxford: Clarendon Press, 1997.

Macey, David. *The Lives of Foucault: A Biography*. New York: Pantheon Books, 1993.

Mack, John E. *A Prince of Our Disorder: The Life of T. E. Lawrence*. Boston: Little Brown, 1976.

Mack, Maynard. *Alexander Pope: A Life*. New Haven: Yale University Press, 1985.

McKay, Nellie Y. *Jean Toomer: Artist*. Chapel Hill: University of North Carolina Press, 1984.

McLynn, Frank. *Robert Louis Stevenson: A Biography*. New York: Random House, 1994.

Maddox, Brenda. *D. H. Lawrence: The Story of a Marriage*. New York: Simon & Schuster, 1994.

———. *Nora: A Biography of Nora Joyce*. London: Hamish Hamilton, 1988.

Mariani, Paul. *Lost Puritan: A Life of Robert Lowell*. New York: W. W. Norton, 1994.

———. *Dream Song: The Life of John Berryman*. New York: W. Morrow, 1990.

———. *William Carlos Williams*. Chicago: American Library Association, 1975.

Markus, Julia. *Dared and Done: The Marriage of Elizabeth Barrett Browning and Robert Browning*. New York: A. A. Knopf, 1995.

Marsh, Margaret. *Anarchist Women: 1870–1920*. Philadelphia: Temple University Press, 1981.

Massie, Robert. *Peter the Great*. New York: A. A. Knopf, 1980.

Mellen, Joan. *Hellman and Hammett: The Legendary Passion of Lillian Hellman and Dashiell Hammett*. New York: HarperCollins, 1996.

Meyers, Jeffrey. *Robert Frost: A Biography*. Boston: Houghton-Mifflin, 1996.

———. *Hemingway: A Biography*. New York: Harper and Row, 1985.

———. *Katherine Mansfield: A Biography*. New York: New Directions Publication Corporation, 1980.

———. *The Enemy: A Biography of Wyndam Lewis*. London: Routledge & Kegan Paul, 1980.

Middlebrook, Diane Wood. *Suits Me: The Double Life of Billy Tipton*. Boston: Houghton-Mifflin, 1998.

———. *Anne Sexton: A Biography*. Boston: Houghton-Mifflin, 1991.

Miles, Jack. *God: A Biography*. New York: A. A. Knopf, 1995.

Milford, Nancy. *Zelda: A Biography*. New York: Harper & Row, 1970.

Miller, James. *The Passion of Michel Foucault*. New York: Simon & Schuster, 1993.

Mills, Kay. *This Little Light of Mine: The Life of Fannie Lou Hamer*. New York: Dutton, 1993.

Milton, Joyce. *Loss of Eden: A Biography of Charles and Anne Morrow Lindbergh*. New York: HarperCollins Publishers, 1993.

Moi, Toril. *Simone de Beauvoir: The Making of an Intellectual Woman*. Oxford: Blackwell, 1994.

Monk, Ray. *Bertrand Russell: The Spirit of Solitude, 1872–1921*. London: J. Cape, 1996.

Moorehead, Caroline. *Bertrand Russell: A Life*. New York: Viking Press, 1993.

Morison, Samuel Eliot. *John Paul Jones: A Sailor's Biography*. Boston: Little, Brown and Company, 1959.

——. *Admiral of the Ocean Sea: A Life of Christopher Columbus*. 2 vols. Boston: Little, Brown and Company, 1942.

Morris, Edmund. *The Rise of Theodore Roosevelt*. New York: Coward, McCann, and Geoghegan, 1979.

Motion, Andrew. *Keats*. London: Faber & Faber, 1997.

Neale, John E. *Queen Elizabeth*. London: J. Cape, 1934.

Nicolson, Harold. *King George V: His Life and Reign*. London: Constable, 1952.

——. *Benjamin Constant*. Garden City: Doubleday, 1949.

——. *Tennyson: Aspects of His Life, Character and Poetry*. Boston: Houghton-Mifflin, 1930.

——. *Swinburne*. New York: Macmillan Company, 1926.

Nicolson, Nigel. *Mary Curzon*. London: Weidenfeld & Nicolson, 1977.

——. *Alex: The Life of Field Marshall Earl Alexander of Tunis*. London: Weidenfeld & Nicolson, 1973.

——. *Portrait of a Marriage*. New York: Atheneum, 1973.

Novick, Sheldon. *Henry James: The Young Master*. New York: Random House, 1996.

Nye, David. *The Invented Self: An Anti-Biography, From Documents of Thomas Edison*. Odense, Denmark: Odense University Press, 1983.

Origo, Iris. *Leopardi*. Milano: Rizzoli, 1974.

Owen, D. D. R. *Eleanor of Aquitaine: Queen and Legend*. Oxford: Blackwell, 1993.

Paris, Barry. *Garbo: A Biography*. New York: A. A. Knopf, 1995.

Paris, Reine-Marie. *Camille Claudel: The Life of Rodin's Muse and Mistress*. New York: Seaver Books, 1988.

——. *Camille Claudel: 1864–1943*. Paris: Gallimard, 1984.

Paulson, Ronald. *Hogarth*. 3 vols. New Brunswick: Rutgers University Press, 1991–3.

——. *Hogarth: His Life, Art, and Times*. New Haven: Yale University Press, 1971.

Phelps, Glenn. *George Washington and the American Constitutionalism*. Lawrence, Kan.: University Press of Kansas, 1993.

Phillips-Matz, Mary Jane. *Verdi: A Biography*. Oxford: Oxford University Press, 1993.

Plutarch. *Lives of Noble Grecians and Romans*. Oxford: Blackwell, 1928.

Pringle, Henry. *Theodore Roosevelt*. New York: Harcourt Brace, 1931.

Peters, Margot. *May Sarton: A Biography*. New York: A. A. Knopf, 1997.

Quinn, Susan. *Marie Curie: A Life*. New York: Simon & Schuster, 1995.

Rampersad, Arnold. *The Life of Langston Hughes*, I, 1902–41, *I, Too, Sing America*. New York: Oxford University Press, 1986.

——. *The Life of Langston Hughes*, II, 1941–67, *I Dream A World*. New York: Oxford University Press, 1988.

Reid, B. L. *The Man From New York: John Quinn and His Friends*. New York: Oxford University Press, 1968.

Reid, Constance. *Hilbert*. New York: Springer-Verlag, 1986.

Richards, Laura Elizabeth Howe and Maude Howe Elliot, assisted by Florence Howe Hall. *Julia Ward Howe*. 1915; Dunwoody, Ga.: N. S. Berg, 1970.

Richardson, Robert. *Emerson, The Mind on Fire: A Biography*. Berkeley: University of California Press, 1995.

Robb, Graham. *Balzac: A Biography*. London: Picador, 1994.

Rodger, N. A. M. *The Insatiable Earl: A Life of John Montagu, Fourth Earl of Sandwich, 1712–1792*. London: Harper Collins, 1993.

Rose, Kenneth. *King George V*. New York: A. A. Knopf, 1984.

Rose, Norman. *Churchill: The Unruly Giant*. New York: Free Press, 1995.

Rose, Phyllis. *Woman of Letters: A Life of Virginia Woolf*. New York: Oxford University Press, 1978.

Rosengarten, Theodore. *Tombee: A Portrait of a Cotton Planter*. New York: Morrow, 1986.

Rowley, Hazel. *Christina Stead: A Biography*. Port Melbourne, Victoria: W. Heinemann Australia, 1993.

Russell, Bertrand. *The Autobiography of Bertrand Russell, 1872–1914*. Boston: Little, Brown and Company, 1967.

Ryan, Alan. *Bertrand Russell: A Political Life*. New York: Hill and Wang, 1988.

Sackville-West, Vita. *Knole and the Sackvilles*. London: E. Benn, 1958.

Sanders, Charles R. *Lytton Strachey: His Mind and Art*. New Haven: Yale University Press, 1957.

Sandford, Christopher. *Mick Jagger: Primitive Cool*. London: V. Gollancz, 1993.

Sartre, Jean-Paul. *Saint Genet: Actor and Martyr*. Translated by Bernard Frectman. New York: George Braziller, 1963.

Saul, Nigel. *Richard II*. New Haven: Yale University Press, 1997.

Scammell, Michael. *Solzhenitsyn: A Biography*. New York: W. W. Norton, 1984.

Sewall, Richard B. *The Life of Emily Dickinson*. 2 vols. New York: Farrar, Strauss, and Giroux, 1974.

Seymour-Smith, Martin. *Hardy*. New York: St Martin's Press, 1994.

Sherwood, Frances. *Vindication*. New York: Farrar, Straus, and Giroux, 1993.

Smith, John E. *Jonathan Edwards: Puritan, Preacher, Philosopher*. Notre Dame: University of Notre Dame Press, 1992.

Sobel, Dava. *Longitude: The True Story of a Lone Genius Who Solved the Greatest Scientific Problem of His Time*. New York: Walker and Company, 1995.

Stevenson, Anne. *Bitter Fame: A Life of Sylvia Plath*. Boston: Houghton-Mifflin, 1989.

Strachey, Lytton. *Elizabeth and Essex: A Tragic History*. New York: Harcourt Brace, 1928.

——. *Queen Victoria*. New York: Harcourt, Brace, and Company, 1921.

——. *Eminent Victorians*. Garden City, NY: Garden City Press, 1918.

Strouse, Jean. *Alice James: A Biography*. Boston: Houghton-Mifflin, 1980.

Super, R. H. *The Chronicler of Barsetshire: A Life of Anthony Trollope.* Ann Arbor: University of Michigan Press, 1988.

Taibo, Paco. *Guevara, Also Known as Che.* New York: St Martin's Press, 1997.

Tanner, Stephen. 'The Western Context of *One Flew Over the Cuckoo's Nest*'. In *Biographies of Books*, ed. James Barbour and Tom Quirk, 291–320. Columbia: University of Missouri Press, 1996.

Thomas, D. M. *Alexander Solzhenitsyn: A Century in His Life.* New York: St Martin's Press, 1998.

Thompson, E. P. *Witness Against the Beast: William Blake and Moral Law.* New York: New Press, 1993.

Thurman, Judith. *Isak Dinesen: The Life of a Storyteller.* New York: St Martin's Press, 1982.

Thwaite, Ann. *A. A. Milne: The Man Behind Winnie-the-Pooh.* New York: Random House, 1990.

Tomalin, Claire. *Invisible Woman: The Story of Nelly Ternan and Charles Dickens.* New York: A. A. Knopf/Random House, 1991.

Tomkins, Calvin. *Duchamp: A Biography.* New York: Henry Holt, 1996.

Trzebinski, Errol. *The Lives of Beryl Markham: Out of Africa's Hidden Free Spirit and Denys Finch Hatton's Last Great Love.* New York: W. W. Norton, 1993.

Uglow, Jennifer. *Elizabeth Gaskell: A Habit of Stories.* New York: Farrar, Straus, and Giroux, 1993.

Ulrich, Laurel Thatcher. *A Midwife's Tale: The Life of Martha Ballard.* New York: A. A. Knopf, 1990.

Urquhart, Brian. *Ralph Bunche—An American Life.* New York: W. W. Norton, 1993.

Wagner-Martin, Linda. '*Favored Strangers*': *Gertrude Stein and Her Family.* New Brunswick, NJ: Rutgers University Press, 1995.

——. *Sylvia Plath: A Biography.* New York: Simon and Schuster, 1987.

Waid, Candace. 'Building *The House of Mirth*.' In *Biographies of Books*, ed. James Barbour and Tom Quirk, 160–86. Columbia: University of Missouri Press, 1996.

Wain, John. *Samuel Johnson.* New York: Viking Press, 1974.

Walton, Izaak. *The Lives of Dr. John Donne, Sir Henry Wotton, Mr. Richard Hooker, Mr. George Herbert.* London: 1670.

Ward, Aileen. *John Keats: The Making of a Poet.* New York: Viking Press, 1963.

Ware, Susan. *Partner and I: Molly Dawson, Feminism and New Deal Politics.* New Haven: Yale University Press, 1987.

Weintraub, Stanley. *The Four Rosettis.* New York: Weybright and Talley, 1977.

Weir, Alison. *The Children of Henry VIII.* New York: Ballantine Books, 1996.

Wendorf, Richard. *Sir Joshua Reynolds.* Cambridge: Harvard University Press, 1996.

Westfall, Richard. *Never at Rest: A Biography of Isaac Newton.* 1980; Cambridge: Cambridge University Press, 1983.

Wexler, Alice. *Emma Goldman: An Intimate Life.* New York: Pantheon Books, 1984.

Willcox, William Bradford. *Portrait of a General: Sir Henry Clinton in the War of Independence.* New York: A. A. Knopf, 1964.

Williams, T. Harry. *Huey Long.* 1969; New York: Vintage, 1981.

Wilson, Robert Forrest. *Crusader in Crinoline: The Life of Harriet Beecher Stowe.* Philadelphia: J. B. Lippincott Company, 1941.

Winn, James. *John Dryden and His World*. New Haven: Yale University Press, 1987.

Winslow, Ola Elizabeth. *Jonathan Edwards, 1703–1758: A Biography*. New York: The Macmillan Company, 1940.

Wolfe, Linnie Marsh. *Son of the Wilderness: The Life of John Muir*. New York: A. A. Knopf, 1945.

Wolfe, Tom. *The Right Stuff*. New York: Farrar, Straus, and Giroux, 1979.

Wolff, Cynthia Griffin. *Emily Dickinson*. New York: A. A. Knopf, 1986.

Woolf, Virginia. *Flush: A Biography*. 1933; New York: Harcourt, Brace, Jovanovich, 1976.

——. *Roger Fry: A Biography*. 1940; London: Hogarth Press, 1969.

Wright, Richard. *Black Boy*. New York: Harper and Brothers, 1945.

Wright, Thomas. *Biographica Britannica Literaria*. 2 vols. London: J. M. Parker, 1842–6.

Wright, William. *Lillian Hellman: The Image, The Woman*. New York: Simon & Schuster, 1986.

X, Malcolm. *Autobiography of Malcolm X*. With the assistance of Alex Haley. Introduction by M. S. Handler, and Epilogue by Alex Haley. New York: Grove Press, 1966.

Young-Bruehl, Elisabeth. *Hannah Arendt, For Love of the World*. New Haven: Yale University Press, 1982.

THEORY AND PRACTICE OF BIOGRAPHY

Aaron, Daniel, ed. *Studies in Biography*. Cambridge: Harvard University Press, 1978.

Alpern, Sarah, Joyce Antler, Elisabeth Israels Perry, and Ingrid Winther Scobie, ed. *The Challenge of Feminist Biography: Writing the Lives of Modern American Women*. Urbana: University of Illinois Press, 1992.

Altick, Richard. *The Scholar Adventurers*. New York: Free Press, 1950.

Ascher, Carol, Louise DeSalvo, and Sara Ruddick, ed. *Between Women: Biographers, Novelists, Critics, Teachers, and Artists Write about Their Work on Women*. Boston: Beacon Press, 1984.

Backscheider, Paula. 'Biographer: Both Ally and Enemy'. *Research Frontiers* (Fall 1989): 20.

Baron, Samuel H., and Carl Pletsch, ed. *Introspection in Biography*. London: Analytic Press, 1985.

Batchelor, John, ed. *The Art of Literary Biography*. Oxford: Clarendon Press, 1989.

Bell, Susan Groag, and Marilyn Yalom, ed. *Revealing Lives: Autobiography, Biography, and Gender*. Albany: SUNY Press, 1990.

Benstock, Shari, ed. *The Private Self: Theory and Practice of Women's Autobiographical Writings*. Chapel Hill: University of North Carolina Press, 1988.

Bloom, Lynn Z. 'Reunion and Reinterpretation: Group Biography in Process'. *Biography*, 13 (1990): 222–34.

Bowen, Catherine Drinker. *Biography: The Craft and the Calling*. Boston: Little, Brown and Company, 1969.

——. *Adventures of a Biographer*. Boston: Little, Brown and Company, 1959.

Bradbury, Malcolm. 'The Telling Life: Some Thoughts on Literary Biography'. In *The Troubled Face of Biography*, ed. Eric Homberger and John Charmley, 131–40. New York: St Martin's Press, 1988.

Brogan, Hugh. 'The Biographer's Chains'. In *The Troubled Face of Biography*, ed. Eric Homberger and John Charmley, 104–12. New York: St Martin's Press, 1988.

Bromwich, David. 'The Uses of Biography'. *Yale Review*, 73 (Winter 1984): 161–75.

Browning, J. D. *Biography in the Eighteenth-Century*. New York: Garland, 1980.

Bush, Jamie. 'Authorial Authority: Johnson's *Life of Savage* and Nabokov's *Nikolai Gogol*'. *Biography*, 19 (1996): 29.

Chevigny, Bell Gale. 'Daughters Writing: Toward a Theory of Women's Biography'. *Feminist Studies*, 9 (1983): 79–102.

Christianson, Gale. *Writing Lives is the Devil!* Hamden, Conn.: Archon Books, 1993.

Clifford, James L. *From Puzzles to Portraits: Problems of a Literary Biographer*. Chapel Hill: University of North Carolina Press, 1970.

——. *Biography as Art: Selected Criticism*. London: Oxford University Press, 1962.

Daghlian, Philip B., ed. *Essays in Eighteenth-Century Biography*. Bloomington: Indiana University Press, 1968.

Davenport, William H., and Ben Siegel, ed. *Biography: Past and Present*. New York: Charles Scribner's Sons, 1965.

Davis, Linda. 'The Red Room: Stephen Crane and Me'. In *The Literary Biography: Problems and Solutions*, ed. Dale Salwak, 66–79. Iowa City: University of Iowa Press, 1996.

De Voto, Bernard. 'The Skeptical Biographer'. In *Biography: Past and Present*, ed. William Davenport and Ben Siegel, 276–92. New York: Charles Scribner's Sons, 1965.

Dyson, Michael. 'Inventing and Interpreting Malcolm X'. In *Seductions of Biography*, ed. Mary Rhiel and David Suchoff, 43–53. New York: Routledge, 1996.

Edel, Leon. 'Biography and the Science of Man'. In *New Directions in Biography*, ed. Anthony Friedson, 1–11. Honolulu: University of Hawaii Press, 1981.

——. 'The Figure Under the Carpet'. In *Telling Lives*, ed. Mark Pachter, 17–34. Washington, DC: New Republic Books, 1979.

——. *Writing Lives: Principia Biographica*. 1959; New York: W. W. Norton, 1984.

——. *Literary Biography*. Toronto: University of Toronto Press, 1957.

Ellmann, Richard. 'Freud and Literary Biography'. *Diogenes*, 139 (1987): 70–86.

——. *Golden Codgers: Biographical Speculations*. New York: Oxford University Press, 1973.

Elms, Alan C. *Uncovering Lives: The Uneasy Alliance of Biography and Psychology*. Oxford: Oxford University Press, 1994.

Epstein, William, ed. *Contesting the Subject*. West Lafayette, Ind.: Purdue University Press, 1991.

——. *Recognizing Biography*. Philadelphia: University of Pennsylvania Press, 1987.

Erikson, Erik. 'On the Nature of Psycho-Historical Evidence: In Search of Gandhi'. *Daedalus*, 97 (1968): 695–730.

Fox-Genovese, Elizabeth. 'First Lady-Like Behavior'. *TLS* (21 May 1993): 13–14.

Frank, Katherine. 'Writing Lives: Theory and Practice in Literary Biography'. *Genre*, 13 (1980): 499–516.

Friedman, Susan Stanford. 'Women's Autobiographical Selves'. In *The Private Self: Theory and Practice of Women's Autobiographical Writings*, ed. Shari Benstock, 34–62. Chapel Hill: University of North Carolina Press, 1988.

Friedson, Anthony M., ed. *New Directions in Biography*. Honolulu: University of Hawaii Press, 1981.

Fromm, Gloria G., ed. *Essaying Biography*. Manoa: University of Hawaii Press, 1986.

Fromm, Harold. 'Holroyd/Strachey/Shaw: Art and Archives in Literary Biography.' *Hudson Review*, 42 (1989): 201–21.

Galtung, Johan. 'Macro-History as Metaphor for Biography: An Essay on Macro and Micro History'. *Biography*, 13 (1990): 283–99.

Garber, Marjorie. 'Bisexuality and Celebrity'. In *Seductions of Biography*, ed. Mary Rhiel and David Suchoff, 13–30. New York: Routledge, 1996.

Garraty, John A. *The Nature of Biography*. New York: Garland, 1985.

Garrison, Dee. 'Writing the Biography of Mary Heaton Vorse'. In *The Challenge of Feminist Biography*, ed. Sara Alpern, Joyce Antler, Elisabeth Perry, and Ingrid Winther Scobie, 65–78. Urbana: University of Illinois Press, 1992.

Givner, Joan. *The Self-Portrait of a Literary Biographer*. Athens, Ga.: University of Georgia Press, 1993.

Glasser, Leah Blatt. '"She is the One You Call Sister"'. In *Between Women: Biographers, Novelists, Critics, Teachers, and Artists Write About Their Work on Women*, ed. Carol Ascher, Louise DeSalvo, and Sara Ruddick, 187–211. Boston: Beacon Press, 1984.

Glendinning, Victoria. 'Lies and Silences'. In *The Troubled Face of Biography*, ed. Eric Homberger and John Charmley, 49–62. New York: St Martin's Press, 1988.

Gordon, Lyndall. 'Women's Lives: The Unmapped Country'. In *The Art of Literary Biography*, ed. John Batchelor, 87–98. Oxford: Clarendon Press, 1995.

Gutiérrez, Rachel. 'What is Feminist Biography?' In *All Sides of the Subject: Women and Biography*, ed. Theresa Iles, 48–55. New York: Teachers College Press, 1992.

Hall, N. John. 'Those Wonderful Youths and Maidens, My Reviewers'. In *The Literary Biography: Problems and Solutions*, ed. Dale Salwak, 22–31. Iowa City: University of Iowa Press, 1996.

Hamilton, Ian. *Keepers of the Flame: Literary Estates and the Rise of Biography*. London: Hutchinson, 1992.

Hamilton, Nigel. 'Thomas Mann'. In *The Craft of Literary Biography*, ed. Jeffrey Meyers, 106–17. New York: Schoken Books, 1985.

Hedrick, Joan. 'The Paradox of Biography'. Paper given at the 1996 Modern Language Association Conference, *The Future of Biography I*, 29 December 1996.

Heilbrun, Carolyn. *Writing a Woman's Life*. New York: W. W. Norton, 1988.

Hoberman, Ruth. *Modernizing Lives: Experiments in English Biography, 1918–1939*. Carbondale: Southern Illinois University Press, 1987.

Holmes, Richard. 'Biography: Inventing the Truth'. In *The Art of Literary Biography*, ed. John Batchelor, 15–25. Oxford: Clarendon Press, 1995.

——. *Footsteps: Adventures of a Romantic Biographer*. London: Hodder and Stoughton, 1985.

Holroyd, Michael. 'How I Fell into Biography'. In *The Troubled Face of Biography*, ed. Eric Homberger and John Charmley, 94–103. New York: St Martin's Press, 1988.

Homberger, Eric, and John Charmley, eds. *The Troubled Face of Biography*. New York: St Martin's Press, 1988.

Honan, Park. *Author's Lives: On Literary Biography and the Arts of Language*. New York: St Martin's Press, 1990.

Hooten, Joy. 'Autobiography and Gender'. In *Writing Lives: Feminist Biography and Autobiography*, ed. Susan Magarey, 25–42. Adelaide: Australian Feminist Studies Publications, 1992.

Iles, Theresa, ed. *All Sides of the Subject: Women and Biography*. New York: Teachers College Press, 1992.

Josselson, Ruthelken and Amia Lieblich, ed. *The Narrative Study of Lives*. London: Sage Publications, 1993.

Kaplan, Justin. 'A Culture of Biography'. In *The Literary Biography: Problems and Solutions*, ed. Dale Salwak, 1–11. Iowa City: University of Iowa Press, 1996.

Karl, Frederick. *Biography and Source Studies*. I. New York: AMS Press, 1994.

Kendall, Paul M. *The Art of Biography*. 1965; New York: W. W. Norton, 1985.

Kimbrel, William W. *Necessary Illusions: Biography and the Problem of Narrative Truth*. Amherst: University of Massachusetts Press, 1992.

King, Richard H. 'Martin Luther King: Problems of History and Biography'. *Southern Review*, 24 (1988): 132–5.

Langness, Lewis, and Gelya Frank. *Lives: An Anthropological Approach to Biography*. Novaro, Calif.: Chandler and Sharp Publishers, 1981.

Lichtenberg, Joseph D. 'Psychoanalysis and Biography'. In *Introspection in Biography*, ed. Samuel H. Baron and Carl Pletsch, 33–65. London: Analytic Press, 1985.

McFeely, William. 'Why Biography?' In *Seductions of Biography*, ed. Mary Rhiel and David Suchoff, xi–xiii. New York: Routledge, 1996.

Mack, John E. 'D. H. Lawrence and the Psychology of Heroism'. In *Introspection in Biography*, ed. Samuel H. Baron and Carl Pletsch, 273–96. London: Analytic Press, 1985.

Magarey, Susan, ed., with Caroline Guerin and Paula Hamilton. *Writing Lives: Feminist Biography and Autobiography*. Adelaide: Australian Feminist Studies, 1992.

Malcolm, Janet. *In the Freud Archives*. New York: A. A. Knopf, 1984.

Mandell, Gail Porter. *Life Into Art: Conversations with Seven Contemporary Biographers*. Fayetteville: University of Arkansas Press, 1991.

Mariani, Paul. 'Conversation with Paul Mariani'. In *Life Into Art: Conversations with Seven Contemporary Biographers*, interview by Gail Mandell Porter, 15–42. Fayetteville: University of Arkansas Press, 1991.

Martin, Jay. 'Historical Truth and Narrative Reliability: Three Biographical Stories'. In *Biography and Source Studies*, I, ed. Frederick R. Karl, 25–72. New York: AMS Press, 1994.

May, Georges. ' "His Life, His Works": Some Observations on Literary Biography'. *Diogenes*, 139 (1987): 28–48.

Meyers, Jeffrey, ed. *The Craft of Literary Biography*. New York: Schocken Books, 1985.

——. ed. *The Biographer's Art: New Essays*. New York: New Amsterdam, 1989.

——. *The Spirit of Biography*. Ann Arbor: University of Michigan Research Press, 1989.

Middlebrook, Diane Wood. 'Postmodernism and the Biographer'. In *Revealing Lives: Autobiography, Biography, and Gender*, ed. Susan G. Bell and Marilyn Yalom, 155–65. Albany: State University of New York Press, 1990.

Minnich, Elizabeth Kamarck. 'Friendship Between Women: The Act of Feminist Biography'. *Feminist Studies*, 11 (1985): 287–305.

Moraitis, George. 'The Psychoanalyst's Role in the Biographer's Quest for Self-Awareness'. In *Introspection in Biography*, ed. Samuel H. Baron and Carl Pletsch, 319–54. London: Analytic Press, 1985.

Nadel, Ira B. 'Biography as Cultural Discourse'. In *Biography and Source Studies*, I, ed. Frederick R. Karl, 73–84. New York: AMS Press, 1994.

——. *Biography: Fiction, Fact, and Form*. New York: St Martin's Press, 1984.

Novarr, David. *The Lines of Life: Theories of Biography, 1880–1970*. West Lafayette, Ind.: Purdue University Press, 1986.

O'Brien, Sharon. 'Feminist Theory and Literary Biography'. In *Contesting the Subject*, ed. William Epstein, 123–34. West Lafayette, Ind.: Purdue University Press, 1991.

O'Connor, Ulick. *Biographers and the Art of Biography*. Dublin: Wolfhound Press, 1991.

Oates, Stephen B. *Biography as High Adventure: Life-Writers Speak on their Art*. Amherst: University of Massachusetts Press, 1986.

——. 'Responses'. In *The Biographer's Gift: Life Histories and Humanism*, ed. James F. Veninga, 30–6. College Station: Texas A&M University Press, 1983.

Origo, Iris. 'Biography, True and False'. In *Biography: Past and Present*, ed. William Davenport and Ben Siegel, 368–79. New York: Charles Scribner's Sons, 1965.

Pachter, Mark, ed. *Telling Lives: The Biographer's Art*. Washington, DC: New Republic Books, 1979.

Parke, Catherine. *Biography: Writing Lives*. New York: Twayne, 1996.

Personal Narratives Group. *Interpreting Women's Lives: Feminist Theory and Personal Narratives*. Bloomington: Indiana University Press, 1989.

Quilligan, Maureen. 'Rewriting History: The Difference of Feminist Biography'. *Yale Review*, 77 (1988): 250–86.

Rampersad, Arnold. 'Conversation with Arnold Rampersad'. In *Life Into Art: Conversations with Seven Contemporary Biographers*, interview by Gail Porter Mandell, 44–67. Fayetteville: University of Arkansas Press, 1991.

——. 'Psychology and Afro-American Biography'. *Yale Review*, 78 (1988): 6.

——. 'Biography, Autobiography, and Afro-American Culture'. *Yale Review* 73 (1983): 1–16.

Reid, B. L. *Necessary Lives: Biographical Reflections*. Columbia: University of Missouri Press, 1990.

Rhiel, Mary, and David Suchoff, ed. *The Seductions of Biography*. New York: Routledge, 1996.

Rich, Adrienne. *On Lies, Secrets, and Silence*. New York: W. W. Norton, 1979.

Rollyson, Carl. 'Biography as Genre.' *Choice* 35 (1997): 249–58.

Rose, Phyllis. *Parallel Lives*. New York: A. A. Knopf, 1983.

Salwak, Dale, ed. *The Literary Biography: Problems and Solutions*. Iowa City: University of Iowa Press, 1996.

Sharistanian, Janet. 'Introduction.' *a/b: Auto/biography Studies*, 8 (1993): 155–270.

Silverman, Kenneth. 'Mather, Poe, Houdini'. In *The Literary Biography: Problems and Solutions*, ed. Dale Salwak, 107–16. Iowa City: University of Iowa Press, 1996.

Sinclair, Andrew. 'Vivat Alius Ergo Sum'. In *The Troubled Face of Biography*, ed. Eric Homberger and John Charmley, 123–30. New York: St Martin's Press, 1990.

Skikelsky, Robert. 'Only Connect: Biography and Truth'. In *The Troubled Face of Biography*, ed. Eric Homberger and John Charmley, 1–16. New York: St Martin's Press, 1990.

Sklar, Kathryn Kish. 'Coming to Terms with Florence Kelley'. In *The Challenge of Feminist Biography: Writing the Lives of Modern American Women*, ed. Sara Alpern, Joyce Antler, Elisabeth Israels Perry, and Ingrid Winther Scobie, 17–33. Urbana: University of Illinois Press, 1992.

Snipes, Wilson. 'Authorial Typology in Literary Biography'. *Biography*, 13 (Summer 1990): 235–50.

Spector, Judith, ed. *Gender Studies: New Directions in Feminist Criticism*. Bowling Green, OH: Bowling Green State University Popular Press, 1986.

Stanley, Liz. *The auto/biographical I: The theory and practice of feminist auto/biography*. Manchester: Manchester University Press, 1992.

——. 'Moments of Writing: Is There a Feminist Auto/Biography?' *Gender and History*, 2 (1990): 62.

Stannard, Martin. 'The Necrophiliac Art?' In *The Literary Biography: Problems and Solutions*, ed. Dale Salwak, 32–40. Iowa City: University of Iowa Press, 1996.

Stone, Lawrence. 'Prosopography'. *Daedalus*, 100 (1971): 46–79.

Storr, Anthony. 'Psychiatry and Literary Biography'. In *The Art of Literary Biography*, ed. John Batchelor, 73–86. Oxford: Clarendon Press, 1995.

Thwaite, Ann. 'Writing Lives'. In *The Troubled Face of Biography*, ed. Eric Homberger and John Charmley, 17–32. New York: St Martin's Press, 1988.

Uglow, Jennifer, ed. *The Macmillian Dictionary of Women's Biography*. London: Macmillan, 1989.

Vaught, Bonny. 'Trying to Make Things Real'. In *Between Women: Biographers, Novelists, Critics, Teachers and Artists Write about Their Work on Women*, ed. Carol Ascher, Louise DeSalvo, and Sara Ruddick, 55–69. Boston: Beacon Press, 1984.

Veninga, James F., ed. *The Biographer's Gift: Life Histories and Humanism*. College Station: Texas A&M University Press, 1983.

Voss, Norine. '"Saying the Unsayable": An Introduction to Women's Autobiography'. In *Gender Studies: New Directions in Feminist Criticism*, ed. Judith Spector, 218–33. Bowling Green, OH: Bowling Green State University Popular Press, 1986.

Wagner-Martin, Linda. *Telling Women's Lives: The New Biography*. New Brunswick, NJ: Rutgers University Press, 1994.

Walker, Cheryl. 'Feminist Literary Criticism and the Author'. *Critical Inquiry*, 16 (1990): 551–71.

Walker, Nancy. '"Wider Than the Sky": Public Presence and Private Self in Dickinson, James, and Woolf'. In *The Private Self: Theory and Practice of Women's Autobiographical Writings*, ed. Shari Benstock, 272–303. Chapel Hill: University of North Carolina Press, 1988.

Walter, James, and Raija Nugent, ed. *Biographers at Work*. Queensland: Institute for Modern Biography, 1984.

Ward, Aileen. 'William Blake and the Hagiographers'. In *Biography and Source Studies*, ed. Frederick R. Karl, 1–24. New York: AMS Press, 1994.

Weinberg, Steve. *Telling the Untold Story: How Investigative Reporters are Changing the Craft of Biography.* Columbia: University of Missouri Press, 1992.

Westfall, Richard. 'Newton and His Biographer'. In *Introspection in Biography*, ed. Samuel H. Baron and Carl Pletsch, 175–90. London: Analytic Press, 1985.

Wexler, Alice. 'Emma Goldman and the Anxiety of Biography'. In *The Challenge of Feminist Biography: Writing the Lives of Modern American Women*, ed. Sara Alpern, Joyce Antler, Elisabeth Israels Perry, and Ingrid Winther Scobie, 34–50. Urbana: University of Illinois Press, 1992.

Whittemore, Reed. *Whole Lives: Shapers of Modern Biography.* Baltimore: Johns Hopkins University Press, 1989.

——. *Pure Lives: The Early Biographers.* Baltimore: Johns Hopkins University Press, 1988.

Winkler, Karen J. 'Seduction of Biography'. *Chronicle of Higher Education*, 27 Oct. 1993, A14.

Worthen, John. 'The Necessary Ignorance of a Biographer'. In *The Art of Literary Biography*, ed. John Batchelor, 227–44. Oxford: Clarendon Press, 1995.

Young-Bruehl, Elizabeth. 'Conversation with Elizabeth Young-Bruehl'. In *Life Into Art: Conversations with Seven Contemporary Biographers*, interview by Gail Porter Mandell, 170–213. Fayetteville: University of Arkansas Press, 1991.

Zinsser, William, ed. *Extraordinary Lives: The Art and Craft of American Biography.* New York: American Heritage, 1986.

GENERAL

Ackroyd, Peter. *Chatterton.* New York: Grove Press, 1987.

——. 'Interview with Peter Ackroyd'. Interviewed by Susana Onega. *Twentieth-Century Literature*, 42 (Summer 1996): 208–20.

——. 'The Three Sisters'. *The New Yorker*, 18 September 1995, 99–102 and 104.

——. *The Last Testament of Oscar Wilde.* New York: Harper & Row, 1983.

American Society of Genealogists. *Genealogical Research Methods and Sources.* 2 vols. Edited by Milton Rubin and Jean Stephenson. Washington, DC: American Society of Genealogists, 1960.

Anderson, Benedict. *Imagined Communities: Reflections on the Origin and Spread of Nationalism.* London: Thetford Press, 1983.

Antler, Joyce. 'A Purposeful Journey'. *The Nation*, 13 July 1992, 58–60.

Aptheker, Bettina. *Tapestries of Life: Women's Work, Women's Consciousness, and the Meaning of Daily Experience.* Amherst: University of Massachusetts Press, 1989.

Armstrong, Nancy, and Leonard Tennenhouse. *The Imaginary Puritan.* Berkeley: University of California Press, 1992.

Arthur, Diane. *Workplace Testing.* New York: American Management Association, 1994.

Atlas, James. 'Holmes on the Case'. *New Yorker*, 19 September 1994, 57–65.

——. 'The Biographer and the Murderer'. *New York Times Magazine*, 12 December 1993, 74.

Avery, Gillian. 'With Family and Friends'. *TLS* (12 February 1993): 8.

Backscheider, Paula. *Spectacular Politics*. Baltimore: Johns Hopkins University Press, 1993.

Bakhtin, Mikhail. *The Dialogic Imagination: Four Essays*. Translated by Caryl Emerson and Michael Holquist. Austin: University of Texas Press, 1981.

Balibar, Etienne. 'The Nation Form: History and Ideology'. In *Race, Nation, Class: Ambiguous Identities*, ed. Etienne Balibar and Immanuel Wallerstein, 86–106. London: Verso, 1988.

Balibar, Etienne, and Immanuel Wallerstein, ed. *Race, Nation, Class: Ambiguous Identities*. London: Verso, 1988.

Barr, Catherine, ed. 'American Book Title Production'. *The Bowker Annual: Library and Trade Almanac*. New Providence, NJ: R. R. Bowker, 1995.

Barton, Anne. 'Over the Dark River'. Review of *Dr. Johnson and Mr. Savage*, by Richard Holmes. *New York Review of Books* (15 February 1995): 6–8.

Bateson, F. W. 'The Application of Thought to an 18th C. Text: The School for Scandal'. In *Evidence in Literary Scholarship: Essays in Memory of James Marshall Osborn*, ed. René Wellek and Alvaro Ribeiro, 321–35. Oxford: Clarendon Press, 1979.

Battersby, Christine. *Gender and Genius*. Bloomington: Indiana University Press, 1989.

Bawer, Bruce. Review of *God: A Biography*. *Wilson Quarterly* 19 (Summer 1995): 90–1.

——. 'God on the Bestseller List'. *Hudson Review*, 48 (Autumn 1995): 397–410.

Baym, Nina. *American Women Writers and the Work of History, 1790–1860*. New Brunswick, NJ: Rutgers University Press, 1995.

Beattie, J. M. *Crime and the Courts of England*. Oxford: Clarendon Press, 1986.

Beauvoir, Simone de. *The Second Sex*. Translated and edited by H. M. Parshley. New York: Bantam Books, 1961.

Beecher, Lyman. *Autobiography, Correspondence, etc. of Lyman Beecher*. Edited by Charles Beecher. New York: Harper, 1866.

Bell, Millicent. Review of *Henry James: The Young Master*, by Sheldon Novick. *TLS* (6 December 1996): 3.

Ben-Shakhar, Gershon and Efrat Neter. 'The Predictive Validity of Graphological Inferences'. *Personality and Individual Difference*, 10 (1989): 737–45.

Beyerstein, Barry L., and Dale F. Beyerstein, ed. *The Write Stuff: Evaluations of Graphology, the Study of Handwriting*. Buffalo: Prometheus Books, 1992.

Bianchi, Alessandra. 'The Character-Revealing Handwriting Analysis'. *Inc.*, 18 (February 1996): 77–9.

Bogan, Louise. *Body of This Death*. New York: Robert M. McBride, 1923.

Bostock, Kate. 'Interview with Michael Holroyd.' *Literature Matters*, 9 (1991): 4–5.

Bowers, Kenneth S. 'There's More to Iago Than Meets the Eye: A Clinical Account of Personal Consistency'. In *Personality at the Crossroads*, ed. David Magnusson and Norman S. Endler, 65–81. Hillsdale, NJ: Lawrence Erlbaum Associates, 1977.

Bowers, Toni. *The Politics of Motherhood: British Writing and Culture*. Cambridge: Cambridge University Press, 1996.

Bowman, Marilyn. 'Difficulties in Assessing Personality and Predicting Behavior'. In *The Write Stuff*, ed. Barry L. Beyerstein and Dale F. Beyerstein, 203–31. Buffalo: Prometheus Books, 1992.

Boyer, Abel. *The Political State of Great Britain*. 60 vols. London: 1711–40.

Bradshaw, Graham. 'Current Literature: Biography, Literary Theory and Criticism'. *English Studies*, 72 (December 1991): 530–44.

Branch, Taylor. *Parting the Waters: America in the King Years, 1954–63*. New York: Simon & Schuster, 1988.

Breslin, James. 'An Artist's Tortured Life'. Interview by Peter Monaghan. *Chronicle of Higher Education* (2 February 1994): A6–A7.

Brinkley, Alan. 'Young Jack's Triumph'. *TLS* (21 May 1993): 5.

Brodzki, Bella, and Celeste Schenck. *Life/Lines: Theorizing Women's Autobiography*. Ithaca: Cornell University Press, 1988.

Brontë, Charlotte. *Villette*. London: Smith, Elder and Company, 1853.

——. *Jane Eyre*. London: Smith, Elder and Company, 1847.

Bunyan, John. *The Pilgrim's Progress from this World to That Which Is to Come*. London: 1678.

Burke, Kenneth. *Language as Symbolic Action*. Berkeley: University of California Press, 1966.

Byatt, Antonia Susan. *Possession*. New York: Random House, 1990.

Caldwell, Gail. 'A Life of France's "sacred monster"'. *Books, The Boston Globe* (15 April 1990): A16–A17.

Cameron, Elspeth, and Janice Dickin, ed. *Great Dames*. Toronto: University of Toronto Press, 1997.

Cannon, John. Review of *The Insatiable Earl: A Life of John Montagu, Fourth Earl of Sandwich*, by N. A. M. Rodgers. *TLS* (30 July 1993): 23.

Carlisle, Rodney. *The Roots of Black Nationalism*. Port Washington, NY: Kennikat Press, 1975.

Carr, David. *Time, Narrative, and History*. Bloomington: Indiana University Press, 1986.

Carson, Clayborne. 'King Scholarship and Iconoclastic Myths'. *Reviews in American History* 16 (March 1988): 130–6.

Chernaik, Judith. *The Lyrics of Shelley*. Cleveland: Press of Case Western Reserve University, 1972.

Chodorow, Nancy. *The Reproduction of Mothering*. Berkeley: University of California Press, 1974.

Cimbala, Paul A., and Robert F. Himmelberg, ed. *Historians and Race: Autobiography and the Writing of History*. Bloomington: Indiana University Press, 1996.

Colie, Rosalie. *The Resources of Kind: Genre Theory in the Renaissance*. Berkeley: University of California Press, 1973.

Congdon, Thomas. 'Lives That Matter'. *Humanities*, 5 (1988): 4.

Cose, Ellis. *The Rage of a Privileged Class*. New York: Harper Collins, 1993.

Costa, Paul T., jun., and Robert R. McCrae. *Emerging Lives, Enduring Dispositions: Personality in Adulthood*. Boston: Little, Brown and Company, 1984.

——. 'Still Stable After All These Years: Personality as a Key to Some Issues in Adulthood and Old Age'. In *Life-Span Development and Behavior*, III, ed. Paul B. Baltes and Orville Brim, 66–90. New York: Academic Press, 1980.

Courtivan, Isabelle de. 'The Body as Battleground'. Review of *The Passion of Michel Foucault*, by James Miller. *New York Times Book Review* (10 January 1993): 1, 29–30.

Cuddon, J. A. *A Dictionary of Literary Terms*. Garden City, NY: Doubleday Press, 1977.

Culler, Jonathan. *Structuralist Poetics: Structuralism, Linguistics, and the Study of Literature*. Ithaca: Cornell University Press, 1975.

Davis, Allison. *Leadership, Love, and Aggression*. Boston: Harcourt, Brace, Jovanovich, 1983.

Defoe, Daniel. *A Journal of the Plague Year*. London: 1722.

——. *Serious Reflections*. London: 1720.

——. *The Life and Adventures of Robinson Crusoe*. London: 1719.

——. *The Family Instructor*. London: 1715.

——. *History of the Kentish Petition*. London: 1701.

Delaney, Samuel. *The Motion of Light in Water: Sex and Science Fiction Writing in the East Village*. New York: Arbor House, 1988.

Denvir, Barnard. Review of *Matisse: A Portrait*, by Hayden Herrera. *New York Times Book Review* (10 October 1993): 28.

Digman, John M. 'Personality Structure: Emergence of the Five-Factor Model'. In *Annual Review of Psychology*, 41 (1990), ed. Mark Rosenzweig and Lyman Porter, 418–40.

Doctorow, E. L. Review of *Harriet Beecher Stowe: A Life*, by Joan Hedrick. *New York Times Book Review* (13 February 1994): 3 and 33.

Dodgson, Charles. *Lewis Carroll's Symbolic Logic*. Ed. William Warren Bartley, III. New York: C. N. Potter, 1986.

Doody, Margaret. Review of *The Married Man: A Life of D. H. Lawrence*, by Brenda Maddox. *TLS* (4 November 1994): 4–6.

——. Review of *The Life of Jane Austen*, by John Halperin. *Nineteenth-Century Fiction* 40 (September 1985): 225–7.

Draper, Roger. Review of *JFK: Reckless Youth*, by Nigel Hamilton. *The New Leader*, 14–28 December 1992, 3–4.

DuBois, W. E. Burghardt. *The Philadelphia Negro: A Social Study*. New York: B. Blom, 1967.

——. *Dusk of Dawn: An Essay Toward an Autobiography of a Race Concept*. 1940; New York: Schocken Books, 1968.

——. *The Souls of Black Folk*. Chicago: A. C. McClurg, 1904.

Duguid, Lindsay. 'City Lights'. *TLS* (21 August 1992): 4.

Earle, Peter. *The World of Defoe*. London: Weidenfeld & Nicolson, 1976.

Edwards, Paul, ed. *The Encyclopedia of Philosophy*. 8 vols. New York: Macmillian, 1967.

Erickson, Amy L. 'Common Law versus Common Practice: The Use of Marriage Settlements in Early Modern England'. *Economic History Review* 2, ser. 43 (1990): 21–39.

Erikson, Erik. *Childhood and Society*. New York: W. W. Norton, 1964.

Felski, Rita. *Beyond Feminist Aesthetics*. Cambridge: Harvard University Press, 1989.

Fenton, Matthew McCann. 'Shaking up the House'. *Biography*, 2:1 (1998): 60–6.

Feynman, Richard, Robert Leighton, and Matthew Sands. *Feynman Lectures on Physics*, 3 vols. Reading, Mass.: Addison-Wesley Publishing Company, 1963–5.

Finney, Brian. 'Ackroyd, Postmodernist Play and *Chatterton*'. *Twentieth-Century Literature* 38 (Summer 1992): 240–61.

Fitzpatrick, Ellen F. *Endless Crusade: Women Social Scientists and Progressive Reform*. New York: Oxford University Press, 1990.

Foucault, Michel. *Discipline and Punish: The Birth of the Prison*. New York: Pantheon Books, 1977.

Frendel-Brunswik, Elsa. *Childhood and Society*. New York: W. W. Norton, 1950.

Frost, Robert. *The Poetry of Robert Frost*, ed. Edward C. Lathem. New York: Holt, Rinehart, and Winston, 1969.

Froude, James Anthony. *Short Studies on Great Subjects*. 4 vols. New York: Charles Scribner's Sons, 1900–1.

Gardner, Howard. *Creating Minds*. New York: Basic Books, 1993.

Garnet, David. 'Brown Beauty'. *TLS* (5 October 1933): 667.

——. 'Current Literature'. *New Statesmen and Nation* (7 October 1933): 416.

Gassner, John. 'Tragic Perspectives: A Sequence of Queries'. *Tulane Drama Review* 2 (May 1958): 7–22.

Gates, Henry Louis, jun., and K. A. Appaih, ed. *Langston Hughes: Critical Perspectives Past and Present*. New York: Amistad Press, 1993.

Gay, Peter. *Freud for Historians*. New York: Oxford University Press, 1994.

Geertz, Clifford. *The Interpretation of Cultures: Selected Essays*. New York: Basic Books, 1973.

Gergen, Kenneth. 'The Emerging Crisis in Life-Span Developmental Theory'. In *Life-Span Development and Behavior*, III, ed. Paul B. Baltes and Orville Brim, 33–7. New York: Academic Press, 1980.

Gergen, Mary M. and Kenneth Gergen. 'Narratives of the Gendered Body in Popular Autobiography'. In *The Narrative Study of Lives*, ed. Ruthellen Josselson and Amia Lieblich, 191–218. London: Sage Publications, 1993.

Gergen, Mary M. 'The Social Construction of Personal Histories.' In *Constructing the Social*, ed. Theodore Sarbin and John I. Kitsuse. London: Sage Publications, 1994.

Gewen, Barry. 'By the Light of Burning Crosses'. Review of *The Schoolhouse Door: Segregation's Last Stand at the University of Alabama*, by E. Culpepper Clark. *NYTBR* (1 August 1993): 12.

Gilbert, Elliot. 'Rescuing Reality'. *Victorian Studies* 34 (1991): 295–314.

Gilligan, Carol. *In a Different Voice: Psychological Theory and Women's Development*. Cambridge, Mass.: Harvard University Press, 1982.

Gittelson, Celia. *Biography: A Novel*. New York: A. A. Knopf, 1991.

Glazer, Penina Migdal, and Miriam Slater. *Unequal Colleagues: The Entrance of Women into the Professions, 1890–1940*. New Brunswick, NJ: Rutgers University Press, 1987.

Gleick, James. *Chaos: Making a New Science*. New York: Viking Press, 1987.

Gordon, Colin. Review of *The Lives of Foucault*, by David Macey. *TLS* (27 August 1993): 27.

Goreau, Angeline. Review of *May Sarton: A Biography*, by Margot Peters. *NYTBR* (6 April 1997): 9.

——. 'Oh, Shut Up, Voltaire'. Review of *Madame Du Deffand and Her World*, by Benedetta Craveri, translated by Teresa Waugh. *NYTBR* (1 January 1995): 13.

Graunt, John. *Reflections on the Weekly Bills of Mortality*. London, 1665.

Greene, Jack P. Review of *Founding Father: Rediscovering George Washington*, by Richard Brookhiser. *TLS* (15 November 1996): 5–6.

Grier, William H., and Price M. Cobbs. *Black Rage*. New York: Basic Books, 1992.

Gross, John. Review of *Anthony Trollope*, by Victoria Glendinning. *NYRB* (8 April 1993): 9–11.

Grundy, Isobel, ed. *Romance Writings* by Lady Mary Wortley Montagu. Oxford: Clarendon Press, 1996.

Hacking, Ian. *The Emergence of Probability*. Cambridge: Cambridge University Press, 1975.

Hamel, Gildas. 'Lives of God'. *Judaism*, 45 (1996): 377.

Hamilton, Ian. 'The Tatty Wreckage of Her Life'. *NYTBR* (25 October 1987): 12–13.

Harris, Richard. 'A divine character?' Review of *God: A Biography*, by Jack Miles. *TLS* (8 December 1995): 26.

Haydon, Benjamin Robert. *Lectures on Painting and Design*. London: Longman, Brown, Green, and Longmans, 1844–6.

Hellman, Lillian. *An Unfinished Woman: A Memoir*. Boston: Little, Brown and Company, 1969.

Hemingway, Ernest. *A Farewell to Arms*. New York: Charles Scribner's Sons, 1957.

Herrnstein-Smith, Barbara. *Contingencies of Value: Alternative Perspectives for Critical Theory*. Cambridge: Harvard University Press, 1988.

——. *On the Margins of Discourse: The Relation of Literature to Language*. Chicago: University of Chicago Press, 1978.

Himmelfarb, Gertrude. 'The Company He Kept'. Review of *Eminent Churchillians*, by Andrew Roberts. *NYTBR* (16 July 1995): 6.

Hoffman, Lois, Scott Paris, and Elizabeth Hall, ed. *Developmental Psychology Today*, 6th edn. New York: McGraw Hill, 1994.

Holman, C. Hugh. *A Handbook to Literature*. Indianapolis and New York: Odyssey, 1972.

Holmes, Richard. 'Leon Edel: A Literary Obsession'. *New York Times Magazine*, 4 January 1998, 42–3.

Holroyd, Michael. 'Interview with Michael Holroyd'. Interviewed by Kate Bostock. *Literature Matters*, 9 (1991): 4–5.

——. Interviewed by Michelle Field. *Publisher's Weekly*, October 14 1988, 45–6.

Hopper, Mark A. and Karen Stanford. 'A Script for Screening'. *Security Management*, 36 (1992): 72–81.

Hynes, Samuel. 'The Blocked Keyhole'. Review of *Hardy*, by Martin Seymour-Smith. *TLS* (18 March 1994): 3–4.

Imlah, Nick. 'A Friend of the Poet?' Review of *Tennyson*, by Peter Levi. *TLS* (2 July 1993): 14.

Inglis, Fred. Review of *JKF: Reckless Youth*, by Nigel Hamilton. *The Nation*, 28 December 1992, 813–15.

International Bibliography of Biography, 1970–1987. 12 vols. London: Published for British Library, 1988.

James, Henry. *Aspern Papers*. London: J. M. Dent, 1935.

Jenkyns, Richard. 'The Distant Shaw'. Review of *Bernard Shaw: The Search for Love*, by Michael Holroyd. *The New Republic*, 14 November 1988, 38–41.

John, Oliver P. 'The "Big Five" Factor Taxonomy: Dimensions of Personality in the Natural Language and in Questionnaires'. In *Handbook of Personality: Theory and Research*, ed. Lawrence A. Pervin, 66–100. New York: Guilford, 1990.

Johnson, Barbara. *A World of Difference*. Baltimore: Johns Hopkins University Press, 1987.

Johnson, Diane. Review of *Simone de Beauvoir: A Biography*, by Deidre Bair. *NYTBR* (15 April 1990): 1 and 24.

Johnson, James Weldon. *The Autobiography of an Ex-Coloured Man* in *Three Negro Classics*. Introduction by John Hope Franklin. New York: Avon Books, 1965.

Johnson, James Welden. *Negro Americans, What Now?* New York: Viking Press, 1934.
———. *The Book of American Negro Poetry.* New York: Harcourt, Brace, and World, 1931.
Johnson, Luke. 'What A Character!' *Commonweal*, 122 (19 May 1995): 32–4.
Johnson, Paul. 'Reading the Mystery'. *Commentary*, 100 (July 1995): 55–6.
Johnson, Samuel. *The History of Rasselas, Prince of Abyssinia.* London: 1759.
———. *Rambler*, 60 (15 May 1751).
Johnston, Claire. *Notes on Women's Cinema.* London: Society for Education in Film and Television, 1973.
Keats, John. *John Keats.* Edited by Elizabeth Coole. Oxford: Oxford University Press, 1990.
Keinan, Giora. 'Can Graphologists Identify Individuals Under Stress?' In *Scientific Aspects of Graphology*, ed. Baruch Nevo, 141–50. Springfield, Ill.: Charles C. Thomas, 1986.
Kennedy, David M. 'Up From Hyde Park'. *NYTBR* (19 April 1992): 1, 19, and 21.
Kenyon, J. P. Review of *The Other Pepys*, by Vincent Brome. *TLS* (30 July 1993): 23.
Kesey, Ken. *One Flew Over the Cuckoo's Nest.* New York: New American Library, 1962.
King, Richard H. 'Martin Luther King: Problems of History and Biography'. *Southern Review*, 24 (1988): 979–85.
Kissinger, Henry. 'With Faint Praise'. Review of *Churchill: The Unruly Giant*, by Norman Rose. *NYTBR* (16 July 1995): 7.
Koenig, Rhoda. Review of *JFK: Reckless Youth*, by Nigel Hamilton. *New York* (16 November 1992), 76–8.
Kramer, Hilton. 'The Passion of Mark Rothko'. *NYTBR* (26 December 1993): 21.
Kurtz, David, *et al.* 'CEOs: A Handwriting Analysis'. *Business Horizons*, 32 (1989): 41–3.
LaCapra, Dominick, ed. *The Bounds of Race: Perspectives on Hegemony and Resistance.* Ithaca: Cornell University Press, 1991.
Ladd, Everett C. 'Giving Form to the New'. *TLS* (21 May 1993): 6–7.
Lauretis, Teresa de. 'Feminist Studies/Critical Studies: Issues, Terms and Contexts'. *Feminist Studies/Critical Studies.* Bloomington: University of Indiana Press, 1986, 1–19.
Lee, Hermoine. 'The Man Who Didn't Sleep'. Review of *Dickens*, by Peter Ackroyd. *The New Republic*, 10 June 1991, 35–8.
Leivick, Laura. 'Following the Ghost of Dickens'. *New York Times Magazine*, 22 December 1991, 26–8, 30–1, and 36.
Lenin, Vladimir. *Imperialism, the Highest Stage of Capitalism: A Popular Outline.* Moscow: Progress, 1968.
Lerner, Gerda. 'Priorities and Challenges in Women's History'. *Perspectives* (April 1988): 19.
Lewis, David Levering. 'From Eurocentrism to Polycentrism'. In *Historians and Race*, ed. Paul A. Cimbala and Robert Himmelberg, 66–90. Bloomington: Indiana University Press, 1996.
Lewis, Naomi. 'A Camberwell Beauty'. *Encounter*, 25 (August 1965): 76–9.
Lewis, Paul. 'The Art of Peace'. Review of *Ralph Bunche*, by Brian Urquhart. *NYTBR* (26 September 1993): 25.
Lewis, Roger. 'Review of *The Last Testament of Oscar Wilde*'. *American Spectator*, 17 (1984): 39–41.

Lilla, Mark. 'A Taste for Pain'. *TLS* (26 March 1993): 4.

Linde, Charlotte. *Life Stories: The Creation of Coherence*. Oxford: Oxford University Press, 1993.

Locke, John. *Essay Concerning Human Understanding*. London: 1689.

Lockwood, Thomas. 'Cross-Channel Dramatics in the Little Haymarket Theatre Riot of 1738'. In *Studies in Eighteenth-Century Culture*, 25, ed. Syndy M. Conger and Julie C. Hayes, 63–74.

Lubow, Arthur. 'Charms and the Man'. *Vanity Fair*, September 1991, 214–18, 236, 238, and 240.

Lukács, Georg. *The Theory of the Novel*. 1920; Cambridge: MIT Press, 1989.

Lurie, Alison. *The Truth About Lorin Jones*. Boston: Little, Brown and Company, 1988.

Lustig, Irma, and Frederick A. Pottle, ed. *Boswell: The English Experiment, 1785–1789*. New York: McGraw-Hill, 1986.

Lytton, Edward Robert Bulwer. *Poetical Works of Owen Meredith*. Boston: Houghton-Mifflin, 1900.

McCarthy, Abigail. 'Out of Her Husband's Shadow'. *Washington Post Book World* (19 April 1992): 5.

McGilligan, Patrick. Review of *Garbo: A Biography*, by Barry Paris. *NYTBR* (2 April 1995): 3.

McKay, Nellie. 'Naming the Problem that Led to the Question "Who Shall Teach African American Literature?", or Are We Ready to Disband the Wheatley Court?' 113, *PMLA* (1998): 359–69.

McKeon, Michael. *The Origins of the English Novel*. Baltimore: Johns Hopkins University Press, 1987.

McNeill, William H. *The Rise of the West: A History of the Human Community*. Chicago: University of Chicago Press, 1963.

Magnusson, David, and N. S. Endler, ed. *Personality at the Crossroads*. Hillsdale, NJ: Erlbaum, 1977.

Malcolm, Janet. 'The Silent Woman'. *The New Yorker* (23 August 1993), 94.

———. 'The Mortality of Journalism'. *New York Review of Books* (1 March 1990): 20–1.

Maslin, Janet. 'Katharine the Great'. Review of *Katharine Hepburn*, by Barbara Leaning. *NYTBR* (16 April 1995): 10.

Mayne, Judith. *Private Novels, Public Films*. Athens: University of Georgia Press, 1988.

Mee, John. *Dangerous Enthusiasm*. Oxford: Oxford University Press, 1992.

Mehew, Ernest. 'The True Stevenson?' Review of *Robert Louis Stevenson: A Biography*, by Frank McLynn. *TLS* (2 July 1993): 15–16.

Meir, Elchanan I. 'Testing Graphology: Is Graphology a Test?' In *Scientific Aspects of Graphology*, ed. Baruch Nevo, 311–14. Springfield, Ill.: Charles C. Thomas, 1986.

Mellow, James R. 'Storming the gates'. Review of Beth Brombert's *Edouard Manet: Rebel in a Frock Coat*. *NYTBR* (24 March 1996): 13–14.

Melville, Herman. *Journals*. Revised by Howard C. Horsford, with Lynn Horsford. Evanston: Northwestern University Press, 1989.

Miller, Arthur. *Death of a Salesman*. New York: Bantam Books, 1951.

Miller, James. *The Coffee-House*. London: 1734.

Millon, Theodore. 'The Disorders of Personality'. In *Handbook of Personality: Theory and Research*, ed. Lawrence A. Pervin, 339–69. New York: Guilford Press, 1990.

Mills, Nicolas. 'She Scared L. B. J'. Review of *This Little Light of Mine: The Life of Fannie Lou Hamer*, by Kay Mills. *NYTBR* (7 February 1993): 15–16.

Mitford, Mary Russell. *Our Village*. 5 vols. London: 1824.

Monagan, Peter. 'An Artist's Tortured Life'. *Chronicle of Higher Education* (2 February 1994): A47.

Montagu, Elizabeth Robinson. *An Essay on the Writings and Genius of Shakespeare*. London, 1753.

Montagu, Lady Mary Wortley. *Romance Writings*. Ed. Isobel Grundy. Oxford: Clarendon Press, 1996.

Montefiore, Hugh. 'Unguarded Bishops'. Review of *Robert Runcie*, by Humphrey Carpenter. *TLS* (4 October 1996): 29.

Moraitis, George, and George H. Pollock. *Psychoanalytic Studies of Biography*. Madison, Conn.: International Universities Press, Inc., 1987.

Morris, Roger. 'More Than a Rake's Progress'. Review of *JFK: Reckless Youth*, by Nigel Hamilton. *NYTBR* (22 November 1992): 1, 36–7.

Morrison, Phillip. 'Her Brilliant Career'. Review of *Marie Curie: A Life*, by Susan Quinn. *NYTBR* (2 April 1995): 17.

Neagles, James C., assisted by Mark C. Neagles. *Library of Congress: A Guide to Genealogical and Historical Research*. Salt Lake City, UT: Ancestry Press, 1990.

Nell, Victor. *Lost in a Book: The Psychology of Reading for Pleasure*. New Haven: Yale University Press, 1988.

Neugarten, Bernice L. *Middle-Age and Aging*. Chicago: University of Chicago Press, 1968.

Neve, Michael. 'Gathering Moss'. Review of *Mick Jagger: Primitive Cool*, by Christopher Sandford, *Jagger Unauthorized*, by Christopher Andersen, and *Keith Richards: The Biography*, by Victor Bockris. *TLS* (9 July 1993): 9.

Nevo, Baruch. 'Reliability of Graphology: A Survey of the Literature'. *Scientific Aspects of Graphology*, 253–62. Springfield, Ill.: Charles C. Thomas, 1986.

Newman, Richard. 'Sara Lawrence-Lightfoot: "To Chart Different Journeys"'. *Publisher's Weekly* (5 September 1994): 80.

Nicolson, Harold. *Diaries and Letters by Harold Nicolson*. Ed. Nigel Nicolson. 3 vols. New York: Atheneum, 1966.

Noble, Peter. 'Beyond Imagining'. Review of *Eleanor of Aquitaine: Queen and Legend*, by D. D. R. Owen. *TLS* (17 September 1993): 25.

Novick, Peter. *That Noble Dream: The 'Objectivity Question'*. Cambridge: Cambridge University Press, 1988.

Onega, Susan. 'Interview with Peter Ackroyd'. *Twentieth-Century Literature*, 42 (1996): 208–20.

Origo, Iris. *The World of San Bernardino*. New York: Harcourt, Brace, and World, 1962.

Ozick, Cynthia. *Art and Ardor: Essays*. New York: A. A. Knopf, 1983.

Parini, Jay. Review of *Emerson*, by Robert Richardson. *TLS* (21 July 1995): 6.

Pervin, Lawrence A., ed. *Handbook of Personality: Theory and Research*. New York: Guilford Press, 1990.

Peters, Catherine. 'Secondary Lives: Biography in Context'. In *The Art of Literary Biography*, ed. John Batchelor, 43–56. Oxford: Clarendon Press, 1995.

Peters, Margot. Review of *Tracings: A Book of Partial Portraits*, by Paul Horgan. *NYTBR* (10 October 1993): 11.

Phillips, William. 'Eliot and Kafka'. *Partisan Review*, 52: 4 (1985): 444–8.

Plath, Sylvia. *The Bell Jar*. New York: Harper & Row, 1971.

——. *Ariel*. New York: Harper and Row, 1965.

Porter, Dorothy, ed. *Early Negro Writing, 1760–1837*. Boston: Beacon Press, 1971.

'Portraits in Prose'. Review of *Biography as an Art*, ed. James L. Clifford. *TLS* (2 March 1962): 130.

Prendergast, Christopher. 'The Appetites of the Colosus'. Review of *Balzac: A Biography*, by Graham Robb and *Honoré de Balzac*, by Roger Pierrot. *TLS* (17 June 1994): 8–9.

Reeves, F. D. Letter on a Biography of Robert Frost. *NYTBR* (23 June 1996): 4.

Robinson, Abraham. 'On the Construction of Models'. In *Essays on the Foundations of Mathematics*, ed. Yehoshua Bar-Hillel, *et al.*, 207–17. Jerusalem: Magnes Press, 1961.

Roosevelt, Theodore. *The Rough Riders*. New York: Charles Scribner's Sons, 1899.

Rothman, Shelia. Review of *Back Talk*, by Joan Weimer. *NYTBR* (16 October 1994): 32.

Rothstein, Edward. 'The Furious Man from Busseto'. Review of *Verdi: A Biography*, by Mary Jane Phillips-Matz. *NYTBR* (2 January 1994): 3–4.

Ryan, Alan. 'Out of his Shell'. Review of *Bertrand Russell*, by Ray Monk. *TLS* (21 June 1996): 5–6.

Sacks, Oliver. 'Making Up the Mind'. Review of *Bright Air, Brilliant Fire: On the Matter of the Mind*, by Gerald M. Edelman. *New York Review of Books* (8 April 1993): 42.

Sage, Lorna. 'A Necessary Cruelty'. Review of *Christina Stead: A Biography*, by Hazel Lowley. *TLS* (20 August 1993): 3–4.

Salwak, Dale. 'Sketches from Life: Philip Larkin—An American View'. *Biography: An Interdisciplinary Quarterly*, 21 (1998): 195–205.

Sarbin, Theodore R. and John I. Kitsuse, ed. *Constructing the Social*. London: Sage Publications, 1994.

Schweinitz, George de. '*Death of a Salesman*: A Note on Epic and Tragedy'. *Western Humanities Review*, 14 (1960): 91–6.

Scott, Joan W. 'The Evidence of Experience'. *Critical Inquiry*, 17 (1991): 773–97.

Sennett, Richard. *The Fall of Public Man*. New York: A. A. Knopf, 1977.

Sexton, Linda Gray. 'A Daughter's Story: I Knew Her Best'. *NYTBR* (18 August 1991): 20.

Seymour, Miranda. 'Stopping by Woods for Seduction'. Review of *Robert Frost: A Biography*, by Jeffrey Meyers. *NYTBR* (19 May 1996): 8.

Shakespeare, William. *As You Like It*. London: 1599.

Shapiro, Barbara. '*Beyond Reasonable Doubt*' and '*Probable Cause*': Historical Perspectives on the Anglo-Amercian Law of Evidence. Berkeley: University of California Press, 1991.

——. *Probability and Certainty in Seventeenth-Century England*. Princeton: Princeton University Press, 1983.

Shawe-Taylor, Desmond. *Genial Company: The Theme of Genius in 18th-Century British Portraiture*. London: White Brothers, 1987.

Shelley, Percy Bysshe. *Adonais: An Elegy on the Death of John Keats*. Pisa: 1821.

Smith, Gaddis. 'Whose Finest Hour?' Review of *Churchill: The End of Glory*, by John Charmley. *NYTBR* (29 August 1993): 3.

Soloman, Deborah. 'Ready Made Genuis'. Review of *Duchamp: A Biography*, by Calvin Tomkin. *NYTBR* (1 December 1996): 9.

Solzhenitsyn, Alexander. *Gulag Archipelago, 1918–1956*. Barcelona: Plaza and Janés, 1974.

Stambusky, Alan A. 'Arthur Miller: Aristotelian Canons in the Twentieth-Century Drama'. In *Modern American Drama*, ed. W. E. Taylor. Deland, Fl.: Everett/ Edwards, Inc., 1968.

Stansell, Christine. 'Wonder Woman'. *The New Republic* (25 May 1992): 36–9.

Stavans, Ilan. 'Questions of Legitimacy'. Review of *In Search of Bernabé*, by Graciela Limon. *NYTBR* (14 November 1993): 66.

Staves, Susan. *Players' Scepters*. Lincoln: Univerisity of Nebraska Press, 1979.

Steinbeck, John. *The Grapes of Wrath*. New York: Modern Library, 1939.

Strickland, Geoffrey. 'The Accuser'. Review of *Zola: A Life*, by Frederick Brown. *NYTBR* (4 June 1995): 10.

Swift, Jonathan. *The Correspondence of Jonathan Swift*. 5 vols. ed. Harold Williams, Oxford: Clarendon Press, 1963.

——. *A Proposal for the Universal Use of Irish Manufactures*. Dublin: 1720.

Tandon, Bharat. 'A Novelist's Nightmare'. Review of *Wonder Boys*, by Michael Chabon. *TLS* (21 April 1995): 20.

Tate, Claudia, ed. *Black Women Writers at Work*. New York: Continuum, 1983.

Taylor, William E. *Modern American Drama: Essays in Criticism*. Deland, Fl.: Everett/Edwards. Inc., 1968.

Thomas, Peter. 'The Old Block'. Review of *Pitt the Elder*, by Jeremy Black. *TLS* (21 May 1993): 28.

Tomalin, Claire. 'Mrs Jordan'. *TLS* (4 November 1994): 17.

Toomer, Jean. Foreword by Waldo Frank. *Cane*. New York: University Place Press, 1951.

Trotman, C. James, ed. Keynote essay by Arnold Rampersad. *Langston Hughes: The Man, His Art, and His Continuing Influence*. New York: Garland Publishing, 1995.

Turbin, Carole. *Working Women of Collar City: Gender, Class, and Community in Troy, New York*. Urbana: University of Illinois Press, 1991.

United States National Archives and Records Service. *Guide to Genealogical Research in the National Archives*. Washington, DC: National Archives and Records Office, 1982.

United States National Historical Publications and Records Commission. *Directory of Archives and Manuscript Repositories in the United States*. Washington, DC: National Historical and Public Records Commmission, 1978.

Updike, John. 'Eliot Without Words'. *The New Yorker*, 61 (25 March 1985): 120, 123–30.

Ure, John. 'A Series of Escapes'. Review of *Flora MacDonald*, by Hugh Douglas. *TLS* (24 September 1993): 26.

Walker, Keith. Review of *The Life of Samuel Johnson*, by Robert DeMaria, jun. and *Johnson*, by Pat Rogers. *TLS* (24 September 1993): 26.

Walter, James, and Raiji Nugent, ed. *Biographers at Work*. Queensland: Institute for Modern Biography, 1984.

Walton, Hanes, jun. Review of *W. E. B. Dubois*, by David L. Lewis. *Journal of Negro Education*, 63 (1994): 649.

Wandor, Michelene. *Look Back in Gender*. London: Methuen Press, 1987.

Ward, Geoffrey. 'Outing Mrs. Roosevelt'. Review of *Eleanor Roosevelt*, by Blanche Wiesen Cook. *New York Review of Books* (24 September 1992): 49–56.

Watt, Ian. *Myths of Modern Individualism*. Cambridge: Cambridge University Press, 1996.

Weimann, Robert. *Structure and Society in Literary History*. Charlottesville, Va.: University Press of Virginia, 1976.

Weimer, Joan. *Back Talk: Teaching Lost Selves to Speak*. New York: Random House, 1994.

——, ed. *Women Artists, Women Exiles*. New Brunswick: Rutgers University Press, 1988.

——. 'Women Artists as Exiles in the Fiction of Constance Fenimore Woolson'. *Legacy: A Journal of Nineteenth-Century American Women Writers*, 3 (1986): 3–15.

Wellek, René, and Alvaro Ribeiro, ed. *Evidence in Literary Scholarship*. Oxford: Clarendon Press, 1979.

Welsh, Alexander. *Strong Representations: Narrative and Circumstantial Evidence in England*. Baltimore: Johns Hopkins University Press, 1992.

Wharton, Edith. *The House of Mirth*. New York: Charles Scribner, 1905.

White, Hayden. *The Content of the Form: Narrative Discourse and Historical Representation*. Baltimore: Johns Hopkins University Press, 1987.

——. 'The Problem of Style in Realistic Representation: Marx and Flaubert'. In *The Concept of Style*, ed. Berel Lang, 279–98. 1979; Ithaca: Cornell University Press, 1987.

——. *Tropics of Discourse: Essays in Cultural Criticism*. Baltimore: Johns Hopkins University Press, 1978.

Whitman, Walt. *Leaves of Grass*. New York: New York University Press, 1965.

Wilde, Oscar. *The Picture of Dorian Gray*. London: Ward, Lock, 1891.

Wilson, A. N. Review of *A Sultry Month*, by Althea Hayter. *The Spectator* (21 November 1992): 39.

Wilson, Robin. 'A Graduate Student Searches for a Job Teaching Literature'. *Chronicle of Higher Education* (25 April 1997): A10–11.

Wofford, Harris. 'A Righteous Alabamian'. Review of *Taming the Storm*, by Jack Bass. *NYTBR* (7 February 1993): 13–14.

Wolfe, Tom. *The New Journalism*. New York: Harper and Row, 1973.

Woolf, Virginia. *The Diary of Virginia Woolf*. 5 vols. New York: Harcourt, Brace, Jovanovich, 1989.

——. *The Letters of Virginia Woolf*. 6 vols. Ed. Nigel Nicolson and Joanne Trautmann. New York: Harcourt, Brace, Jovanovich, 1975.

——. *Collected Essays*. 4 vols. London: Harcourt, Brace and World, 1967.

——. *The Waves*. 1929; New York: Harcourt, Brace and World, 1959.

——. *A Room of One's Own*. New York: Harcourt, Brace, Jovanovich, 1957.

——. *Orlando: A Biography*. New York: Harcourt, Brace and Company, 1928.

Zimmerman, Everett. *The Boundaries of Fiction: History and the Eighteenth-Century British Novel*. Ithaca: Cornell University Press, 1996.

Index

academic biography xix–xx; 219, 229, 232–3
Ackroyd, Peter xxi, 182–4, 187–90, 192–3, 195, 250 n. 5
Adams, Abigail 44–5
Adams, Clover 136
Adams, Susan B. 222
Addison, Joseph xviii, 76
African-Americans xxi, 108, 155–6, 182, 200–25, 230, 251 n. 38; and Communist Party membership 223; language for experience 22, 206–7, 215, 218; as a people 210–11, 216; relation to US history 200–1, 210–12, 216, 223–4; unknown history 213–15, 251 n. 36
Ali, Muhammad xiii
Allport, Gordon 93
Alpern, Sara 157, 159
Alpers, Antony 86
Altick, Richard 67, 70, 89
Aptheker, Bettina 35
archetypes 47–8
Arendt, Hannah xiv, xxi, 34, 48, 132, 163–4
Aristotle 15, 237 n. 12, 237 n. 14
Armstrong, Nancy 16
Ascher, Carol 42–4, 119–20, 239 n. 21, 246 nn. 62, 64
Ashe, Arthur 34–5, 219, 221, 222; and race 201, 202–4, 207, 210
Atkinson, Brooks 15
Atlas, James 42
Aubrey, John, *Brief Lives* 127
Auden, W. H. xv, 155
Austen, Jane 134–5, 144, 193, 194
authority 84, 85–6, 188–9, 234–5
autobiography 17, 41, 150
Autobiography of Malcolm X 219
Avery, Gillian 116

Backscheider, Paula, writing *Daniel Defoe* xiv, xvi–xvii, 19, 38, 59, 86–7; research for *Defoe* 61–71, 110, 242 n. 56
Bainton, Roland 11, 49
Bair, Deirdre 60, 61–2, 134, 154, 157; relation to subject 20, 28, 31–2, 42–4
Baker, Ella 221–2
Bakhtin, Mikhail 16, 237 n. 12
Balibar, Etienne 211
Ballard, Martha 49
Bancroft Prize xviii, 20–8, 148, 215, *and see* prizes
Barbour, James, and John Quirk, *Biographies of*

Books 178–81
Barnum, P. T. 169
Barrett, Elizabeth, *see* Browning, Elizabeth Barrett
Barton, Anne 185, 193
Bate, Walter Jackson xx, 4, 10, 21–2, 36, 121; *Keats* 24, 47–8, 195–9, 238 n. 6
Beattie, J. M. 68
Beauregard, P. G. T. 46
Beauvoir, Simone de 19, 31, 120, 131, 134, 154, 237 n. 19; emblematic woman 32, 35, 42–4, 48, 119
Beckett, Samuel 61–2, 75
Bell, Quentin 73
Benstock, Shari 132, 161, 171
Berg, Scott 33
Bernoulli, Johann 50
Berryman, John xvi, xvii, 118
Best, William 83
Bethune, Mary McLeod 214
biographer 234; feminist 129, 153, 156, 161, 246 n. 3; literary 12–13, 118, 186–7; responsibilities of 76–7, 107, 163–4, 169–70, 199–200, 221, 224–5, 228–9, 235; roles of xxi–xxii, 34, 86–7, 100, 118–19, 226
biographer: relationship to subject xv–xvi, 28, 30–60, 184–8, 190, 246 n. 64, 250 n. 9; adversarial 45; collaborative 32, 45, 107, 219–21, 226; personal 121, 160–2, 246 n. 62, 250 n. 8
biographical contexts, model of 132–40, 167
biographies, types of: academic, *see* academic biography; Black, *see* Black biography; ideological 14, 43, 163, 212–13, 229–30; literary, *see* literary biography; psychoanalytic, *see* psychoanalytic biography; television xiii, 230, 231, 232, 233
Biographies of Books, see James Barbour
biography: commercialization of xiii, 174, 232; composite 17; English tradition 189–91, 193; ethical function xxi–xxii, 9–10, 127, 188–90, 193, 199, 219, 232, 241 n. 29; fixes image 9, 10, 47–8, 63, 188, 196–7, 216, 236 n. 2; form unfriendly to women 150–1, 156; group 17, 167–72, 215, 249 n. 10; and journalism 186, 230–2; limits of the form xix, 17, 163–4, 169–70, 181; and other literary forms 107, 110–11, 127, 142, 150, 170–1, 180–1, 186, 220–1; methods in other forms 174–6; and novelistic qualities xxi, 7, 12, 183, 198, 226,

biography (*cont.*):
231–2; openings 21–6; poetics of 14–18, 26, 90, 163, 226–8, 235, 237 n. 12, 241 n. 29, 252 n. 3; popularity of xiii–xiv, xviii, 226–35; power of 8–9, 49, 163–4, 216, 226, 227–30, 236 n. 2; purposes of xviii–x, xxi–xxii, 8–9, 17, 43–4, 59–60, 149–50, 163–4, 193, 221–3, 225, 226–30, 235; as reference books xix, 85, 229, 242 n. 52; reviewing xiv–xv, 86, 106, 141, 235, 248 n. 1; stakes in contemporary debates 100–1; theoretical study xiv, 16–17, 43, 235, 250 n. 16; *see also* novel, similarities to biography
biography and nationhood xv, 8–9, 39, 99, 101, 104–5, 167, 225, 227–30; and British nationhood 190, 229–30; and English nationhood 25, 36, 189–90, 210, 243 n. 13; and Russian nationhood 3–4, 7, 45; and US nationhood 8, 25, 40–1, 71, 99, 105, 179, 211–12, 223–4
Biography, magazine xiii
Bishop, Elizabeth 118
Black biography xxi, 182, 200–25
Black Nationalism 216–17
Blake, William 63, 182, 185
Bogan, Louise 23, 92, 139–40, 145, 153, 155
Bolivar, Simon 167
Bonaparte, Napoleon 48, 87
Boswell, James 66, 84, 186; *Life of Johnson* 127, 241 n. 30
Bowen, Catherine Drinker xv, 20, 22–3, 31, 58, 91; on evidence 63, 71, 74–5, 81, 85, 137; on writing 13, 25, 37, 111, 119
Bowers, Kenneth 118
Bowers, Toni 146, 247 nn. 19, 21
Boydson *et al.*, *Limits of Sisterhood* 172
Boyer, Abel 91–2
Brabazon, James 36
Bradbury, Malcolm 250 n. 16
Bradley, Bill 203
Branch, Taylor 223
Brawne, Fanny 197–9
Breslaw, Elaine 233
Breslin, James 41, 59, 87, 231
Brightman, Carol 20, 26, 105, 133, 147, 153; with Mary McCarthy 11, 24, 28, 157
Brinkley, Alan 75
Brome, Vincent 36
Bromwich, David 47, 109, 236 n. 2
Brontë, Charlotte, *Jane Eyre* 154; *Villette* 154
Brown, John 214
Browning, Elizabeth Barrett 168–70, 176–7
Browning, Robert 109, 168–70
Brutus 161
Buck, Pearl 151
Bunyan, John 48
Burke, Edmund 175

Burke, Kenneth 15
Burney, Frances 70, 142
Burns, James 21, 25–6, 117–18
Burton, Richard 181
Bush, Douglas 40
Bush, Jamie 194
Bute, John Stuart, Lord 167
Byatt, A. S. 227
Byron, George Noel Gordon, Lord 108, 170, 190

Caldwell, Gail 131
Campbell, Joseph 103
canon, of biography 127, 161, 223, 234
Cantor, Georg 53
Capper, Charles 23, 32
Carey, John xiv
Carlyle, Jane Welsh (Mrs Thomas) 72, 168
Carlyle, Thomas 51, 168
Carmichael, Stokeley 216
Caro, Robert 231, 232
Carpenter, Humphrey 231
Carroll, Lewis (Charles Lutwidge Dodgson) 44
Carson, Clayborne 9, 214–15, 221–2
Castañeda, Jorge 231
Castro, Fidel 167, 231
Cauchy, Augustin-Louis 54
cause–effect 18, 119, 169, 176, 230
Caw, Mary Ann 171
Cecil, David 189
Chalmers, George 110
Chanler, Margaret Terry 131
Chaplin, Thomas 49
Charles XII, of Sweden 87–8
Chatterton, Thomas 184, 191
Chernaik, Judith 170–1, 181
Chesler, Ellen 134, 148–9
Chevigny, Bell Gale 159
Christensen, Jerome, *Practicing Enlightenment* xix, 227
Churchill, Winston 9–10, 133, 165, 184, 244 n. 25
Cicero 16
Civil Rights Movement, US 39, 49
Clairmont, Jane (Claire) 170–1
Clapp, Margaret 20, 26, 46
Clark, Ronald 85
class 33, 70, 129, 171, 217; markers of 36, 71, 232, 243–4 n. 25; new willingness to address 70, 228, 299–30
Claudel, Camille 145–6, 153, 247 n. 16
Claudel, Paul 145–6, 153, 247 n. 16
Clegg, Claude 231
Cleopatra 48, 150
Clinton, Bill 39, 144
Coit, Margaret 20
Coke, Edward 72

Coleridge, Samuel Taylor xiii, 48, 182, 184, 188, 190–1, 195
Colie, Rosalie 15, 17, 18, 237 n. 13
Columbus, Christopher 32, *and see* Morison, Samuel Eliot
Cone, James 216
Confucius 48, 167
Congdon, Thomas 34
Conrad, Joseph xiii, 193
consciousness, coming to 142–3, 205–6, 208–9, 224
constructed person 50, 100, 103–5, 118
Cook, Blanche Wiesen 133, 151–3, 157, 163
Cose, Ellis 202
Cowley, Malcolm 179
Critics' Circle Prize xviii, 20–8, 49, *and see* prizes
Crocker, Ruth 140, 249 n. 12
Cromwell, Oliver 48, 49, 92, 239 n. 27
Culler, Jonathan 16
Curie, Marie 48
Curry, Izola 223
Curzon, Mary 130–2, 135–8, 140, 144, *and see* Nicolson, Nigel

Dauben, Joseph 53–5, 57
Davis, Allison 202
Davis, Linda 42
Days of Grace, see Ashe, Arthur; Rampersad, Arnold
death 91–2, 107–8, 175–6, 177, 202, 206–7
Defoe, Daniel 63–5, 68–72, 112, 123, 135, 138, 165, 193, 246 n. 7; biographers of 31; mysteries in life xvi–xviii, 21, 40, 59, 61–2, 87, 110; and women xvi, 88–9, 129, 148
Delbée, Anne 153
DeMott, Robert 178–81
Dewey, John 123
Dickens, Charles xv, 63, 75, 182, 187–90, 193, 228, *and see* Ackroyd, Peter
Dickinson, Emily 143, 150, 152
Dinesen, Isak 28, 57, 96, 118, 138, 143–5, 154, *and see* Thurman, Judith
Dinnage, Rosemary xiv
Dix, Dorothea 134
Doney, Gayle Rice 96–8
Doody, Margaret 70, 154–5
Dryden, John xvii, 127
DuBois, W. E. B. 150, 205, 207–14, 216, 218–20, 225; lives of 224; and racism 150, 201–3, 225; reputation 222, 223; *and see* Lewis, David Levering
Dunbar, Paul Laurence 108
Dyson, Michael 216

Earle, Peter 40
Earls, Felton (Tony) 220

Edel, Leon xv, xx, 22, 39, 77, 106, 164, 233; method 50, 67, 71–3, 104, 107
Edwards, Jonathan 134
Ehrenpreis, Irvin 113
Einstein, Albert 149
Eliot, George 63, 72, 127, 139, 193
Eliot, T. S. 187–8, 190, 192, 195, *and see* Ackroyd, Peter
Eliot, Vivien (Mrs T. S.) 195
Elizabeth I, Queen of England 48, 71, 186
Elliott, Maud Howe 4; *Julia Ward Howe* 20
Ellmann, Richard xx, 22, 32, 114, 161–2, 193, 226; his method 12–14, 25, 84, 86, 96, 104, 106, 123, 189–92; *James Joyce* 12–13, 32, 123, 226, 227, 234; *Oscar Wilde* 13, 25
Elms, Alan 100, 114, 229
Emerson, Ralph Waldo 32, 234–5
emotional centres 87
Epstein, William 18, 105; *Recognizing Biography* 16–17
Erasmus 49
Erikson, Erik 120, 124, 133, 246 n. 64; influence on the form 114, 116; life stages 103, 106–7, 243 n. 23
Evanzz, Karl 231
Events 133–4
evidence: legal heritage 80–1, 241 nn. 37–9, 242 n. 41; reliability of 74, 100; too much 13, 23, 85–6

facts 10, 75, 81–2, 86–7, 183–4, 227; confusion over 3, 61–3; 'fertile' 87–8
Father Divine (George Baker) 216
Faubus, Orville 39
Fauset, Jessie 214
feminism: defined 128–9, 246 n. 3; perspectives 28, 79, 105–6, 128–62, 151, 157–8, 217–18, 230
feminist xxi, 128–9; feminist biographer, *see* biographer, feminist; language for experience 22, 144, 151, 237 n. 18, 238 n. 23; research on language 19–20, 247 n. 26; urgency 159–60
Feynman, Richard 52, 57–8, 118
Field, Andrew 44–6, 173
Field, Michele 191
filing xvii, 13, 62–4, 66, 240 n. 9
Fitzgerald, F. Scott 141, 161
Fitzgerald, Zelda 161
Foltz, Clara Shortridge 144
Forbes, Esther 21
Frady, Marshall 203
Fraenkel, Abraham 54
Frank, Elizabeth 20, 28, 92, 140, 155
Franklin, John Hope 249 n. 2
Fraser, Antonia 92, 172, 239 n. 27
Frederick the Wise, Frederick III, elector of Saxony 49

Freeman, Mary Wilkins 160
Frendel-Brunswik, Elsa 103
Freud, Anna xiv
Freud, Sigmund 103, 109, 114, 116, 124; *Eine Kindheitserinnerung des Leonard da Vinci* 229
Freudian psychology 75, 96, 101, 108, 114, 127
Friedman, Susan 142
Fromm, Harold 185, 191
Frost, Robert 94, 149, 234; 'Tree at my Window' 94
Froude, James 51
Fuller, Margaret 23, 32
Furbank, Nick xx

Gambinos xiii
Gandhi, Mohandas Karamchand (Mahatma) 106–7, 120, 150, 243–4 n. 25; protest philosophy 224
Garber, Marjorie 191
Garbo, Greta 48, 227
Garnett, David 177, 249 n. 15
Garraty, John 74, 127, 202
Garrick, David 46, 181
Garrison, Dee 146
Garrow, David, 10, 11, 25, 205–6; *Bearing the Cross* 9, 49, 205–6, 221–2
Garvey, Marcus 216
Gaskell, Elizabeth 23, 116, 128
Gassner, John 15
Gates, Henry Louis 218, 251 n. 36
Gattégno, Jean 44
Gauss, Carl 50
Gay, Peter 114
Geertz, Clifford 49, 69–70, 239 n. 28
Gelles, Edith 44–5
gender 19–21, 26–8, 33, 105–6, 128–9, 140–2; biographers writing specifically about 33, 120, 136, 140–2, 229–30; differences 132, 141–51
Genet, Jean 114
genius 40, 47, 48, 50–9, 104
Gergen, Kenneth 102
Gergen, Mary 147
Gérin, Winifred 20
Gibson, Dana 130
Gielgud, John 181
Gitting, Robert 197
Givner, Joan 160
Glasser, Leah Blatt 160
Gleick, James 57–8, 118
Glendinning, Victoria xxi, 20, 28, 35, 75–6, 114, 119, 182–3; on evidence 74, 81, 86, 242 n. 55; method 4, 12, 14, 24, 137, 156–7, 191, 193–5
Godwin, Mary 170–1
Godwin, William 170
Goldman, Emma 154, 156

Goodwin, Doris Kearns 20, 73, 152–3, 155–7, 210
Gosse, Edmund 33, 73
Grant, Ulysses S. 37
group identity 142, 201–2, 204–9
Grundy, Isobel 31, 35–6
Guevara, Ernesto (Che) 167, 232
Guiney, Louise, 'The Talisman' 139

Hacking, Ian 81–2
Hale, Matthew 82
Hale, Nathan 223
Haley, Alex 219
Hall, N. John 30, 163
Hall, Tord 52, 59
Halperin, John 154–5
Halsband, Robert 31
Hamer, Fanny Lou 49
Hamilton, Ian 78–9
Hamilton, Nigel 75–6, 80, 94, 156
handwriting analysis 111–13, 244–5 nn. 39, 41
Hardy, G. H. 52, 55
Hardy, Thomas xiii, 193
Harlan, Louis 182, 208–10, 215, 223–4
Harriman, Averell xvii
Haydon, Benjamin 47, 168–9, 196, 198
Hayes, Rutherford 213
Hayter, Alethea 167–70, 249 n. 8
Haywood, Eliza 184
Hedrick, Joan xiv, xx, 20, 26–7, 94–5; *Harriet Beecher Stowe* 227
Heilbrun, Carolyn 19, 36, 134, 161, 193; expanding subjects of 144, 172, 174; on language 19, 237 n. 18, 247 n. 26
Hellman, Lillian 17, 141
Hemenway, Robert 182
Hemingway, Ernest xvi, xx, 21, 65, 72, 91
Herivel, John 232
hero 106, 109, 116, 128, 243 n. 13; defined 8–9, 48, 122; types 99, 104
Hilbert, David 55–6, 58, 149
Hill, Christopher 49, 92, 239 n. 27
Himmelfarb, Gertrude 9–10
historians, 77, 152, 157, 172, 219, 230
history xxi, 18, 178–9, 232; in African-American biography 200, 210–13, 216–17, 223, 225; biography's power to define 8, 229–30
Hitler, Adolf 48, 87
Hogarth, William 71
Holland, Norman 116
Holmes, Amelia Lee Jackson (Mrs Oliver Wendell) 137
Holmes, Oliver Wendell 74
Holmes, Richard 30, 190–3, 195, 233; method 72, 182–5, 199–200; and purpose of biography xx–xxi, 187–8, 212, 230

Holroyd, Michael xxi, 30, 182–94, 219, 249 n. 4, 250 n. 9
Homer 190
Honan, Park 4, 12, 13, 84, 86, 123
Hooten, Joy 137
Hoover, Herbert 9, 222
Hope, John 214
Horgan, Paul 71
Howe, Irving 136
Howe, Julia Ward 32, 151; *see also* Elliott, Maud Howe; Richards, Laura Howe
Hughes, Langston 35, 223, 225, 251 n. 43; poetry 206–7, 212, 218, 251 n. 36; and racism 201, 204–5, 209, 212–13
Hughes, Ted xv, 77–80
Hutchinson, Lucy 128
Huxley, Aldous 189

identity, definition 122, 243 n. 23, 247 n. 13
illustrations 72–3, 155–6
Imlay, Fanny 170–1
Imlay, Gilbert 171
individual, independence of 100–1, 201
interior life 50, 94, 101, 121, 221, 246 n. 66; interior/exterior 108, 188–9, 225; models of 114–16, 136–9; how revealed 88, 154, 185
interpretation 97–100, 123, 180, 208–9, 234; blended into narration 5–7, 32–3, 166–7, 197; how done 18, 92, 98–100, 116–18, 171, 184–5, 232; responsibility of biographer 3, 188–9, 227
interviews, 45, 73–4, 109, 166
Iococca, Lee 147

Jackson, Andrew 167, 210
Jackson, Jesse 203, 205, 220
Jagger, Mick 93–4
James, Alice 23–4, 136, 154, 160
James, Henry xv, 67, 75, 110; *Aspern Papers* 227; *and see* Edel, Leon
James, William 24, 160
Jarrell, Randall 118
Jefferson, Thomas 210
Jenkyns, Richard 191
John Paul II, Pope xiii
Johnson, James Weldon 201, 205, 208, 210, 221, 224, 251 n. 45
Johnson, Lyndon 73, 167
Johnson, Samuel xxii, 36, 46, 60, 111, 121, 176, 182; on biography 76–7, 115, 188–90, 193; *Life of Savage* xxi, 76–7, 127, 161, 188–9, 241 n. 30
Jordan, Dorothy xiii
Julia Ward Howe 20

Kanigel, Robert 35, 52, 55
Kaplan, Justin 37

Keats, John 23, 47–8, 147, 169, 173, 190–9
Kelley, Kitty, *His Way* 227
Kemble, Fanny 168
Kennedy, David 26, 28, 105, 134, 147–8
Kennedy, Jacqueline, *see* Onassis, Jacqueline Kennedy
Kennedy, Joe, Sr. 75
Kennedy, John 76
Kennedys (American political family) 44, 75
Kenyon, J. P. 36
Kerouac, Jack 179
Kesey, Ken 179–80
Keynes, Maynard 191
King, Coretta Scott 203
King, Martin Luther 11, 122, 205–7, 214–15, 218, 223, 224; interpretations of 9, 150, 216, 222; and racism 203, 209, 213; and US history 212, 222
King, Richard 221–2
Kingsmill, Hugh 186, 189
Kissinger, Henry 9–10
Knowlson, James 62, 234
Koenig, Rhoda 75
Kozol, Jonathan 251 n. 43
Kramer, Lloyd 14, 59–60, 227, 233
Kumin, Maxine 79–80
Kurlansky, Mark 174–6

language, translation from disciplines 52, 54, 59, 73
Lash, Joseph 152–3
Lauretis, Teresa de 202
Lawrence, D. H. 39, 147, 173–4, 192
Lawrence, Frieda 147, 172–4, 192
Lawrence, T. E. 118, 243 n. 13
Lawrence-Lightfoot, Sara 219–20
LeBeau, Bryan 232–3
Lee, Hermione 190
Leivick, Laura 185
Lenin, Nikolai 167, 207–8
Lerner, Gerda 151, 161, 171
letters, as evidence 65, 74–5, 84–5, 110, 138, 148, 169, 198
Levison, Stanley 223
Lewis, David Levering 150, 207, 218–19, 222, 223; defining field 182, 204, 230
Lewis, R. W. B. 10, 14, 18, 24, 28, 39; *Edith Wharton* 21
liberal arts 55
Lichtenberg, Joseph 108–9
life sciences xxi
life shape xxi, 88, 100, 102–8, 121–2, 224–5, 243 n. 18
Lincoln, Abraham 26, 213
literary biography 11–13, 30–1, 40, 78–9, 123, 185–7, 195–9; appeal of xviii–xx, 47–8, 104, 177; methods of 63, 178–80, 190–1

literary criticism xviii, 152, 177–8, 180–1; methods of used in biography 12, 45, 249 n. 16; within biography 4, 188, 198, 206–7
literary marketplace 34, 36–40, 128; pre-twentieth-century 70
Locke, John 83
Lockhart, John Gibson 186
Long, Huey 32, 224, *and see* Williams, T. Harry
Long, Russell 32
Lowell, Robert 78, 118, 155
Lukács, Georg 17
Lurie, Alison 227
Luther, Martin 49, 106, 150
Lytton, Edward 51

Macauley, Thomas Babington 19
McCarthy, Mary 105–6, 109, 132–3, 135–6, 145–7, 153–4, 224
MacCartney, Paul 168
McCullough, David 22, 23, 27, 46, 70, 176; *Mornings on Horseback* 5–7, 14, 27, 46; *Truman* 25, 70
MacDowell, Paula, *Women of Grub Street* 232
Mack, John E. 118, 122, 243 n. 13
Mack, Maynard 34
McKay, Claude 10
McKay, Nellie 200–1
McKeon, Michael 16
Macready, William 168
Maddox, Brenda 20, 26, 147, 172–4, 192–3
Malcolm X 216, see also *Autobiography of Malcolm X*
manic depression 53, 118
Mann, Thomas 156
Mansfield, Katherine 73, 86, 129–30
Mariani, Paul xvi, xvii, 13, 34, 41, 154–5
marriage, as subject 45, 141, 145–6, 152–3, 156, 161, 172–3, 249 n. 13
Marsh, Margaret 171
Martin, Jay 123
Marvell, Andrew 92
Marx, Karl 207
Massie, Robert 3–4, 7, 87–8
mathematics 10–11, 15, 50–9, 164–5, 227
Maurois, André 230
Mehew, Ernest 61–2
memory 73–4, 90, 97, 176
meta-biography 120
metonymy, 7–8
Meyers, Jeffrey 65, 67, 72–4, 129–30, 149, 228, 250 n. 8
Middlebrook, Diane Wood 34, 39, 77–80, 118, 232; on biography 154–5, 162, 238 n. 26, 241 n. 31
Miles, Jack 165–7, 180–1, 248 n. 4, 249 n. 17
Milford, Nancy, *Zelda* xiv, 128, 161
Miller, Arthur, *Death of a Salesman* 15, 16, 236–7 n. 8, 237 n. 9

Miller, Dorie 212
Miller, Henry 85
Miller, James (eighteenth century) 184
Miller, James (twentieth century) 25
Millon, Theodore 117
Mills, Kay 49
Milne, A. A. 95, *and see* Thwaite, Ann
Minnich, Elizabeth 132
Mitchell, Lucy Sprague 134
Mitford, Mary Russell 144
Moers, Ellen 151
Moi, Toril 35, 43–4, 48, 237 n. 19
Monk, Ray 84–5
Monroe, Marilyn 150
Montagu, Elizabeth 48
Montagu, Lady Mary Wortley 31, 35–6
Montgomery, Bernard 167
Montgomery, M. R. 75
Moraitis, George 116
Morison, Samuel Eliot 21, 23, 32
Morris, Edmund 5–8, 14, 25–6, 99
Morrison, Toni 98, 101, 202, 211
motherhood, as subject 43–5, 79–80, 110, 146–9, 152, 247 nn. 19, 21, 22
Motherwell, Robert 87
Motion, Andrew 182–3, 187, 190–9
motive xviii, 12, 94, 109, 121–2, 210; assignment of 69, 96–100, 184, 188
myths, use of 110–11, 122, 127, 152–3, 171, 215; popular 63, 93–4, 104–5

Nabokov, Véra 45–6, 173
Nabokov, Vladimir 44–6, 173
Nadel, Ira xiv, 189
narrative 12, 108, 119, 123–4, 165–7, 193–5, 232; as mode of understanding 11, 18, 35–6, 229–30; persuasive power 83–4, 230
National Book Award xviii, 5, 6, 20–8, 31, 37, *and see* prizes
national self-image 8–9, 59–60, 104–5, 117–18, 167
nature vs. nurture 100
Neale, John 71
Nelson, Horatio 46, 147
nest and adventure 98, 101, 108, *and see* Morrison, Toni
Neve, Michael 93–4
New Journalism 230–2
Newman, Richard 220
Newton, Isaac 50–1, 55, 57–8, 70, 91–2
Newton, Mary 88–9, 129
Nicolson, Harold 14, 18, 74, 130, 156–7, 186, 189, 228
Nicolson, Nigel 27–8, 35, 130–1, 135–8, 144
Nietzche, Friedrich Wilhelm 110
Nin, Anaïs 172
Noonan, John T. 40–1
North, Francis 81

novel, similarities to biography 15–17, 163, 177, 183, 191, 192–3; to popular novels 106, 191, 244 n. 28; nonfiction novel 230–1; to nineteenth-century 18, 106, 193–5, 231–2; theoretically 127–8, 227–8

Oates, Stephen xiii, 228
Onassis, Jacqueline Kennedy xiii, 151–2, 167
Oppenheimer, J. Robert 52
Origo, Iris 86
Ozick, Cynthia 73

papers, ownership of xv, 53, 77–9, 241 nn. 32–5
parents 95–6
Paris, Barry 227
Parks, Rosa 11, 214
patriarchy 79, 129
Paulson, Ronald 71
Peel, Robert 168
Pepys, Samuel 133
Perkins, Max 33
person: 'core' xvi, 9–10, 93–4, 96, 121–2, 138–9; essential 93–4, 138–9, 192, 228–9, 250 n. 26
personality: Big Five descriptive model 114–15, 245 n. 51; clinical domains of 117–18; defined 93, 101–2, 228–9; disorders 118; see also trait; syndromes
Peter, the Great, Czar of Russia 4, 87–8, 167
Peters, Catherine 228
Pippin, Horace 217
place, importance of 6, 53, 71–3, 176–7, 205, 231–2; collecting evidence about 71–2, 168–9, 185; given thematic weight 7, 53, 95, 137–8, 197
Plath, Sylvia xv, 77–80, 91, 92, 136
Plutarch, Lives of the Noble Grecians and Romans 127, 149–50
Poincaré, Henri 57
Politt, Katha 77
Pope, Alexander xv, 34, 127
Porter, Katherine Anne 90, 160
Porter, Roy 199
Pound, Ezra 67
Powell, Adam Clayton 204–5
Pringle, Henry 3, 5–7, 13–14, 99–100, 251 n. 44
prizes, for biography xviii, 5, 19–22, 31, 39, 91, 196
psychoanalytic biography 114, 119–21
psychobiography 114, 121, 246 n. 65
Pulitzer Prize xiv, xviii, 5, 19–28, 35, 37, 46, 78, 111, 165; and see prizes
Pushkin, Aleksander 45

Quilligan, Maureen 141, 159

race 104, 129, 150, 202–4, 208–9
racism, US, examples of 202–4, 208–9, 211–12, 214, 217, 223, 224
Raleigh, Sir Walter 111
Ramanujan, Srinivasa 35, 52, 55
Rampersad, Arnold xx, 34–5, 182, 219, 223, 232, 251 n. 43; as biographer 203, 205–6; on biography 208, 221, 251 nn. 38, 45
Randolph, Philip 214
readers, of biography xiii, xx–xxii, 3–4, 10, 86, 99–100, 233–5; demands 92, 94–5, 103, 141–2, 163–5, 234; desires 13, 43–4, 100, 103–4, 116, 226; expectations 17, 93, 104, 148–9, 226–7, 230–1; relationship to material xvii–xviii, 17; resistances 44, 55, 79, 90, 163–4, 214–15
record offices, process for working in them 65–9
Reich, Robert 144
Reid, B. L. 111
Reid, Constance 10–11, 56–8, 149
religion 36, 48–9, 104, 190, 248 n. 4
reviewers xiv, 93, 106, 160–1, 163–5, 177; as hyper-readers 73, 84, 234–5, 236 n. 2; and see biography, reviewing
Reynolds, Joshua 46
Rich, Adrienne 143
Richard the Lion Hearted 167
Richards, Laura Howe 4; Julia Ward Howe 20
Rinehart, Mary Roberts 13
Robinson, Abraham 53–5, 133
Rochefoucauld, François de Marsillac, Duc de la 72
Rodin, August 145–6, 153
Roethke, Theodore 118, 155
Roosevelt, Alice 5–7
Roosevelt, Eleanor 133, 142–3, 210, 224; contrasting representations of 151–3, 155–8; and women 136, 139, 158, 222
Roosevelt, Franklin 25, 46, 117–18, 133, 135, 141–3, 152–3, 155–6
Roosevelt, Theodore 3, 5–8, 13–14, 22, 23, 98–100, 105; and race 213, 223, 224, 251 n. 44
Rose, Kenneth 20, 22
Rose, Phyllis 42, 142, 226
Rosengarten, Theodore 49
Rothko, Mark 41, 87
Rowley, Hazel 40
Runcie, Robert 231
Russell, Bertrand 57, 84–5
Ryan, Alan 84–5

Sacks, Oliver 123
Sackville-West, Vita 74, 130, 137, 156–7, 191, 194–5
Sage, Margaret Olivia, Mrs Russell 140
Salinger, J. D. 78–9
Salwak, Dale 191
Sand, George 48, 151
Sanders, Charles 191

Sanger, Margaret 105, 122, 147–51, *and see*
 Kennedy, David
Sartre, Jean-Paul 19, 31, 42, 113–14
Saul, Nigel 234
Savage, Richard xxii, 161, 184–5; *see also*
 Johnson, Samuel, *Life of Savage*
Sayers, Dorothy 36
Scammell, Michael 156
Schwartz, Delmore 118, 135–6
Seale, Bobby 216
Sennet, Richard 82
Sewall, Richard 23, 38–9, 49, 150, 229
Sexton, Anne 77–80, 91, 92, 118, 206
Sexton, Linda 77–8
Shakespeare, William 190, 198; *Hamlet* 15,
 180–1
Shapiro, Barbara 81, 241 nn. 37–9, 242 n. 41
Shaw, George Bernard 185, 188, 191–2,
 250 n. 9, *and see* Holroyd, Michael
Shelley, Percy Bysshe 48, 170, 187, 196
Sherwood, Frances 171, 181; *Vindication* 171
Siddons, Sarah 46, 73
Silverman, Kenneth xx, 30, 39, 61
Skidelsky, Robert xx
Sklar, Kathryn 159
Smith, Gaddis 9–10
Smith, John E. 134
Smollett, Tobias 193
society, as text 104–5
Solzhenitsyn, Alexander 156
Solzhenitsyn, Natasha 156
Spencer, Herbert 207
Spurling, Hilary 183, 195, 249 n. 1
Staël, Germaine Necker, Mme de 23, 48
Stalin, Joseph 167
Stallworthy, Jon 189–90
Stanley, Liz 156–7
Stannard, Martin 18
Stead, Christina 40
Steele, Danielle 39
Steele, Richard 76
Stein, Gertrude 136
Steinbeck, John 178–80
Steinum, Gloria 134
Stevenson, Anne 78
Stevenson, Robert Lewis 185
Stone, Irving 39
stories, cultural 39, 119, 204, 243 n. 21, 243 n.
 24; favorite 48–9, 91–2, 102–4, 106–8, 193,
 248 n. 29; stakes in 79–80, 115–16, 229–31;
 as ways of knowing 35–6
Storr, Anthony 118
Stowe, Harriet Beecher 27, 108–9, 134–5,
 150–2, 180; and her sisters, 172; *and see*
 Hedrick, Joan; Wilson, Robert Forrest
Strachey, Lytton 3, 14, 18–19, 177, 237 n. 17,
 249 n. 15; as groundbreaking biographer 127,

161, 189; as subject 183–7, 190–2, 194, 199;
 Eminent Victorians 127, 186; *and see* Holroyd,
 Michael
Strickland, Geoffrey 61–2
Strouse, Jean 20, 23–4, 136, 160
Stukeley, William 58
Sturken, Marita 225
Super, R. H. 30–1
Swift, Jonathan 113, 115, 182
syndromes 116–17

Taibo, Paco 231
Tanner, Stephen 179–80
Tanner, Tony xix
Tennenhouse, Leonard 16
Thatcher, Margaret 229–30
thick description 49, 69–70, 219
Thomas, Donald 156
Thoreau, Henry David 32
Thumb, Tom 169
Thurman, Judith 20, 28, 57, 96, 118, 128, 144
Thwaite, Ann 20, 23, 33–4, 73, 95, 249 n. 1
Till, Emmett 221
Tomalin, Claire 35, 228, 249 n. 1
trait 101–2, 115–17
Truman, Harry 39, 70, 72, 133, 176, *and see*
 McCullough, David
Trzebinski, Errol 116

Uglow, Jenny 116, 152
Ulrich, Laurel Thatcher 20, 21, 49, 153
underclass 17, 176–7
Updike, John 187

Vaught, Bonny 42
Victoria, Queen 19, 184, 186, 187, 237 n. 17
Victorians 19, 34, 189
voice xx–xxi, 3–29, 37; biographer's audible
 xx–xxi, 3–5, 14–15, 34, 43, 157–8 (decision to
 be 90, 118–20, 194–5, 219, 220); hearing
 subject's 71; magisterial 18–20, 22–3, 28–9,
 91, 188–9, 234, 238 n. 26; need for consistent
 10, 14, 119–21; subject speaks for self 14, 84,
 90, 119
Vorse, Mary Heaton 134, 146

Wagner-Martin, Linda 77–8, 128, 136, 153,
 171–2
Waid, Candace 178, 180
Wain, John 36
Walker, Alice 182
Walton, Izaak 127
Walton, Sam xiii
Wandor, Michelene 141
Ward, Aileen 20, 196–9
Ware, Susan 155

Washington, Booker T. 203–4, 208–10, 213, 214–15, 216, 222–4
Washington, George 147, 165, 167, 210
Weil, Simone 48
Weimer, Joan 42
Weinberg, Steve xix
Wellington, Arthur Wellesley, Duke of 168
Wells, Ida B. 214
Welsh, Alexander 83
Wendorf, Richard, *Sir Joshua Reynolds* xviii, 46, 232–3
Wesley, Charles 48
Wesley, Susannah 151–2
Westbrook, Harriet 170–1
Westfall, Richard 51–2, 57–8, 70, 90–2
Wexler, Alice 154
Wharton, Edith 94, 161, 178, *and see* Benstock, Shari; Lewis, R. W. B.
Whitbread Prize xviii, 20–8, 172, 183, *and see* prizes
White, Hayden 83, 134
White, Ralph 113
Whitman, Walt 17
Whittemore, Reed 107
Wilde, Oscar xv, 184–5, 189
Wilkes, John 167
Wilkins, Roy 205, 214
Willcox, William 46
Williams, T. Harry 32–3

Wilson, A. N. 249 n. 1
Wilson, Edmund 29, 71, 105, 146–7, 153–4
Wilson, Robert Forrest 26–7, 95, 107–8, 150, 247 n. 25
Wilson, Woodrow 109
Winn, James xvii, 34
Winslow, Ola 20, 95, 134
Wolfe, Linny Marsh 20, 35
Wolfe, Tom 164, 231–2
Wollstonecraft, Mary 171
women, intelligent 34, 35, 48, 97, 131–2, 172–3, 247 n. 9; and clothing 79, 105; emblematic 28, 42–3
women's culture 94–5, 128
Woolf, Cynthia Griffin 63
Woolf, Leonard 14, 18
Woolf, Virginia 4, 48, 128, 130, 146, 164, 183; on biography 13, 14, 17–19, 30, 61, 76–7, 86–7; writings about 42, 142; *Flush* 176–7, 249 n. 15; *Roger Fry: A Biography* 17, 18, 61, 76, 77, 177
Wordsworth, William 168, 178, 196
Worthen, John 93, 193
Wright, Richard 113, 202, 224

Yeats, George Hyde-Lees (Mrs William Butler) 32
Young, Charles 213, 214
Young-Bruehl, Elisabeth xiv, 34, 61, 132, 163–4